Psychosis and Spirituality

Psychosis and Spirituality
Consolidating the New Paradigm

Second Edition

Edited by

Isabel Clarke
Hampshire Partnership NHS Foundation Trust

WILEY-BLACKWELL

A John Wiley & Sons, Ltd., Publication

This second edition first published 2010
© 2010 John Wiley & Sons Ltd

Edition history: Whurr Publishers (2001)

Wiley-Blackwell is an imprint of John Wiley & Sons, formed by the merger of Wiley's global Scientific, Technical, and Medical business with Blackwell Publishing.

Registered Office
John Wiley & Sons Ltd, The Atrium, Southern Gate, Chichester, West Sussex, PO19 8SQ, UK

Editorial Offices
The Atrium, Southern Gate, Chichester, West Sussex, PO19 8SQ, UK
9600 Garsington Road, Oxford, OX4 2DQ, UK
350 Main Street, Malden, MA 02148-5020, USA

For details of our global editorial offices, for customer services, and for information about how to apply for permission to reuse the copyright material in this book please see our website at www.wiley.com/wiley-blackwell.

The right of Isabel Clarke to be identified as the author of the editorial material in this work has been asserted in accordance with the Copyright, Designs and Patents Act 1988.

Wiley also publishes its books in a variety of electronic formats. Some content that appears in print may not be available in electronic books.

Designations used by companies to distinguish their products are often claimed as trademarks. All brand names and product names used in this book are trade names, service marks, trademarks or registered trademarks of their respective owners. The publisher is not associated with any product or vendor mentioned in this book. This publication is designed to provide accurate and authoritative information in regard to the subject matter covered. It is sold on the understanding that the publisher is not engaged in rendering professional services. If professional advice or other expert assistance is required, the services of a competent professional should be sought.

Library of Congress Cataloging-in-Publication Data

Psychosis and spirituality : consolidating the new paradigm / edited by Isabel Clarke. – 2nd ed.
     p. ; cm.
  Includes bibliographical references and index.
  ISBN 978-0-470-68348-4 (cloth) – ISBN 978-0-470-68347-7 (pbk.) 1. Psychoses–Religious aspects. 2. Psychiatry and religion. I. Clarke, Isabel.
  [DNLM: 1. Psychotic Disorders. 2. Delusions–psychology. 3. Religion and Psychology. WM 200 P9727 2010]
  RC512.P738 2010
  616.89–dc22

                                                                                    2010016273

HB ISBN: 9780470683484
PB ISBN: 9780470683477

A catalogue record for this book is available from the British Library.

Set in 10.5/13pt Minion by Thomson Digital, Noida, India.

1   2010

Contents

List of Figures

Acknowledgement

I would like to acknowledge the members of the Spiritual Crisis Network, people I have encountered in my work and all other experiencers who have inspired this enterprise; but above all, Chris Clarke, who has been my invaluable collaborator in all the detailed and technical tasks involved in the editing – it should really read 'edited by Clarke and Clarke'.

Notes on Editor and Contributors

Isabel Clarke, MA, BA, C Clin Psychol   Isabel Clarke is a Consultant Clinical Psychologist, currently Psychological Therapies Lead in an NHS Acute Inpatient Unit (Woodhaven, New Forest). She has published, organised conferences etc. on Psychosis and Spirituality. She studied history at Cambridge, is a lifelong practicing Anglican, and founder member of the Spiritual Crisis Network. Her general interest book, 'Madness, Mystery and the Survival of God' was published by O Books in 2008. For further details, see: www.isabelclarke.org.

Peter Fenwick, FRCPsych, DPM, MB BChir   Dr Peter Fenwick is an Emeritus Neuropsychiatrist of the Maudsley Hospital and an Honorary Senior Lecturer, Kings College Institute of Psychiatry and the Neurosychiatry Department, Southampton University. He has studied transcendent states of consciousness and brain mechanisms underpinning consciousness. With his wife, he has written a book on NDEs, "The Truth in the Light" and last year "The Art of Dying" describing transcendent phenomena occurring as we die.

Brian Les Lancaster, PhD   Les Lancaster is Professor of Transpersonal Psychology at Liverpool John Moores University, Honorary Research Fellow in the Centre for Jewish Studies at Manchester University, and part of the Adjunct Research Faculty at the Institute of Transpersonal Psychology, California. Les's published works include Mind Brain and Human Potential, winner of a Science and Medical Network Best Book Award, Approaches to Consciousness: the Marriage of Science and Mysticism (Palgrave-Macmiillan, 2004), and The Essence of Kabbalah (Arcturus, 2005).

Natalie Tobert, PhD   Dr Natalie Tobert, medical anthropologist and Course Director of Medicine Beyond Materialism, a programme which invites debate among medical and allied healthcare practitioners, on varieties of human experience. Seminars offer a forum for discussion about BME cultural explanatory models for experiences which may attract psychiatric attention. Courses are run in hospitals (People Like Us project) and medical schools (Barts & the London, Brighton & Sussex). Natalie has published 70 + articles and three books. http://www.medicine-beyond-materialism.com/natalietobert@aol.com.

Neil Douglas-Klotz, PhD   Dr Neil Douglas-Klotz focuses his research in the boundary areas between somatic psychology and religious studies in the area of hermeneutics. He is the director of the Edinburgh Institute for Advanced Learning. His books include Prayers of the Cosmos (1990), Desert Wisdom (1995), The Hidden Gospel (1999), The Genesis Meditations (2003), The Sufi Book of Life (2005), Blessings of the Cosmos (2006) and The Tent of Abraham (2006, with Sr Joan Chittister and Rabbi Arthur Waskow).

Peter Chadwick, MSc, DIC, PhD, PhD, C Psychol   Dr Peter Chadwick, now retired, was a lecturer in psychology at Birkbeck College, Faculty of Community Education, University of London, and at The Open University, Anglia and London Regions. He has written three books and about 50 articles since 1975; two of the books: Borderline (Routledge 1992) and Schizophrenia: The Positive Perspective (Routledge 1997) do deal with the spiritual aspects of psychosis.

Gordon Claridge, DSc   Dr Gordon Claridge is the now retired Professor of Abnormal Psychology in the Oxford University Department of Experimental Psychology. Over many years, he has pursued a programme of research examining the more positive aspects (e.g. creativity) of psychosis and psychotic personality traits. His approach steers a way between an unduly medical ('broken brain') and a purely psychological view of psychosis. A good summary of the work is his edited volume Schizotypy: implications for illness and health (Oxford University Press, 1997).

Richard House, MA, PhD, Cert Couns   Dr House, originally a Geographer with a PhD in environmental Sciences, now practices as a counsellor (AHPP and BAC accredited), course tutor in counselling (University of East Anglia) and supervisor-trainer with Waveney Counselling Service, Lowestoft. He is co-editor (with Nick Totton) of the anthology: Implausible Professions: Arguments for Pluralism and Autonomy in Psychotherapy and Counselling. (PCCS Books, Ross-on-Wye, 1997). He is currently writing a book on New Paradigm thinking and the teachings of J. Krishnamurti.

Chris Clarke, PhD   Chris Clarke was Professor of Applied Mathematics at the University of Southampton, researching Astrophysics, Quantum theory and the physics of the brain, until moving to free-lance work in 1999 to focus on the philosophical and spiritual connections of science. He has been chair of GreenSpirit (a charity promoting eco-spirituality) and The Scientific and Medical Network.

Most recent publication: 'Ways of Knowing: science and mysticism today', Imprint Academic, 2005; forthcoming: 'Weaving the Cosmos', O Books.

Emmanuelle Peters, PhD, C Clin Psychol   Dr Emmanuelle Peters is a Senior Lecturer in Clinical Psychology (Institute of Psychiatry) and a Consultant Clinical Psychologist (South London and Maudsley NHS Foundation Trust). She is the Director of an award-winning specialist out-patients psychology service for psychosis (PICuP). She has specialised in psychosis for the last 20 years, and provides supervision and teaches in a wide variety of contexts. She has published many scientific journal articles and book chapters on psychological approaches to psychosis.

Mike Jackson, PhD, C Clin Psychol   Dr Mike Jackson, is a Consultant Clinical Psychologist with Betsi Cadwaladr University Health Board and Honorary Lecturer, University of Bangor. After studying psychology and philosophy at Oxford, he worked for the Religious Experience Research Centre, MIND and completed his D.Phil there. Relevant Publications: (with Fulford) 'Spiritual experience and psychopathology', in Philosophy, Psychiatry, & Psychology, and 'Benign schizotypy? The case of spiritual experience', in Claridge's: Schizotypy. Implications for Illness and Health.

Caroline Brett, PhD, MSc   Dr. Caroline Brett is currently carrying out a Doctorate in Clinical Psychology at Salomons, Christ Church Canterbury University. She followed her Oxford BA in Philosophy and Psychology with an an MSc in Philosophy of Mental Disorder and then a PhD at the Institute of Psychiatry, King's College London. Recent publication: Brett *et al.*, 'Appraisals of Anomalous Experiences Interview (AANEX): a multidimensional measure of psychological responses to anomalies associated with psychosis, The British Journal of Psychiatry (2007).

Roger Waldram, MA   Roger Waldram is a UKCP Registered Integrative Psychotherapist working in private practice in Peterborough. A qualified general nurse, he worked for 20 years as Employee Welfare Advisor in the Occupational Health Service of a national organisation. He qualified as a humanistic psychotherapist with a research-based Masters Degree in 2000. His research, title: 'How Does the Phenomenology of Spirituality and Madness Compare and What Are the Implications for Psychotherapeutic Practice?' was for his doctorate of integrative psychotherapy practice.

Sharon Warwick, MSc, BA   After 16 years in the commercial marketing world, Sharon is a now a counsellor and psychotherapist in private practice, focusing upon transliminal experience in research and practice. Founder and Director of Apertum Associates Ltd. She also works as consultant and facilitator with individuals, teams, and organisations wishing to respond to the changes and challenges of the modern workplace. She is a founder member of the Spiritual Crisis Network and East Midlands Spirituality and Mental Health Network.

David Lukoff, PhD   Dr Lukoff is a Professor of Psychology at the Institute for Transpersonal Psychology and co-author of the DSM-IV diagnostic category 'Religious or Spiritual Problem'. His areas of expertise include treatment of schizophrenia, transpersonal psychotherapy, and spiritual issues in clinical practice. He is author of 70 articles and chapters on spiritual issues and mental health; co-president of the Institute for Spirituality and Psychology and of the Association for Transpersonal Psychology; maintains the Spiritual Competency Resource Center.

Nigel Mills, C Clin Psychol   Nigel trained as a Clinical Psychologist at the Institute of Psychiatry in London. He worked in the NHS, for over 22 years before moving into independent practice. He has further trained extensively in QiGong/Chigung and as a Cranio-Sacral Therapist. He has written a book about the therapeutic use of Qigong for people with multiple sclerosis. He has also had several articles and book chapters published on body-based approaches to therapy.

Janice Hartley, BA   Janice writes from personal experience. Following her own acute psychotic episode she went on to study psychology, transpersonal psychology and counselling. She has conducted research into negative paranormal and spiritual experience, and is an active member and director of the Spiritual Crisis Network. Janice is passionately committed to challenging the stigma and prejudice surrounding psychosis, and to promoting alternatives to medical and pharmacological treatments. She currently conducts training workshops with service users in the voluntary sector.

David Kingdon, MD, MRC Psych   David Kingdon is Professor of Mental Health Care Delivery at the University of Southampton. Previously, he worked as Medical Director in Nottingham, Senior Medical Officer at the Department of Health and as an Adult Psychiatrist in Bassetlaw, Nottinghamshire. He chairs the Committee of Experts in Human Rights and Psychiatry, Council of Europe, and is a member of the NHSE National Service Framework External Reference Group. His extensive publications include the co-authored Cognitive Behavioural Therapy of Schizophrenia.

Ron Siddle is Consultant Psychologist & Clinical Lead for the Cumbria Early Interventions Service with Cumbria Partnership NHS Foundation Trust.

Dr Shanaya Rathod is Associate Medical Director and Consultant Psychiatrist with Hampshire Partnership Foundation Trust.

Dr Farooq Naeem, PhD student, University of Southampton, practicing psychiatrist in Pakistan and engaged in adapting CBT cross-culturally.

1

Psychosis and Spirituality Revisited: The Frontier is Opening Up!

Isabel Clarke

The first edition of this book began by observing that the connection between spirituality and psychosis was not new or surprising. Anyone familiar with the recurring themes of psychosis would recognise religious pre-occupations as commonplace. Similarly, psychotic experience could be said to lie outside the domain of logical discourse and many would say the same of religious belief. Rather it was the way in which psychosis and spirituality had been kept so distinct that demanded explanation. The 'New Frontier' referred to in the title was explained as the breaking through into an area beyond the efforts to draw distinction between psychosis and spirituality, and an exploration of the creative possibilities that this vista revealed.

The challenge lay in linking the *highest* realms of human consciousness and the *depths* of madness. It was recognised that this challenge would feel uncomfortable to many. It required a rethinking of the nature of both psychosis and spirituality. I argued then that the psychological research, accounts from marginalised areas of discourse (such as the cross-cultural and anthropological perspectives) and data from personal experience brought together in the chapters of that volume demanded that this challenging new perspective be taken seriously.

That edition came out in 2001, but the material was essentially gathered in 1999. In the intervening 10 years, this perspective has emerged from the shadows into the light in a way that makes any special pleading about the need for a second edition of this book redundant. Instead, I will sketch in some of the developments that I am aware of that have contributed to this change of intellectual climate, and then trace the part played by the process that was started by the first edition of this book. That process began with conferences arising out of the book itself, and has ultimately contributed to the founding of a Spiritual Crisis Network in the United Kingdom.

Psychosis and Spirituality: Consolidating the New Paradigm Second Edition   Edited by Isabel Clarke
© 2010 John Wiley & Sons, Ltd.

Developing Interest in Spirituality in The Health Service

A number of developments have transformed a situation when spirituality was not talked about, in the late 1980s (when I entered the NHS) and today. There is a belated recognition that the religious and spiritual priorities of other cultural groups cannot be ignored in our multicultural society. The Royal College of Psychiatrists Spirituality Special Interest Group started in 1999. The National Institute for Mental Health in England (NIMHE) and the Mental Health Foundation (MHF), started their 5 year spirituality project in 2002. Gilbert *et al.* (2003), launched the 'Inspiring Hope' manifesto. The project has now ended, with the launch of another joint publication (Coyte, Gilbert and Nicholls, 2007). This project had represented an alliance between NIMHE, the body charged with leading progressive thinking in the health service, and the MHF, a service user-led organisation. At the same time, John Swinton and others were very active in raising the profile of spirituality in the nursing field (Swinton, 2001a, b; Swinton and Pattison 2001). Publications and research on spirituality in the nursing journals have flourished ever since.

Recognition of the relevance of spirituality for psychosis was slower in emerging and does not sit easily with the 'illness' model of psychosis. However, there are some straws in the wind here. In 2006, I was invited to contribute a paper to the Royal College's *Spirituality SIG Newsletter* and present at a Spirituality and Mental Health Conference organised by the International Society for the Psychological Treatment of the Schizophrenias. The Somerset service user-led research project (Somerset Spirituality Project Group, 2002) was prominent among the pioneers of a new attitude to psychosis and spirituality.

The Recovery Approach

This service user-inspired movement which has been adopted by NHS Mental Health Services (see Ralph, Lambric and Steele, 1996, for the original research), identifies spirituality as a vital element in enabling people with serious mental health difficulties to rebuild a meaningful life. Within my own Trust, not trust, spirituality workshops run at recovery events laid the foundation for Spirituality Awareness Training for staff and now a Spirituality Network. There is increasing recognition that, irrespective of their personal position as regards spirituality, staff have a duty to those in their care to take this aspect of their lives seriously. In the context of the acute inpatient unit, this means no longer dismissing the spiritual content of psychotic communication as merely 'illness'.

Psychosis and Spirituality: Launch of a Conversation

This conversation about the psychosis and spirituality overlap, a conversation amongst friends and allies, started a while before the book came out. During

1997–1998, I was on a learning curve. I had spent many years pondering the phenomenon of spirituality and its enduring place in human experience, despite the intellectual triumph of the scientific world view, which accorded it no role. As I studied psychology as a second degree, I applied psychological thinking to my sense that human beings had access to two, qualitatively different and non-overlapping ways of experiencing. I first lighted upon Kelly's Construct Theory (Bannister and Fransella, 1971) as a way into this. As a clinical psychologist working in a setting (a psychiatric rehabilitation service) that enabled me to offer CBT for psychosis to people who had long sought to make sense of their experience, but until then had been denied therapy, I was struck by the way the psychotic experience matched the spiritual literature with which I was familiar. Coming across Peter Chadwick's book, 'Borderline' (Chadwick, 1992) was the catalyst that prompted me to organise my ideas and attempt to publish them. It was Paul Chadwick (no relation of Peter's!), my then boss, who suggested an edited volume and urged me to contact Gordon Claridge because of the relevance of Schizotypy to my subject. This invaluable advice proved the key. I wrote to all my heroes with the chapter I had prepared, Peter Chadwick, Mike Jackson, Peter Fenwick and many other contributors to the book, and was amazed when they replied, one and all, in the affirmative to my request for chapters. I began to conclude that this was an idea whose time was coming.

Bringing the contributors together as part of that process led to the suggestion of a conference on Psychosis and Spirituality that was made possible by Professor Kingdon and organised by the Southampton University Mental Health Unit's Education and Development Department. The success of the September 2000 conference led to the second in 2001, both held in or near Winchester, attended by about 60 delegates, with a good mixture of service users/experiencers, professionals and interested others. Both conferences ended with the sense of a conversation that needed to continue. Chris Clarke responded to this by setting up a closed Yahoo psychosis and spirituality discussion list, which flourishes on the World-Wide Web to this day.

The Psychosis and Spirituality Web Discussion List

This conversation has displayed respect for the individual's experience, open-mindedness about interpretation, a bias against dogmatism and a respect for mystery. Time and again, members of the list comment that this is an accepting and supportive place. There are little bursts of real intellectual excitement, but the main function seems to be to hold that space so that it can contain psychosis and spirituality together without judgement and without the need for ultimatum answers, but with real support and companionship through both dark and suffering, and exhilerating times.

Such accounts of experience featured in a special issue of the *Journal of Critical Psychology, Counselling and Psychotherapy*, which came out in 2002 (Clarke, 2002).

A final conference, with a wider focus on 'Ways of Knowing' was organised by Chris Clarke in Winchester in 2005 (Clarke, 2005). However, that was by no means the end of conferences! Conferences on spirituality, on recovery and spirituality, and even on psychosis and spirituality have abounded over the last few years.

The UK Spiritual Crisis Network

Just as our enthusiasm for organising conferences started to wane, the 'Revisioning Mental Health' conferences, organised by Catherine Lucas, which started in 2004 took up the baton. Significantly, these three successful conferences led directly to the formation of the Spiritual Crisis Network in the United Kingdom.

Our ultimate vision for the Spiritual Crisis Network (I am a member of the development group) is for a network of groups of people in every locality who could support someone going through a crisis, at the same time as receiving support from each other to provide this. Of course, where the risks are judged to be too great, the individual would be supported to access the local mental health services. At present, only groups exist in a few localities, but our website is up and running, and well used; the email advice line is contacted by one or two people every week, and at least there is evidence of another perspective on such crises for people experiencing them and their carers/supporters. The web address is listed at the end of this book.

Members of the Spiritual Crisis Network have contributed some of the new material in this second edition. The network has a thriving Kundalini Section and a member of the section has added an account of her own experience to House's (2001) chapter on Kundalini. Other contributors from the network are Sharon Warwick and Janice Hartley. Janice's contribution to the clinical section gives a striking account of her own experience, uses this as a therapeutic tool to help other people make sense of theirs and incorporates a powerful plea for an alternative to the conventional psychiatric approach.

An Explosion of Research

The explosion of research into this subject area that has taken place since 1999 gives me real optimism that the conceptual map is being redrawn. The first edition included all the research I was aware of 10 years ago; Mike Jackson's comprehensive study of the overlap between spiritual and psychotic experience, and Emmanuelle Peters' comparisons between diagnosed samples and members of new religious movements. It would be impossible to encompass the field in that way any longer. All I can do is to include examples of some of the most significant and interesting research that I am aware of, namely Caroline Brett's study, supervised by Peters, of anomalous experiences, and two examples of qualitative research by Sharon Warwick and Roger Waldram.

Rethinking Psychosis

I would like to think that this reconceptualisation of psychosis is set to move beyond a frontier and towards a paradigm shift. In my daily work as a clinical psychologist in an NHS acute mental health hospital, I am constantly confronted with the damage to hope and sense of self that the prevailing conceptualisation of psychosis produces. I am aware that there is a long way to go here, but at least we have started. The research explosion is producing the evidence and we are building on that research to develop new, more valuing and less stigmatising ways of working with people who have received that diagnosis. My prediction is that this new research stream will force those of us who work in the mental health services to look long and hard at how we handle the phenomenon of psychosis.

The conclusions of this research are inescapable. The apparatus of labelling, stigmatising and presenting medication as the only option is creating more and more persistent and serious dysfunctions than it aims to relieve. This research points to a new and more creative conceptualisation and attitude, which in turn can open the door to new and more creative treatment and response. The final, clinical, section of the book explores such responses, again with two new chapters. The first edition opened the door a little way to this new vision. Between the two editions, I have sought to open this debate to a wider audience with the generally accessible, 'Madness, Mystery and the Survival of God' (Clarke, 2008). My hope is that this second edition will move the discourse yet further and help to consolidate the new paradigm.

Section 1

Neuropsychology

Rethinking the interface between psychosis and spirituality raises major questions at the neuropsychological level, the inescapable scientific foundation for any consideration of non-ordinary experience. These questions concern both the neuropsychological correlates experience, and how the human mind/brain might transcend the confines of individual consciousness and reach beyond.

This field has developed momentously since Fenwick's classical consideration, a development that is comprehensively covered by Lancaster. Both contributors firmly reject the reductionist viewpoint that this area of experience can be explained away by the peculiarities of the brain.

2

The Neurophysiology of Religious Experience

Peter Fenwick

Introduction

Throughout the ages, there have always been a small number of people who claim to have had more far-reaching and wider experiences than their fellows. How these experiences are regarded depends on the time and the culture. Joan of Arc's voices led her onto the battlefield. In more primitive cultures, the Shaman was viewed as powerful and his experiences were revered. In ancient Greece, the epileptic falling was believed to show the signs of the sacred disease and some epileptic experiences were regarded as mystical. Today, hearing voices and experiencing altered states of consciousness are no longer thought of as seeing through the veil of reality into its true structure but as the misfiring of a disordered brain distorting the everyday world.

Our culture is now becoming more tolerant of deviant experience, and the age-old question of the nature of subjective experience is coming once again to the top of both the public and the scientific agendas. The hippie era of the 1960s, when the taking of hallucinogenic agents became widespread, had a powerful influence on this process. Many people had the 'veil of perception' torn and perceived a different world of altered sensory experience, subjective time and strong emotions. The widespread nature of these experiences has called into question their special value, as it would appear that under particular circumstances they are common to us all. This raises the question of how they can be explained by science and whether some of these experiences do have a special meaning for the experiencer and a special value for society.

The Nature of Consciousness

For many centuries, there appeared to be no place in the physical universe for consciousness. Newtonian mechanics in the eighteenth century, at the time of the age

---

Psychosis and Spirituality: Consolidating the New Paradigm Second Edition   Edited by Isabel Clarke
© 2010 John Wiley & Sons, Ltd.

of enlightenment, assumed a totally materialistic universe without consciousness, evolving according to a set of unchanging physical laws. It is this Newtonian mechanical model of the world which has led modern mainstream science to conclude that mind cannot exist as a separate entity.

Neuropsychiatry deals with brain science and is based on the correlation of mental states with the complex patterns of activity arising from diffuse nets of interconnected neurones. It is impossible to predict subjective experience by the study of objective firing patterns, and therefore impossible to explain the subjective aspects of mind or consciousness. Conscious stuff and brain stuff are different. The idea of a mechanical universe which excludes consciousness is unsatisfactory from an experiential point of view. Both psychology and psychiatry suffer from the lack of a satisfactory theoretical framework for the investigation and explanation of consciousness.

The electrical probe of the neurophysiologist defines only the objective electrical mechanisms of cellular action, whereas the psychologist defines the objective aspects of subjective experience. There is as yet no clear understanding of how these two are linked. Our current science has reached a point of extreme sophistication with the techniques of positron emission tomography (PET), functional magnetic resonance imaging and magnetoencephalography, where there at last appears to be a possible point of contact between subjective experience and physical structure and brain function. But if consciousness is to be reintegrated into science, it is important to understand why and how it came to be excluded from it.

The Changing Scientific View

Our science is based on the rationalism of Galileo, Descartes, Locke and Newton. Galileo defined a two-stuff universe: matter and energy. These stuffs, he said, had primary and secondary qualities. The primary qualities were those aspects of nature that could be measured, such as velocity, acceleration, weight, mass, etc. There were also secondary qualities, the qualities of subjective experience such as smell, vision, truth, beauty, love, etc. Galileo maintained that the domain of science was the domain of primary qualities. Secondary qualities were too complex to be investigated, and should be ignored as non-scientific.

This view has conditioned science ever since and has led to science's rejection of secondary qualities or subjective experience. Descartes, in the seventeenth century, contributed to the exclusion of consciousness. He also maintained, like Galileo, that there are two radically different kinds of stuff, the *res extensa*, the extended substance, which has length, breadth and depth, and can therefore be measured and divided; and a thinking substance, the *res cogitans*, which is unextended in physical space (and thus other-worldly, the soul, a sop to the Church of that time) and indivisible.

This picture started to shift in the twentieth century. Quantum mechanics suggested that matter, rather than being seen as discrete particles, could also exist in wave packets, each one of which is theoretically distributed throughout the universe, but has a statistical probability of appearing in a limited region of space. This point of view admits the possibility of a highly interconnected universe; the idea of a discrete particulate universe, each particle of which is independent, now falls by the wayside. It also allows the possibility that the effects of matter are not necessarily limited to one specific area, and may be non-local. Quantum mechanics adds another important component that the presence of an observer in a quantum mechanical experiment, by his interaction, determines that there is a definite outcome to the experiment. The consciousness of the experimenter seems important in limiting the outcome of the experiment, although this is a matter of debate among physicists at the present time. This view of quantum mechanics would suggest that subjective experience and consciousness may be interwoven into the objective world.

Current Explanatory Philosophies

There is as yet no explanation of religious experience that satisfies both those who have had the experiences and those who seek a scientific basis for them. Two major philosophical schools currently attempt to explain consciousness and brain function. Dennett's neurophilosophy characterises one extreme. He argues that consciousness and subjective experience are just the functions of neural nets. Nothing else is required to explain personal and religious consciousness except a detailed knowledge of neural nets. This is clearly a reductionist approach and a strong form of the brain identity theory, which equates subjective experience with neural mechanisms (Dennett, 1991).

The other extreme is characterised by the philosophy of Nagel (1974), who argues that it is never possible to learn from an objective third-person point of view what it is like to have a first-person experience. Subjective experience is not available to the scientific method, as it is not in the third person and cannot be validated in the public domain. Nagel argues that however much we understand about the neurophysiology or anatomy of the functioning of a bat's brain, we will never know what it is like to be a bat. This view suggests that the explanation of subjective experience requires a new principle which is beyond neural nets. Others such as Searle (1992) argue from an intermediate position.

Until there is a satisfactory philosophical explanation of the nature of mind, it will be impossible to answer questions relating to the nature of subjective experience, religious experience and the possibility of extra-sensory perception. These areas are still by definition beyond the confines of science. At present, any scientific theory of consciousness and subjective experience must explain everything in terms of brain functioning. However, I expect there are many people who, like Schrödinger (1967), feel claustrophobic when asked to accept that the broad sweep of the soul is contained only within the grey porridge of the brain. Will 'soul stuff' ever be probed by the microelectrode, or does it exist in a different dimension?

Features of Religious Experience

Religious experience is very common in the population. There are many studies of the frequency of mystical or religious experience. Surveys of the percentage of the United States or UK population reporting having had a religious or mystical experience (Glock and Starck, 1965; Back and Bourque, 1970) have varied between 20% and 44%.

In Britain, David Hay organised an NOP survey in 1976, asking a similar question, and found a similar rate of reply: about 36% gave positive responses. Of interest is the finding that although about a third of all people have had the experience, only 18% have had it more than twice and only 8% 'often and more'. There was no correlation with age, but positive replies were commonest in those whose education went beyond 20 years, e.g. the more articulate university graduates. There was also, interestingly, a sex difference: 41% of women gave positive replies against 31% of men. Fifty-one per cent said their experiences lasted between seconds and minutes; 74% said it lasted 'less than a day'.

Ecstatic mystical states, in which the subjects describe a feeling of universal love, become identified with some aspect of the cosmos and occur much less often. These states can occur spontaneously, but they, or fragments of them, may also occur in other circumstances, as in the near-death experience, for example. Such alterations in mental state can also be induced by a number of quite common meditation techniques. Some hallucinogenic drugs can induce similar mental states. They can occasionally occur in temporal lobe epilepsy (TLE), and frequently in psychosis, when they are usually associated with an elevation of mood.

It therefore seems probable that the ability to experience these wide mystical states is a normal part of brain function, and indeed, there are techniques in many eastern religions directed at inducing these wide feelings of universal love at will. Bucke (1961), a nineteenth-century Canadian psychiatrist, was one of the first Western scientists to attempt to define mystical experience. In his book *Cosmic Consciousness*, he examined many very deep experiences:

> Now came a period of rapture so intense that the universe stood still as if amazed at the unutterable majesty of the spectacle: only one in all the infinite universe. The all-caring, perfect one, perfect wisdom, truth, love and purity: and with rapture came insight. In that same wonderful moment of what might be called supernal bliss came illumination... What joy when I saw there was no break in the chain – not a link left out – everything in its place and time, worlds, systems, all blended in one harmonious world, universal, synonymous with universal love.

[handwritten marginalia, left margin:] Perhaps the longer the rift between a person & the divine the more careful they must be when approaching it again?

[handwritten marginalia, lower left:] experiences of this suddenly plummet into a state of horrified terror.? Why did my (stoned) ... ?

Bucke and others have listed nine features which characterise the main elements of the mystical experience. These are:

1. feelings of unity;
2. feelings of objectivity and reality; ?
3. transcendence of space and time; ✓
4. a sense of sacredness; ✓
5. deeply felt positive mood – joy, blessedness, peace and bliss; ✓
6. containing paradox – mystical consciousness, which is often felt to be true, despite a violation of Aristotelian logic; ✓
7. ineffability – language is inadequate to express the experiences; ✓
8. transiency; ?
9. positive change in attitude or behaviour following the experience.

Although all these features are quoted widely in the mystical literature, they are not in any way limited to rare spontaneous mystical states, but are part of normal human experience. They are also a feature of pathological experiences such as psychoses. If mystical experience is so common, then it is logical to assume that there must be a brain mechanism which allows expression of the experience. The question then is, what mechanism? Much of the evidence we have about the brain mechanism which mediates that state has been acquired through the study of pathologically induced mystical experiences. Epileptic and drug states are two such examples.

A door that can be opened, a telescope through which we can look

A Mainly Right Hemisphere Experience?

Because emotional synthesis appears to be predominantly a function of the right hemisphere, it has been argued that changes in right hemisphere function may be the basis of mystical experience. The evidence for this is as follows. The ineffability of the experience would suggest that there are insufficient verbal concepts or words to characterise it. Left hemisphere function is known to be associated with categorisation, and thus the absence of categories and words for the experiences could suggest that the right hemisphere plays a leading role. *FASCINATING*

A major feature of the experience is the loss of boundaries, both spatial and personal. When looking at the world, there is a deep feeling of unity. Spatial integration is known to be a function of the right hemisphere, and thus a loss of spatial boundaries is probably caused by an alteration in right hemisphere function. Time alters during the experience and is usually stretched out to form an eternity. Disorientation in time and misordering of events in time is a right hemisphere, either right temporal or right parietal, function (Davidson, 1941; Wagner, 1943). Speeding up and slowing down of subjective time are found in right temporal lobe seizures and with right temporal damage (Penfield and Perrott, 1963; Pichler, 1943).

Many people who have mystical experiences report entering a heavenly scene and hearing heavenly music. They often describe this 'heavenly music' as being like traditional church music sung by angelic choirs. Traditional church music is essentially concordant and rhythmic music; it was not until the twentieth century that discordant arrhythmic music came to be widely played. I have yet to hear of an experience in which heavenly music was described as being discordant. Wieser and Mazzola (1986) report a limited study on one patient undergoing epilepsy surgery, who had implanted foramen ovale electrodes, a procedure in which the electrodes come to lie alongside the right and left medial temporal structures. It was found that concordant tones stimulated the right hippocampus and discordant tones on the left.

A wide range of similar experiments reinforce this association with the right hemisphere. The response to emotional sounds (Beaton, 1979; Carmon and Nachson, 1973) and visual emotion (Habid, 1986), as well as the effects on mood control of sodium amytal injections (Terzian, 1964) and temporal damage or right-sided fits (Hurwitz *et al.*, 1985), suggests that the right hemisphere is dominant for emotion. Emotional involvement in deja vu perception and strong emotional experiences associated with TLE are exclusively right-sided (Mullan and Penfield, 1959). All this evidence points towards a major right hemisphere contribution to mystical experiences. It is thus likely that fragments of the mystical experiences could be found in patients who have right temporal lobe damage or pathology.

Temporal Lobe Epilepsy and Mystical Experience

It is difficult to know why epilepsy was known as the sacred disease. Patients with epilepsy seldom talk coherently during a seizure, or during the confusional state following a seizure. It has been suggested that the sudden falling to the ground accompanied by the motor movements of a generalised seizure, the post-ictal period of unconsciousness when the sufferer lies apparently dead and the subsequent return of consciousness could only be seen as caused by some divine act, rather than by the neurophysiological impairment of brain structures. Perhaps, it was the ability to die and be reborn that gave epilepsy sufferers apparent magical powers.

An alternative view is that the correlation between brain damage and epilepsy is the important link. There are anecdotal accounts of subjects developing psychic gifts (clairaudience and clairvoyance) after a head injury. We set out to test this observation on 17 mediums from the College of Psychic Studies, with the prediction that the psychic gifts would have developed after a head injury, particularly an injury to the right temporal lobe. The study confirmed that those who claimed to have psychic gifts had had more head injuries and more right hemisphere deficits on psychometric testing than the control group. Two subjects in the control group who had had mystical experiences also developed these after a blow to the head and subsequent right temporal impairment. It would thus not be surprising if some patients who developed epilepsy after a head injury claimed psychic gifts and this would reinforce the idea of epilepsy as a 'sacred disease' (Fenwick *et al.*, 1985).

The best example of a mystical experience directly associated with an epileptic seizure is that of Prince Mishkin in Dostoevsky's *The Idiot*:

*[handwritten margin note: * Bashes head against wall *]*

Perhaps an important endeavor is not just the experiencing of the divine, but the capacity to live with it sustainably and non-compensatorily, rather than manically? fruitfully.

...there was a moment or two in his epileptic condition...when suddenly amid the sadness, spiritual darkness and depression his brain seemed to catch fire at brief moments...All his agitation, all his doubts and worries, seemed composed in a twinkling, culminating in a great calm full of serene and harmonious joy, full of understanding and knowledge of the final cause.

Dostoevsky was known to have epilepsy, and so it seems reasonable to assume that he was describing his own experience. However, others have suggested that the experience occurred independently of a seizure, but in fictionalising it he ascribed it to the epilepsy.

In any event, positive experiences as part of the aura of a partial complex arising in the temporal lobe are extremely rare. In Gowers' (1881) study of 505 epileptic auras, only 3% were said to be emotional, and none positive. Lennox (1960), in a study of 1017 auras, found only nine which were said to be pleasant (0.9%), and of these, only a few showed 'positive pleasure'. Penfield and Kristianson (1951) cite only one case of an aura with a pleasant sensation, followed by an epigastric feeling of discomfort. However, Cirignotta *et al.* (1980) published an account of a patient who had an aura similar to that described by Dostoevsky before a temporal lobe seizure arising from his right temporal lobe. Thus, there is evidence that such auras do exist as part of a seizure, and that they are likely to be associated with the right side of the brain. A patient of mine had an aura very similar to that described above, and had been having it for a number of years before I saw him. His aura was an ecstatic feeling and one he greatly valued. It was not until after having experienced his first grand mal seizure, which was very unpleasant, that he sought medical care. EEG and MRI investigations showed that his seizures were arising from the right temporal lobe, and he was started on the anti-epileptic drug carbamazepine. Since that time he has been seizure free, and in the clinic, when discussing his epilepsy, he looks longingly back to the time when he could experience his auras. However, he is so frightened of having another grand mal seizure that despite his sense of loss he still takes his carbamazepine.

Dewhurst and Beard (1970) looked at cases of TLE collected from the Maudsley and Queen Square Hospitals, which showed religious conversion. The conversion usually occurred suddenly, and was not always related to a mystical aura. Of greater interest, the majority of these cases had previously had a psychotic illness. It was thus difficult to know whether their experience was related to their epilepsy or their psychosis.

It seems that the temporal lobe is, to some extent, involved in the synthesis of mystical feelings and states, but that these states are related equally with normal brain function and in illness with psychosis. A parsimonious view would be that mystical experiences are normal and temporal lobe structures are involved in their synthesis, but that their expression in fragmented form is frequently associated with pathology.

A study by Sensky and Fenwick (1982) investigated the relationship between epilepsy and religious experience. Subjects were taken from the Maudsley Hospital Clinic and compared with samples of the general population obtained from other studies. Mystical states were assessed by questionnaire. The questions included 'Did your faith come gradually or was there a point at which you suddenly saw the light?' and 'Have you ever felt at one with the universe and in touch with the universal?' Any responses which were part of a psychotic illness were discounted. There was a 76% response rate to the questionnaire, males and females being equally represented. Twenty-six per cent had generalised epilepsy, and 56% had a diagnosis of TLE.

The results of this study showed that our subjects with TLE were no more inclined towards religion than those with generalised epilepsy. Nor did they repeat more frequently a belief in or an experience of mystical or psychic states. Of more importance, the epileptics under-reported mystical and psychic states compared with the general population. This finding would seem to be at variance with American workers who find religiosity over-represented in their temporal lobe epileptics. It does suggest that the term 'religiosity' may not be travelling across the Atlantic very well, and that part of the confusion is a confusion of terminology.

Hallucinations

[handwritten margin note: Can two people see "the same" hallucination (in the way they see "the same" chair – both convinced the other knows what they're talking about)?]

Everyone knows what a hallucination is. It is defined as a false perception. Voices are heard, although no one is speaking. Visions are seen that nobody else can see. The body is stimulated in a variety of ways, although no one is there to stimulate it. Hallucinations have been thought of as defining pathology, although they are extremely common in the population and may have no pathological significance. It is very common, for example, for a bereaved husband or wife to hallucinate the *[handwritten: !!]* dead partner. In one study, over half the people hallucinated the dead spouse, with equal proportions of men and women. The hallucinations frequently lasted many years, although they were most common during the first 10 years after bereavement. There is no variation with culture, site of residence, etc. The authors of this study saw hallucinations as normal and helpful.

But do we really know what a hallucination is? The current scientific explanation depends on the abnormal functioning of different cortical regions. A good example of this view is shown by the occurrence of the phantom limb syndrome. If a limb is evulsed in a car accident, or removed by surgery, then frequently the image of having a limb remains, although it is degraded. However, after a number of months it has been shown that the area of brain which was responsible for representing the limb is invaded by cells from neighbouring cortex. These new cell connections then activate the old area and the patient becomes aware of a phantom limb which has a life of its own. It will take up different positions, feel different and sometimes feel severe pain.

This concept of abnormal activity in an area of cortex leading to an abnormal perception is found throughout the hallucination literature. Our current understanding of auditory hallucinations in schizophrenia is that it is the patient's own voice which is the basis of the hallucination, but it no longer carries the tag with it that it is being generated by its owner. The same structures are seen to be active on neural imaging when the patient imagines a voice as when he hallucinates (Frith, 1995). Damage to the tegmentum of the brain, which regulates the flow of information to the

[handwritten margin note: What is the nature of the mental act of perceiving a thought as "not mine"? is "not mine"?]

[handwritten note at bottom: "limits"??]

cortex and is part of the mechanism of attention, leads to wonderfully detailed, rich and colourful hallucinations of everyday scenes, which the sufferer may take to be real.

There have been a number of studies looking at the functioning of the brain after the ingestion of psychoactive drugs. Dr Vollenweider, a researcher in Switzerland, has looked at blood flow in the cerebral cortex by means of a PET scan during drug-induced mystical states. He defines three major sets of experiences. The first are wide mystical states with oceanic feelings. These show an increase in blood flow, predominantly in the frontal region. Hallucinogenic experiences are accompanied by a marked increase in blood flow in the sensory cortices of the brain. Those 'bad trips' in which the ego feels as if it is disintegrating, and the subjects are terrified, are accompanied by a general reduction in blood flow throughout the cortex, but an increase in blood flow in the thalamus. It is thus possible to see that even the wide experiential states of mystical experience are accompanied by an altered brain state based in cerebral functioning. *So what?*

Conclusion

It is now possible to outline the various brain areas which are active during mystical *— what about the rest of the body?* states. There is little doubt that the right temporal lobe is important, but there is also evidence that mystical states involve much more of the brain, with both a large frontal and a thalamic component. Even though we are able to suggest what brain areas may be involved during such experiences, as far as explaining the experiences themselves, we are no further forward. The reductionist, who argues strongly for a mind-brain-identity theory, will leave the matter at this point, stating that as mind and brain are essentially the same, little further information can be gathered by looking into the topic in more depth.

However, there are those of us who feel that the postulates of reductionist science, though adequate to describe brain structure, are quite inadequate when it comes to explaining subjective experience. It is thus time to formulate theories which will allow the integration of conscious experience into brain states. If this could be done, then when the mystic says that he looks through into the structure of the universe, we would have a theory which would be able to correlate accurately the mental state? which would arise with any pre-defined brain state. More important, the subjective side of experience would become a part of our science and consciousness and a greater understanding of the spiritual nature of man would come to the fore.

3

Cognitive Neuroscience, Spirituality and Mysticism: Recent Developments

B. Les Lancaster

The challenge to integrate cognitive neuroscience with the domain of spirituality and mysticism has advanced considerably over recent years. Developments since the 1990s have come about not only as a result of the ever increasing sophistication in our ability to detail brain function but also as a consequence of more subtle analyses of the spiritual domain. As far as the latter is concerned, it is fallacious to think in terms of one over-arching spiritual state to which we might correlate brain function. Rather there are various spiritual objectives, each perhaps relating to a distinctive form of religious practice, and the need to be specific when attempting to 'explain' spiritual states in terms of the functioning of the brain has been increasingly realised. Moreover, many involved in the project to develop a spiritually sensitive cognitive neuroscience have recognised the distorting effect of assuming that spirituality is only concerned with cultivating certain experiential states. There is more to the project than simply imaging the brains of meditators, for example. The spiritual traditions have, over millennia, cultivated highly insightful analyses of the nature of the mind, and the core of the project to integrate spirituality and cognitive neuroscience lies in the recognition that we have two powerful instruments for understanding the mind, the one entails *observation from within* and the other, *observation from without*. The most potent expressions of these are found within the two domains of our interest here – spiritual traditions and cognitive neuroscience, respectively.

It is this focus on understanding the mind which renders the project important. It will be self-evident that all our endeavours to improve the human condition must hold a central place for understanding the mind. Cognitive neuroscience is the partner of neurology in our endeavours to bring healing to those in whom brain damage has disrupted the normal operation of mind. Its links with psychiatry and psychotherapy can offer important perspectives for those suffering because of a

Psychosis and Spirituality: Consolidating the New Paradigm Second Edition   Edited by Isabel Clarke
© 2010 John Wiley & Sons, Ltd.

disturbed mind. But the spiritual traditions have held up the candle of a *more-than-normal* mind, a mind that realises a potential beyond our immediate repertoire of abilities, and it is in its engagement with these traditions, that cognitive neuroscience may bring the most profound service to humankind.

There are three approaches to the relationship between cognitive neuroscience and spirituality, each of which will take up a section of this chapter. The first concerns the effects of spiritual practice both on the brain and on cognitive processes. Generally, spiritual practices are adopted because they are deemed to be beneficial in cognitive terms (e.g. improving control of attention, developing *mindfulness*) and/or *transpersonal* terms (e.g. effecting contact with a higher self, or with the divine). This first area of our interest reviews studies examining the extent to which these claimed benefits may be real in terms of brain regions activated by the practice and changes in cognitive functions. As we shall see, such studies have demonstrated that meditation, for example, does bring about changes in brain activity and in cognitive functions in line with predictions. Accordingly, this line of research lends significant credence to the value of such meditative practice.

The second area of connection between cognitive neuroscience and spiritual traditions entails examining their respective analyses of specific functions of the mind (e.g. perception, thought, memory). This approach can not only establish concordances between these analyses, but may also indicate where insights in one area can sharpen the approach in the other. A Buddhist analysis of the process of perception may, for example, suggest ways of understanding seemingly anomalous observations in the neuroscience of vision.

The third aspect of this discourse between cognitive neuroscience and the spiritual traditions takes us further from the materialist worldview that underpins most work in science. As Fenwick (this volume) implies, it may be fallacious to think that at root consciousness is simply a product of the physical brain. Consciousness may, in ways that we do not yet fully understand, be *irreducible* to physical structure and processes. The third area for consideration, then, explores ideas articulated within the more esoteric aspects of spiritual or mystical traditions, which see the brain as reflective of a higher, transpersonal level of the intellect, a dimension to which the word *soul* most aptly applies. Although it is clearly beyond the remit of psychological science to demonstrate the *reality* of the soul, I shall explore material which suggests that cognitive neuroscience may nevertheless have a role to play in substantiating more mystical views of the further ramifications of the psyche.

Although in each of these areas our primary interest focuses on the data that directly forge links between cognitive neuroscience and spirituality, there are two issues in the background that I should like to address briefly here. First is *ontology*, the issue of what we believe to be real. In introducing the word *soul*, I have hinted already at this question of what is real. But the question is not limited to the third area of our interest concerning esoteric speculation. Even when considering the neural changes brought about by prayer or meditation we might question whether or not the data fit into a belief that the brain is the sole seat of the mind. As we shall see, the author of one such study claims that his data do not fit within a materialistic mould, suggesting

[margin, top left, handwritten:] Curious the relationship; similarities and differences between physical brain - matter damage and trauma emotional / psychological / spiritual -

[margin, handwritten:] fascinating

[margin, handwritten:] such as?

[margin, bottom left, handwritten:] perhaps meditation + other things ↓ does "brain" + "mind" stuff too?

rather that those whose brains he was investigating were connecting with 'the divine Ground of Being' (Beauregard and O'Leary 2007, p. 293)

The second issue concerns the *value* of the spiritual path. A sceptical position might hold that even if a practice such as meditation brings about changes in brain activity, such changes may be of no value in that they are inconsequential or perhaps ephemeral. However, a believer might feel that their practice is of ultimate value whether or not psychology demonstrates any effects; they know, for example, that their contact with the divine is real whatever scientific experimentation may show. This matter of value is conveyed by the Christian theological term *soteriology*, meaning the teachings about salvation. All religions self-evidently teach their own path to perfection, and justify these teachings in terms such as *revelation* that are not open to scientific enquiry. An undercurrent in the research we shall be considering here is whether some aspects of these teachings can be justified in terms other than those of the religion itself. In this sense, cognitive neuroscience might become not only a yardstick by which to measure effects of spiritual practice but also an arbiter of the claimed transformational effects of adherence to the disciplines of religion. It is worth noting here at the outset the danger of *psychologisation*, that is, of substituting the evaluative constructs of neuroscience and psychology for those to which the religion properly appeals. In short, if the soul is a 'portion of God from above' (Hebrew Bible, *Job* 31:2) then trying to find evidence for it in the categories of psychological science would be misguided.

These two, ontology and soteriology, are effectively two sides of one coin, for it is perhaps a defining feature of religion that its practices are directed to goals which are not of this material realm. Even the non-theistic Buddhism presents its ultimate goal in terms of detachment from the wheel of life, a concept that can hardly be squeezed into a materialistic worldview. Nevertheless, all religions do discuss the workings of the mind, most notably in their mystical teachings, and it is legitimate to explore the extent to which these discussions stand up in the face of the scientific study of the mind in our day.

Of Religion, Spirituality and Mysticism

The terms 'religion', 'spirituality' and 'mysticism' have peppered my introductory comments above. It is time to tighten up on the terminology. To my mind, it is their respective relation to the 'sacred', which unites these terms, giving us a fourth word whose meaning needs clarification. The term 'religion' refers to that which has become *canonical*, meaning that at its core are writings, teachings and organisational structures which are viewed as somehow essential for devotees to connect with the sacred. 'Spirituality' is a more inward concept in that it connotes one's personal sense of the sacred, and those places, practices and times that enrich that sense and promote growth towards more continuous experience of the sacred. That sense is not merely intellectual but is primarily emotional. Hill *et al.* (2000, p. 66) thus define spirituality as, 'The feelings, thoughts, experiences and behaviours that arise from a search for the sacred'. 'Mysticism' includes teachings and practices that encourage a quest to unite with the source of the sacred. For theistic religions, this entails knowledge of the inner workings of the divine as it intersects with the human world (the *Godhead*).

There is considerable overlap between these terms, most especially in the way I have related them all to the sacred. Critically for our purposes, there has been a historical shift in relation to which of the terms might be regarded as central within this trinity. The twentieth century seems to mark a boundary between 'religion' being the central, overarching term and its replacement by 'spirituality'. The story of this shift is deeply important, drawing together as it does historical trends and our collective journey to understanding the psyche in psychological terms. Here is not the place to detail that story. Suffice it say that the move away from religion reflects a changing attitude to authority[1], with 'spirituality' implying a need to personally evaluate the value of given teachings; as Pappas and Friedman (2007, p. 28) put it, spirituality 'is based on a personally constructed philosophy grounded in experience'. Another reason for this shift has been the widespread availability of teachings from diverse religions, which brought challenges to traditional acceptance of religious authority. The consequence of all this has been that personal experience and scientific credibility have become the major arbiters of value. The reason I wrote that this historical shift is 'critical for our purposes' is that it places our interest in inter-relating cognitive neuroscience (as well as psychology more generally) and spirituality in context. Scientific corroboration may be irrelevant to the claims of *religion*, but it is becoming critical for the tenets of *spirituality*.

What then of the *sacred*? Hill *et al* (2000, p. 66) expand on their definition cited above by stating that, 'The term 'sacred' refers to a divine being, divine object, Ultimate Reality, or Ultimate Truth as perceived by the individual'. Although not disputing the importance of these Ultimates, I would suggest that this definition is perhaps placing the bar too high! As Emmons and Crumpler (1999) suggest, even seemingly mundane pursuits can take on the quality of the sacred. In his highly influential study of the *holy*, Otto (1917/1958) uses the term *numinous* to convey the non-rational, feeling quality that characterises the sacred. It is a consciousness of the 'wholly other' that is essentially incapable of being conveyed to one who has not experienced it. A reflection of the shift towards less-religiously focused spirituality in our day may be found in the fact that many associate such a numinous quality with non-Ultimates, such as football, management styles or environmental concerns. Traditionally, the notion of *separation* from the mundane has been the hallmark of the holy: a place, object or practice becomes sacred to the extent that it is intentionally *set aside* from matters of the mundane, being related instead to the religious sphere.

---

[1] I would see the First World War as marking the turning point inasmuch as the authority of rulers was effectively bankrupted by their inability to bring wisdom to the situation they faced. The move towards spirituality was hastened by the individualistic explorations of the 'sixties', but these came about largely in the wake of the post-WW2 period, and most historians would see the Second World War as effectively a continuation of the First.

The shift in our day has led to this act of setting aside becoming concerned with whatever the person construes as the larger sphere within which they are embedded. The sense of being connected with a larger consciousness, or with some kind of global *being* becomes, together with Otto's notion of the numinous feeling-tone, central to any definition of spirituality. A third factor is *quest*; that the individual must embark on a journey to increase contact with the numinous and to consolidate their connection with the larger sphere. Although the specifically Christian overtones of the term may have been attenuated in much contemporary spirituality, a spiritual journey is quintessentially *soteriological* inasmuch as some form of transformation to a more desired state of being is the primary motivation.

The Cognitive Neuroscience of Spiritual Practice

A review of research in this area shows that spiritual practices are effective at achieving the kinds of cognitive goals discernible in traditional teachings. To take my first research example, the Buddhist Vipassana practice is traditionally described as developing a form of *meta-awareness* (Lutz, Dunne and Davidson, 2007), meaning that practitioners might be expected to develop increased ability to avoid their attention being grabbed by distracting stimuli. A study by Slagter *et al.* (2007) put this claim to the test by examining the *attentional blink* in participants before and after a 3-month Vipassana retreat, during which the participants meditated 10–12 h/day. As the term implies, the attentional blink is a cognitive equivalent to the blink of the eyelid; when two visual stimuli are presented in quick succession amongst a stream of such stimuli, our awareness of the second is often obscured by processing of the first. This obscuring effect is operative with inter-stimulus intervals between about 200 and 500 ms. Results from the study showed greater improvements in the ability to detect the second stimulus when presented within this inter-stimulus time frame amongst the retreat participants than amongst controls (novice meditators). In addition to this behavioural measure, the study examined electrophysiological responses to the visual stimuli. Amongst those attending the retreat, there was a relative decrease in the amplitude of the evoked P3b wave to the first visual stimuli. This positive wave in the evoked potential is thought to relate to attentional resource allocation, and the authors suggest that the increased ability to detect the second stimulus came about because of a lowering in the level of cognitive resources being devoted to the first stimulus. This lowering of resources being devoted to the first stimulus is clearly in accord with the goal of cultivating 'bare attention' as promoted traditionally in the teachings about Vipassana. In other words, in cognitive and neurophysiological terms, Vipassana meditation seemed to be achieving exactly what the teachings state that it should achieve.

Connected to our control of attention is the ability to detach from habitual modes of cognitive processing. Such *cognitive flexibility* requires us to assert control to overcome the way that features of our world automatically grab our attention. Only by stopping the automaticity (Deikman, 1966a) we can re-frame the approach we adopt in a given situation. A classic example of such a habitual mode leading to inappropriate processing is the *Stroop effect*. Stroop (1935) demonstrated that our ability to read a colour word (e.g. 'red') was compromised when the word was written in ink of a colour that conflicted with the word (e.g. 'red' written in blue ink). The Stroop effect demonstrates that the colour that is before our eyes captures our attention, even when we have been instructed to ignore it. An obvious question therefore arises in relation to meditation given the claimed effects on attention: does meditation lead to increased cognitive flexibility as evidenced through decreased interference on a Stroop task? Studies by Wenk-Sormaz (2005) and Moore and Malinowski (2009) answer this question affirmatively. Moore and Malinowski's study showed that participants' scores on a scale of mindfulness correlated with their accuracy on the Stroop task, and that meditators achieved higher mindfulness scores than non-meditators.

A further example of automatic processing is found in the phenomenon of *binocular rivalry*. When two different images are presented to the two eyes simultaneously, we generally see one or the other, not some kind of superimposition of one on the other. Typically, the image we see alternates randomly. Carter *et al.* (2005) studied this phenomenon on a group of Tibetan Buddhist monks. In an interesting methodological strategy, the researchers had the monks act as their own controls by engaging in two different meditative practices, each predicted to have different consequences for the rivalry task. One was a practice the authors translate as 'one-point', which entailed maintaining attention on a single object and reducing distraction by other internal or external events. The other practice was to develop compassion and to emanate loving-kindness. For obvious reasons in terms of the goals of the practices, the one-point meditation was hypothesised as likely to give greater stability on the binocular rivalry test. This was indeed the outcome: the compassion practice resulted in no changes from the baseline level of perceptual stability, whereas 50% of monks had highly increased stability both during, and following, the one-point practice.

In addition to these various cognitive effects, meditation has been reported to have positive consequences for our emotional lives, with periods of practice resulting in 'positive mood, emotional stability and resilience to stress and negative life events' (Rubia, 2009, p. 2). Many studies have demonstrated these effects using behavioural and social measures, and conclusions are reinforced by research using brain imaging techniques, which have shown that emotionally oriented meditation activates areas of the brain known to have important roles in emotion-related processing. Lutz *et al.* (2008a) studied the areas of the brain activated by emotional stimuli whereas expert meditators engaged in loving–kindness–compassion meditation. They found that meditators had increased levels of activity in areas of the limbic system (insular and cingulate cortices) long recognised as playing central roles in emotion. Moreover, these neural changes were correlated with changes in heart rate, suggesting that compassion meditation induces a recalibration of the neural systems that co-ordinate peripheral indices of emotion (Lutz *et al.*, 2009).

An earlier study (Lutz *et al.*, 2004) showed that those with long-term experience of Tibetan compassion meditation had developed greater integration across widespread regions of the brain. The researchers studied the power in the gamma band of the EEG, a measure of synchrony in neural patterns of firing. Compared with controls, the long-term practitioners displayed high levels of such synchrony not only during their meditation but also at baseline prior to meditating. This latter observation is striking because it suggests the influence of meditation on the individuals' general state. After all, the purpose of a regular practice is not simply to engender a given state at the time of the practice but to transform the practitioner in the longer term. As the goal of the meditation in this study is to bring about a global state of compassion, the global coupling amongst widespread brain regions is especially suggestive. As the authors suggest, it seems that the meditators' brains have indeed been transformed to a more unified state.

A primary objective of many forms of meditation is a state of equanimity, in which one becomes detached from emotional disturbance. Neurophysiological support for the effectiveness in this regard of a form of Yoga meditation (*Sahaja Yoga*), intended to generate thoughtless awareness, comes from an EEG-based study by Aftanas and Golocheikine (2005), in which participants were shown emotionally distressing movie clips. Controls showed increases in EEG gamma synchrony over frontal brain regions in response to the clips. Long-term meditators, by comparison, displayed none of these changes in their EEG patterns, implying that some degree of equanimity on this measure had been achieved. *This could become DE-humanizing*

Other changes in brain activity associated with meditations have been reviewed by Cahn and Polich (2006) and Lutz *et al.* (2008b). As a generalisation, meditation directed at control of attention results in activation of frontal areas known to be involved in higher-order executive functions; and 'open monitoring' meditation, in which there is no specific focus for the attention, with the meditator monitoring internal and/or external events more generally, activates brain regions concerned with vigilance and monitoring of signals arriving through the sensory systems. As I stated above in relation to the study of cognitive functions behaviourally, the data from study of the brain indicate that the practices are doing precisely what they are traditionally said to be doing.

But what of the more numinous aspects of spiritual practice? Can we point to neural concomitants of an experience of the divine, for example? And, if we can, are these patterns of brain activity all there is to such mystical experience?

Beauregard and Paquette (2006, 2008) approached these questions through studies of Carmelite nuns who had experienced mystical states of union with God. Clearly, it is not possible to turn on such encounters at will, simply to fit in with the researchers' monitoring of the brain. The closest the authors could come to studying these mystical states was to ask the nuns to remember and attempt to relive the most intense mystical experience they had encountered. As it turned out, recalling the experience did lead to significant 'reliving' inasmuch as self-reports following the study gave high scores on measures designed to evaluate mystical experience.

Beauregard and Paquette were assessing brain activity through functional magnetic resonance imaging (fMRI; the 2006 study) and EEG analysis (2008). The studies
made comparisons across a baseline condition of rest, a control condition in which
the nuns were asked to recall and relive their most intense encounter with a *human*,
and the above condition in which the encounter had been with *God*. The fMRI study
showed patterns of activity in the control and mystical conditions consistent with a
lowered sense of self, as might be expected if one were merging with another
(increases in activity of left and right superiror parietal lobes); increased emotion,
which related to the nuns' subjective reports of peace and unconditional love
(left caudate nucleus and left cingulate); and imagery (regions of visual cortex).
The particular observations of interest concern the comparison between the control
and mystical conditions. Amongst a range of difference between these two conditions, activity in the right middle temporal cortex was higher in the mystical
condition, an observation that accords with Fenwick's (this volume) view that the
right temporal lobe is active in mystical states. Beauregard and Paquette suggest that
the right temporal activation during the mystical condition reflected the subjective
sense of having contacted a *spiritual*, rather than a *human*, entity.

This conclusion regarding the role of the right temporal cortex was reinforced by
the EEG study, which showed greater gamma power over this region in the mystical
versus control conditions. Other findings included increased theta power over
frontal regions, interpreted by the authors as relating to feelings of peace, joy and
unconditional love; and long-distance alpha synchrony over regions of the right
hemisphere, considered to reflect an inhibition of sensory processing during the
mystical condition.

Studies such as this leave many questions unanswered. From a neuropsychological perspective, the proposed functions of particular areas involve much
supposition; it is one thing to note commonalities in activations associated with
emotion in general, for example, but quite another to suggest that a particular
aspect of such activation relates to 'unconditional love'. There is a questionable
level of circularity involved in the way in which categories obtained through
subjective reports are imposed on the brain imaging data. The most defensible
conclusion is the one the authors make to the effect that the substitution of a divine,
for a human, *other* does generate a distinctive pattern of activity in the brain. The
scientific data alone cannot, however, indicate whether the spiritual experience is
more than a *subjective* reality. Nevertheless, Beauregard and O'Leary (2007, p. 290)
assert that, '[T]he evidence supports the view that individuals who have RSMEs
[religious, spiritual, and/or mystical experiences] do in fact contact an objectively
real "force" that exists outside themselves'.

In closing this section, I would like to emphasise briefly the strengths and
limitations of this experimental work in the cognitive neuroscience of spiritual
practice. It has been clearly demonstrated that practices generate changes in line with
the emotional and cognitive consequences to be expected according to the psychological aspects of the relevant spiritual teachings. Moreover, these changes can be
long term and have beneficial consequences for health and well-being. However,

there are cases of *over-interpretation* of neuroscientific data, and, more generally, this branch of our enquiry can cast very little light, if any, on the genuinely *spiritual* aspects of the traditional teachings. The jury remains out . . .

Towards a Triangulation of Mental Processes

The question to be addressed in this section asks whether insights into the nature of mind presented in spiritual traditions accord with data from cognitive neuroscience. It would be a mistake to think that the various spiritual traditions are concerned only with Ultimates. Buddhism has much to say about the minutiae of perception; Kabbalah explores the nature of thought beneath the limen of consciousness; Sufism is rich in its discussions of imagination; and the Advaita Vedanta school of Hinduism details the propensity of mind to split reality into subjects and objects. In all cases, the goal is not simply to specify the function of these mental processes for its own sake, but to advance the transformational quest. It is through coming to know the inner processes that we are able to harness them in quest of the aspiration to a higher state of being.

I have previously examined in detail the view of perception in the Wisdom literature (*Abhidhamma*) of Therevadan Buddhism and its relation to perceptual processes as understood in cognitive neuroscience (Lancaster, 1997a, b, 2004). The degree of 'fit' between these diverse approaches is epitomised by their respective approaches to 'moments' of consciousness. The Abhidhamma holds that there are several successive moments of consciousness in the perceptual process. This idea is itself consistent with the fundamental Buddhist notion of *impermanence* that everything rises and decays in its own time-scale. For the Abhidhamma, then, consciousness is not a continuous stream, but a succession of consciousnesses, each of which arises as a conditioned response to previous events, endures briefly, then falls, having itself triggered the next moment in the sequence. Our sense of consciousness being a continuous stream is, on this view, illusory. According to Abhidhamma, a normal act of perception comprises 17 moments of consciousness, which are grouped into a number of stages. Using the example of vision, Aung (1910/ 1972) names these stages as follows:

> [First] consciousness of the kind that apprehends sensations . . . rises and ceases. Immediately after this, there rise and cease in order – visual consciousness, seeing just that visible object; recipient consciousness receiving it; investigating consciousness investigating it; determining consciousness determining it (p. 126).

These moments of consciousness are understood as being incredibly brief; according to the Buddhist texts, millions of such moments may occur in the duration of one lightning flash! Such a time-scale (allowing for hyperbole in the texts) places them in the same time-scale as the brain processes occurring en route to perception. It is, then, of considerable interest that one recent formulation of the cognitive neuroscience of perception holds that successive stages in the brain's processing of sensory data give rise to 'micro-consciousnesses' (Zeki, 2003; Zeki and Bartels, 1999), a concept that tightly parallels the Buddhist formulation. Zeki argues that the processing that occurs in distinct visual regions of the brain – processing of colour information, of movement information, etc. – eventuates in distinct micro-consciousness. As he succinctly puts it, 'a processing site is also a perceptual site' (2003, p. 214). The central point he makes is that, despite our introspective sense to the contrary, consciousness *is not unified,* that there are many conscious-nes*ses* distributed in time and space. The parallel here with Buddhist ideas is striking.

I have argued that such a parallel extends into specific details of the stages identified in the Abhidhamma. In my formulation, the following parallels may be discerned:

1. The Abhidhamma stage of *visual consciousness* corresponds to the neural activities in the various areas of the visual cortex through which specific properties of the visual stimulus (colour, movement, etc.) become encoded as patterns of firing amongst specialised neural groups. This stage very much equates to Zeki's micro-consciousnesses arising from primary processing sites.

2. *Recipient consciousness* corresponds to the oscillations in neural responses which signal involvement of (preconscious)[2] memory systems. The neural systems in 'lower' processing areas (stage 1) connect with those in 'higher' areas where connections with objects previously experienced are established. These lower-higher connections are crucial for intelligible perceptions to arise. Putting it simply, we do not merely see colours, shapes, movements, etc., we see mean-ingful objects and their meaningfulness can only arise through memory connections.

3. *Investigating consciousness* corresponds to activation of memory structures ('engrams') which have elements in common with the current visual stimulus (as mediated through the visual processing areas in stage 1).

4. *Determining consciousness* corresponds to the matching between sensory neural activity (stage 1) and the output from memory (stage 3). The engram which most closely matches the sensory pattern becomes dominant with other,

---

[2] Confusion arises on account of problems with terminology. Most cognitive neuroscientists would refer to the very rapid early stages of perceptual processing as being *preconscious*. Thus, the memory activity mentioned here is not the normal conscious function of recall, which comes later. Rather, this stage is one in which the initial perception is being constructed through relating the incoming stimuli with stored images to which they relate. It is occurring within a few hundred milliseconds of the stimulus falling on the retina, before normal conscious perception comes about. Zeki, with his arguments about micro-consciousnesses – which very much fit with the Buddhist view – is, in fact, out of step with most neuroscientists in this regard. Here is not the place to go further into this issue (see Lancaster, 2004), involving, as it does, the differing reasons why Buddhists and neuroscientists would be interested in processes of the mind such as perception.

competing, engrams being inhibited. In this sense, the meaning of the object is determined.

These four stages in the neural account follow each other automatically. The pattern in the sensory array results in a specific pattern of activation in the higher, memory-related neural areas, and competing patterns are inhibited as a dominant pattern arises. It is significant to note that the Buddhist scheme makes the same point: that these four stages come as an all-or-none package.

There are two further stages, not mentioned in the earlier quote from Aung: *running consciousness* and *registering consciousness*. To complete my account:

5. *Running consciousness* corresponds to the incorporation of whatever has been determined through stage 4 into the ongoing 'I-narrative', which is the normal, everyday state of consciousness. In brief, the sense of 'I' is viewed as arising through a constructive process which generates this sense of self as a coherent centre to the mind (as Buddhism asserts, there is no ongoing, substantive 'I'; the sense of self is a moment-to-moment construction). This centre seems to be the receiver of impressions, the director of thinking and instigator of free-willed actions. Much research in cognitive neuroscience attests to the fact, consistent with Buddhist theory, that it is none of these things. My term, 'I-narrative', emphasises the way in which successive perceptions become incorporated into what seems to be a coherent and temporally unfolding narrative, within which 'I' is the central character.

6. *Registering consciousness* is the final stage identified by the Abhidhamma texts and corresponds to the way in which the experience arising through stage 5 becomes stored in memory.

Considerably, more detail of these stages as they are described in the Abhidhamma, and of the evidence for relating them to stages in neural processing will be found in Lancaster (1997a, and 2004). Not only is the evidence for the correspondences given here strong, but also the incorporation of the Buddhist ideas into our understanding of the nature of perception clarifies aspects which are unclear from the neuroscientific data themselves. Theories in cognitive neuroscience depend on researchers' insight as to how to interpret their data. There seems little doubt to me that the masters of the Abhidhamma developed the highest levels of insight into mental processes, and that their insights are invaluable for cognitive neuroscience in its attempts to make sense of data on perception.

A similar conclusion may be drawn from the insights into the mental process of *grasping* developed in the Advaita-Vedanta school in Hinduism. Kaplan (2009) has demonstrated strong parallels between the Advaitans' analysis of the role of mental grasping in establishing the sense of subject and object and the view from cognitive neuroscience of the way in which the brain's parietal lobe is involved in establishing our sense of self. Research into the role of the parietal lobe in this regard can be summarised by stating that it generates the sense of being an embodied subject in a world where objects constitute an external space; the parietal lobe is crucial for being able to situate oneself in relation to the 'objective' world. The point of interest here concerns how this crucial cognitive skill develops. There is much neuropsychological evidence to support the view that the parietal lobe is central to the ability to grasp for objects. In cases where it is damaged, for example, the patient may lose this ability to reach for an object in its correct spatial location. d'Aquili and Newberg (1999, p. 34) argue that the ability to grasp accurately is the primitive forerunner of the spatial awareness that we take for granted, though which 'self' is localised in relation to the 'objective' world it inhabits.

It is, accordingly, of considerable interest that, as Kaplan (2009) informs us, the etymology of the Sanskrit term *grah*, meaning 'to grasp', relates it to the act of perception and the division between 'perceiver' and 'perceived', subject and object. This etymology becomes an explicit teaching about the manner in which a sense of self is established by mental grasping. From a soteriological perspective such grasping is to be eschewed, for the resulting sense of separation between subject and object is an illusion which holds us back on the path of transformation. Leaving aside the soteriological claim, we have a clear parallel to the neuroscientific understanding of the role of the parietal lobe in its spatial functions: physical grasping is viewed by both approaches as the primary determinant of the full-blown mental state in which self is established as separate from the outer world.

Kaplan summarises the major aspects of Advaitan philosophy in three points:

> First, the fundamental human problem is the appearance of the duality of the grasper and the grasped. Second, this presentation of duality is associated with sense perception. Third, the highest truth, the ultimate aim of the religious life, cannot be realised until the nature of the duality of grāhaka–grāhya ['grasper'–'grasped'] is realised (p. 258).

The Advaitan tradition asserts that the general human condition is one in which we fail to see that this distinction between the subject and the object, the 'grasper' and the 'grasped', is only a function of the mind. The distinction is in actuality *maya*, illusion, for there is no reality outside the mind in which these distinctions exist. To transcend this illusion, the mind must cease from grasping.

Kaplan concludes, much as I have from my examination of the Abhidhamma's view of perception, that there is 'a fascinating confluence of ideas' (p. 262) between these two traditions, of Advaita and cognitive neuroscience. Both traditions have come to the conclusion that this fundamental distinction between the embodied self and objects existing spatially beyond the self comes about as a construction of the mind, and that the grasping function lies at the root of the distinction.

This 'confluence of ideas' is not only 'fascinating', but has the potential to lead to new understandings and generative hypotheses. By interrelating the two divergent vantage points on the mind – the one scientific and the other introspective and spiritual – we can achieve a form of *triangulation*. As with the geographical equivalent, the use of two perspectives enables a more accurate picture to be built up than that produced by either alone.

Cognitive Neuroscience and The Soul

I mentioned above the Sufi understanding of imagination and the Kabbalistic notion of the unconscious roots of thought as exemplifying spiritual insights that may be ranged alongside modern psychological or neuroscientific approaches to the mind. Although imagination and unconscious processing are increasingly being examined in neuroscientific terms, the Sufi and Kabbalistic contexts in which imagination and the unconscious are discussed relate more to their respective traditions' understanding of the *soul* and of the psyche's role in connecting to a *higher world*. For these reasons, I shall explore these ideas and their relationship to cognitive neuroscience in a way that differs from my treatment above of Buddhist and Advaitan insights. Essentially, as we have seen, these Buddhist and Advaitan ideas relate *directly* to processes researched in cognitive neuroscience; the Kabbalistic and Sufi sources are concerned more with *indirect* connections with the brain.

It is the essentially reductionistic stance of cognitive neuroscience that renders any direct linkage with Sufi and Kabbalistic ideas untenable. In the worldview of these traditions, the essential function of the imagination and thought is to connect with a non-physical realm of being[3]. In his study of the Sufi understanding of imagination, Corbin (1958/1969) emphasises the distinction between *fantasy* and *imagination*, which may serve to amplify the limitation of reductionism in this regard. Fantasy is the result of undisciplined viewing of alternatives in a given situation, and most probably is understandable in neurological terms as the spreading of activation amongst interconnected groups of neurones. Imagination for Sufism is of a totally different order, being the essential faculty through which God creates; it is the 'organ of Creation' (p. 190), and human imagination is but a dimension of this divine power: 'our own Imagination *is* Imagination in His Imagination' (p. 191). The fact that the brain displays a form of activity which sustains fantasy exemplifies the *principle of correspondence* that operates across different levels in the created hierarchy. Such brain activity, correlating with the experience of fantasy, may correspond to the higher faculty of true imagination. Thus, cognitive neuroscience relates to these spiritual teachings not in the direct way we examined in the previous section, but indirectly as a result of the principle of correspondence.

Human imagination and thought are viewed in Sufism and Kabbalah as agents of connection to a higher world. Corbin explains that the imagination connects objects or events experienced to the 'World of Imagination', through which sensible forms are linked to their essential inner meaning in the highest realm. For the Kabbalist, human thought can be elevated to its source in the divine mind: 'Human thought has the ability to strip itself and to ascend to and arrive at the place of its source. Then it unites with the supernal entity whence it comes, and it [the thought] and it

---

[3] Of course, this interest in non-physical realms is not unique to Judaism and Islam but is true of all religions. I am singling out Sufism and Kabbalah in this section because this interest in the non-physical takes shape in ways that are psychologically interesting and therefore worthy of examination in relation to the theme of this chapter.

[its source] become one entity' (anonymous thirteenth-century Kabbalist, cited in Idel 2005, p. 219).

Such excursions into rarefied realms of 'higher worlds' would have no place in a chapter dealing with cognitive neuroscience were it not for the principle of corre- spondence between 'lower' and 'higher', 'microcosm' and 'macrocosm', which is a cornerstone of these traditions. As Corbin (1958/1969) expresses it in his study of Sufism, '...to everything that is apparent, literal external, exoteric ... there corre- sponds something hidden, spiritual, internal, esoteric' (p. 78). As he remarks, this concept is the 'central postulate of esotericism and esoteric hermeneutics'. In the words of the *Zohar*, the major text of Kabbalah: 'The Holy One, blessed be He ... made this world corresponding to the world above, and everything which is above has its counterpart here below', and He 'made man corresponding to the pattern above, for all is according to wisdom and there is not a single part of man which is not based on the supernal wisdom' (*Zohar* 2:20a and 1:186b). This is the crucial point for this section of my chapter: God and man are *isomorphic* in that they 'share the same structure and are logically equivalent' (Shokek, 2001, p. 6). Or, as Wolfson poetically puts it, 'God, world, and human are intertwined in a reciprocal mirroring' (2005, p. 32).

In the previous section, I addressed the insights perpetuated in spiritual traditions by showing that certain key ideas about perception and self taught in Buddhism and Hinduism appear uncannily accurate when viewed in the light of cognitive neuro- science. The question I wish to address here concerns how Kabbalistic ideas of the functioning of the brain, as they may be discerned through the more fundamental Kabbalistic teachings about the workings of the macrocosm, stand up to research in cognitive neuroscience. Kabbalah does not concern itself directly with the physical brain and its functions. Rather, it addresses the 'brains' in the higher realms of the Godhead. It is only by implication, and by dint of the principle of correspondence, that its teachings about the Godhead may be evaluated in terms of the understanding of the brain revealed by cognitive neuroscience.

In a nutshell, the same 'fascinating confluence of ideas' as we discerned in the previous section is evident here. Core Kabbalistic teachings about the macrocosm reveal an uncanny degree of fit with key principles of brain operation, in particular as these principles relate to consciousness. Again, I have given extensive details in other publications (Lancaster, 2004, 2009, in press), and confine myself here to the basics.

There are two key principles of the brain's operation which have been correlated with consciousness: *binding*, meaning the generation of coherence amongst assem- blies of neurones, and *recurrent processing*, which refers to the impact of 'descending' neural pathways on activity in 'ascending' pathways. The Kabbalistic teachings to which these seem to relate are those of *unification* and *reflexivity*, respectively.

As far as the consonance between binding and unification is concerned, both involve harnessing diverse elements together by means of establishing coherence. In the brain, it is the coherence in oscillatory firing patterns between diverse groups of neurones that signals their integration. As eloquently argued by von der Malsburg (1997, pp. 196–197), the level of consciousness correlating with brain activity depends critically on such coherence:

We experience mind states of different degrees of consciousness, and . . . the difference is made by the difference in the degree of coherence, or order . . . between different parts of the brain. Let us, then, describe a state of highest consciousness as one characterised by global order among all the different active processes. . . A globally coupled state could be one in which all the different [parts] are phase-locked to each other.

The analogy with Kabbalistic teaching is that coherence across different levels in the created hierarchy is viewed as bringing about the highest mystical states:

> 'One' – to unify everything from there upwards as one; to raise the will to bind everything in a single bond; to raise the will in fear and love higher and higher as far as *En-Sof* [the limitless essence of God]. And not to let the will stray from all the levels and limbs but let it ascend with them all to make them adhere to each other, so that all shall be one bond with *En-Sof* (*Zohar* 2:216b)

Moving on to the fit between recurrent processing and reflexivity, both depend on activity at a 'lower' level triggering activity in a 'higher' level, which in turn acts back on the lower level bringing about the intended effect. In neuroscience, this system has been identified in relation to the brain's sensory processing systems, with the 'lower' level comprising brain structures concerned with immediate properties of the sensory stimulus and the 'higher' structures being those dealing with memory. The *meaning* of the sensory stimulus is determined when the activity from the higher centres impacts on the lower regions though recurrent processing. Indeed, Lamme (2006, p. 499) argues that such recurrent processing 'is the key neural ingredient of consciousness'. As he asserts, 'We could even define consciousness as recurrent processing'.

The analogous teachings in Kabbalah need some unpacking from their context in order that the parallel with these findings in neuroscience might become evident. The *Zohar* enunciates the core teaching in its poetic language:

> Come and see. Through the impulse from below is awakened an impulse above, and through the impulse from above there is awakened a yet higher impulse, until the impulse reaches the place where the lamp is to be lit and it is lit . . . and all the worlds receive blessing from it (*Zohar* 1: 244a).

The central imagery of the Kabbalah presents a picture of the realms existing between man and the Ultimate. The 'impulse from below' arises through human spiritual work and brings about resonances throughout the successive intermediary realms reaching to the Ultimate. The 'lamp' refers to an aspect of the Godhead which is capable of bestowing the 'divine' influx, or 'blessings' back into the human sphere. Clearly the imagery of the lamp being 'lit' equates to the activation of this higher aspect of the Godhead.

We see here the fundamental operational pattern of the macrocosm as understood in Kabbalah. It is but a small stretch of the imagination, I think, to see this pattern in the brain systems for consciousness mentioned above in terms of recurrent processing. A sensory stimulus triggers activity in lower centres, which 'awakens' activity in higher centres, through which the 'lamp' that brings the 'blessing' of consciousness is kindled.

Just as we discovered in the previous section more directly, we have in these indirect allusions from spiritual traditions evidence that their accumulated wisdom stands the test of being measured against research findings in cognitive neuroscience. Perhaps, we should put it the other way round: our latest research is catching up, as it were, with the spiritual wisdom which, through diverse teachings around the globe, has built up a highly sophisticated view of the mind and its organ, the brain. But, I think it would be better still to express the point as a recognition that we are reaching towards a unified stance through which the fruits of insight and revelation coming from the spiritual traditions blend with the scientific research effort into consciousness. The spiritual traditions bring not only knowledge but also the ways of transformation; science brings the power to subject claims that are measurable in neuroscientific and psychological terms to rigorous investigation. We have seen in this chapter how far that blending of disciplines has advanced over recent years.

But don't this happen even without some kind of spiritual ascendency? Maybe I'm confusing the "higher functions with "numinous".?

Section 2

Spirituality Revisited

To engage with the argument of this book, it is necessary to rethink many received notions of spirituality as well as of psychosis. Anthropological data are essential here as other cultures have retained a sense of the reality and centrality of spiritual perspectives that ours has lost. Natalie Tobert clarifies how boundary states or liminality, whether between life/birth and death or moving between different sorts of consciousness, are conceptualised in other cultures. She provides a wealth of example to illustrate this, both from anthropological study of cultures distant in time and place, adding for this edition her familiarity with the immigrant cultures in our midst. Neil Douglas-Klotz disinters the mystical understanding buried in over-familiar texts, and through this presents a way of conceptualising that shimmers between the everyday and the spiritual. Both writers also address psychosis, and the wider argument of the book, bringing insights from their singular perspectives.

4

The Polarities of Consciousness

Natalie Tobert

Introduction: An Anthropological Perspective

During the 1990s, in the period leading up to the first edition version of this chapter, the over-riding view of spirituality in the West seemed to concern meditation practices or peak experiences of interconnected consciousness with the universe. It was never clear where religious experience and mental well being fitted into this model. In those days, we were unsure as to whether spirituality was a belief or an experience, a practice, a process or a religious dogma. We tended to value religious practice more than religious experience. Using the discipline of medical anthropology, this chapter explores the term 'spirituality' within a cross-cultural framework, addressing in particular beliefs and explanatory models about the causes of experience.

These days, there is much more literature on aspects of spirituality and health (Barker and Buchanan-Barker, 2004; McSherry, 2006; Koenig, 2007; Swinton *et al.*, 2007). Universities are also covering the area now: Aberdeen has a centre for Spirituality, Health and Disability, Durham University is developing courses for health-care providers, Coventry has a centre for students' pastoral well being, and Staffordshire University now offers a Masters level degree in spirituality and health.

In 2009, there is a much wider understanding of race, culture, religion and mental health as part of the Delivering Race Equality agenda, while the Department of Health has written a guide including the role of religion and belief (Department of Health, 2009a, b). Also NIMHE prepared a guide on spirituality (Gilbert *et al.*, 2003). Our efforts in the West to classify what we observe, indicates that our education system appears to fragment 'life' into certain categories of knowledge. For example, religion, health and consciousness studies used to be discrete scholarly disciplines in which research was undertaken by specialists, whereas in other cultures the concepts are inter-related. Within the field of 'mental health', research into treatment was

Psychosis and Spirituality: Consolidating the New Paradigm Second Edition   Edited by Isabel Clarke
© 2010 John Wiley & Sons, Ltd.

biological or humanistic, although a more holistic approach is now being explored. In the West, some practitioners assessed 'mental health' experience within a social, environmental or spiritual framework (Tobert, 2007a), some did not. In many non-Western societies, the indigenous boundaries concerning concepts about life are interwoven: anthropology libraries abound with monographs about autochthonous interpretations of consciousness within the context of 'life' rather than 'religion' or 'health'. Today's psychologists and psychiatrists offer much more holistic assessments and treatments, following the example set in some non Western societies (Tobert, forthcoming). There is also a far greater exploration of science and human experiences (Laszlo, 2009) than there was 10 years ago when the earlier version of this appeared.

Relationship Between Spirituality and Psychosis

To explore the relationship between spirituality and psychosis, several factors are examined from Western and non-Western viewpoints. These include beliefs about the nature of physical existence from birth to death, and 'non-ordinary' states of consciousness.[1]

Three hypotheses are put forward: that spiritual or religious experience and certain symptoms of psychosis exist within a continuum. They are the polarities of consciousness. Secondly, that a non-physical dimension exists. Thirdly, that our own beliefs about both the nature of physical existence and consciousness after death influence the diagnosis and treatment of mental health cases.

Many of the peoples mentioned below believe in some kind of non-physical world. This fundamentally affects the nature of their beliefs around life and death, human consciousness and mental health.

For example, the anthropologist Reichel-Dolmatoff explains that Tukano peoples of the Northwest Amazon Basin in South America believe that humans on earth are inextricably linked to the cosmos, and they have a framework for understanding different states of consciousness (1997). They believe all their activities are interconnected: the relationship between human existence, the physical world of nature and the spiritual dimension is explicit.

The Tukano believe in two inter-locking worlds whereby the physical world of material things and the spirit world are discrete but co-exist. Human beings interact with nature and the spirits: they are considered incapable of existing independently. During his fieldwork, Reichel-Dolmatoff often heard people talk about 'the other house' or 'the double house'. He said it took him nearly 2 years to understand they were speaking about the other dimension, the abode of spirits, or the non-physical dimension. When he asked his informants why they had never explained, they replied, 'You never asked us'. Like so many anthropologists, when he first

---

[1] The author is teaching these topics in course modules at UK medical schools, universities and in seminars for medical and health-care providers in Harrow.

began his fieldwork he conducted research within the boundaries of his own knowledge. However, later he meticulously recorded native people's interpretation of the material he collected and his work is exceptionally sensitive to the culture (Reichel-Dolmatoff, 1997).

Among the Tukano, ill health is seen as 'the ecologically inadequate behaviour of the patient'. That is, sickness can be a consequence of that person having upset the ecological balance. Shamans do not operate at an individual level: they work to assess which part of the eco-system has been disturbed. In contrast, the Western bio-medical system has tended to assume that illness occurs as a result of organic disorder within the patient's body, although research into psychosomatism suggests patients themselves perceive a variety of wide-ranging explanations (Helman, 1985). The Testimony Project archive suggests peoples' triggers for mental distress can be social, economic or environmental (http://www.insidestories.org/archive). Non-Western societies also often have a multiplicity of explanatory models for ill health, which include both physical and non-physical causes.

Beliefs about Birth and Death

A Question of Interpretation...

The ideas of indigenous peoples concerning the nature of existence fill anthropology publications. However, in the past, we may have subtly discounted the concepts they offered us as false, irrational or culture-bound. In the West, we used to talk about certain groups of people having 'culture-bound beliefs' but we were not always self-reflexive enough to ask whether our own Western beliefs were 'culture-bound'. The case studies below explore whether the biological theory of procreation is universal, or whether there might be additional explanatory models. Often concepts which fall outside the boundaries of our own belief system are considered to be 'other people's beliefs', which may be irrational and not part of empirical reality; and we assume that the biological model is the only empirical model. With regard to the term 'belief', Byron Good suggested that its use did 'indeed connote error or falsehood' although this was seldom explicit (1994; 17). Good claims that the word 'belief' has long been used to connote 'mistaken understandings' whereas 'knowledge' is assumed to mean 'correct explanations'. Today anthropologists use the phrase 'culture-bound knowledge' but it may be a Eurocentric way to mean the same thing as 'belief'.

In the West, we seemed to hold certain beliefs about the human body. We said we knew we were born – conceived by an act of intercourse between people of different gender (though with technological developments this is not necessarily the case). We assumed people lived a certain amount of time on earth, then died, and we often said that we did not know what happened after death. But the version of life presented above is simply one 'belief system' of the West. The understanding of human identity within the cosmos is quite different in other parts of the world, and today we are much more aware of different models of reality and cultural explanations for mental health.

This section engages in a discussion of cross-cultural explanatory causes for life transitions. The aim is to explore the possibility of an alternative framework for understanding psychosis, which could be used to complement bio-medical practice. Different explanatory models may also help patients' coping mechanisms and support their health seeking strategies for treatment.

I propose that the definition of psychosis was developed and maintained from a Western culture-bound materialist belief system. The relevance of the material to understanding psychosis will become clear as the chapter progresses.

Assumptions Around Birth

In the 1920s, the anthropologist Malinowski conducted fieldwork amongst the Trobriand Islanders of Papua New Guinea. He had to learn about reincarnation before he could speak about conception. He said Trobriand Islanders 'are so mixed up with beliefs about the incarnations of spiritual beings' that he had to present biological and spiritual ideas together (Malinowski, 1929, p. 145). Similarly, the Dinkas of Sudan explained that men and women engage in coitus and then 'Divinity' creates a child inside a woman's belly and 'has a creative function in the formation of every human being' (Lienhardt, 1990, p. 39). In each case, sexual intercourse is considered essential, but not enough.

Among the Laboya peoples of Indonesia, pregnant women are considered to be containers of ancestral breath and spirit and as such they are temporarily in touch with the 'realm of the dead'. People believe that a newborn is an unidentified being, coming from the wilderness and 'from foreign realms related to the realms of ancestors' (Geirnaert-Martin, 1992, p. 230).

A new-born's identity appears to have several components: as well as biological aspects there is another factor the Sabarl considered essential for a human being to be born. This is *hinona* (essence of life) or the vital substance, which makes the body breathe (Battaglia, 1990, p. 39). The Laboya people believe that a newborn baby has a soul, the elements of which need to be welded together using a loom swift, in the same way that yarn is wound from a skein into a ball, otherwise their *mawo* (breath, life force) may become restless and leave their body (Geirnaert-Martin, 1992, p. 102). Among the Muslim Malay people, the subtle energy components of a newborn are: the soul (*ruh*); the breath of life (*nyawa*); and the spirit of life (*semangat*, Laderman, 1983; 144). Once a baby has been born there are various ceremonies, which take place to ensure it stays on earth (Heinze, 1982, p. 5).

The main points mentioned above suggest that to create babies, people believe a spiritual input is needed as well as the biological practice of sexual intercourse. In addition to the physical body, a new baby is considered to be made up of non-physical elements which include: life force, breath and soul. A non-physical element is believed to exist, which can leave the body during sleep, or at will later in life. This concept is pertinent to the suggested faculties of 'non-corporeal consciousness' which are discussed later.

Assumptions Around Death

The possibility that conception occurs by the will of an ancestral soul results in various cultures' concern with having a 'good' death, so that ancestors may reincarnate and not remain in limbo like ghosts (Parry, 1994; Obeyesekere, 1981; Fuller, 1992). Furthermore, the Asian concern with 'karmic carry-over' creates an awareness that behaviour in this life may affect a subsequent birth. In India, people who died a 'good' death were cremated, which resulted in rebirth and renewal. Those who died a 'bad' death were blocked from being reborn. Much human misfortune was attributed to ghosts of those who died an untimely death (Parry, 1994, p. 226). It is only when the deceased is reunited with the ancestors that the 'ghost' becomes an 'ancestor'. Upon becoming an ancestor, the deceased can confer blessings on the living and increase their fertility and material abundance. Sometime after its stay in the abode of the ancestors, its soul can be recycled as a new baby. However, someone who dies a bad death, may get stuck in a liminal state as a ghost, for a long period. They draw attention to themselves by molesting the living, in the hope that they will take measures to improve their situation. Physical and mental illness, childlessness and other misfortunes may be attributed to the spirits of the 'untimely' dead (Fuller, 1992). People believe malevolent spirits take possession of the living and control their minds and bodies. Recent research suggests these beliefs are current in parts of the United Kingdom that have a multi-ethnic population, and with first generation migrants in particular (Bhui *et al.*, 2008).

Ancestral relationships are considered to affect the health and well being of people in different ways. In the West, if a discarnate being appears to the recently bereaved, as a hallucination or apparition, this may be considered delusional or a case of 'complicated grief', whereas in other societies it might be a welcome vision. In Sri Lanka, discarnate beings are perceived to 'overshadow' the minds or bodies of living relatives, taking possession to a lesser or greater degree. A 'bad' case of possession is unsolicited, and a 'good' case is solicited whereby the incoming spirit is transformed into a benevolent healer or clairvoyant. There are two options for cure: the spirit can be exorcised or honoured (Obeyesekere, 1981).

Victor Turner (1968) conducted fieldwork among the Ndembu, in Zambia, Africa. He noted that in the past when people became ill, they propitiated the ancestors. During the ritual to release one man from ancestral beings, which troubled him, the participant spoke all his troubles aloud. During the ceremony, it was socially acceptable for secret grudges and hidden animosities within the group to be voiced. The patient could not get better until all villagers' tensions had been expressed or confessed. Speaking private matters in public was perceived to allow the angry spirit, which caused sickness, a gateway to leave. Turner suggested the purpose of the rituals served to consolidate village unity, stabilise personal relationships, and alleviate body pains and misfortune. Similar group ceremonies to address mental well being are familiar to today's Somali residents in UK (Tobert, forthcoming). The parallels with psychotherapy and family therapy in our society are obvious, and this also impacts on mental health care for people of different ethnicity, and their understanding of 'privacy' which are often different from euro-centric assumptions.

Reincarnation

The idea that discarnate beings might exist in some kind of non-physical dimension and overshadow human beings is found in many societies which have a belief in existence after death. This is often accompanied by a belief in the possibility of rebirth or reincarnation. These beliefs are current among Hindu populations in Harrow. Many religions have some concept of rebirth after death and the continuance of the soul beyond physical life. Belief in reincarnation is widespread and underlies many Eastern faiths, whereby the soul is eternal and reborn repeatedly. The main aim of Hindu, Jain and Buddhist religions is liberation from human cycles of rebirth. This process is seen as governed by the concepts of *karma*, enduring consequences of behaviour in previous lives, *moksha*, release from repeated cycles of existences, and *samsara*, the struggle is to renounce life and achieve enlightenment.

India is only one place among many to hold a belief in reincarnation: it was recognised as being central to African and Native American beliefs and cosmologies. It was known by different labels and came under polytheism or pantheism, or was subsumed by other cosmologies. Stevenson (1997) has brought a professional approach to the study of reincarnation and has made attempts to verify the information. He presented an analysis of 225 examples where people had been born with birth marks or birth defects and claimed these related to past lives or the manner of past deaths. In particular, lives which ended in violent deaths seemed to be more remembered. Charles Tart (1997) speculates that extra-cerebral memories can be transferred from one life to another. The above examples suggest that human bodies and consciousness are not necessarily limited by time and space. Tart's (2009) more recent work addresses this, as does Laszlo's (2009).

Opening to New Explanations

There may be a relationship between our beliefs about consciousness after death and our mental well-being. There may be a correlation between Western beliefs about the nature of human existence which influence peoples' access to health care, and the diagnosis and treatment of a mentally or emotionally disturbed person. Many non-Western peoples believe that once the physical body dies, consciousness and some form of identity continue. There is a belief that the method of death can affect the nature of the non-physical aspect of a discarnate being. A human being is thought to be made up of various non-physical components, some of which precede and survive death.

In the name of cultural diversity, we can take an emic perspective that acknowledges the beliefs and explanatory models of different cultures in accounting for mental distress ('Emic' means people's own explanations, rather than 'etic', the observer's explanations). This would consider the possibility of reincarnation, communication with disincarnate beings and the reality of possession, with psychosis entailing slipping into a non-physical dimension, picking up material and confusing it with common consensus reality. Such beliefs are common both among first generation migrants to the United Kingdom from South Asia and Africa. In autochthonous societies, a 'being's identity' is rooted within the local cosmology even before conception and the human body is considered to be 'permeable'. People believe the body can be made sick by physical and non-physical elements. Csordas (1994, p. 2) has suggested that in the West we tend to understand the body as a 'bounded entity' with the surface of the skin serving as the boundary between the individual inside and the world outside. Illness occurs within the body, but may be caused by certain things, which permeate the body: through the skin, breathed in, ingested through the mouth (or transmitted via any other opening), or after injury via intrusion of a foreign object (e.g. a thorn or knife).

Addressing the concept of permeability, Canault gives examples of French psychologists who claim an individual may experience trans-generational sickness, whereby hidden grief or unresolved trauma is suppressed but surfaces in the memory or behaviour of subsequent generations. In such cases, becoming conscious of a secret promotes healing and enhances mental health (Canault, 1998). These examples suggest that there is a plurality of frameworks for understanding human existence; belief in one model of existence does not exclude the others from existing.

Altered States of Consciousness

The material in the previous section highlighted the fact that many non-Western societies have different beliefs about the human condition and the nature of birth and death, shared by migrants (e.g. from India or Pakistan) to the United Kingdom today. This section is written from the emic premise of acknowledging the existence of a spiritual dimension (a non-physical world) and it presents a summary of various people who claim to 'go between' the worlds. This includes both specialists like shamans and mediums who claim to focus deliberately on inter-dimensional reality, and also those who have involuntary episodes like out of the body experiences, (OBE)s, or near death experiences (NDE)s or 'religious experience'. One difference between spiritual experience and psychosis is that usually when the experience is solicited it does not overwhelm the individual (or the community), as illustrated by Caroline Brett's research (Chapter 13).

Inter-Dimensional Reality

Throughout the world, most societies have specialists, who claim to work inter-dimensionally, that is they claim to see, talk to, interact or negotiate with non-physical entities. In our society, they are called psychics or mediums, elsewhere they may be known as shamans or healers (Tobert, 2005, 2007b). In the Diagnostic and Statistical Manual of Mental Disorders (DSM) certain diagnostic criteria for schizophrenia are rather similar to the desired conditions of shamans in an altered state of consciousness. Within the bio-medical model, the first-rank symptoms 'have formed the basis for most modern systems of diagnosing schizophrenia' (Thomas, 1997. p. 19). Both biological and psychological models of schizophrenia suggest that its origins are located in the brain or mind of the individual (Thomas, 1997, p. 51). However, he notes 'there is considerable evidence that society, including family, social, economic and political factors, is inextricably linked to the nature of schizophrenia' (Thomas, 1997). Social factors have an important influence on the diagnosis and outcome of schizophrenia, with those people who live in a non-industrial society having a better outcome (Thomas, 1997, p. 28). Research into 'religious experiences' that were said to warrant psychiatric attention suggests there was a tendency to pathologise experiences that people around the sufferer did not understand (Tobert, 2007a).

The National Schizophrenia Fellowship (now Rethink) noted that 50% of those experiencing schizophrenia in India and Africa are cured, compared with 6% in Denmark and 25% in Britain (Kirkness, 1997, p. 10). How can we explain the differences in cure rates? Thomas (1997, p. 24) notes that psychological pathology pre-supposes that 'hallucinations are inherently abnormal' and are believed to arise out of a disease of the mind.

The following section looks at emic explanations for inter-dimensional activity.

Shamans

A shaman is a man or woman who intentionally communicates with the non-physical world. They may undertake a journey to the non-physical dimensions for various reasons: on behalf of others, for the benefit of the community, to gain information, or to effect healing. During journeys to non-physical realms, time and space are said to collapse. Although spirits do sometimes possess the bodies of shamans, shamans do not need to be possessed to do healing work or undertake remote vision. The practice is linked with ecological stability and is a powerful force in controlling and managing the relationship between humans and natural resources. Shamans deliberately choose to experience alternative states of reality. However, a person who remains in the spirit world and cannot function in everyday reality is not respected.

Among the Daur Mongols of Manchuria, mental suffering is thought to be caused by soul loss or spirit possession. There the shamans 'divined the causes of unexplained illness and misfortunes; ... explained dreams; "enlivened" the spirit-placings people kept at home; invoked and bargained with spirits; magically expelled or calmed spirits attacking people; exorcised spirits through substitute objects; retrieved human souls stolen by spirits; ... invoked and propitiated the souls of dead shamans... Daur shamans were invited above all to cure mental illness and depression ...' (Humphrey, 1996, p. 184). The Daur have various definitions of 'madness', each with its own origin. Some, but not all are caused by spirit attack. Different cultures interpret alternative states of consciousness differently and what is considered 'normal' varies from society to society. In the Western Christian situation, trance has sometimes been considered on a par with mental disability, and Christian mystics were sometimes deterred from speaking out by the threat of heresy (Lewis, 1991, p. 34). In the West however, treatments of psychiatry and psychotherapy have been using procedures like hypnotherapy, which provoke a trance like state, and their patients are encouraged to release repressed experiences, which may result in a cathartic shaking of the physical body. Fernando notes that in Western psychiatry, mystical or trance states are associated with 'loss of ego control' and seen as pathological because 'self control' is considered important in Western culture, leading to over-diagnosis of people of African descent, Hispanics and Native Americans in the United States (Fernando, 1991, p. 190).

Religious Experience

Mysticism and schizophrenia have often been linked (Wapnick, 1981, p. 321). Psychosis was said to be an incomplete withdrawal from the spirit state, a failure to return to this reality, whereas in comparison, the mystic was controlled and came back completely to everyday reality.

Visionary and auditory experiences come within the category of religious experience. Perhaps the same phenomenon is called 'religious experience' if the individual is of a stable mental disposition, and 'psychotic' if the individual is unstable?

A number of religions were begun when charismatic people heard voices, which inspired them. These include the Quakers and Shakers, the Seventh Day Adventists, Mormons, Paul on the road to Damascus, Joan of Arc, and Mohammed and the Koran. The health services in the United Kingdom were inspired by Florence Nightingale who heard the voice of god in 1837 (Keighley, 1999). Others experienced visions: Moses saw the burning bush and many people saw the Resurrection of Christ. There seems to be different weighting given to 'The Central Christian Revelation' seen by a number of people and, private revelations seen by individuals. Today, in Western society, religious practice is valued, whereas religious experience is feared.

Liminality

The concept of liminality is interesting with regard to understanding psychosis. Arnold Van Gennep (1960, p. 21) identified three stages of transition: 'separation' (from an earlier condition), liminal (the condition of being in transition), and post-liminal (incorporation into a new situation). I wonder how many individuals have been diagnosed in the West as suffering from psychosis who have simply switched, unsolicited into liminal space, and are anxious about this.

This concept is also covered by the psychiatrist Barrett (1998, p. 478), who suggests that patients with schizophrenia are in a state of 'suspended liminality'. Barrett suggests that psychiatric institutions may 'freeze liminality into a permanent state'.

The Polarities of Consciousness

Non-Physical Dimension and Verity

This section explores whether the ethnographic case studies mentioned above have any relevance to psychosis as diagnosed in the West. It asks whether we ignore non-physical attributes of existence, assuming they are figments of a culture-bound imagination. The material presented in the section above suggests the existence of a non-physical dimension. We will explore below how this may have a relevance to the interpretation of psychosis.

In Western society, in earlier years, it seems that interpretation of an experience depends on the belief system of the observer. May I explain? I undertook research at the Religious Experience Research Centre at University of Wales, Lampeter (Tobert, 2007a). I explored explanatory models for 'unusual human experience' that were perceived by society as negative, or in need of psychiatric assistance. This study explored the gap between: public perception, psychiatry's health care strategy and practices in different locations, and found a link between silence about an experience and a fear of being thought insane. Some people assumed there was a relationship between unusual human experience and mental illness, and between schizophrenia and visionary experiences. Popular misperceptions endured, in spite of professional reassurance (Tobert, 2007a).

There are cases where anthropologists working in the field have seen things that affected their belief system. Edie Turner is an anthropologist with the University of Virginia who conducted fieldwork in Zambia in 1985 and tried to understand Ndembu ways of harnessing spiritual power. While she participated in a Ndembu ceremony she actually saw a spirit manifestation (Turner, 1992, p. 1), and she was not willing to push this experience aside. What is seen is considered to be 'out there' and not projected through the mind. She quotes Paul Stoller who experienced sorcery while working among the Songhay of Niger with a priestess called Dunguri. He says 'all of my assumptions about the world were uprooted from their foundation on the plain of Western metaphysics. Nothing that I had learned or could learn within the parameters of anthropological theory could have prepared me for Dunguri'. These 'visions' Edie Turner claims, 'are not projected through the mind' (Turner, 1992, p. 171).

The question as to whether the psychic occurs in us, in our consciousness, or whether it is actually external to us has concerned numerous researchers. Carl

Gustave Jung (1933, p. 170) framed the question 'Were the dissociated psychic contents – to use our modern terms – ever part of the psyches of individuals, or were they rather from the beginning psychic entities existing in themselves according to the primitive view as ghosts, ancestral spirits and the like?'. He noted that native peoples believed ancestral spirits were not hallucinations: it was not their imagination; rather the spirits appeared of their own volition. If we acknowledge what the seers, psychics, shamans and quantum physicists are saying with an open mind, perhaps we might address psychosis in a different way.

A Different Explanatory Model?

Let us suppose that what we assume to be delusional is veridical; that mystics can spontaneously see visions and hear voices; that specialists can recall past lives, their own and other peoples', communicate with the dead, become deliberately over-shadowed by spirits, experience 'extended empathy', and undertake remote viewing (within various geographical locations and time frames). Is it possible that 'normal' human faculties could include: past-life memory recall (whereby consciousness stays in the same place, but at 'other times'); remote viewing (whereby the body stays within the same time frame, but non-corporeal consciousness moves to and reports back on 'other places'); perceiving individual consciousness remotely from the body; seeing spirits of the dead (whereby consciousness exists at the same time/place, but tunes into discarnate entities in other dimensions); experiencing spirit possession (whereby a human body is 'porous' and can be overshadowed by incarnate or non-incarnate beings); hearing voices (whereby live and dead beings verbally assault/assist the client); and other discarnate presences are felt. The self is made up of pre-natal and extra-corporeal experiences as well as postnatal psychological responses. While acknowledging the triggering role of trauma and anxiety (bodily, personal, social, environmental and political), and that the mind can create or generate any of the above, as well as hallucinations and delusional thinking, is it possible to consider an alternative framework at the same time, and use this to develop different treatment strategies, and more cultural or religious interventions?

Mental illness is said to exist when a combination of symptoms occurs, including deteriorating ability to function within social or occupational contexts, deteriorating care for themselves and threats to harm self or others. Most societies are clear about the meaning of 'inappropriate' behaviour, even though this may mean different things. In practice, the RERC archive records indicated that the presence of a 'religious experience' episode on its own was sometimes enough for mental health pathology to be considered. There was clearly a difference between the ideal response to an unusual human experience event and the actual response (Tobert, 2007a).

Although there are university modules for medical and health-care practitioners on 'trans-cultural psychiatry' in the United Kingdom (e.g. at Queen Mary's college or University College in London), there is still a gap in the ordinary training of front line mental health-care providers. This needs to be addressed, so that cultural diversity in its widest sense becomes a normal part of training in all educational establishments for those working in mental health care.

In Harrow, UK, Somali and Gujarati residents are suggesting research into the effectiveness of religious practitioners, to test their interventions with patients' well being. This could be ascertained by clinical psychiatric assessment before and after alternative techniques for therapy.

In our society, is it perhaps because we have not had an ontological model for life after death, that we experience confusion when trying to understand psychosis? Although we are beginning to accept the idea of consciousness after death, we may still find it problematic to embrace the concept of non-corporeal discarnate entities with personality. Likewise there has been reticence to perceiving that the human body is in some way porous or permeable and, like a radio transmitter, can tune into different times and spaces, or be tuned into by non-corporeal entities. Stemming from our denial regarding consciousness continuing after bodily death, and our poor understanding regarding non-physical aspects of humans, have we developed our own culture-bound explanations for certain symptoms of individual mental suffering?

5

Missing Stories: Psychosis, Spirituality and the Development of Western Religious Hermeneutics

Neil Douglas-Klotz

This chapter puts the discussion of 'spiritual' and 'psychotic' in the context of the tension between the way Christianity has developed in the West and the language of Middle Eastern mysticism from which it springs. For the West, this is an alien and misunderstood culture. The history of Western interpretation theory (i.e. hermeneutics) sheds new light on the split between Western 'religion' and 'science', which underlies questions about the differences or similarities between spiritual and psychotic states. I propose that, beginning with the imperialisation of Christianity under the Roman Empire, European culture extracted a limited language concerning these states from an underlying Middle Eastern context, but without fully understanding the language or worldview involved. Because of this, Western culture developed a massive split between 'inner' psychic and 'outer' normative consciousness, as well as splits between cosmology and psychology, body and soul, and humanity and natural environment. The same split led to the division of religion and science that informs the current discussion. Whether by following an orthodox religious interpretation or by reacting against this interpretation in the form of the Enlightenment and the Western scientific revolutions, Western culture evolves without a language or worldview that can conceptualise expanded states of consciousness in a healthy way. Traditions of mystical hermeneutics in Judaism and Islam preserve these ways of using language and so allow for a continuum of consciousness(es). I give examples of the application of these interpretive methods to particular texts that reveal so-called spiritual/psychotic states. Finally, I give an example of the way that a living tradition of Middle Eastern mysticism would assess various types of spiritual states, including so-called normal consciousness, and use various practices, including stories, breathing and body awareness, to prepare for shifts in consciousness in a healthy way.

Psychosis and Spirituality: Consolidating the New Paradigm Second Edition   Edited by Isabel Clarke
© 2010 John Wiley & Sons, Ltd.

In this chapter, I am drawing on doctoral and post-doctoral research in the fields of somatic psychology and religious studies (Douglas-Klotz, 1995, 1999a, 1999b). I am also drawing on 23 years of personal experience of spiritual states as a student and later teacher of meditation in the Sufi tradition. The first half of the article uses the language of hermeneutics; the second half uses language reflecting a preliminary comparison of 'non-ordinary' states from both a Western somatic psychological viewpoint and Middle Eastern mystical one.

The Domain of Hermes and the Limits of Language

In Greek mythology, the god Hermes held several titles: the messenger of the gods, the inventor of language, healer, the god of science and the protector of boundaries. In the Islamic tradition, Hermes is further identified with Enoch (Idrîs), who walked with god and was taken to heaven without dying (Burckhardt, 1971, p. 18). Hermeneutics, the branch of philosophy, literature, religion and social science dealing with interpretation takes his name. So does the word *hermetic*, which deals with alchemy and non-Western versions of the natural sciences. As the alchemist, Hermes transforms material substance (just as he does language) so that it recovers a harmonious relationship with the rest of the natural world. As this discussion lies at the common boundary of spirituality, cosmology and somatic psychology, it is implicated in all of Hermes' domains.

Interesting

As the inventor of language, Hermes was called a trickster, a thief and a bargainer. According to Socrates in Plato's Cratylus (408c), all of these attributes have to do with the fact that Hermes creates through language, and that words have the ability to reveal as well as conceal: 'speech can signify all things, but it also turns things this way and that' (Hoy, 1978, p. 1).

also Interesting

In his reading of Plato, Jean-Luc Nancy argues that it is, in fact, the word that mediates the experience of 'all things'. Language, specifically in the form of dialogue, determines how one understands the ideas and objects one encounters, what one understands about them, and whether understanding is even possible (Nancy, 1989, pp. 230–248).

Throughout the history of both Western and Eastern thought, language, creation, healing and the sacred have been associated. Since Plato, the Western hermeneutical discourse has grappled in various ways with the way we interpret reality and the nature of the reality that we are capable of interpreting. As Ludwig (1967) writes in Zettel, 'Like everything metaphysical, the harmony between thought and reality is to be found in the grammar of the language' (section 55). Or as he says succinctly elsewhere, 'The limits of my language are the limits of my world'.

Hm

For previous generations in the modern West, primarily philosophers and linguists debated these issues. Today, the importance of language and the way that it determines the 'limits of our world' have increased dramatically. The reach of communications has become virtually global yet increasingly narrowed in both form and content, the former determined by the mass media and the latter by economic and commercial interests. To put the question posed by one modern example bluntly: what is the proper language to use when discussing the possibility of genetic engineering: ethical, religious, political, sociological or economic?

Means tho...

In investigating any two areas that seem to lie in separate domains, such as psychosis and spiritual states, or religion and science, a hermeneutical approach looks at the possibility that the grounds for separating the categories may lie in an unacknowledged language problem. What we call a 'limit of language' in discussing such states may in fact be only a limit of modern Western language and the way in which it is used currently by both psychology and theology. Behind the actual words used may lie unstated presumptions about the nature of reality, presumptions that are not held by all cultures. However, as Western dominance of mass media increases, these presumptions increasingly colonise the discourse of the rest of the world.

With these issues in mind, both scientists and theologians have noted the current limits of Western language and interpretation. The former questions whether Western language, influenced by Newtonian physics, can express the new findings about either the development of the cosmos or its behaviour at the sub-atomic level. The latter notes that new interpretations of old scriptures need to be brought to bear to speak cogently to the problems of the day.

For instance, physicist Brian Swimme and theologian Thomas Berry (Swimme and Berry, 1992) point out that, while in the classical era science formerly repudiated any 'anthropomorphic' language in speaking about the universe – i.e. any description of the cosmos acting like a human being – it made an equally grievous error in seeking to describe the universe in terms of a machine.

> [During the rise of Newtonian science] the western mind had become completely fascinated with the physical dimensions of the universe ... A univocal language was needed, one whose words were in direct, one-to-one relationship with the particular physical aspects under consideration. In this way, anthropomorphic language was abandoned in favour of mechanomorphic language. (p. 36)

This machine model for language also infected the translations and study of sacred scriptures in the West for the past several hundred years. It led first to an over-emphasis on 'literalism' – the study of what was supposedly present in the original with nothing added or deleted – and second to the extreme relativism of literary criticism which ended up dividing and analysing virtually all meaning and wisdom out of sacred texts.

The Christian theologian Matthew Fox (1990, forward) notes:

> A paradigm shift requires a new pair of glasses by which to look anew at our inherited treasures. Just as all translations of our mystics are affected by the ideology or worldview of the translator, so the same is true of our Scriptures. Those who have lost a cosmology and the mysticism that accompanies it hardly recognise that fact when they translate the Bible for us. (ix)

The Need for a New Language

These voices of both Western science and religion are looking for a language that can describe more nuanced views both of the human relationship to the cosmos and of its psychic life. To find such a view, this discussion looks at the origins of Western science and religion and the way that both are extracted from a ground of Middle Eastern language and cosmology. The process of extraction was also a refining – what was left behind was greater than what was used – similar to the extraction and refining of oil. I am proposing here that both Western Christian theology and Western science arise from a divided vision of human, nature and cosmos that implicates their entire development to this day. It also impacts the way that both Western science and religion view 'non-ordinary' states of awareness, whether labelled 'spiritual' or 'psychotic'.

For instance, from the standpoint of Middle Eastern Semitic languages like Hebrew, Aramaic or Arabic, which were spoken by all of the named prophets of Judaism, Christianity and Islam, the word that means 'spirit' also stands for breath, air, wind or atmosphere. If Jesus said anything about 'Holy Spirit', then from a Middle Eastern interpretative viewpoint, he was also saying something about Sacred Breath, that is, the source from which all breathing – human and non-human comes. This is what might be called today a psychophysical construct. Correspondingly, these languages do not divide the life of a being – human or non-human – into the separate categories of mind, body, psyche or spirit. These categories stem from primarily Greek philosophy. The Middle Eastern languages articulate different types of diversity within the life of a being, but not these.

This use of language might be called 'multivalent' as opposed to the univalent use that dominates Western scientific or theological categories, where one places a value on exactitude: one word means one thing. However, in evaluating spiritual/psychotic states that are, by definition, multivalent and subject to shifts in category, there is value in investigating a use of language that can express subtlety and paradox in an area that cuts across the received mind–body–psyche–spirit boundaries.

We find such a use of language in the so-called mystical hermeneutics of both Judaism (called midrash) and Islam (called *ta'wil*). The word 'mystical' must again be taken cautiously, because the Semitic languages do not distinguish between the Western sense of mystical (meaning an inner, esoteric way) and the prophetic (an outer, exoteric engagement). The way in which most expressions of European Christianity lost their ability to use such language has to do with the history of hermeneutics in this tradition and the way in which it influenced the development of Western science, including psychology.

Jewish and Islamic Mystical Hermeneutics

To get to grips with the limits of current language and conceptualisation when faced with the subject area embraced by both psychosis and spirituality, we need to consider this other, 'mystical' use of language in some depth. It may provide a model that could express a non-linear, yet comprehensible and useful, language of 'non-ordinary' states. Our source material for this will be sacred texts drawn from Jewish and Islamic traditions.

A number of texts and oral traditions from the Jewish and Islamic mystical traditions mention a multileveled, symbolic and interpretative approach to sacred texts. The basis for these traditions lies in qualities of the Semitic languages which, as I touched upon above, can lead to ambiguity in the meaning of a particular text. Both Jewish and Islamic traditions of mystical hermeneutic point to the importance of individual letters and letter-combinations called roots. The Semitic languages depend upon root-and-pattern systems that allow a text to be rendered literally in several different ways.

The root-and-pattern system of Hebrew, Aramaic and Arabic, and the interpretative methods that evolved from it, could be compared with the musical system of Indian *ragas* in which families of notes and scales interlink and 'intermarry' to produce other scales. The closest equivalent in Western music is the free-form improvisations on a theme found in jazz. Like jazz and raga, learning midrashic interpretation, especially in the mystical trends in Judaism and Islam, seemed to depend as much upon feeling as upon technique, as much upon individual contemplative experience as upon scholarship. Particularly in the Kabbalistic and later Hasidic circles, these techniques were passed on in an oral tradition, that included a community of voices, both present and past, upon which subsequent interpretations were built, using the possibilities in the language as well as traditional stories and folklore.

A number of the earliest texts from the Jewish mystical traditions mention a symbolic, interpretative approach to sacred texts. This approach begins with a study of the letters of the Hebrew alphabet themselves, which come to symbolise cosmic or universal patterns of energy. One of the earliest Jewish mystical texts (first to sixth century, C.E.), the Sepher Yitzirah (Book of Creation), establishes the unique properties of the Hebrew language in an ontological sense – i.e. as a language that not only communicates meaning but also can create being. Later Kabbalistic texts, such as the Sepher ha-Zohar ('Book of Splendour') promote the ideas that the interpretation of a given text can vary according to the cycle of existence in which the community is currently living, and that every letter, word, sentence and phrase of the scripture may exist simultaneously on several levels of meaning.

Expressing a post-modern Jewish voice, Jewish linguist Shulamith Hareven notes certain unique features of the Hebrew language that make word-for-word translation misleading, if not impossible:

> Hebrew, a synchronic language, holds certain precise ethical and philosophical value concepts that belong only to Hebrew and to Judaism and that are really untranslatable. Such words cannot be learned simply as words, without their philosophical context. Some are whole teachings ... As a written language Hebrew is basically a skeletal, shorthand structure, in which the main process takes place in thought
>
> (Hareven, 1995, p. 41).

In mystical Islam, a virtually identical hermeneutical approach concerns the rendering and translation of the 99 'Beautiful Names' of Allah as well as the translation/interpretation of the Arabic letters and words of the Quran itself (Friedlander, 1978, p. 7, Name of Allah).

In this regard, the most profound and complex mystical hermeneutic, called ta'wíl, has been preserved primarily by mystics in the Shi'ite branches of Islam. Similar to the Kabbalistic approaches to midrash, ta'wíl uses the sacred text or word as a symbolic means to contact a greater cosmic reality.

Islamic scholar Seyyed Hossain Nasr relates the practice of ta'wíl to Islam's unified cosmology of human, nature and divine. Nature is considered the ultimate sacred text (al-Qur'an al takwini), of which the Quran revealed to Muhammad is a reflection (al-Qur'an al-tadwini). The approach to nature as the ultimate sacred text is interdependent with a living, symbolic relationship to the written or spoken revelation (Nasr, 1968, p. 95).

The main Middle Eastern languages spoken by the prophets of Judaism, Christianity and Islam lend themselves to these symbolic, poetic, multileveled and open-ended interpretations. One word can literally have many different meanings. Word play in the form of assonance, alliteration and parallelism abounds. The words of a prophet or mystic in this tradition – stories, prayers and visionary statements – seem virtually guaranteed to challenge listeners to understand them according to their own life experience.

Imagine trying to read a Poem as if it were a legal text

Other Stories and Other States of Consciousness

For instance, the Hebrew words that Genesis uses for 'heaven' and 'earth' can be understood, from a cosmological standpoint, as the two major ways our universe has developed. From a psychological perspective, they can be seen as the two major ways that we can encounter our universe. 'Heaven' can refer to the way in which everything is united in community as though by one sound, ray of light or vibrating wave. 'Earth' can refer to the individuality of every being – the way that the universe has mysteriously produced such abundant diversity that no two clouds, blades of grass or human beings are exactly the same. The Hebrew word for 'heaven' refers to the psychological sense of 'we', a shared sense of connectedness with other beings or the entire cosmos. The word for 'earth' refers to our sense of 'I', one's own individual sense of purpose. A contemporary midrash might compare Genesis 1:1 to the way physicists talk about seeing light as wave and particle simultaneously. Another layer of the midrashic process might look at the way I balance the communal and individual aspects of my personal life. Or the way in which one handles visionary (wave-based, vibratory) life in relation to everyday (particle-based, material) life.

The concept of heaven as a reward in the future, for some definition of the well-lived life or for believing a particular set of principles, is a latter innovation of Western Christian theology, as is the notion of 'earth' as a place flawed by 'original sin'. Neither concept would have been known to the Hebrew prophets or Jesus.

So one completely accurate way to translate the first verse of Genesis in a midrashic sense would be:

In the time before time,
in principle and archetype,
in beginningness,
the One and the Many,
the unnameable Force behind the universe
that was, is and will be,
established two fundamental ways the universe works:
the particle and the wave,
the 'I' and 'we' of existence.

Likewise, the Hebrew, Aramaic and Arabic words usually translated 'self' or 'soul' (nephesh, naphsha or nafs) present the image of a community of voices that can be experienced either inside or outside (within or among). I do not *have* a soul, I *am* a soul. That is, one does not possess a 'self' or 'soul' in this sense, nor is the self or soul housed within an un-souled 'body' or 'mind'. Instead, one experiences life as a self-soul in various ways. One way, expressed by the words above, reflects the 'earth' or particle reality of the self, the 'I-ness', as it were. The other way (expressed by the words ruach, Heb.; ruha, Aramaic, or ruh, Arabic) reflects the 'heaven' or wave reality of the self, the 'we-ness'. These are also the words that can be translated as breath or spirit. In this 'we' dimension occur various sorts of 'non-ordinary' (from a Western viewpoint) states of awareness.

We also find the notion of the self as a collection of voices stated poetically in Jewish Wisdom literature. Viewed in the original language, using a midrashic interpretative style, the Hebrew book of Proverbs speaks of a psychic process or archetype in all beings that gathers the various, seemingly separate, voices into a *Integration* harmonious and healthy 'I'. This gathering, relating voice in the self is called in Hebrew Hokhmah, which can be translated as the 'nurturing breath from underneath and within', or as Sacred Sense or Holy Wisdom. This archetype or psychic organising force is better known by her later Greek name, Sophia.

To deal with such texts, I have proposed (Douglas-Klotz, 1999b) an open translation method that combines traditional midrashic techniques with postmodern poetic language in a 'hermeneutic of indeterminacy'. All the meanings in this translation from Proverbs 8 come from the possibilities present in the Hebrew words themselves.

From the primordial, chaotic 'within'
Hokhmah–the breath of nourishing insight–
has created a separate place to live:
By enclosing her unknowable, inner mystery,
Holy Wisdom has created an address for her temple.
She has done this by dividing the Dark,
pushing from outside until the

foundations of her dwelling–the necessary basic 'selves'–
join together by their own mutual attraction:
this natural union creates the first conscious 'I am.'

We can combine the multivalence of the words 'spirit', 'soul', 'heaven' and 'earth' in Semitic languages to apply midrash to another reported saying of Jesus:

> Verily I say unto you, Whatsoever ye shall bind on earth shall be bound in heaven: and whatsoever ye shall loose on earth shall be loosed in heaven.
>
> (Matthew 18:18-19, KJV)

This passage has often been interpreted to mean that Jesus gave particular followers of his (later identified in various ways with church hierarchies) a special ability to forgive sins. However, the Aramaic text presents another picture. The word 'bind' in Aramaic can mean to tie oneself to something, as well as to engage or enmesh oneself in some aspect of material existence. It can mean to harness one's energies or, symbolically, to enclose fire in a circle. The Aramaic word for 'loose' is related by root and sound to this. It presents the symbolic image of a circle opening up, of liberation, or of the umbilical cord being severed after birth (for more exact linguistic analysis, see Douglas-Klotz, 1999a, pp. 99–113).

Given that the worlds of 'heaven' and 'earth' interpenetrate at all times, a person then has a choice about how to use his or her energies: some of them invested in the world of vision and vibration, some in the world of form and manifestation. For instance, we can invest time and energy to envision a new vocation, or to change the conditions of the one we have. If we want something new to happen, we have to be willing to let go, to some extent, of what has already manifested to allow the possibility for what could be. If we want to preserve what we already have, we need to invest energy into caring for and nurturing it. So a more open or midrashic reading of the above passage, using the traditional Aramaic Christian text as a basis for a poetic interpretation, could be:

What you hold onto in form
will also be fixed in vision.
The energy you contain in
an individual effect or possession
will also be bound in
the field of vibrating cause.

What you release from form
will be available for vision.
The energy you allow to grow
beyond your own creation,
cutting the cord that keeps
you and it dependent,
will liberate both into the larger
cosmos of unlimited creation.

Generally, Western psychology views those who spend too much time in the visionary or 'heaven' world as more in need of help than those who invest too much creating and protecting possessions in the 'earth' one. However, the problem of being overly caught up in material existence has also been recognised as the cause of various stress disorders. Again, the degree of the 'problem' depends upon the social construction given to word 'reality'. From the interpretation expressed here, Jesus is talking about finding a balance between states of awareness that would allow one to find a sense of 'kingdom' (reign or empowerment) both within oneself and among all one's outer relations.

The Development of Western Christian Hermeneutics

If the reader finds such interpretations far-fetched or obscure, it is because dominant Western culture has, for more than 1500 years, steadily excised the ability to see in multivalent, even paradoxical ways from its language and psyche. In the Western Christian tradition, a symbolic hermeneutic that relates humanity, nature and the divine faced a more difficult history and was gradually eliminated from the tradition by a number of factors.

First, when Christianity became the official religion of the Roman Empire after the conversion of Constantine, it increasingly lost touch with its roots in the Middle East, and specifically in the Semitic language spoken by Jesus, Aramaic. With the exception of the Aramaic-speaking churches that broke away during the formation of the Nicene and later creeds in the fourth to fifth centuries, Greek became the official language of European Christianity. As Jesus did not preach in Greek, the marginalisation of Aramaic as a language of interpretation and commentary closed access to the Middle Eastern worldview embedded in the language and to the multileveled, symbolic system embedded in its letters and roots.

According to Assyrian Aramaic Christian scholar George Lamsa (1947/1976, p. 1), the emphasis on Greek as the 'original' Christian language was prompted by the imperialisation of Christianity after Constantine and by anti-Semitism. Middle Eastern Aramaic-speaking Christians had access to written scriptures from the earliest times, said Lamsa; consequently, he felt that the theological formulations of Christianity after Constantine based solely on Greek texts were flawed from the outset. This ignorance of Christianity's Middle Eastern cultural roots persisted into the nineteenth and twentieth centuries (Lamsa, 1947/1976, pp. 17–18).

Second, when Christianity felt itself called upon to 'save the world' rather than simply to maintain its survival in a hostile empire, it organised itself in such a way as to eliminate elements of experiential spirituality related to Gnosticism that it felt to be unhealthy. According to biblical scholar Elaine Pagels (1979), these elements included the feminine aspects of the divine, shared authority in ritual and decision-making and the importance of individual spiritual experience as the basis for the interpretation and exegesis of scripture.

Third, the choices that organised Western Christianity after its imperialisation further weakened its cosmology – the world view of humanity in relation to sacred nature – in favour of its theology, the relationship of humanity to God, excluding nature.

Because Western Christianity tended to restrict inquiry and diversity in favour of the newly developed concept of 'orthodoxy', the rise of Western science developed in reaction to it. Yet both the institution of Western Christianity, divorced from the Middle Eastern worldview that was its origin, as well as the reaction against it in the form of the scientific revolution, suffered from the same divided worldview.

Woa

With the rupture of the relationships between science, religion, nature and sacred literature, the modern use of the term *hermeneutics* in the Christian West first became associated with various 'regional' hermeneutic approaches; that is, a separate method of interpretation for sacred, literary, legal and philological texts.

A major shift towards modern hermeneutical theory occurs with the work of Martin Heidegger and Hans-Geog Gadamer. In their work, interpretation no longer becomes a process directed towards understanding one's place in the natural cosmos or towards uniting with the mind of another, but rather an example of the everyday process by which one makes sense the world. Interpretation is always based on a 'fore-knowledge' which pre-determines how and what we understand (Heidegger, 1927/1962, pp. 115–139).

This insight nears that of midrash and ta'wil, in that the observer, observed and their relationship can be all considered part of the field of interpretation. However, as the domains of religion and science had already divided from one another, neither field was large enough to include a language of 'non-ordinary' experience. In the case of religion, inquiry was limited by orthodoxy: faith was more important than experience. In the field of science, the non-rational was by definition to be avoided or stigmatised.

Despite this history, and even after the influence of various redactions, portions of the Judeo-Christian scriptures point to insights about non-ordinary states of awareness that may still be relevant today. As demonstrated above, if a ground of Middle Eastern cosmology and psychology is used for interpretation, we may gain insights about states of awareness that have developed because of the lack of a proper cognitive ground.

Breath and Self

In this final section, I bring insights gained from a midrashic approach to Western sacred scripture into dialogue with those of somatic psychology, particularly as they regard 'unhealthy' and 'healthy' experiences of non-ordinary states of consciousness. I propose that Middle Eastern mystical psychology, in conjunction with aspects of somatic and cognitive psychology, can provide a context for re-interpreting these states. Although Jewish Kabalistic mystical practice shares much in common with Islamic Sufism, particularly the way that both use breathing practice, body awareness, sound awareness and poetic language, I primarily use examples from the latter for the sake of continuity.

Both somatic psychology and Middle Eastern mystical practice emphasise the importance of breathing awareness in determining answers to the questions: Who or what is doing the feeling and perceiving? Does the awareness of breathing help to build a healthy 'self', however defined, or does it lead to the dissolution of the 'self'.

In the somatic psychology field, we can compare Wilhelm Reich's analysis of this area. Reich considered the detailed witnessing of small proprioceptive differences essential to his approach with both neurotic and psychotic patients. These differences included feelings of tension (called 'armouring') in the muscles and connective tissue that are arranged in rings around the eyes, throat, chest, solar plexus, genitals and pelvic floor. Reich associated this armouring with a patient's subconscious attempts to suppress breathing, sensation and feeling.

In other patients, Reich found the reverse of armouring in these areas – an excessive softness (hypotonia) and lack of feeling. In these cases, Reich felt that patients' awareness of bodily sensations and feelings had become 'split' from their *Huh* sense of identity. In extreme cases, he felt that this splitting of body awareness from identity was the functional definition of schizophrenia. He noted in an extensive case history of a person with schizophrenia:

> [The] degree of clarity and oneness [of consciousness] depends, to judge from observations in schizophrenic processes, not so much on the strength or intensity of self-perception, as on the more or less complete integration of the innumerable elements of self-perception into one single experience of the SELF ...
>
> *Nihilistic "mindfulness" vs integration*
>
> (Reich, 1949, p. 442, emphasis in the original).

> Besides the abilities to see, hear, smell, taste, touch, there existed unmistakably in healthy individuals a sense of organ functions, an orgonotic sense, as it were, which was completely lacking or was disturbed in biopathies. The compulsion neurotic has lost this sixth sense completely. The schizophrenic has displaced this sense and has transformed it into certain patterns of his delusional system, such as 'forces', 'the devil', 'voices', 'electrical currents', 'worms in the brain or in the intestines', etc.
>
> *Interesting ...*
>
> (Reich, 1949, p. 454).

What the schizophrenic experiences on the level of body awareness, Reich maintained, is not so different from the experience of the inspired poet or mystic:

> The functions which appear in the schizophrenic, if only one learns to read them accurately, are COSMIC FUNCTIONS, that is, functions of the cosmic orgone energy in undisguised form...
>
> In schizophrenia, as well as in true religion and in true art and science, the awareness of these deep functions is great and overwhelming. The schizophrenic is distinguished from the great artist, scientist or founder of religions in that his organism is not equipped or is too split up to accept and to carry the experience of this identity of functions inside and outside the organism
>
> *It's REAL, it's just overwhelming / terrifying rather than inspiring, animating.*
>
> (Reich, 1949, pp. 442, 448, emphasis in original).

In Sufism as well as Kaballah, breathing is related to ruh (ruach, Heb.); as we have seen, this is another name for the spiritual or 'wave-reality' soul. The splitting of the subconscious personality into multiple fragmented 'I's' is also a spiritual problem approached by several branches of Middle Eastern mysticism, including Sufism. Reich's orgonotic 'sixth sense' could be seen in relationship to the witnessing or gathering self in Middle Eastern psychology. In Sufi psychology, this is called the awareness of 'Reality' (haqiqa, Arabic). In the interpretation of Jewish mystical psychology mentioned earlier, the same function is served by the 'Sacred Sense' or 'Holy Wisdom' (Hokhmah, based on the same root as the Arabic), which organises the healthy sense of an 'I'.

Without this gathering or witnessing awareness, which is intimately tied up with the body's proprioceptive awareness, the subconscious self (*nafs* in Arabic, *nephesh* in Hebrew) splits into a multiplicity of discordant voices forgetful of the divine Unity (the source of all 'I am-ness'). The personal sense of 'I am-ness' is not developed once for all time, but shifts depending upon the degree to which a person is aware of the multiplicity within and yet is still able to integrate it. In Sufism, this has been expressed by the saying, 'Whosoever knows him/her self, knows the One Self (a literal translation of the word *Allah*)'. This could be seen as a foundational view of the psyche that underlies the entire range of Middle Eastern mysticism. (Douglas-Klotz, 1995).

To help distinguish the progress of a student of the inner school, Sufism distinguishes between states of expanded awareness (called hal) and the ability to integrate the states in everyday life (the so-called 'station' or makam). Although many Sufi practices (like breathing, chanting or, in certain traditions, whirling) engender expanded or ecstatic states, the practitioner is directed to disregard so-called psychic effects like voices, colours or out-of-body experiences and to focus on the integration or 'perfection' of hal in makam. As I pointed out in an earlier study, various stages of makam can be related to degrees of awareness and flexibility in body awareness. This includes not only the muscular rings posited by Reich but also proprioceptive awareness of ligaments, bones, blood pulsation and skin contact (Douglas-Klotz, 1984).

Like the multivalent language used in mystical hermeneutics and the consideration of sacred texts, most Sufi stories aim to help students 'unlearn', that is, to go beyond the emotional boundaries and mental concepts that enclose the sense of who they think they are. What one sees is dependant not only upon who is doing the seeing, but also upon which aspects of the self (which state of consciousness) is involved.

As students gradually go beyond these boundaries, they become acclimatised to the province of what one may call 'wild mind'. This wild mind is like an inner landscape that is both richer and less controlled than the safety of fixed ideas and rules. It is a fluid and changing reality that one must constantly relate to the sense of 'I am' in the way that a potter centres a lump of clay on the wheel. By comparison, Gregory Bateson (1991) called a similar approach to epistemology and psychology the 'ecology of mind', recognising that consciousness operates much more like an ecosystem than anything else, and that 'mind' is embedded in an ecological reality, within and without.

All of this happens in an ideal development, as the student learns to balance states (*hal*) with station (*makam*), and as a sense of the *nafs* (the 'particle' self) enlarges to meet and merge with the *ruh* (the 'wave' self). A Sufi teacher might analyse the tendency towards what Western psychology calls borderline states by pointing to the lack of development of a 'gathering self' (*Hokhmah*) from earlier life. The sense of love and compassion that would embrace the opposites within a child was not present in sufficiently healthy a form to allow the child's own 'I am' to form. In a native Middle Eastern view, as we gather our inner selves, we create a soul. As they scatter, we lose our souls.

Not only do individuals experience this alienation of a fragmented self, so does society as a whole. Those who experience the breakdown of a unified 'I' in our society, mostly from early traumatic abuse, point to the way in which our entire cultural self has become fragmented and alienated from each other and nature. In such a case, both Sufism and Kaballah point to the difficulty of engendering enough love to overcome the splits that have occurred.

Summary

This chapter places the discussion of models of psychosis and spiritual states of consciousness within the context of the evolution of Western sacred hermeneutics. Both Western religion and science lack the cognitive models and language to describe such states in a nuanced way, just as Western culture fails to support those experiencing these states with a viable cultural language. The possibility for such a language was left behind when Western Christianity, in abandoning its Middle Eastern roots, emphasised univalence and consistency in the language of faith and exiled language that expressed multivalence and diversity. The framework for multivalence in language still exists in the form of Jewish and Islamic mystical hermeneutical styles, methods that can also be applied to the words of Jesus when using an Aramaic version of the Gospels. These interpretative methods describe a unity of altered states of awareness in a 'wave-heaven' reality that distinguishes itself from a 'particle-earth' reality. From a Middle Eastern mystical viewpoint, differences between states ('healthy') or ('unhealthy') can be framed as more or less complete contact with a healthy 'I am' that can integrate both wave and particle views of life. Methods historically used in Middle Eastern mysticism to build a dynamic 'I am', capable of fluid changes of consciousness, include story, poetic language, breathing and body awareness.

Section 3

The Mystical Face of Psychosis: The Psychotic Face of Mysticism. The New Continuum

Personal experience is the core data for considering this topic, and the normalisation of the continuum between non-ordinary and everyday experience is also key. This section tackles these linked themes. Gordon Claridge and his group's extensive research on Schizotypy supplies the theoretical and research framework for this continuum.

Peter Chadwick's rewritten version of his own experience and Richard House's consideration of the mysterious but persistent phenomenon of Kundalini, which cuts across any supposed divide between spirituality and psychosis and challenges notions of diagnosis, supplies the data. The postscript to House's chapter adds a contemporary personal account of the process of Kundalini as it weaves through the life of an anonymous member of the Spiritual Crisis Network. The theme of the transformative potential of such transliminal experience starts to emerge in this section.

6

'On Not Drinking Soup with a Fork': From Spiritual Experience to Madness to Growth – A Personal Journey

Peter K. Chadwick

For me, a spiritual experience is an awareness of being open to forces as if from beyond oneself. All religions are based on spiritual experiences, even if not all religious people, in these terms, need necessarily be particularly spiritual. My own access to such realms of experience, as outlined in this chapter, was centrally an openness to God, to me the positive spiritual presence of the cosmos, but also an openness to The Infernal, the ever-present downside for all such questers in this territory of human endeavour.

Since both share the individual's permeability to 'the beyond', spiritual experiences are far from rare during psychotic crises and this is how I came across such domains. There are some misinformed researchers who would scorn access to the sacred if it is associated with subsequent psychosis. This chapter, by a psychologist, myself, who has himself been psychotic, will I hope show that such experiences, can plant seeds that one can cultivate later in one's own personal development, growth and search for peace.

The Conditions for Psychosis

The access to the psychotic state is, in many ways, a life process and recovery to a fulfilling and meaningful way of being is very much the same. In my case there were, however, likely genetic vulnerabilities as my brother George, 28 years my senior, had my mother allowed him to be diagnosed in the 1950s and 60s, would almost certainly have been regarded by psychiatrists as a hebephrenic schizophrenic. In turn, my mother's attitude to people, life and the world would very likely have prompted the diagnosis of paranoid personality disorder. In 1979 I received the diagnosis

Psychosis and Spirituality: Consolidating the New Paradigm Second Edition   Edited by Isabel Clarke
© 2010 John Wiley & Sons, Ltd.

of schizoaffective psychosis with the affective component being an atypical form of hypomania – a mood enhancement however that was concealing a profound depression.

<u>There was a lifelong problem within me in the *integration* of cognition and affect, typical of the schizoid mind, and I despaired of ever being able to *love*.</u>

At the individual level it is tremendously difficult to disentangle nature and nurture (and of course nurture tends to 'bring out' nature) but certainly it seems to me that difficulties in our household at least exacerbated vulnerabilities of a constitutional character. In my childhood, though I only became consciously mindful of this when I was 17, my feelings of *the right to exist* were extremely fragile.

Because of quite dreadful events concerning the way the Chadwick family had treated my mother, Edith, she had a deep-seated hatred for them which often she took out on myself and my brother (e.g. (following my father's death when I was 7): 'What have I done to be left with a pair of no-good Chadwicks?!' Tragically the ambience in our home did have this effect... or at least brought out this vulnerability.

In my case, being also rather feminine in temperament and a trace bisexual, the nature of my personality was utterly at odds with the loud, aggressive model of man paraded as the way to be in the culture in which I grew up (early post-war Manchester). In effect I was born into hatred at home and at school and in the community.

In my chapter in the first edition of this book (Chadwick, 2001) I made a great deal out of the paranoia I suffered due to misaligning myself with the tough north of England culture of the day in respect of gender role behaviour and sexuality. In other words I was 'too poofy' for Manchester males. Certainly I was stigmatised and genuinely persecuted for 'not measuring up' as a 'real man' or as 'one of the lads'. In this second edition however I wish to go deeper than this in saying that I need not have reacted to the bullying, scorn and discrimination I did receive had I been brought up to be stronger in self-pride, self respect and self belief. Being brought up to feel that I was a 'no good Chadwick', a rotter, not really respected for what I was, gave me no secure, solid existential foundation to my being. When I asked my mother when I was about 23 why she had not *cultivated* my undoubted protectiveness feelings, sensitivity and delicacy of spirit as real positives in me she said, with a forlorn expression: 'Oh. . . . I tried to knock all that out of yer'. . . . . Manchester.

Existential Fragility

In the study of psychiatric morbidity, the focus on existential difficulties has particularly been associated with the name of R.D. Laing (1960, 1967, 1970) though other significant figures such as Ludwig Binswanger (1958, 1963) and Medard Boss (1963, 1977) also have made great strides in this area. In relating the psychotic to the spiritual I think the examination of a person's existential ground is especially important.

If the very foundations of one's sense of being are compromised, one's capacity both to give and receive love also is damaged. Lack of existential solidity, in addition, gives one a sense of being 'blurry', of not having clear boundaries, of being permeable and implodable. This openness to without and within can have advantages for insight, sensitivity and creativity and also for access to spiritual experiences but on an everyday level such 'skinlessness' undoubtedly is a burden – and a fear-inducing burden at that. Having no right to be also is hardly a good basis for a secure relationship with God.

A feminine man in the north of England and a 'Chadwick' living with a Chadwick-hating mother, Edie Burghall, no wonder I used to feel *hated*. Was it the anger in me, that I used to hold myself together at the unfairness of it all, that broke me down? Perhaps it was. George, Edie and me all had problems with anger. Was it the high sex drive that made me focus on the pleasures of the flesh and the joys of orgasm to intensify my feelings of being 'there' at all? If I was, at core, 'no good', at least I could 'feel good', it was the next best thing. Such negative perceptions of the Self that can make one permeable to the Infernal.

From Wretchedness to Spirituality

In 1979, given my 'no good sissy boy' self-perception, I felt battered by the hatred and gossip of the world. Bullied at school by football people for assumed homosexuality, scorned by my mother as 'a right bloody Chadwick swine' and of course, 'not good enough' (indeed, as she said '*never* good enough') my identity was utterly wretched. For a time, I involved myself in transvestism, causing more gossip and slander, nowhere could I find peace, love and acceptance, either without or within.

In the summer of 1979, having resigned a university lecturing post in psychology because of increasing paranoia, I hit the base of my fortunes. Living in a bedsitter in Hackney, East London, I was essentially alone, penniless, unemployed, felt scorned, hated, with no future now and an horrific past, it was as if a portal opened and I was overwhelmed by a positive, euphoric, spiritual experience. It was like being an empty vessel being filled with the Divine Light of God. The transgressions of my many persecutors quickly became trivial. Hate turned to love, anger and revenge wishes turned to forgiveness. From being a scorned speck of a being, I became an agent of The Almighty! The emotions of anger, fear and sex were totally dormant; the tortuous agonies of my past were forgotten. I was as if reborn with a new self-perception and a new purpose, to bring God into the world. The damage to the integrity of my Self was solved by losing myself in God.

From Euphoria to Damnation

At the time of my positive experience, God was a real presence, as if hovering behind a thin membrane. Great power and energy surged through me, my eyes were bright, my movements sturdy and dynamic, my hopes high. The world, the very cosmos, I saw as the instantiation of meaning, an interconnected unity, a living organic totality pervaded by the mind of God. At a personal level, I was as if floating, devoid of ego, in touch with all that is. My life was both portentous and insignificant but my destiny was both with God and in God. I felt I had great forgiveness powers, that I sensed everyone's thoughts and even the very unconscious of the world.

At this time, I was writing furiously. Surely now I had attained innocence and absolution? But then I noticed how self-justificatory my narratives were – and hence how defensive and one-sided. Now I began to doubt myself again. Musing on my many past failings and transgressions, from petty vanities and hubris to the murderous wishes I had entertained towards my mother, once this happened the experience began to flip side into something quite abominable.

In the positive state, I was as if devoid of a past and devoid of lower emotions. I was therefore 'empty' of my history and 'cleaned out and excavated' of lower affects. Hence the feelings of being a vacant receptacle. It was a state that hardly could be maintained, certainly not in somebody like me who for years had been steeped in psychoanalysis!

Nonetheless, to this day I value that positive experience as it enabled me to as if touch something experientially that my cynical, critical, scientific upbringing had always masked and heavily veiled. As decades went by, the experience of that positive permeability helped me in my creative work and it opened up for me the worlds of art and spirituality. Even my sexual life was enriched by it. The experience therefore helped kindle flames within that could not have been conceived in any other way.

However, in the summer of 1979 I had to deal, temporary though it proved to be, with the reversal from that state. As my self-justificatory dam began firstly to crack and then to crumble under my own self analysis, I pondered the possibility that far from being an agent of God, a worthless 'no good pansy' like me was more likely an agent of Satan. At this point in my musings, ushered in by reading a book entitled 'The Devil in Art and Literature', an incredible barrage of coincidences shifted me from what had been a fragile euphoric 'Supersanity' to insanity.

As I sat on a bench in the middle of Hackney Downs with my dog Penny, a mother and her small daughter walked by. The daughter said, 'Mummy, is that man possessed by The Devil?' referring to me. The mother took one glance at me and said, 'Yes dear'. It was like having a knife plunged into my mind, as that was what I was wondering at that very moment!

Back in my bedsitter, I noticed that as my own thoughts calmed, the rain beating against the window pane then also calmed, as my thoughts accelerated the rain then became heavier. Was my mind somehow in tune paranormally with the world? I noticed a red van and a green van parked across the road outside the front door. I felt that somehow this was 'significant' and so switched on the radio. Incredibly the talk on the radio was indeed about the hermeneutics of red and green! The boundary between within and without, always diffuse in me, now seemed to be totally evaporating. I was becoming at one with all that is but now in very specific ways, actual events were demonstrating this at-oneness to me and it was unnerving.

I wrote to colleagues about my distressing life situation, referring to my female transvestic alter ego that I had in those days as 'a cherub girl'. A few days later, the DJ Pete Murray scornfully mocked 'a cherub girl' in his talk on the radio. Then I made my fatal bridging inference to explain this. Obviously my letters had been passed on to the media for amusement. Now not only bullies at school and neighbourhood gossips were persecuting me (they *really would* have passed them on), now the media itself was having a go at me! At this point, as we say in England, I 'lost the plot' of everyday life. Now I had passed from being the talk of the district, which as an openly practising transvestite I was, to being the talk of the media. Now I was insane with paranoia.

Psychotic Consciousness

Clearly, so I thought, the media persecution, which uncannily kept on coming (hence rubbing the belief in) must have some connection with the 'fact' that I was possessed by the Devil or maybe even be the Antichrist. As the comments on the radio seemed sometimes to be guiding and therapeutic, I interpreted this to mean that there was an organised plan to *cure* me of my evil, sybaritic, transvestic lifestyle of those days and turn me into a nice, clean-living, well-behaved, decent person. The people who were doing this I came to call 'The Organisation' and they were sending in subtle messages to me via the radio and occasionally via television and via comments people would be told to make as they walked past me in the street. Even headlines on newspapers deliberately placed on rain-sodden pavements were being used by them to influence me. They were very clever and seemed to know perfectly how my mind worked.

To this day, rather disconcerting, although this may be for some readers, I am nonetheless absolutely DISGUSTED with myself for succumbing to this silly, outrageous delusion and am appalled at myself for losing my sanity. Indeed this somewhat irascible attitude has helped to deter me from ever going mad again. Getting well again since this episode has involved sailing in completely the opposite direction to that which I took when deluded.

Nonetheless, between July and September 1979 all manner of jolts and jogs to my consciousness were given by these 'subtle messages' and indeed I did try to live a more clean-living life. I stopped smoking, gave up sugar, changed my reading habits to more worldly, externally oriented topics and became a more well-behaved person generally. After all, they were trying to cure me of possession by Satan, I had to make an effort!

In this state of mind, what previously had been mystical thoughts such as 'All is Meaning' now became psychotic thoughts such as 'Everything means something, even street signs, advertisements and car number plates'. What previously had been 'The cosmos is an interconnected unity' now became 'Everyone and everything is together against me'. I had returned to being a speck and a nothing but least, in some bizarre way, a person of consequence. After all, it must be important and I must be a special person to justify all *this* going on! In that kind of respect, the episode was defensively compensatory and self-inflating.

All the time, I only would process events or comments that somehow fitted with or confirmed my delusional concerns – a massive amplification of Peter Wason's (1960) 'confirmation bias'. It never occurred to me to use evidence to discredit my delusion, so much fitted it *surely* had to be true?! Such is the character of a psychotic delusion.

One night in September 1979, towards the end of the episode, I erupted out loud, in my bedsitter, into a monologue against The Organisation – which I assumed could hear me via hidden sensors and microphones.

At about this time, the subtle messages began to change and became more ominous. Cliff Richard's new record, 'We don't talk any more' was being played a lot on the radio, I took this to mean that The Organisation had given up on me, I was a lost soul, a waste of space and time. Their plan now surely was to induce me to kill myself. After all, the whole character of The Organisation's messages had been, 'Change or die!'

As I was sat in the office at Argus Press, where I had a temporary job, contemplating how they wanted me to 'do it', a man, Arthur, came out of the manager's side office and shouted back to him, 'So he's got to do it by bus then?!' 'Yes!' came the manager's reply. Doubtless it was about a delivery but to me it was yet another perfectly timed message. The Organisation knew my very thoughts. That was how I had to do it.

At a club, I was at that evening a trans-sexual friend had a spasm of the muscles of her scalp and gripped her head as if it was being crushed. I interpreted this event to be a deliberate, set-up message that the wheels of the bus had to crush my head so as to thrust Satan out of my brain and mind. It obviously was The Organisation's last resort to get Satan out of this world.

New King's Road in Fulham obviously was the perfect location for my nemesis. Me, the Antichrist, must be destroyed on 'the road of the new king'. When I was dead, Satan, 'the old king' would be thrust out of my mind and Jesus, 'the new king' would come into the world to reign. As usual, it all fitted so well it surely had to be true! This was no delusion, this was *really happening*!

How the bus missed me when I threw myself down into the path of its left nearside wheel I have, to this day, no idea. I ended up in the gutter on New King's Road, blood dripping from my right hand onto the tar of the road, people filing out of the bus and gathering on the pavement by my prostrate form. I was absolutely mortified that I had survived. A woman lent over me as I garbled and said, 'He's trying to say something'.

The ambulance arrived quickly, called for by the driver, and I was taken by two ambulance men, Peter and Paul, to Charing Cross hospital (to me 'the hospital of the charring cross'). I was put in Ward J for treatment. Still the fitting events kept on coming, even after I'd tried to kill myself.

There were three further suicide attempts in hospital over the next 2 or 3 days, in response to rappings, clicks and taps (in reaction to my thoughts) that started and came from the walls and ceilings of my side ward: one tap for 'Yes', two taps for 'No'. After my final, fourth suicide attempt (I flung myself headlong down a flight of about

30 steps in the hospital staircase between floors) the rapping tapped 'Yes' to the thought, 'This is Hell, I am in torment for ever!!' Needless to say I broke down screaming. I was then, at last, injected with anti-psychotic drugs and fell asleep immediately. After my hand was operated on, I finally awoke in my bed in the psychiatric unit at Charing Cross. The delusion, the rappings, had totally VANISHED! It was like waking up from a bad dream.

Recovery and Reflections

There was only one brief crisis in my recovery period that is worthy of note, particularly in the context of this volume. It is important for the reader to realise that the rappings I referred to above that began in Charing Cross were actually audible to other people. They were not hallucinations. I have them at times to this day and even our cats can hear them and orient their heads quickly to the source. They particularly come from wood and metal.

In September 1981, 2 years after the episode, I was living in a basement flat in Perham Road, West Kensington with my future wife Jill, who I had first met in the day hospital. The rappings began again over a period of a couple of weeks, gradually at first but eventually they became more intense, reacting to my every thought. Jill could hear them and would flee the kitchen when they built up. They were now frequently tapping 'Yes' to the thought that I should rush out and throw myself under a lorry.

At times like this, one sees and fully realises how useless the attitude of sceptics in the field of the paranormal can be. In that situation, a sceptic would not have had the faintest idea what to do. It seemed to me that as the rappings began to really gallop, science and psychology were of no use to me now. I asked Jill if she could find my Bible and when she brought it to me I sat at the kitchen table, turned to The New Testament and began to read. It seemed to me that I really needed to call upon a Higher Power to defeat what was definitely looking like a manifestation of The Demonic. Jill's belief was, 'The Devil's trying to kill you'.

As I started to read The New Testament the *timing* of the rappings started, very slightly at first, to go awry. This gave me hope and I kept on reading. By the second page, their timing was definitely 'off', by the third they were 'missing thoughts' and not tapping at all to some things that crossed my mind. By the fourth and fifth pages, their timing was totally haywire, it was like the sound of a machine that was completely malfunctioning and there was a quality of panic, even desperation, in the air. Then very suddenly they stopped completely. The kitchen was quiet.

It took years for there to be any recurrence of these rappings, I do occasionally suffer them when I am spiritually afraid, as for example after watching a frightening ghost story on television late at night, but as a *problem* they have now lost their power. However, in September 1981, had we not had a Bible in the house at that time, happily a present from my mother, I really do *not* know what we would have done or what would have happened to me physically and mentally.

It is obvious from a crisis such as this that one cannot ignore spiritual dimensions in recovery when they intrude so blatantly into the psychosis itself. It was important to me that many vicars I spoke with corrected the very savage view of God I had received as a child and eased me into seeing in Him Ultimate Understanding, compassion, and love. In the three decades, that have passed since this episode I have come to see God as understanding one's life and struggles through one's *own* eyes not with the outsider mentality of a judgemental neighbourhood gossip. God really is there *in* all of us, He is man, woman, heterosexual, homosexual, beggar and king. In all and through all.

My Pantheistic beliefs have been central and critical to me for many years now. Although I still regularly take a tiny amount of anti-psychotic medication (halo-peridol), being at peace spiritually seems to have helped the orchestration and integration of lower-level psychological processes top-down. Even in my own work, I have come to think that it is better if our reason is grounded in something deeper than itself. I consider that my many years of deep immersion in such a cynical, materialistic atmosphere, in the 1970s, did me more damage mentally and spiritually than, at the time, I at all realised.

My current attitude is, however, still 'knowledge-seeking' (Latin *scientia*) but I look upon this endeavour as best conceived as a blend of science, art and spirituality not as pre-emptively scientistic. Because of this, I write not only for psychological and mental health periodicals but for literature journals (e.g. Chadwick, 2005, 2006, 2007) and give talks and write on art as therapy and on the spiritual dimension in psychosis (e.g. Chadwick, 2004).

There seems to me no reason why spiritual considerations in therapy could not be blended with those of a cognitive and psychodynamic character. In my own self-therapy, as a psychologist who has himself 'been there', all these directions have proved profitable.

My own experience and indeed my own quite long life has convinced me, with Zoroastrians (Burke, 2004) that there are both positive *and* negative spiritual forces at work in the cosmos. One must always learn to defocus from the newsworthy and salient negative to the stronger and more all-pervading positive. To be mindful of this is critical and one even can apply such an attitude to schizophrenia itself – often seen wrongly as negative through-and-through (see Chadwick, 1997, 2008). Indeed pessimistic clinicians in this field can be seriously demoralising for sufferers, it is vital after such traumatic experiences to have an attitude of hope, resolve and self-belief. Cynicism about outcome is damaging not only for patients/clients but for the very staff assisting them.

I am hopeful that a chapter such as this, written by someone who is both a professional and a peer of the patients, will encourage sufferers to write about the background and causes of their crises. Service user research which focuses only on evaluation of services, as so much of it does, is a particularly one-eyed view of the contribution former sufferers can make to the psychosis field. Research by people with inside knowledge into causes and precipitating factors, in my view, should be 'the dominant eye' of service user research and could contribute greatly to understanding, stigma reduction, prevention and early intervention.

Conclusions

The single case study presented here reminds us starkly that no one singular perspective, be it biochemical, cognitive or whatever, can totally embrace the understanding of psychosis nor should it dominate recovery from it. Here, we have seen likely genetic factors, family processes, cognitive biases, social stigma, moral issues, spiritual and existential problems, indeed it is clear that a whole reticular potpourri of factors are involved in leading a person both into and out of psychosis.

This offering also is obviously a study in qualitative psychology and implicitly argues for the value of the single case study in psychology and psychiatry. It is clear that 'all is *not* number' [a position not entirely fairly attributed to Pythagoras (Waterfield, 2000)] and it would hardly have been nourishing, satisfying or meaningful to have recounted the above only in an arid analytical way. One does not drink soup with a fork and it often is the case, that if one wants more clarity one has to settle for less truth – but if one wants more truth, one has to suffer less clarity.

The integration of science, art and spirituality which I have tried to orchestrate in my own work on psychosis (e.g. Chadwick, 2008) will I hope help students and practitioners not feel embarrassed (as usually they are) about putting God on the page in what they write. Delusional thinking, as well as involving intriguing issues in information processing psychology, can also be the release of a fiction-making ability and an encounter with the very outer reaches of human phenomenology. It would be absurd, and wrong, to reduce this via a model based only on the physical sciences.

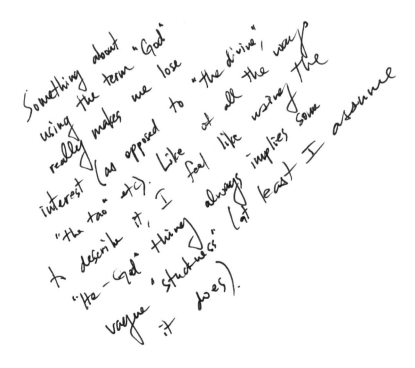

Something about "God" using the term really makes us lose interest (as opposed to "the divine", "the tao" etc). Like at all the ways the God thing implies some structures (at least I assume to describe it, I feel like using "He-God" always does). vague ✝ ✝

7

Spiritual Experience: Healthy Psychoticism?

Gordon Claridge

Preamble

It is appropriate to open this chapter by considering the fundamental dilemma concerning the manner in which individually we are inclined to interpret the putative connection between psychosis and spirituality. The dilemma can be stated as follows. If it is the case that spiritual beliefs and experiences are phenomenologically similar to a psychotic world view, then should we not conclude that religions are just a form of madness and the religious merely insane? Or could we not equally well decide that those diagnosed as clinically psychotic are really misunderstood visionaries, wrongly labelled and disparaged by others who fail to share their sensitivities? Of course, few would adopt either of those two extreme positions, at least as generalisations about all examples. But the point is made and the contributors to this book have been obliged, in one way or another, explicitly or implicitly, to touch upon the issue. The debate has several strands.

For example, it need not be argued, just because spiritual experience and psychosis superficially look alike, that they share the same 'aetiology', whether this is construed sociologically, psychologically or biologically. There are many phenomena whose similarity does not extend throughout the whole range of causal relationships. And even if in this instance the isomorphism was to prove to be complete, there is still plenty of scope for individual expression – for in nature the general rule is, not identicality, but variability.

In the present instance, the sources for such variation are many. Socio-cultural influences often dictate whom we label mystic and whom we label psychotic. Within the same society that decision (and the behaviours and experiences leading to it) will be shaped by the person's life history, current emotional relationships, scarcely fathomable personal strengths and weaknesses, as well as economic circumstances, timing, and sheer luck. Since as yet we really have no idea what madness is, we are

We're all mad here

Psychosis and Spirituality: Consolidating the New Paradigm Second Edition   Edited by Isabel Clarke
© 2010 John Wiley & Sons, Ltd.

perhaps entitled to shelve for the moment trying to answer the 'big question' in the spirituality/psychosis dilemma; concentrating instead on seeking clues as to what the answer might, eventually, be.

The present chapter is written in that vein. It offers a particular view of the topic, drawing upon what, it must be admitted, is a rather messy concoction of clinical and abnormal psychology, on the one hand, and some parts of contemporary personality theory, on the other. Where the chapter connects to others in the book it is mostly to those by Chadwick, Peters, and, especially, Jackson, whose work provided important evidence and insights for the ideas to be discussed here.

Three themes – crucial to an understanding of what is to be presented – need to be stated at the outset. First is the proposition that there are inherent personality differences between people that are substantially constitutional, even partly genetic, in origin: such characteristics form traits – or, as clusters of traits, dimensions – that run through the general population and describe the structure of human individual differences. Secondly, it is assumed that these characteristics also act as dispositions to varying forms of mental illness and personality dysfunction: if people do become ill they will be more likely to develop the disorder to which their underlying personality makes them vulnerable. Thirdly, because of the intrinsic connection envisaged between healthy personality and mental disorder, there is nothing inevitable about the former resulting in the latter; on the contrary, traits that in one context lead, or contribute, to psychological breakdown can, in another context, be perfectly adaptive and beneficial to the mental well-being of the person.

There is little in any of the above three points that would be regarded as particularly controversial by most clinicians and academics in psychiatry and abnormal psychology, except where a 'dimensional' perspective to psychotic disorders, i.e. their being seen as rooted in some sense in otherwise healthy functioning, has seemed unacceptable. The idea therefore needs some special consideration.

Psychosis as Dimension

For most of this century, insanity has been seen to belong firmly in the medical domain, with the promised discovery of a neurobiological 'lesion' as cause always just around the corner. The working models for madness have generally been, and continue to be, sought in the domain of the degenerative neurological illnesses, such as Alzheimer's disease.

Admittedly, there were (relatively brief) challenges to this viewpoint during the 1960s and early 70s: in the United States from the anti-psychiatry of Thomas Szasz (1974) and, in Britain, from the existentialist radical psychiatry of R.D. Laing (1960). In many ways, both of these movements actually did a disservice to attempts to provide a corrective to the overly medical view of the time. The Laingian analysis of madness, for example, although certainly reawakening us to the fact that there is meaning in the psychotic experience, went too far in that direction, neglecting the suffering of genuinely sick people, entirely ignoring an evident biology in mental illness, and confusing the notions of blame and cause in the determined search for an entirely sociogenic explanation.

The arrival and folklore popularity of the combined (although by no means concordant) Szasz/Laing ideologies had practical consequences that constrained subsequent thinking about the nature of psychosis, in two ways. First, the eventual backlash in mainstream psychiatry against what were perceived as the excesses of these alternative movements was such that, boosted by fresh discoveries in neurobiology, the old-style medical model of psychosis became even more entrenched than it was before. Secondly, the excitement and furore generated by the debate within psychiatry (indeed society at large) between conventionalists and rebels distracted attention from the fact that there was – and always had been – a third, alternative, theory of madness; one that could accommodate some parts of both sides in the argument. It was from this background that the dimensional model of psychosis drawn upon here originated. Historically, it had two roots.

The first was, ironically, in psychiatry itself. Even with attempts around the end of the nineteenth century to identify discrete forms of psychotic disease there was a recognition that the boundaries of these illnesses were blurred. For example, Bleuler (1911), in describing schizophrenia, also recognised the schizoid personality, either as a mild variant of the illness or as a cluster of 'odd' temperamental traits related to it (he was never quite sure which). Then, somewhat later, another concept – 'schizotypy' – emerged, defined more explicitly in terms of the presence in a person of mild schizophrenic or schizophrenic-like symptoms (Rado, 1953; Meehl, 1962). Both terms articulated the notion of a continuum of functioning, of which full-blown schizophrenic illness was just the extreme. Of the two, schizotypy became the more used; indeed it has now emerged as a pivotal construct for guiding investigations into the dimensional aspects of psychosis (for edited collections of research on this topic see Raine, Lencz and Mednick, 1995; Claridge, 1997).

The second influence has come more from psychology, from personality theory, and specifically from the work of the late H.J. Eysenck. Eysenck is best known for identifying dimensions of personality which, in the clinical sphere, relate to and try to explain the less severe, neurotic disorders, such as those stemming from anxiety and mild depression. But very early on, he also proposed and subsequently developed a comparable personality dimension associated with psychosis (Eysenck, 1952; Eysenck and Eysenck, 1976). It should be noted that Eysenck construed this dimensionality more broadly than researchers who came to the question from a clinical direction (and who concentrated mostly on the *schizophrenic* form of psychosis). Eysenck subsumed, under the general heading of 'psychoticism', dispositions to psychoses of *all types*; viz including bipolar (manic-depression) forms, as well as schizophrenia. In doing so, he was following some old traditions in both psychiatry and personality description. In the former case, this refers to an early school of thought that there was just one psychosis, with several variants (Berrios, 1995). In the latter case, it refers, in personality theory, to the dimensionalising, also, of manic-depressive psychosis, under descriptors like 'cyclothymia' and 'cycloid' (Kretschmer, 1925).

It turns out that Eysenck's broader conceptualisation is probably more accurate; or at least for the moment provides a better working model for studying psychosis and its dimensionality. This is supported on two fronts. One is clinical evidence about the psychotic illnesses themselves, coming from comparisons of symptom patterns, genetics and treatment response in the different forms of psychosis (Kendell, 1991; Baron and Gruen, 1991; Taylor, 1992). The other is from statistical analyses of the self-report scales used for measuring psychotic traits in healthy subjects. Over the last two decades, many such scales have been developed and tested out in non-clinical, clinical and borderline clinical populations (for reviews see Chapman, Chapman and Kwapil, 1995; Mason, Claridge and Williams, 1997). Most of this work has been carried out under the rubric of schizotypy research, but the findings clearly point to the fact that, not only is there not a single dimension of 'schizotypy', the latter term seems too narrow to describe the full spectrum of psychotic traits. Thus, several components have been discovered in which, importantly, schizophrenic *and* manic depressive features intermingle (Claridge *et al.*, 1996).

Four components can be recognised. The first two correspond to the so-called 'positive' or active symptoms of psychosis. One of these components concerns the disposition to unusual perceptual and other cognitive experiences – such as hallucinations and magical, or superstitious, belief and interpretation of events. The second, also cognitive, covers more disorganised forms of thinking, such as the tendency for thoughts to become derailed in states of anxiety. A third component – mapping on to 'negative' psychotic symptoms (or signs of absence of behaviours) – describes introverted, rather schizoid, features, associated with a deficiency in the ability to feel pleasure from social and physical stimulation (anhedonia). Finally, 'impulsive non-conformity' refers, as the label implies, to unstable mood and behaviour and the tendency to break rules or adopt unconventional attitudes. These four clusters of characteristics map well on to the clinical syndromes to which they are intended to relate, show the same overlapping features, and, between them, seem to account well for most of the variation in psychosis and psychoticism. The latter, rather than 'schizotypy', is therefore probably the better generic term to use from here on – notwithstanding the fact that, perversely, Eysenck (1992) himself eventually narrowed down his own usage of 'psychoticism' to denote something closer to only the fourth, anti-social, component referred to above.

In summary, then, the contemporary scene contains a number of ideas that express the notion of insanity as a continuum, doing so in a form more digestible for mainstream psychiatry than the anti-medical challenges of an earlier era. Indeed there is nothing in current-dimensional theories that contradict the idea of psychosis as illness, or preclude conventional scientific investigations of cause, nature and treatment. Research in the field now has a broad remit: the genetic basis of psychoticism; its cognitive, neuropsychological, neuroanatomical and psychophysiological correlates; the possible mechanisms whereby it acts as a vehicle for psychotic experiences; and whether high levels in childhood can predict later mental breakdown (for regular reviews of these, and related, aspects see, particularly, continuing issues of *Schizophrenia Bulletin*).

Despite an apparent confluence of purpose and interest, there is, nevertheless, within the dimensionality debate itself, a subtext that is rarely articulated. It happens to be of particular – indeed crucial – relevance to the subject matter of this book and concerns the precise interpretation to be placed on the notion of a continuity between psychotic and non-psychotic.

Psychoticism: Personality Dimension or Mild Illness?

As pointed out in the previous section, the dimensional view of psychosis had two origins: one, psychological, in personality theory, and the other medical, as an extension of the clinical description of mental illness. Although leading to superficially similar conclusions, the underlying philosophies of these two schools of thought were, and remain, actually very different, giving rise to a schism of opinion among those researching psychoticism. The point at issue is whether psychoticism is truly a personality trait (or set of traits), or whether it merely signifies a subclinical form of disease. Elsewhere (Claridge, 1997). I have referred to these two versions of continuity as, respectively, the 'quasi-dimensional' and the 'fully dimensional' models (see Figure 7.1). As shown in the figure, the quasi-dimensional model – which originated in the medical tradition – rests on the assumption of *forme fruste* of disease, the well-established notion that the symptoms of illness can present themselves in varying degree, forming a continuum of severity.

Applied to schizotypy (the issue has usually been debated under that heading) 'dimensionality' has then been seen as strictly confined to the clinical sphere, intended to refer solely to a so-called 'schizophrenia spectrum' of psychotic disease.

In contrast, the fully dimensional theory – which encloses the quasi-dimensional model – is precisely as outlined at the beginning of this chapter and further illustrated in Figure 1. That is to say, psychotic traits of personality are assumed to exist – just like any other personality characteristics – as descriptors of individual differences

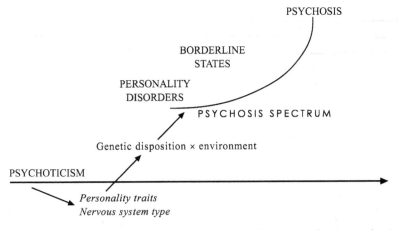

Figure 7.1 Comparison of two interpretations of dimensionality in psychosis

between people. They certainly pre-dispose to psychotic disorder, and if this happens, the individual passes into the clinical domain (represented schematically in the diagram as being above the line): there he or she can potentially show the same spectrum of mild to severe symptoms assumed by the quasi-dimensionalists. But the important point is that, according to the fully dimensional view of continuity, psychotic traits, in and of themselves, are not pathological, but merely represent personality variation.[1]

The way workers in the two camps have chosen to interpret the dimensionality of psychoticism has sometimes had strong consequences: one conference critic of the present writer once described the fully dimensional view as an 'impossible idea'! Certainly, the distinction has noticeably influenced their respective research methodologies, the hypotheses tested and how results have been interpreted. For example, in their search for an underlying biology, quasi-dimensionalists assume that what they are looking for is some neurological deficit: true to the *forme fruste* idea, this is expected to express itself as degrees of malfunction, resulting in a continuum of disordered behaviour which, at the very mild end, might even look like a natural personality variation.

Those preferring a fully continuous view, though equally concerned to understand the biology, tend to start at the other (low) end of the dimension. In line with the notion that personality differences partly represent natural variations in the way in which normal nervous systems can be organised, they seek to characterise the biology of psychoticism as one such variant. The biology of psychotic illness then merely represents an exaggerated form of that type of central nervous functioning. A good analogy here is with anxiety. People of anxious temperament have nervous systems that make them unusually sensitive to fear-provoking stimuli. This makes them more susceptible to phobias, panic attacks and so on. But it can be beneficial in situations where a moderate degree of apprehension helps to promote peak performance on some task. At a biological level, anxiety *disorder* therefore merely represents a transformation of processes that mediate healthy anxiety. So it is, the argument goes, with psychosis and psychoticism.

Evidence from a range of studies examining the extent to which laboratory phenomena ascribed to clinical psychotics can be found in perfectly normal subjects strongly favours the fully dimensional view (Broks, 1984; Chapman and Chapman, 1980; Mason and Claridge, 1999). Some of the most persuasive observations – of special interest here of course – come from work on the personality correlates of spiritual experience, as described by Jackson in Chapter 12 of this book. From his research, it is clear that the psychoticism (schizotypy) of some individuals can express itself in a form which, in some respects, is phenomenologically similar to

---

[1] It should be noted that, although historically the two models of continuity described are split along medical versus psychological lines, on the contemporary scene the distinction is also to some extent transatlantic. Thus, North American *psychologists* working in the field also tend to espouse the quasi-dimensional view, the fully dimensional alternative being favoured more by those, mostly European, writers influenced, directly or indirectly, by Eysenck and his followers.

clinical psychosis, even though, in some other respects, the person's mental state is quite different.

The case of spiritual experience is only one of a number of examples where psychoticism can be seen to have a perfectly healthy outcome. McCreery and Claridge (1995), in parallel research on the phenomenon of out-of-the-body experience (OBE), showed that individuals reporting OBEs were also high in psychotic traits. Yet they, too, were mentally quite healthy. Then, on a broader front, there is the established association between creativity and psychoticism, indicating that styles of perception and associative thinking that, in one context or one individual, can lead to aberrant mentation can, in another, result in products of exceptional originality and worth (Jamison, 1993; Claridge, Pryor and Watkins, 1998). Given this kind of evidence, it would be difficult, I believe, to dismiss the idea that psychosis has elements within it that are entirely compatible with normal mental health – or better. The conclusion raises several other questions that are pertinent to the supposed connection between spirituality and psychosis.

Further Questions

The thesis of this chapter has been that certain individuals, because of their so-called 'psychotic' personalities are more likely to have (or report) perceptions, thoughts and beliefs which, in one way or another, are peculiar, idiosyncratic, outside the usual range of everyday experience. But what are the mechanisms of this susceptibility? What biological or other processes could explain the psychology of such individuals? And what determines whether the expression of their psychoticism is judged sick or inspired?

On the question of the underlying mechanisms of psychoticism, experimental abnormal psychology has thrown up several possibilities, drawing upon cognitive, neuropsychological and psychophysiological paradigms (for edited reviews see Claridge, 1997). One that chimes well with some of the ideas discussed in this book draws upon the notion that in psychotic and psychotic-like states there is a breakdown in the 'stimulus barrier' that ordinarily excludes information from awareness (Deikman, 1966b). Or, as Frith (1979) later put it, psychotic individuals have difficulty 'limiting the contents of consciousness'. More technically, this quality has been construed as caused by variations in 'cognitive inhibition', a hypothetical mechanism used to account for some individual differences in modes of attention and thinking. Thus, the inhibitory mechanism necessary for focused attention is weaker in some individuals. Several experimental procedures to test this idea have emerged and been successfully tested in the laboratory in both non-clinical and clinical subjects (Bullen, Hemsley and Dixon, 1987; Williams and Beech, 1997; Peters, Pickering and Hemsley, 1994; Evans, 1997). Results of that work suggest that there is, in the notion of cognitive inhibition, a plausible mechanism for explaining why, in certain susceptible people, out of the ordinary experiences come easily from the fringes into the centre of awareness and form a fertile ground for elaborated systems of thought and belief.

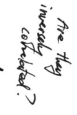
Are they inversely correlated?

A writer who has gathered these and other related themes together most comprehensively is Thalbourne (Thalbourne and Delin, 1994; Thalbourne *et al.*, 1997). He has performed so under the heading of 'transliminality', a term designed to capture the cognitive differences discussed above, but sufficiently non-judgemental to avoid the pejorative overtones associated with terms like psychosis and psychoticism. As defined by Thalbourne, transliminality refers to individual differences in the extent to which ideas, affects and other mental contents cross the threshold between subliminal and supraliminal: in some people, he argues, the barrier is simply more permeable. Thalbourne paints across a broad canvas in outlining the consequences and correlates of transliminality. Quoting a range of psychometric, clinical and experimental evidence, he argues that a high degree of transliminality is associated with strong belief in and reporting of paranormal phenomena; enhanced creativity; a greater tendency to indulge in magical thinking; more frequent mystical experiences; and a susceptibility to psychotic and psychotic-like symptoms.[2] On the last score. Thalbourne has focused his own research particularly on the manic-depressive aspects of psychosis, and corresponding cyclothymic personality traits (It is worth noting in passing that in Thalbourne's work these correlate highly with several features studied elsewhere as 'schizotypy', again confirming the validity of the general psychoticism concept).

Thalbourne's (1991) concentration on the mood (especially manic) element in psychoticism is significant because he uses this as a particular vehicle for exploring how transliminality relates to mystical (or spiritual) experience. Like other writers (e.g. Goodwin and Jamison, 1990), he notes that there is much in common between religious ecstasy and the type of elation and 'flight of ideas' seen in mania. In comparing the two, he enumerates many similarities: sudden onset; a sense of external or internal light; profound joy; difficulty in verbalising the mental state; a feeling of purpose in the experience; an insight into the connectedness of previously unrelated events and their subsuming under a 'Oneness' or Unity; an utter conviction that the information imparted is absolutely true and a sense that the experience is extremely valuable; transcendence of the usual ego-boundaries and a merging into a greater Being; and, despite a temporary duration of the experience, the belief, while it lasts, in one's own immortality.

Thalbourne writes here very much from his own personal experience because he admits (Thalbourne, 1991) to be himself a sufferer from manic-depression. He is therefore well-placed to judge the similarities and differences between psychotic illness and the spiritual state, and where the border between them lies. Clinical psychosis, Thalbourne points out, is more riven with aggressive outburst, paranoia, personalised themes. Yet despite this, it does make a difference – as Chadwick

---

[2] A similar idea – construed as 'thin and thick mental boundaries' – has been proposed independently by Hartmann (1991) as an explanation of individual differences in dream and nightmare experience. Here, according to Thalbourne, is another manifestation of transliminality; so it is not surprising to find that that nightmare susceptibility is also correlated with psychoticism (Levin and Raulin, 1991; Claridge, Clark and Davis, 1997).

(Chapter 6) states – if others take psychotic thoughts seriously, as a meaningful part of the person's experience, with its own genuine, if distorted, insight; and not something to be dismissed outright, as delusional rubbish. Then, to a sympathetic observer, judging solely from the possible underlying processes responsible for the two states, there could appear to be an almost entirely arbitrary distinction between them. They differ, it might be argued, only in content and context, being otherwise identical expressions of the same kind of, to use Thalbourne's term, transliminal nervous system.

But other questions lurk here. Not all, perhaps relatively few, people who suffer clinical psychosis also report experiences of a positive, spiritual kind. And by the same token, not all mystics are easily regarded as clinically mad. Are the distinctions we are seeking therefore to be found elsewhere, perhaps in the life circumstances or personal history of the individual? There are really two separate questions here, one *intraindividual* and the other *interindividual*. The former concerns how it can be that, for the vulnerable, an altered state of consciousness can sometimes hover between the healthily spiritual and the mentally ill. Chadwick's graphic account of his own experience illustrates how personal interactions, isolation, misperceptions, pre-existing beliefs, chance encounters, geography and cyclical changes in mood can make all the difference.

The interindividual question is pertinent to the idea introduced here of stable personality traits that make people more or less prone to spiritual and/or psychotic states. Earlier we noted that theories proposing such dispositions generally take a strongly biological stance; to the extent of assuming that the characteristics in question are constitutional, even heritable: types of nervous system genetically programmed to process information in a certain way. But is that an adequate account? Certainly, Thalbourne (1991), accounting for his own propensity to both psychosis and mystical experience, is content to observe that '... I have inherited the gene for manic-depression'. And indeed, there is ample evidence that genetics do make an important contribution to the aetiology of the psychotic disorders (Gottesman, 1991; Torrey *et al.*, 1994).

The genetic explanation offers an inadequate explanation of individual variation in effects of transliminality. We need instead to look towards some environmental factors, such as life experience, that might interact with and shape the biological traits and their expression.

Some clues here come from evidence about the role of early abuse and neglect in the aetiology of mental illness (Mullen *et al.*, 1988; Paris, Zweig-Frank and Guzder, 1994; Sabo, 1997; Wexler *et al.*, 1997). The influence of such factors has been consistently documented, especially in the case of disorders borderline to psychosis. The effects could be twofold. One is through the actual shaping in the individual of psychotic personality traits. This is illustrated in reports (e.g. Lawrence *et al.*, 1995) that the experience of trauma in childhood can increase fantasy and the tendency to adopt paranormal or superstitious explanations of events. Notably, both of these – seen as magical ideation – help to define one of the major components of psychoticism and might be a significant precursor of later 'mystical' styles of thought.

Comparable effects – measured on laboratory tasks of schizotypal cognitive style – have even been observed in otherwise healthy individuals who vary in their experience of a relatively mild form of 'trauma', i.e. insecure parental attachment (Wilson and Costanzo, 1996). In discussing their results, the latter authors raise the obvious dilemma of whether life experiences actually produced psychotic tendencies in their subjects, or merely exacerbated existing biological dispositions to such traits. Either way, it is clear that early life events, in addition to genetic factors, do contribute to an individual's later psychotic profile.

The second possible consequence of abusive early experience is as an effect on the altered state of consciousness itself. This could simply be by increasing the susceptibility to such experiences: clinically identified adult hallucinators, for example, frequently have a history of early abuse (Ensink, 1992; Coombs, 1996). Or the effect could be on the content of the experience, including the discourse heard in auditory hallucinations (Ensink, 1992). The negative, often accusatory, nature of these hallucinations can feed into the person's already existing sense of society's disparagement, and his or her feeling of low self-esteem, to produce the classic constellation of symptoms that define clinical psychosis (Linn, 1977). Where nourishing as opposed to abusive early experience obtains, the same biological susceptibility to transliminality, the break with ordinary reality could be much less threatening, even psychologically rewarding. Associations, found in 'normal' hallucinators, with such traits as enhanced creativity (Posey and Losch, 1983) would be consistent with that conclusion.

Of course, in practice, as Chadwick's story illustrates, the result of this interaction between life experience and biological disposition will often be an untidy spiritual/ psychotic mix. And there will be several reasons for this. For most people, including those high in psychoticism, parental rearing is neither wholly evil nor wholly idyllic. Furthermore, the biological disposition to psychoticism will vary: from strong disposition to psychosis to a tendency only to tip over the threshold in situations of great disadvantage. People also differ in other personal characteristics, quite unconnected to psychoticism. Some such traits (e.g. anxiety or solitariness) might exacerbate the less healthy expressions of psychoticism. Other characteristics, like high intelligence or strong ego-strength, or the tendency not to see things in a self-referential manner, might protect the individual from psychopathology; or they might nourish positive, healthy outcomes, of which enhanced spirituality could be just one example.

A final set of questions, already partly touched upon, concerns the relative contribution to spiritual experience (or illness) of the different components of psychoticism. Is one aspect more likely than the others to constitute a necessary accompaniment or precursor of either state? Does the simultaneous presence in the person of several of the components determine the outcome – benign or pathological? Indeed, are these sorts of comparison a basis for distinguishing the 'genuinely' psychotic from the 'genuinely' mystical?

As noted earlier, Thalbourne has identified manic-depressive (especially manic) features of psychosis as being most linked to the ecstatic states typically seen in both psychotic and mystical experience. As a view of where the important link between the two lies – and where a difficulty in distinguishing between them might arise – this certainly seems convincing and was the conclusion reached, for example, by Buckley (1981) in his phenomenological comparison of schizophrenia and mystical experience. Buckley noted that the two conditions resemble each other most closely where the schizophrenia presents as an acute clinical picture; as contrasted with insidious forms of the disorder, characterised by introversion, withdrawal and flattening of mood – described as negative symptom schizophrenia, and corresponding to the anhedonic, schizoid component of psychoticism.

Huh

So can we conclude that the debate here is really just about a certain subset of unusual experiences, psychiatric diagnoses, or components of psychoticism? Is it these – the manic-depressive elements – that create the difficult distinctions we are seeking to resolve? It may not be as simple as that. Debating the issue of what is mystical and what is mad therefore probably does have to take account of possible similarities and confusions that exist across the whole spectrum of psychotic behaviour and thought, making the distinctions even more blurred than they might seem at the outset. To help illustrate the point consider the following biographical comparison between two famous and contemporaneous mediaeval mystics: Margery Kempe and Julian of Norwich.

Again, who cares?

Margery Kempe (b. circa 1373) is most famous for her dictated (she was illiterate) autobiography, *The Book of Margery Kempe* (Windeat, 1985). In her lifetime she was – to use a more appropriate adjective – notorious for her wild excesses of behaviour; her visions of Christ and subsequent calling to the spiritual life; her continuing hallucinations; her chaotic pilgrimages across Europe; and, most characteristic – as well as troublesome for others – her boisterous expressions of devotion, in the form of loud cries and sobbing, at every opportunity. Even in her own day, Margery was regarded by many as mad; in contemporary diagnostic terminology there is ample justification for placing her somewhere along the spectrum between schizophrenia and mixed schizophrenic/manic state (Pryor in Claridge, Pryor, and Watkins, 1998; Claridge, 1998).

Julian of Norwich (b. 1342) also had hallucinations (of Christ's suffering and the Blessed Virgin), was widely known in her own time as a respected visionary, and was also an authoress, famous for her exquisitely written *Revelations of Divine Love* (Hudleston, 1952). Unlike Margery Kempe, Julian, after her own divine visions, withdrew into the contemplative life of the recluse, and established a reputation that has subsequently stopped short only of sainthood. There has never been, as far as I am aware, any suggestion that she might have been insane.

Does the contrast between these two very different women offer us any guidelines about spirituality and psychosis? On the one hand, Margery Kempe who possessed the very features – of manic psychosis – that cause us difficulty in finding a boundary between madness and mysticism; yet considered insane even at a time when revelations such as hers were a normal part of daily life. On the other hand, Julian of Norwich, whose withdrawal into contemplation after hallucination could be seen, from a present day perspective, as an analogue of the introverted schizophrenic's self-imposed (and self-protective) isolation from the world. A verdict such as that presumably makes us uncomfortable. And rightly so, because it degrades the memory of an obviously talented woman. Yet if we accept one (Margery Kempe) then we should surely also accept the other (Julian) as together representing the several different ways in which psychoticism can find spiritual expression, and both veering – again in different ways – towards clinical psychosis.

Conclusions

As was anticipated, the dilemma used to introduce this chapter has not been resolved in what has followed. We are no nearer to knowing whether the mystic should be considered formally mad, or whether the clinically psychotic sometimes stumble on universal insights of great significance, albeit through the distorted lens of the personalised paranoia to which their nervous systems make them peculiarly susceptible. But hopefully the discussion here has moved the debate on slightly.

In some respects, of course, the perspective on psychosis adopted in this chapter makes it more, rather than less, difficult to solve the puzzle of spirituality by referring to clinical data. Conventional interpretations of psychosis – even some of those grounded in a dimensional viewpoint – are essentially modelled on notions of disease as neurological deficit. If spiritual experience is to be brought within that same domain, then the logical conclusion is surely that the spiritually inspired are merely deranged.

The alternative presented here at least offers a way out of that simplistic equation. Psychosis – or rather psychoticism – could simply be, as suggested, a variation on 'ways of behaving and thinking'. In which case, the judgment, 'mad' or 'inspired', becomes a matter of personal (or societal) evaluation. Well, not quite: it probably *is* the case that some ideas, perceptions, interpretations of events, *are* crazy, having no foundation either in consensual reality or in a theoretically fathomable universal truth. But at least, for the moment, the matter remains open, if we are prepared to accept the view of psychosis offered here.

Of course, one could step completely outside the spirituality/psychosis debate as it has been interpreted in this chapter. Mysticism and psychosis might be completely different universes of discourse; high psychoticism need not be a necessary condition of enhanced spirituality; and, even if it were in some instances, this might not always (or mostly) be the case. It would be difficult to counter that argument entirely. Although a truism, it has to be conceded that behaviour is always multiply determined and the explanations of particular cases rarely identical. Nevertheless, the argument here has been – and the evidence seems in its favour – that psychoticism and psychosis *do* provide a substantive bridge to the understanding of the origins of *most* spiritual, mystical or religious experiences that stem from the personal psychology of the individual – as distinct, that is, from cult or culture bound or mimicked religious versions that originate in ritualised, theological dogmas or the suggestibility of gullible persons.

It's all the same copy, whether you can swallow it or not.

Psychoticism has been assumed to be a substantially constitutional trait, reflecting central nervous system differences between people, but the precise mechanisms which, at that level, mediate the connection between psychoticism and spirituality (or psychosis) are not entirely clear. Given the multi-dimensional nature of psychoticism itself, it is likely that several processes are involved, to do with both affect and cognition, and their interaction. However, one central explanatory construct here probably *is* something like the 'transliminality' quoted by Thalbourne. This or similar notions have existed in various forms throughout the history of attempts to explain the psychotic's wild swings and unpredictable trajectories of ideation and emotion; a condition found as 'skinlessness' (Anthony, 1987), in the characteristic childhood trait said to pre-dispose to such reactions. As a key feature of the psychotic personality, this supersensitivity of perception, thinking and feeling might provide a common mechanism for the phenomena discussed here, the *content* of individual experiences – and whether positive or negative in tone – being shaped by situational, life history, and other contextual factors. In clinical psychosis, such hyperawareness results in a state that fluctuates along a continuum from the real through the misperceived to the seemingly entirely imagined. If we were to try to confront how the same formulation might also account for spiritual or mystical experience, then we might logically be forced to consider that the psychotic person's skinlessness (or transliminality) could even extend to what in conventional terms would be called the 'supernatural'. The possibility is intriguing but takes us to the very far reaches of a topic that is already fraught with philosophical uncertainty and its own brand of irrationality. For the moment therefore that particular theme must remain, unsubstantiated, outside the scope of our discussion.

Instead, the final remarks of this chapter more properly belong, I feel, not with those people whose psychoticism results in a spiritually satisfying, highly valued experience, but rather with those whose similar personality dispositions lead them into mental illness. The possibility that both outcomes represent alternative facets of the same tendency – together with the notion of 'healthy psychoticism' – should surely give hope to the genuinely insane and lead to a better understanding and greater tolerance of their own bizarre, but legitimate, experiences.

8

'Psychopathology', 'Psychosis' and the Kundalini: Post-Modern Perspectives On Unusual Subjective Experience

Richard House

> We should not try to 'get rid' of a neurosis [or psychosis – RH], but rather to experience what it means, what it has to teach us, what its purpose is. . . We do not cure it – it cures us.
>
> C. G. Jung (interpolation added)

Introduction

Despite the existence of major philosophical and clinical objections to the conceptual coherence of the notions of '(ab)normality' (e.g. Buck, 1992a; Caplan, 1995) and 'psychopathology' (e.g. Halling and Nill, 1989; Parker *et al.*, 1995), their stubborn ubiquity in popular and academic discourse suggests that there may exist unconscious, anxiety-driven reasons for their longevity in 'modernist' paradigmatic approaches to human experience. Starting from a critique of these concepts, and the assumptions that underpin 'pathologising diagnosticism' in the mental-health field (Boyle, 2007), I will argue that what is commonly termed 'psychotic' experience may often constitute:

- a struggle towards meaning-making (cf. Bannister, 1985);
- a meaningful *process* (e.g. Halling and Nill, 1989), typically operating at many levels, rather than an 'abnormal malfunction' of the brain; and
- more speculatively, a possible harbinger, albeit often a highly distressing one, of qualitative advances in human consciousness which, as yet, the 'ordinary' Cartesian ego consciousness of modernity finds it difficult if not impossible either to contain or to make sense of.

Psychosis and Spirituality: Consolidating the New Paradigm Second Edition   Edited by Isabel Clarke
© 2010 John Wiley & Sons, Ltd.

I will draw extensively upon the phenomenon of the so-called 'Kundalini awakening experience' to illustrate these propositions.

A constructivist, post-modern perspective on the notion of '(ab)normality' views it far more as an anxiety-induced, socio-emotionally rooted linguistic category whose unacknowledged function is to reduce anxiety in the face of the other's radical difference, rather than as an objective description of an independent reality existing separately from our own emotionally driven 'construction' of it. Such a view leads, in turn, into interesting philosophical questions about perception, objectivity and subjectivity and 'theories of truth', which can only be touched upon in this chapter. There are a number of (inter-related) factors holding the conventional psychiatric approach to abnormality and psychopathology in place, whose common theme can be termed 'the ideology of modernity' (House, 2009). Not least of these factors is the way in which the medicalisation and pathologising of 'unusual subjective experience' (hereafter USE) conveniently locates it outside of the 'comfort-zone' of what is familiar, predictable and 'normal' – in turn distancing mental-health professionals from direct and fearless engagement with the challenging, often disturbing subjective experience of their patients.

In this medicalisation of USE, a perverse alchemy seems to occur, whereby such experience is surreptitiously transformed into what is an essentially circular and self-fulfilling diagnostic system (Parker *et al.*, 1995) which then becomes the guarantee of its own existence within a professional 'regime of truth' (cf. House, 2002–3, 2009). Several deliciously mischievous commentators have humorously dubbed such a process 'Pervasive Labelling Disorder' (Buck, 1992b) and 'Professional Thought Disorder' (Lowson, 1994). Mary Boyle's (1990, 1996) painstaking (and brilliant) unpicking of the evolutionary history of the concept of 'schizophrenia' is highly revealing in this regard; and an increasing number of commentators are indeed highlighting the blindness of the modernist scientific worldview to the spiritual, mystical, non-material dimension (e.g. Berman, 1984).

It follows from this that conventional distinctions between 'psychotic', 'unusual' and 'mystical/transpersonal' experience are not only far from clear-cut, but might well be fundamentally misguided and philosophically unsustainable. The Indian philosopher J. Krishnamurti's life-long struggle with what he called his 'Process' and the phenomenon of Kundalini awakening illustrate these countercultural perspectives very clearly. Any full discussion of these phenomena would need to encompass critical perspectives on 'madness' and 'psychosis'; the phenomenon of 'spiritual emergence/y'; and cross-cultural and historical perspectives in psychiatry (e.g. Heinze, 1999; Benatar, 2006).

I contend that a radical shift in world-view, from naive technocratic scientism and towards a post-modern, more spiritually informed 'new paradigm' perspective, opens up creative, liberating and potentially healing avenues for understanding the widest spectrum of human subjective experience. I have much sympathy with the Laingian view that so-called 'psychotic' symptoms are sometimes, and perhaps often, a *contextually sane* commentary on what is an essentially and unacknowledged *insane* world – whether it be the interpersonal world of the sufferer, or the wider socio-political institutional world. Rather more speculatively, USEs' may constitute an early manifestation of qualitative advances in human consciousness. Thus at least some USEs [e.g. see Glass (1993) on 'multiple personality disorder' and 'schizophrenia'] may have a wider, *evolutionary* or transpersonal function, which should certainly not be ignored in societal decisions about how to respond individually, professionally and culturally to such experiences.

In conventional mental-health treatment, then, psychiatric patients, through the course of repeated diagnostic assessments, come increasingly to define their experiences in accordance with a professional definition of 'psychiatric illness', with 'clinical discourses impact[ing] upon individual autobiography, thereby influencing both the types of subjectivity and identity that are brought into being' (Parker *et al.*, 1995: 73). On this view, professional elites and their 'regimes of (professional) truth' are seen as constructing people's realities (House, 2003), and 'the ubiquity of particular types of discourse makes it impossible for their subjects to "think" or even imagine an "elsewhere"' (Parker *et al.*, 1995: 75).

For Levin (1987a), the 'cultural-evolutionary perspective' is crucial: for 'the diagnoses of clinical medicine are *not* scientific statements of fact referring to "real" disease entities; rather, they are theory-laden *representations*. . . products of culture; symbols of our time, constructs of the "rational" discourse we call "medicine"' (74–5, original emphases). On this view, *all* human maladies are reflections of, and commentaries upon, our culture and the 'ego-logical' Self (Levin's term) which has produced it.

The Kundalini Awakening Experience (Hereafter, KAE)

> the dominant scientific paradigm is still intolerant of the realities encountered in the Kundalini process and spirituality in general. . . [W]e must begin to look again. . . at much of what scientism has tried to debunk as meaningless and worthless fantasy.
> Lee Sannella

Psychiatrist and ophthalmologist Lee Sannella, M.D. (1992) has explored at some length the existing literature and evidence on the KAE, particularly with regard to its association with so-called 'psychosis'. He points out that KAEs, with all their 'psychotic'-like symptoms, 'seem pathological only because the symptoms are not understood in relation to outcome: a psychically transformed human being' (1992: 7). It is all too easy to label behaviour as 'psychotic' when we are unable to understand its logic or point of view – and we tend to jump to the conclusion that the limitation lies with the sanity of the other, rather than with our own limited framework of understanding.

Gopi Krishna's account of his own KAE (Krishna, 1971) provides copious evidence about the subjective aspects of a KAE. Krishna himself refers to how his 'thoughts were in a daze' (p. 14); to his disturbance, depression, fear and uncertainty (p. 15); and to how a condition of horror, on account of the inexplicable change, began to settle on me, from which. . . I could not make myself free by any effort of my will. . . [T]henceforth for a long time I had to live suspended by a thread between. . . sanity and insanity. (pp. 16, 17).

Much later, we read that 'a life and death struggle was going on inside me in which I, the owner of the body, was entirely powerless to take part' (p. 152).

Sannella also refers to the effects of a KAE upon thinking:

> Thinking may be speeded up, slowed down, or altogether inhibited. Thoughts may seem off balance, strange, irrational. The person may feel on the brink of insanity. . . and generally confused. . . The individual may feel that he or she is observing, from a distance, his or her own thoughts, feelings, and sensations.
>
> (Sannella, 1992: 98, 99).

Out-of-body experiences (OBEs) are also typical in a KAE. Conventional psychiatry typically interprets OBEs as delusional – for to accept them as in some sense ontologically 'real' would undermine the very foundations of a Western metaphysical understanding of the relationship between brain, body and consciousness (ibid.: 102). In his appendix to MacIver (1983)MacIver's book (1983), in which she graphically describes her OBEs, Sannella wrote that 'her journeys into the hidden levels of reality had a positive, healing and revelatory effect on her life' (quoted in Sannella, 1992: 102). Psychic capacities are also commonly reported by those undergoing KAEs, which, if authentic, would again require an explanation going far beyond modernity's currently prevailing materialist neurophysiological worldview.

Such perspectives also call into question the usual conceptualisation of the ego. For Sannella,

> The ego-bound rational consciousness is ultimately unfit for life. . . [Where ego and reason] are made the principles by which life is lived, they become destructive. . . Both ego and reason are recent appearances in the history of consciousness. *And both are destined to be surpassed by superior forms of existence.*
>
> (Sannella, pp. 19–20, emphasis added)

Relatedly, in the case of KAEs we also find that attempts to control the process lead to more pain and distress rather than less. Thus, the female psychologist quoted by Sannella did try to control her KAE, and found that 'pain during the physio-Kundalini cycle might be caused by conscious or subconscious resistance to the process' (1992: 97). Sannella himself goes on to argue that resistance to the KAE can 'result in hysteria *or a state akin to schizophrenia*' (99, emphasis added; see also p. 109). This observation in turn suggests that it is perhaps not the symptoms that accompany USEs *per se* which are the problem, but rather, our (ego-dominated) attempt to resist and avoid pain, discomfort or suffering, which in turn disrupts and complicates what would otherwise be a transformative or healing process. On this view, conventional psychiatric 'treatment' would tend to be routinely iatrogenic rather than healing in nature (cf. Breggin, 1993).

Sannella also implies that the stirring up of 'the sediments of the unconscious' is an intrinsic aspect of the KAE, confronting a person with 'just those psychic materials he or she wishes to inspect least of all' (Sannella, 1992: 98–9). Thus, in depth-psychological or psychodynamic terms, repressed or unresolved traumata seem very likely to erupt in the course of a KAE, which suggests that the KAE may be a multifaceted process that includes both the deeply personal *and* the transpersonal. Again, then, it is clear from this how the symptoms of a KAE could easily be (mis) diagnosed as 'psychopathology', with the underlying generative psychospiritual process being completely missed within a medical-model framework. Certainly, Sannella quotes many cases where those undergoing a KAE heard voices (pp. 79, 83, 85, 143) or had profound fears about their own sanity (pp. 60, 64, 72, 87, 88, 113, 115). Where there are 'inherent weaknesses' and 'negative environmental factors' present (Sanella, 1992: 153), it is perhaps in these cases where a KAE can so easily become conflated with 'psychosis'. Yet for Sannella, the KAE constitutes 'an aspect of psychospiritual unfolding' – 'part of an evolutionary mechanism, and . . . as such *it must not be viewed as a pathological development*' (p. 9, emphasis added).

According to Sannella, once Gopi Krishna's active Kundalini was stabilised, 'it formed the basis for the gradual development of extraordinary mental gifts, creativity and tranquillity – [and] to all kinds of mystical experiences' (p. 51). Gopi Krishna himself goes as far as arguing that the KAE is, *inter alia*, 'the real cause of all so-called spiritual and psychic phenomena [and] the master key to the unsolved mystery of creation' (quoted on p. 20; Krishna, 1974).

It does seem that those undergoing a KAE *who possess no previous theoretical framework for understanding it* will very possibly fear for their own sanity (p. 34) – and certainly more so than those who do have the anchor of such a psychospiritual framework. Both Sannella (p. 31) and Jung (quoted on p. 18) refer to the autonomous, self-directing nature of the KAE; and it is little wonder that this can so easily lead to a self-experience of 'madness' in a (Western) evolutionary conjuncture which tends to fetishise ego-control, and creates an 'abnormalising', pathologising discourse around any experience which either lies beyond conscious ego-control (Gopi described being 'completely at its mercy' – p. 51), or which contradicts the rationalist logic of the dominant materialist world-view.

It seems, then, that the KAE is probably multiply determined, being simultaneously a 'purificatory process' (Sannella, 1992: 107), a process of healing deep unconscious psychic material, and a transmutative process into a higher, qualitatively new level of consciousness. On this view, perhaps many if not all of those USEs that are typically labelled as 'psychotic' and treated biologically with psycho-active medication may well have a crucial transpersonal evolutionary aspect that conventional 'treatments', rooted in the prevailing Cartesian paradigm, not only completely miss, but actually do a profound violence towards. However, the chances of alternative, supportive-facilitative modalities gaining ground are alas at present small, given the massively entrenched vested material interests (professional, ideological and pharmaceutical) underpinning the status quo (e.g. Cohen and Timimi, 2008; House, 2009).

Concluding Reflections

We fall ill for our own development.

Rudolf Steiner

There is danger in deducing causal, generative 'mechanisms' from observed symptomatologies – and particularly when one is unaware of the 'truth constructing' effects of one's tacitly held metaphysical world-view. The Kundalini phenomenon seems to be caught between two possible constructions: a transpersonal context of meaning and the pathologised construction offered by orthodox Western medicine.

There is, thankfully, encouraging progress being made towards the depathologisation of USE, with the work of the International Association of Spiritual Psychiatry (IASP) (e.g. O'Callaghan, 1996); with Psychologist David Lukoff's successfully pioneering a new diagnostic category for the *DSM-IV* (APA, 1994: 685), 'psychoreligious or psychospiritual problem' (Lukoff, Lu and Turner, 1998); and following the relatively fallow 'latency' period following R.D. Laing 1960s anti-psychiatry works, there is again a steadily mounting literature that fundamentally challenges the foundational metaphysical assumptions of psychiatric diagnosis (e.g. Boyle, 1990, 1996; Parker *et al.*, 1995; Burston, 2000; Bracken and Thomas, 2005; Cohen and Timimi, 2008; Bentall, 2009; Geekie and Read, 2009; Moncrief, 2009).

Within an authentically post-modern approach to healing and transformation, perhaps the most effective healers are precisely those who do not (need to) take pre-conceived beliefs and defensive 'clinical gazes' into their work with clients or 'patients', but rather, are able to enter into their professional healing relationships in a relatively undefended way that privileges *the healing power of intimacy* and the immediacy of the real I–Thou encounter, as opposed to the objectifying practices that the diagnostic procedures of conventional psychiatry typically entail.

William James said that 'most people live... in a very restricted circle of their potential being' (quoted in Walsh and Vaughan, 1993) – and to such an extent that 'unusual subjective experiences' are routinely psychopathologised, chemically suppressed and brutally categorised as 'abnormal', and in need of remedial 'treatment' by a mental-health industry whose procedures and assumptive base express the anxiety-driven, security-fixated ideology of modernity which still holds sway at this juncture in the development of human consciousness.

Levin, finally, succinctly and beautifully sums up the position taken in this chapter:

> [S]eemingly psychotic experiences are better understood as crises related to the person's efforts to break out of the standard ego-bounded identity: trials of the soul on its spiritual journey. The modern self is nearing the frontier of a historically new spiritual existence... It is time for a real paradigm shift.

(Levin, 1987b; 16)

Post-Script

Kundalini From The Inside: An Anonymous, Contemporary, Experience

Kate (as she wishes to be known) has lived with her process of Kundalini Awakening for nearly 30 years. In her own words. . .

I was 16 when I experienced the first rumblings of what I now know was a spontaneous Kundalini awakening. As unacknowledged tensions and unexpressed pain began to silently fracture my family during my early teens, a deep 'chasm' opened inside my mind. I clung precariously to the edges and began to feel a desperate desire for romance. Maybe I could fill the hole with 'love'.

Sure enough, along came my first boyfriend. Sparks literally flew as an overpoweringly electro-magnetic connection ignited and flowed between us. I started having 'mystical experiences' – a sense of falling through portals in the linear, three-dimensional fabric of space and time and into a 'truer reality'. For several seconds, I was experiencing spiritual insights that hinged on everything around and within us, seen and unseen, as web-like, profoundly inter-connected, utterly paradoxical and 'one'.

When I was duly dumped, however, the coin flipped. The dissolution of the filters in my mind separating the heaven of what lay 'beyond' my everyday consciousness were now exposing me to the hell. I fell into a state of severe depression. Upon re-surfacing, however, the profoundly meaningful aspects of the experience had fully integrated themselves into my being.

Shortly afterwards, a classic Kundalini 'symptom' erupted into the mix. One night I was woken by a tingling electrical energy surging up my spine from the base to the crown of my head whereupon faces of ancient, wizened old men and women flooded my inner field of vision. 'The lights', as I came to dub them, would continue in this particular form nightly for several years.

Despite having recovered from the first episode of depression, the chasm inside was growing deeper as the breakdown within my family become more entrenched. By my early 30s, I had experienced a further five major episodes each lasting several months. Each depression had common characteristics uninfluenced by anti-depressants however heavy the dose. Triggered by loss or anxiety, a tsunami of negative thought and emotion would flood my mind, pushing me into increasingly vicious downward circles.

The depression would then 'bottom out' followed by a gradual move upwards as my mood slowly lifted. Rather than levelling off, however, a sense of feeling intensely alive would grow and expand. Formerly dense energy blocks of negativity were transforming into feelings of joy, confidence, purpose and vision along with profound psychological insights. In time, the feeling of being supercharged would lessen, giving way to a clear sense of having started a new chapter in a more evolved state of consciousness than before.

Meanwhile, a 'bigger picture' was forming. Each episode was lasting longer than the one before, purging deeper and resulting in greater breakthroughs. As each experience swept through me, attachments to people, situations and desired out-comes were loosened, leaving me with an increasing sense of 'filling up from the inside'. The process culminated with two 'mega-depressions' each lasting a year, combined with two corresponding periods of 'mega-chargedness'. They seemed to represent a 'grand climax' by the end of which deeply buried family issues had been excavated, aired and set on the path to healing. The chasm in my mind largely filled itself up and has since dissolved away.

During this time, I experienced intensely meaningful synchronistic and psychic phenomena – two constant threads throughout my process from the outset. Nights were equally intense as I woke feeling highly charged with inner energy. 'The lights' were now evolving into complex, multi-coloured fractal style patterns that swirled and evolved as if being viewed through a child's kaleidoscope.

Although similar in certain ways to 'phosphenes', an entoptic phenomenon featuring colours and patterns commonly witnessed when the eyes are shut (e.g. 'seeing stars'), my experience of the lights was far more complex with a sense of 'coming from a different place'. Like many others who have experienced Kundalini awakenings, the dynamically evolving patterns I was seeing were akin to those that feature in indigenous art across cultures; from depictions of 'dreamworld' Shamanic travel to 60s acid-inspired psychedelia. At other times, faces and recognisable imagery have featured.

During the 12 years since that time, all aspects of the process have become increasingly gentle and manageable. The 'bolt up the spine' energy has evolved into a more subtle and dissipated surge like movement commonly described as a 'whole body orgasm'. Although less intense, the energy continues to produce lights from the simple – a lighthouse sweep of blue light – to complex patterns. Imagery has included Buddha figures, the Christian cross, Aztec-style artwork, a toddler's scrawl and 'alien script'.

I have also routinely experienced nerve sensations such as itching, prickling and crawling in my hands, feet, arms, legs and ears. When I was referred to a specialist to rule out anything serious I was told that such phenomena unattached to specific conditions have been reported by others and are considered something of a mystery. What I did not reveal for fear of further psychiatric labelling was that the sensations come part and parcel of the energy, particularly during times of deep inner change.

I value the fact that my experiences have not taken place within a specific spiritual or religious belief framework. I believe the energy is universal and struggle with 'Kundalini terminology' that I resort to using purely because there is no other established lexicon to describe such experiences. In the meantime, I have formed clear convictions about the nature of this energy within the paradigm of my own experience.

In doing so, I am aware that my particular process mimics Bipolar II Disorder and that certain professionals would diagnose it as such. I and many others who have experienced Kundalini in a similar way dispute the imposition of a biomedical 'illness model' upon such a profound and life-changing psycho-spiritual experi-ences. We argue that extreme mood shifts can be an intrinsic part of this 'vacuum cleaner' type evolutionary process that sucks out, purges and transforms inner blocks and negativity. The stronger the ego-resistance, the stronger the resulting 'bi-polar' style mood swings.

The fundamental truths I have experienced remain with me. That, in line with the conclusions of monks, mystics and ordinary people across times and cultures, the true nature of 'reality' is unitive, interconnected and profoundly paradoxical. A non-scientist, I intuitively understand the principles of quantum physics, the findings of which go some way towards backing up an emerging holistic worldview in which matter, energy and consciousness are one and the same.

Although it has not been easy, I have grown to increasingly trust the intelligent, loving and unfolding design and purpose behind a process that has all too frequently appeared cruel to be kind. Key to facilitating the process has been the art of surrender and co-operation. Therein lies the greatest paradox of all. The more one can surrender control, the more 'in control' one becomes in a deeper sense of the word – able to accept and enjoy the transitory nature of life by living not in the thrall of attachments to the past and future, but in the simplicity of the present moment.

Something strikes me as somewhat... arrogant? Bypass-y? Shame-based? Holier-than-thou? about this chapter. But also much of it, is it resonates. But "stability" inherently pathologizing?

Section 4

The Discontinuity Hypothesis and its Philosophical Implications

In this section, the editor expounds the reconceptualisation of the relationship between psychosis and spirituality that forms the core of this book, grounding it in psychological theory based on experimental data. Chris Clarke's chapter puts this view into a wider, philosophical, context.

9

Psychosis and Spirituality: The Discontinuity Model

Isabel Clarke

In my introduction, I argued that psychosis and spirituality both represent an aspect of universal human experience that is consistently undervalued and ignored in scientific discourse, but which holds relatively uncritical sway in the popular imagination. In this chapter, I will attempt to pin down more precisely this elusive area of experience; to understand its particular characteristics, and the relationship between it and our everyday, logical, understanding of the world around us.

In every paradigm shift, data that did not fit into the old world view and therefore went largely unnoticed, suddenly assume prominence as they acquire significance in the new order. The starting point for this enquiry is the observation of overlap between the phenomenology of religious/spiritual and psychotic experience, and the prevalence of religious/spiritual themes in the pre-occupations of those diagnosed with psychosis. The old paradigm tended to assume that psychosis was mimicking spiritual experience – or was it the other way round? At all events, the agenda was to find a way to distinguish them. The new agenda takes this overlap/area of identity at face value. While fully recognising the danger and diminishment that follows extended retreat into psychosis, and the psychological mechanisms that can suck the individual into this situation, the area of human experience variously labelled spiritual and psychotic is regarded as integral to being human and open to all, with potential for growth and expansion as well as creating vulnerability.

My own experience of working with people diagnosed with psychosis, combined with familiarity with the (Christian) mystical tradition from earlier study of medieval history, caused me to ask these questions. Inevitably, experiences with a mystical, unitive, flavour had immense personal meaning for the individuals undergoing them. In the case of the people I met in the hospital, they cherished them for decades, but because these experiences were followed by paranoia, breakdown of functioning and long-term contact with mental health services, they were dismissed as 'part of the illness'. Furthermore, these accounts are commonly missed in the records because

Psychosis and Spirituality: Consolidating the New Paradigm Second Edition   Edited by Isabel Clarke
© 2010 John Wiley & Sons, Ltd.

such material does not feature in the information sought for the psychiatric history. Consequently, the experiences can go unrecorded and, possibly often, incompletely construed.

Of course, the contrast between these, often early breakdown, experiences and so called 'healthy mysticism' is the disaster that characteristically follows, and which constitutes the generally recognised psychotic experience: paranoia, persecutory voices or some other form of breakdown. However, a glance at the literature of spiritual guidance from various traditions, or the lives of the saints and holy men and women, suggests a less stark contrast. Recognised spiritual experiences often came at times of crisis and were frequently attended by 'spiritual dangers' that read suspiciously like psychosis. Research by Jackson and Brett elucidates this overlap very clearly in modern samples (Jackson, 1997 and Chapters 12 and 13). The present chapter seeks to explain both the opening to a new and exhilarating quality of experience – the discontinuity of the title, and the way in which vulnerability, which can lead to dissolution and overwhelming fear, is intrinsic to the process.

Developing a Language of Comparison

There is a problem about trying to draw objective and generally accepted conclusions about spiritual and psychotic experiences, because they are in their nature individual, subjective and difficult to communicate. Science has turned its back on this area of human experience precisely because it is inaccessible to objective study. The language available to discuss these subjects is inadequate and harbours assumptions that hinder comparison. Psychoanalysts talk of the emergence of un- or sub-conscious contents into consciousness (according to school). The downward spatial metaphor implies inferiority. Words such as spiritual and mystical, with wholly positive connotations, tend to exclude anything dark or pathological. 'Transpersonal' employs a neutral spatial direction – across, but is in practice associated with the positive (e.g. Wilber, 1996, 1997; Ferrer, 2002).

There are exceptions to this dichotomising tendency. C.G. Jung's collective unconscious was an important influence on my thinking. The collective unconscious is a shared area of experience that any individual can access, in dreams and through altered states of consciousness, populated by archetypes that recur in myths and dreams across time and space, with potential for both transformation and dissolution. Jung's concept of individuation entailed encounter with the shadow, involving disintegration in the service of fuller integration (as expounded in 'Symbols of Transformation', Jung, 1956). That this process involved danger and entering states that could be described as psychotic was illustrated by Jung's own personal journey (see 'The seven sermons to the dead', Jung 1961).

Laing (1960) and Grof (1990 e.g.) are similarly important dissenting voices in signalling the positive and transformative potential of states usually dismissed as psychosis. Grof's concept of spiritual emergency is important here. He sees accessing 'non-ordinary states of consciousness' as integral to the process of spiritual development/personal growth, but recognises that experiencing such states can severely compromise normal functioning, so that the individual might require intensive support from others, and possibly be gripped by dangerous, suicidal, impulses, which can be understood metaphorically, but require the provision of exacting conditions of safety (see Grof and Grof 1990).

The culture-bound limitations of accepted conceptualisations of psychosis and spirituality is comprehensively covered in Tobert's chapter 4, along with the way in which our multicultural society has made these limitations impossible to ignore. In many societies, the 'reality' represented by such experiences is accorded higher status than 'ordinary' reality – in contrast to the generally accepted values in our society. Boyce-Tilman discusses the tendency of cultures to favour either this, intuitive and spiritual or the more scientific and logical style of discourse as the existence of a dominant and a subjugated way of knowing (Boyce-Tillman, 2005). Individuals within the society might well find themselves more attracted to the subjugated variety and so be disadvantaged. The recent interest in spirituality, etc. in our society could be viewed as the resurgence of the way of knowing previously subjugated since the middle ages.

Introducing the Transliminal

We have seen that the most generally used terminology incorporates a distinction between the psychotic and the spiritual, and so impedes discussion of the common state that is here argued underlie both. Even Grof, whose spiritual emergency goes a long way to remedying the deficiency, makes a distinction between those who are on a spiritual journey and 'ordinary' psychosis, and frequently deplores the way in which the two are confused. Several of the contributors to this book tackle this lack of a readily understood term that covers both psychotic and spiritual experience, without these reservations. Mike Jackson needed such a term to talk about his research area. He discusses these confusions in the introduction to his thesis on the subject, and invented his own term; p-s experiences, to facilitate comparison across the spectrum. Gordon Claridge (Chapter 7) cites Thalbourne's work (1997, e.g.) and proposes his term: 'transliminality'. This, and Natalie Tobert's term 'liminal' could roughly translate as Peter Chadwick's 'borderline' and these words are not too far in meaning from 'discontinuity'. The 'transliminal' is the descriptor I adopt in what follows where I attempt to pin down this area of experience, and make the distinction between 'transliminal' and 'everyday' functioning in a number of equivalent ways.

It can further be argued that this transliminal area of experience, which embraces both the spiritual and psychotic, also extends to the interpersonal, so that group phenomena, the transpersonal and the collective unconscious are included. All lie beyond the 'limen'; the threshold or boundary of the individual self. What follows is an attempt to explore this elusive domain, using two recognised cognitive models as a basis. The first of these is Kelly's personal construct theory (Bannister and Fransella, 1971) and the second is Teasdale and Barnard's (1993) Interacting Cognitive Subsystems.

Two Sorts of Experience

I start from the recognition of two possible modes in which a human being can encounter their environment. The most normally accessible of these two modes can be described as ordinary consciousness. The other mode is a less focused state in which both psychotic and spiritual experience becomes possible, as well as being the source of creativity and personal growth, to be referred to as 'transliminal' as discussed above.

Let us explore these two modes of operation, starting from problem-focused conscious thought. It is possible to envisage a continuum from such focused thinking towards more automatic modes of operation. An example of the latter is the experience of reverie, of letting the mind wander as opposed to focused thought. Such a state of reverie is easily accessible to all but the most stressed. Most people attain it naturally, whether by listening to music, lying in the bath or on a sunny beach. In this state, the elusive solution will drift into the mind of the person who has been straining fruitlessly at it for weeks. In sleep, we enter deeply into the transliminal, and in the hypnogogic states that precede sleep it is fleetingly accessible. Travelling further along this progression in full awareness, from focused to less focused thought, is where the real discontinuity is encountered.

The first stage towards this is the experience of trying to still and centre the mind, whether in wordless prayer, in meditation, or by participating fully in a relaxation exercise or guided fantasy. This keeps the mind in balance between the ordinary state and the one beyond. A state of reverie is a necessary starting point, but on its own merely leads to daydreaming and unfocussed thoughts. The internal dialogue becomes muted but does not disappear. Switching into a prayer/meditation mode requires a special sort of 'attention' which is recognised in Buddhist practice. I find the writings of Simone Weill, an unconventional mystic in the Christian tradition, particularly helpful in elucidating this area. Weill writes of it thus in 'Gravity and Grace' (1952) 'Absolutely unmixed attention is prayer'. The fact that this is difficult, without considerable practice, and does not appear to come naturally to most people, is my starting point.

A Personal Construct Understanding of the Two Sorts of Experience

Kelly's idea of personal constructs captures the dichotomy well (see 'Inquiring Man' by Bannister and Fransella, 1971, for a good introduction). Kelly saw the human being encountering the world as a scientist, making hypotheses and predictions based on past experience and any other information that lay to hand. These predictions, or constructs, would be recycled and come to constitute the individual's unique model of the world, both shaping his/her perceptions and actions, and being constantly modified by feedback born of experience.

Conditioning isn't INHERENTLY problematic?

Successful living requires a sufficient range of constructs to be able to deal with most situations encountered with relative ease, but with enough flexibility to be able to assimilate the novel situation. When encountering a new situation, the person needs to loosen their construct system sufficiently to accommodate the new material, thereby expanding the system. It is important that this should be followed by a consolidation phase where the constructs are tightened again, or the person will be unable to make valid predictions. Thus, Kelly's conceptualisation contains within it a natural rhythm of expansion and tightening of constructs, very like breathing. According to this analogy, expansion of the system is compared with breathing out, *→ backward ?* and consolidation, to breathing in. A well-functioning construct system is adaptive as it helps the individual to operate successfully in the world.

According to the construct theory model of thought processes, the state of reverie could be viewed as the 'breathing out' part of the metaphor used above. This represents the suspension or loosening of construing appropriate, both when there was no particular need to make any predictions (as on the beach), or when the existing constructs had led up a blind alley (as in problem solving). The trickier *koan ?* activity of entering a truly meditative or prayerful state I would suggest requires (temporary) suspension of, or moving beyond the construct system. In this state, boundaries dissolve and anomalous experiences become accessible.

The relationship between the world as perceived through the 'filter' of the individual's construct system and a postulated 'reality' behind this filter, is an interesting philosophical issue, already touched upon. One construct theorist, MacWilliams (1983) has tackled it, suggesting a model of successive approximations tending towards a final goal of identity between construct system and 'reality', which suggests an ultimate fading away of the construct system. This is in line with the sort of perspective adopted by Laing (1967), and the Buddhist influenced Deikman (1982), as well as the generality of transpersonal psychologists, that the unmediated *Hm* 'reality', that is not filtered by constructs, is somehow superior. According to this type of model, the constructs become a sort of temporary scaffolding that will ultimately be dismantled, and things will be both tidier and more glorious with their passing. I would dispute this assumption of superiority of 'unfiltered' reality. It takes us, once again, into the linguistic realm of hierarchies, and is therefore incompatible with true comparison between spiritual states and psychosis. I reject such distinctions as a fudge, and suggest instead that both reality filtered by the constructs, and the experience outside the construct system are necessary and valid aspects of being human – each in its place, and each necessarily partial. Such is the human condition. These arguments are explored more fully in Clarke (2008).

The Mystical Side of Psychosis

Peter Chadwick's account in Chapter 6 brings the experience of moving beyond the construct system vividly to life. Such a journey entails moving away from the safety net of construction that the individual has created to operate effectively in the world.

It means moving into the unknown. More challengingly, according to this model, as my understanding of the self is essentially a construction, I lose touch with this when I pass beyond the horizon, along with other constructs, and thereby lose the means of making predictions. Laing (1967) writes about this: 'The "ego" is the instrument for living in *this* world. If the "ego" is broken up, or destroyed . . . then the person may be exposed to other worlds, "real" in different ways from the more familiar territory of dreams, imagination, perception or phantasy'.

Some Neuro-Psychological Grounding

The argument that there are two states of experiencing, distinct at the margins, yet merging and weaving between each other in normal life requires grounding in the hardware – what we know about the operation of our brains, and which aspects of this might explain the existence and mechanism of the threshold (limen). Kelly's system is intuitively plausible, but lacks empirical verification at that level. Chapters 2 and 3 explore this topic in more detail. I am currently concerned with the operation of the threshold that allows access to both spiritual states and anomalous experiences, in the context of our incomplete understanding of the relationship between neurophysiology and actual experience.

Following on from Kelly, it does appear that transliminal experience is mediated by a loosening of boundaries and greater connectedness within the brain, whereas focused cognition relies on inhibition of extraneous influences. One of the earliest authorities here, Frith (1979), cites variability in cognitive inhibition, leading to failure in the system of limiting contents of consciousness in people experiencing psychosis, and to the experimental studies which have backed this model up. Cognitive inhibition and limitation of contents of consciousness essentially describe the operation of the construct system, which directs and focuses, and hence limits, attention. It is this focus and limitation that gives precise context to our thinking, and allows us to connect the current content to relevant memories. Hemsley (1993) notes that psychotic experience can be explained by: 'the failure to relate current sensory input to stored regularities'. This disturbance of integration could be an exact descriptor of the disruption of the normal construing process. Hemsley identifies disruption of the sense of self as a consequence of this disturbance (Hemsley, 1998).

The neurophysiological substrate of high schizotypy, implying easier accessibility of the transliminal, is described in the schizotypy literature thus:

> The positive schizotypal nervous system has been described as an 'open nervous system [. . .] where excitatory mechanisms are high and inhibitory processes low'
>   (McCreery and Claridge, 1996, p. 756).

A recent paper by Simmonds-Moore (2009) covers two further related features of the neurophysiological dimension in this study: greater interconnectivity of brain components, and 'boundary thinness (Hartmann, 1991)', whereby thinner boundaries reflect a relative *connectedness* of psychological processes and thicker boundaries reflect a relative *separateness* of psychological processes.

In tackling the issue of greater connectivity as a source of anomalous experiencing, Simmonds-Moore also acknowledges the role of the left/right brain dimension which has long been linked to the logical/intuitive distinction, while doing justice to the true complexity of interconnectedness within the brain by listing other important connections, thus:

> Lateral connectivity (more connectivity between cortical hemispheres; effectively a greater influence of the right hemisphere on the usually dominant left hemisphere), hierarchical connectivity (connectivity between the cortical areas of the brain and the sub-cortical structures of the brain; effectively more influence of sub cortical processes on the usually dominant left cortex of the brain), cognitive–perceptual connectivity (as synaesthesia and the tendency to make associations, find a signal, and find meaning) information processing boundaries (as attentional widening – more information that is usually outside of conscious awareness is available in awareness) and interpersonal boundaries (as a tendency to get very close to other people/experience empathy)
> (Simmonds-Moore, 2009, p. 3).

Pathways in the Brain

From this discussion, it becomes clear that it is the pathways of connection within the brain, and the mechanisms of inhibition and dis-inhibition that determine the flow of information along them, rather than activation of particular brain areas (e.g. left and right hemispheres) that can elucidate the distinct ways of experiencing that have been identified. Cognitive science has provided us with extensive research data into memory, information processing and bottlenecks in information processing that give insight into the operation of these pathways. The problem here is not lack of data, but almost a superfluity, and the consequent problem of discerning the wood for the trees. Teasdale and Barnard's 'Interacting Cognitive Subsystem' model of cognitive architecture (Teasdale and Barnard, 1993; Barnard, 2003) offers a framework for making sense of this data that provides an elegant explanation for the two distinct ways of knowing.

Interacting cognitive subsystems (ICS), as the name implies, offers a modular architecture of the mind, comprising nine subsystems, each with its unique coding and memory store and pattern of interconnection with the others. I do not propose to go into most of that, but will instead concern myself here with only the two higher order, organising, subsystems, and their associated memory stores; the implicational and the propositional. The propositional subsystem represents the logical mind, capable of fine discrimination, and the contents of whose memory store is coded verbally. It can take an objective, dispassionate view of phenomena, and in this way can learn much about the environment. There is probably some rough correspondence between this aspect of human functioning and the neocortex, the newer parts of the brain, although the rich interconnections within the brain make this sort of statement all but impossible to verify. The implicational subsystem, on the other hand, deals with perception of the whole, and with emotional meaning. Its memory system codes vividly in several sensory modalities and its concerns are not the dispassionate study of the external world, but the inner world of the self and, in particular, its worth, and any threats to its survival or position. Again, this subsystem probably represents the older and deeper levels of the brain, to make a sweeping oversimplification of a complex subject.

Kelly's conceptualisation cuts across Teasdale and Barnard's, as Kelly's core constructs undoubtedly belong to the implicational subsystem, while more peripheral discriminations will be made at the propositional level. A key feature of the ICS model is the lack of straightforward communication between these two central subsystems. The implicational subsystem communicates directly with, and is much influenced by, the various sense modalities and the body's arousal system, whereas the propositional system is more removed from this emotional area, and indeed, the vital communication between the two systems, which makes good cognitive functioning possible, can become temporarily disabled by a state of high or low arousal.

It is thus a short step to recognise that, when the two central meaning making systems are not communicating or in asynchrony, to use Barnard's term for this (Barnard, 2003), and the precision afforded by the propositional is temporarily displaced, a different quality of experiencing becomes accessible. Hence, the everyday, scientific state is one where the propositional and implicational subsystems are working nicely together in balance, whereas the spiritual/psychotic state is one where the two are disjoint, and the system is essentially driven by the implicational subsystem.

The characteristics of this subsystem and some of the characteristics of this area of experience match well. The implicational deals in relatively undifferentiated wholes and cannot manage fine discrimination and shades of grey; it is overwhelmingly emotional, and swings between sharp dichotomies such as euphoria and terror, and it is centrally concerned with the self and threats to the self.

Explaining the Transliminal Experience

I now want to use these two cognitive models of this dichotomy to examine in more detail the features and logic of the transliminal dimension. Operating within constructs, or between the propositional and implicational levels, represents normal human functioning. For most people, either some sort of a jolt, or a carefully designed process is needed to move them into the other state. This could be a crisis, a ritual or religious ceremony designed to shift consciousness, a drug or meditative practice. For the person with psychosis, the barrier that makes this sort of experience hard to access for most of us, is dangerously loose.

Once this barrier has been passed, there will be a loss of boundaries and groundedness. For some people, but by no means all, this dissolution of boundaries is experienced as a blissful state of unity with the whole. The implicational subsystem governs relationship, so that this is relationship or connectedness at the extreme. Such euphoria can be understood as an initial reaction to encountering unmediated reality: 'the whole'. When the asynchrony persists and there is not a rapid reconnection of the two main subsystems, this will be followed by loss of bearings because of having drifted out of reach of the construct system, or the propositional subsystem, which people rely on to make sense of their environment. The often cited timelessness of the mystical experience shows that time is one of the parameters lost in this transition. In the case of a mystical experience attained through spiritual practice (or, as often happens, occurring spontaneously, but within a spiritual context that gives it meaning for the experiencer), managing the transition back to construed reality after the experience generally (but not invariably) occurs naturally and after a short space of time. Where the same state is achieved by taking a drug, the return again normally (but not invariably), occurs when the drug wears off.

In psychosis (and drug experiences that go wrong, or shade into psychosis), the orderly return does not happen. The individual finds themselves stranded beyond the reach of their constructs or propositional subsystem, trying to operate in the world. Not surprisingly this is extraordinarily difficult. The familiar boundaries between people, events, time and space are not accessible as before. Telepathy seems normal. Other people can read, and worse, interfere with, the individual's thoughts. Coincidences abound – everything is connected and everything is disconnected. Everything is possible and nothing is possible. Where this new reality might be exhilarating for a short while, the sustained experience is terrifying. The desperate sufferer tries to make sense of the unfamiliar environment, clutching at whatever connections come to hand. In this way, delusions, which usually have their origin in the early stage of the breakdown, are born. In another dissolution of normal boundaries, internal concerns are experienced as external communication and the person hears voices. Normal thought is disrupted – or as the psychiatrist would say, disordered.

The Logic of the Illogical

In the preceding paragraph, I have started to sketch in the way in which a human being encountering reality unmediated by the construct system, or without benefit of the propositional subsystem, will make sense of it. In both psychotic material, and accounts of spiritual experience and religious ideas from different faiths, a parallel logic can be discerned that is strikingly different from, and frequently opposite to, common-sense and scientific logic. This logic was and is better understood and utilised in other cultures and in former times. Perhaps this is because through science, we have gained unprecedented control over the material world, and, at least in the affluent North, created greater comfort and security for ourselves than any of our forefathers. The logic of science has unlocked so many secrets that we have downgraded the whole area of human experience that lies beyond the reach of this logic. I suggest that this area has its own logic, which is even more compelling, but more difficult to pin down.

This is the logic of archetypes; of myths and stories – full of paradox and a sense of mystery. Science discriminates – things are 'either – or'. In this other realm, two contradictory things can be simultaneously valid – a world of 'both – and'. In archetypal stories, such as the traditional fairy tales, the ordinary transitions of every human life, like leaving home and 'seeking your fortune', falling in love and marrying, and death, are vested with cosmic significance. In Christianity, and indeed most religious traditions, the individual is both supremely precious, and insignificant in the context of the whole; God is distant and transcendent, and simultaneously concerned for the individual. Neil Douglas Klotz (Chapter 5) refers to the way in which religious traditions, such as the Sufi, teach the truths of 'the transliminal' through paradoxical stories.

The psychoanalyst, Matte Blanco and his followers (e.g. Bomford, 2005) have written extensively about these two distinct systems of logic which they name as 'symmetric' (implicational/transliminal) and 'asymmetric' (propositional and implicational working together/scientific). They stress the way in which both are constantly present and weave in and out of normal thought.

Paradox is characteristic of symmetric/transliminal logic. There is here an interesting parallel with a familiar strand in the psychotic experience. A conviction of great personal importance – being Jesus Christ or related to the Queen, for instance, is a common element in delusional systems, as is a conviction of personal worthlessness, often reinforced by derogatory auditory hallucinations. The common theme here concerns the self, and the position of the self in the family, in society and in the cosmos. I have already mentioned that the construct of self is among the concepts to be lost in the transition, which can lead to an exhilarating feeling of unity and interconnectedness, as well as the bewilderment of loss of self. The theme of the self links with the central pre-occupation of Teasdale and Barnard's 'implicational subsystem', cited above, which is the self, its value and threats to the self. I would argue that the characteristic themes of psychotic material, whether in the form of voices or delusions, concern issues of self worth, acceptability, sexuality and personal significance, which are all relevant to understanding the self. The paradox central to transliminal logic is the simultaneous significance and insignificance of the self.

In religious traditions, this is a mystery to be pondered, and is normally experienced as a positive, whether in the form of Buddhist negation of self, or Christian assurance of the love of God for the individual and the need for personal humility and acknowledgement of weakness. It is in subtlety and flexibility rather than content that these ideas differ from the psychotic themes. Grandiose delusions fix on the supreme importance of the self, whereas persecutory voices denigrate and crush. Both can be experienced by the same individual, but they are not somehow held in balance. I would agree with many writers, including Laing and Peter Chadwick, who suggest that well foundedness or otherwise of the self of the

[handwritten margin note:] Hm Unintegrated paradoxical logic; split, as opposed to both/and; torn between disparate extremes, rather than holding space for paradoxical facets of being.

individual undergoing the experience (ego strength) will predict whether it is a temporary, life-enhancing, spiritual event, or a damaging psychotic breakdown, from which there is no easy escape.

It's not meant to be nihilistic.

Putting the Model in Perspective

This model does not deny a physical aspect through some disruption of brain functioning for these phenomena. In the case of drug taking, there is a simple physical cause, and indeed some ascetic practices such as fasting and sleep deprivation can create a physical pre-condition for mystical states in the context of spiritual practice. It offers a complementary psychological understanding of the experience of the person suffering from psychosis as one who is trying to make sense of the world, as all human beings do, but with their usual bearings removed. It is in the tradition of the normalising exposition of psychotic symptoms in cognitive therapy for psychosis. Indeed, emphasising the overlap with spiritual experience brings psychosis in from the cold region of the utterly alien and incomprehensible where it is traditionally relegated.

Our society's particular illiteracy in the area of spiritual experience contributes to the even greater isolation of the person with psychosis. In 'Recovery from Schizophrenia', Richard Warner (1994) notes that in societies where experience of the spiritual/psychotic realm is valued, people diagnosed with schizophrenia have a far better prognosis than in modern Western Society.

Another area that requires clarification is the real clinical dilemma of distinguishing between spiritual and psychiatric crisis when someone presents to the services. On the face of it, my response to this situation would be no different from any reasonably enlightened practitioner; that of 'time will tell', or, to be more biblical, 'by their fruits you shall know them'.

The difference between the position I am adopting, and the more conventional one, will be at the level of conceptualisation. Whereas the standard position, informed for instance by psychodynamic or transpersonal thinking, will be that the course of the condition produces information that enables the practitioner to discriminate between two entirely different phenomena; namely the spiritual crisis and the psychotic breakdown, so that the outcome tells him/her which it was *all along*, I would argue that this absolute distinction is invalid and essentially meaningless. A good analogy for the conventional position would be chicken sexing. This is difficult and requires specialist expertise with baby chicks, but as the bird matures, a difference that was there all along becomes obvious. I am arguing *Hah* that the relationship between psychosis and spiritual does not fit into this type of neat dichotomy. This position does not affect the medical care and therapy that should be offered to those who need it and are asking for it. However, it should give pause for reflection and respect for the nature and significance of the experiences that many of the people receiving our services are undergoing or have undergone.

A Personal Perspective

It could be asked, does all this matter? What difference does it make whether we see psychosis in the context of the human capacity for a spiritual/mystical way of knowing, or whether we continue to regard it, perhaps more conveniently, as an illness which confusingly manages to stray into spiritual territory at times? I would argue that it does matter. It enables us to get a truer perspective of what is going on in spiritual and mystical experience, and demonstrates how this aspect is integral to being human – thus contradicting those who consider that religious and spiritual concerns should melt away in the face of science (see Clarke, 2008 for more on this). Furthermore, it is of considerable importance to those diagnosed with psychosis, whom I prefer to call: 'experiencers', in common with others who have had non-ordinary or anomalous experiences without acquiring a diagnosis. In preparation for this second edition, I talked to one 'experiencer' whom I had known through working for the psychiatric rehabilitation service, who was interested in this approach and had attended the 2000 conference on the subject (see the Introduction), and whom I met recently at a spirituality seminar, as he had joined the Trust's chaplaincy team as a volunteer chaplain. I asked him about the impact that this new perspective had had on him. This was his reply:

> The major contribution of the conference in 2000 was in an awareness raising way. It felt very alienating having the experience of being on an acute ward and having the experience of harshly controlling psychiatric medicines. It was alienating because there was a lot of stigma around. At the time of my admission, there had been a lot of newspaper reports about unfortunate things happening leading to public stigma. That went on for some time, and then in 2000 I went to the conference and it was very nice because there were plenty of people who were willing to recognise and accept that spirituality was relevant. It was not simply being in a church where people were friendly to you. It went deeper than that – some of the ideas and concepts; in particular, it normalised the connection with spirituality. It normalised the connection between spiritual thinking and my first breakdown, which they termed psychosis, as they were much interwoven. For me, it was very obvious that there was a connection. It was very much part of my experience.
>
> Another thing was the use of the word 'experiencer', which has become very much part of my vocabulary. I like it much better than 'service user' because 'service user' implies that there is no giving back and I want to give back as much as I possibly can. Obviously, I have limitations in resources, both financial and personal, but if I can at least try and acknowledge the positive things the services have contributed, but also try and contribute something to them if I am allowed to and if I can.
>
> A particular point I remember from the conference was that one of the participants asked one of the more specifically religious speakers about discernment – 'what is from God and what is from the Devil?' is how she put it, but you could characterise it as 'What is helpful and what is unhelpful?'. That was something that had been important for me to work out before the conference. It suggested me that the propensity to be aware of the transliminal brings with it the ability to experience both this negative and this positive

side. Risk and containment come into it, but it is quite personal in the sense of your personal understanding. In my work as chaplain's assistant, very much my role is about listening and it is very important to understand what the other person is going through. It does not matter if other people do not share it. It is not necessary to share the belief to understand what the other person is trying to convey. There may be a wider truth and you have spoken about 'shared understanding'. This is a helpful idea. All these influences have been incorporated into my thinking, not in a very structured way.

I then asked him whether he saw a wider value coming from his excursions into the transliminal. He answered:

Firstly, if you understand something, it is possible to understand other people. That is the most obvious way. The second way is that one might gain some sort of understanding or insight that can be shared; the mystical tradition. For a long time, I was personally isolated from a faith community. I kept my spiritual ideas to myself. I am now finding that you can share some of this stuff and that is personally rewarding and I am finding that the understanding that I have gained can help other people. Occasionally, one can say something to someone that they have not understood themselves before because it can make them think of something that they can have a positive outcome with.

A final thought: perhaps some of the mystery and difficulty in reducing distress and confusion that can sometimes be associated with spiritual/transliminal areas of life (and/or 'treating mental illness') is because it is easy to get the helpful mixed with the unhelpful. . . perhaps that's precisely because 'we walk by Faith and not by [complete] knowledge' . . . for if it were possible to completely understand and extract pure truth from our subjective experience then it would surely be a very different universe where 'mental illnesses' would be much more amenable to treatment through knowing that particular experiences were 'true or false' and hence precisely what to do with them – but science creates hypotheses and not certain truths. Maybe some of what you are saying Isabel is related to us humans needing to accept the reality of this sublime mystery . . . after all we do not 'know' completely because we humans are not God.

I commented that being an 'experiencer' had deepened what he could offer as a chaplain. He answered: 'It is part of the foundation process of accepting myself as I am'.

Conclusion

I have argued for a radical reconceptualisation of the relationship between psychosis and spirituality; for the recognition of an important area of human experiencing that embraces both, and for caution in trying to make rigid distinctions between them. This new perspective, or paradigm, has implications for how we, as mental health professionals, treat the accounts of experience that we are privileged to receive. It further provides a theoretical basis for recognising the potential for growth and transformation, as well as the danger of diminishment, in all these experiences, which is well reflected in many of the chapters in this book (see particularly Hartley's, Chapter 18 and Brett's, Chapter 13). It is my hope that the impressive and growing body of research and clinical practice in the latter chapters of this book will make this new paradigm hard to ignore. This is important because this reconceptualisation has potential to reduce stigma and provide a more acceptable sense of self in the world to many who find themselves floundering in the transliminal.

10

Knowledge and Reality

Chris Clarke

Introduction

Debates about psychosis and spirituality often hinge on the concept of reality. A current psychiatric manual, for example, defines psychosis as involving a "break in reality testing" (First, Frances and Pincus, 2004, p. 160). But what is real and what is not real varies with the culture involved, particularly concerning spirituality and religion; and when we look at the problem more closely the whole concept of "reality" is seen to be highly problematic. In this chapter, I will survey the philosophy of reality and argue that we now have a good understanding of the issues based on the nature of *knowing*.

The history of this area of philosophy falls approximately into two phases separated by the work of Descartes. Prior to this, the debate (initiated by Plato and Aristotle) was mainly about whether one could determine what was real and what was illusion, and if so, how; while from Descartes onwards, the debate mainly focused on how it is that we know things, and hence on what the status might be of the things that we do claim to know. The role of language was important in both these phases. In this study, I deal in turn with attempts in philosophy to specify what is real, language and the nature of knowing – including the role of science.

What is 'Real'?

Plato, the 'founder of Western philosophy' who worked around 380 BCE, set out a mixture of his own ideas and those of his teacher Socrates. He was convinced that there was such a thing as reality and that we could learn to find it. The case of reality which particularly impressed him was the example of mathematics. It was not merely that everyone could agree that 3 + 2 really was 5 and could not possibly be anything else; even more importantly '[arithmetic] draws the mind upward and forces it to

Psychosis and Spirituality: Consolidating the New Paradigm Second Edition Edited by Isabel Clarke
© 2010 John Wiley & Sons, Ltd.

argue about pure numbers, and will not be put off by attempts to confine the argument to collections of visible or tangible objects' (Plato, 1955: p. 293). For him, the 'visible or tangible' was not real, whereas mathematics seemed to offer a whole word that was far more true and real than the world that we could perceive with our senses. In the mathematical world, triangles always had exactly straight lines and angles that added up to exactly 180° whereas in the world around us everything was approximate and reality was fuzzy.

Plato illustrated the universality and certainty of mathematical reality by describing a seminar (almost certainly fictitious) led by Socrates and featuring a visiting scholar called Meno. In the course of this, Socrates asks Meno to call one of his slaves. Socrates then conducts the slave through the proof of a geometrical theorem (Plato, 1924: pp. 259–371), drawing a series of diagrams for this, and at the end the slave 'sees' that a particular geometrical proposition is in fact true. This demonstrates, according to Plato, that all people, of whatever intellectual or social status, have an innate knowledge of an absolutely real mathematical world. All that is needed is a reminder to enable them to recall and 'see' this world. Indeed, the word 'theorem' is derived from the Greek θεωρειν meaning 'to look at'.

Plato's argument is not particularly convincing to us now. Even if it were true that geometrical ideas are implicitly present in all human beings, this could be telling us more about human beings than about 'reality' – a vital point which, as I will describe, would be taken up much later by Immanuel Kant. Plato's claim was credible at the time, however, because it fitted in with a generally current notion of a 'heavenly' repository of truth to which we might have access, as expressed, for instance, by his contemporary Parmenides (1986).

Plato saw these absolute truths (called, in English translations, 'ideas' or 'forms') as ultimate reality. Furthermore, he felt there was some truth in mythological accounts that described the human soul coming from this realm of reality to be incarnated, and this was what enabled the soul to remember, like Meno's slave, the truths that it had previously known.

So Plato's realm of ideas had two aspects, which we would regard as opposed. On the one hand, it was the source of abstract ideas, both statements about geometry and general concepts like 'Cat', which we think of as rather ordinary. On the other hand, it was associated with reincarnation and the divine which we would link with spiritual/mystical experience (or with delusion, depending on our approach). For Plato or his character Socrates, there is always an air of mystery and 'numinosity' about all aspects of this realm. We can note that, although modern thought is concerned with distinguishing rational 'factual' mathematics from numinous (and possibly delusional) spirituality, Plato classes them together and is concerned with distinguishing both from the mere 'appearances' of the material world, though we would regard the latter as 'reality'! We shall see in what follows how subsequent philosophical developments resulted in Plato's 'ideas' being seen as humanly constructed rather than (divinely) ready-made, and undermined his distinction between reality and appearance.

Reality Through Rationality

Although Plato's views were to last for the next 2000 years, an alternative school of thought immediately started to emerge in parallel with Plato's from the work of his pupil Aristotle. He lacked Plato's mystical streak and so had no time for a separate realm of reality. For him, reality was in the here and now. He continued and developed, however, the tradition of careful logical analysis started by Socrates and Plato. In particular, he codified the rules of logic and developed a system for classifying the words used for talking about things into logical categories (such as, 'substance', 'quantity', 'place' and so on). He proposed that by using these one could analyse people's ideas and discover the truth by proceeding from a generally agreed starting point to reliable conclusions (Aristotle, 1989).

Although Aristotle rejected Plato's notion that universal ideas like Cat (as opposed to Tiddles, a particular, solid cat on a particular mat) occupied some special absolute reality, he did assume that there was a real property of 'catness', so to speak, that was contained in actual cats. Plato's 'ideas' (or *universals* as philosophers now call them) were still there for Aristotle, but they had been brought down to earth in the form of properties of actual objects. By the middle ages, however, the reality of such universals started to be questioned. In 1087, the French theologian Roscellinus (D'Onofrio, 2008: p. 140) taught that universals like this had no reality, but were just words that we chose to attach to things, a view called *nominalism* that gradually gained acceptance amidst much controversy. The picture that progressively emerged in the early middle ages on the *avant garde* side was one in which the ordinary physical world of things was real, but we then classified things arbitrarily by attaching words to them. The more conservative side, however, held to a more Platonic view, holding that the ideas had an absolute reality, a view termed *realism*.

We can compare this with the interacting cognitive subsystems (ICS) model described by Isabel Clarke in this volume (p. 107ff.) which makes a distinction between two ways of knowing: one way using language in its Western form rather than its older form (described here by Klotz and Lancaster) and relying mainly the *propositional* subsystem, and the other way going beyond constructs or relying mainly on the *implicational* subsystem. These two ways of knowing loosely correspond, respectively, to Aristotle's logical, categorising approach and the numinous aspect of Plato's 'ideas' which Plato sees as expressed through myths.

As Neil Douglas-Klotz has emphasised in his chapter, whereas Semitic languages held together the different aspects of existence represented by these subsystems, Western language has divided them. All knowing is an active personal engagement with whatever is out there, *Hmm*... to which we bring our particular tools of understanding, including our now narrowed use of language. Different language-uses result in the perception of a somewhat different reality through this way of knowing. When I go out into the garden, for example, I 'see' a lawn; but I know that my botanist friends, with their more nuanced languages, 'see' a complex ecosystem of tens or hundreds of inter-related species. So what we call 'reality' is a product of both what is outside us and the knowing abilities inside us – our ways of knowing. Different people have different ways of knowing and so 'see' different worlds (Clarke, 2005).

Knowing

The Nature of the Knower

Performing a 'reality check' on one's ideas involves checking whether the ideas are based on valid *knowledge,* or whether they are just supposition. So I return now to the historical sequence and the question, how do we come to know things? This goes to the heart of the nature of the human being.

Both Aristotle and Plato held that the distinctive quality of human beings lay in the nature of our soul, and that it was the soul that was the ultimate 'knower' as far as the human being was concerned. Plato felt that there was some truth in mythical accounts of a soul that was reincarnated from one body to another, although he did not claim to be able to prove this. Aristotle, on the other hand, started from thinking about actual physical humans and regarded the soul as a specialised principle possessed by humans which enabled us to discriminate and make judgements about the data coming from our senses. They agreed, however, that the soul (or at least the thinking, intellectual part of it, as opposed to the part that feels hungry, etc.) was, in Aristotle's words, 'imperishable' (ου φθειρεσθαι). Whatever Aristotle himself may have thought about it, this insistence by him and Plato on an unchanging soul as the knower gave human knowing a privileged position related to religion and spirituality.

Aristotle's main argument for this is in fact weak. He is implicitly resorting to a doctrine that nothing can change without some cause to make it change. The only available cause for the soul's perishing seems to be ageing; but ageing pertains to the body and not the soul. Hence, the soul does not age and it is therefore imperishable. But the basic reason why Aristotle accepts such a rocky argument is that, while he makes a considerable advance on his predecessors, he still has an insufficiently clear notion of what, on his approach, pertains to the body and what to the soul, or how they might relate to each other.

It was to be some 2000 years before Aristotle's picture of the human was seriously challenged, through the work of Descartes which completely revolutionised thinking about human beings and reality, work flowing from an episode when he spent several days in a prolonged meditation while sheltering from the cold in a refuge in the hills near Neuburg-on-Danube (Rodis-Lewis, 1998, p. 36). He started from a recognition that, in principle, one could doubt almost all the 'truths' that he and most others of his time would regard as reality, such as: that the world of trees and woods really existed, and that he and the entire world had been created by an omnipotent and benign god. But he was rescued from total nihilism by deciding that his could be sure of his own existence: for, if he doubted his existence, who would it be who was doubting it, other than himself? Thus, arose his famous primary proposition, 'I think, therefore I am'. The 'I' was real and was the ultimate knower.

From this, he then unfolded the essence of his subsequent philosophy, including a proposal for the nature of the human being (Descartes, 1968, pp. 53–65). In the course of this, he derived and so reinstated the wider assumptions about reality that he had earlier put into doubt, starting with the reality of a beneficent God – a crucial step that enabled him to deduce the reality of the external world on the grounds that such a God would not deceive us by displaying an illusory world. The deduction of the existence of God owed more to Descartes' Jesuit education than to rational argument and was not to survive subsequent critiques, but his arguments about human beings set the agenda for philosophy and science until the present day.

Considering the human being, he assumed that the 'I' whose existence he had claimed to have established was to be identified with Aristotle's soul, and then he set out to elucidate the relation between the soul and the body, which had remained obscure for Aristotle. His first move was to invite the reader to imagine, for the sake of argument, that the body was an automaton like the animated models operated by clockwork and pneumatic control that were starting to be made at that time. Just how much of the human body's functions, he asked, could we imagine being performed by a mere machine? Guided by what was then known about anatomy and by his own discoveries from the corpses of animals, as well as by reflecting on the making of automata, he described how the nerves, which could well be bundles of fine tubes, might convey signals to the muscles by means of pulses of 'spirits' sent down them. He speculated that our reflexes and appetites might regulate these signals at their point of generation in the brain by using similar signals from nerves coming from the senses. This regulation, he suggested, took place in a fluid-filled cavity in the brain called the third ventricle which he took to be a control centre through which impulses from the nerves could propagate. A crucial organ in this process might be the pineal gland, which he incorrectly took to be suspended from the top of the third ventricle. Impulses from nerves that originated from the sense organs could shift the position of the pituitary gland, which would in turn affect the flow of other signals across this cavity, so that they entered nerves leading to different muscles (Descartes, 1972, pp. 77–93).

In this way, he developed at considerable length an account of how such an automaton might work. He took it for granted that such a model could only cover the physical aspects of the body, leaving conscious intellectual operations to the soul, which he felt could best carry out its functions by being coupled to the pineal gland. He was in no position to prove that this really was how the body worked, but he made a very convincing case that such a system could be correct in principle.

This was indeed radical stuff. Up to this point, all the functions of the body, such as sense, motion, digestion, growth and so on, had been assigned to mysterious soul-like properties attached to the material body. But on the new picture, all these functions could become completely comprehensible, implemented by mechanical components. In particular, the experiences produced by the senses – the redness of a rose, the sweetness of sugar – corresponded to the impact of 'spirits' on the pineal gland. The rose possessed not redness but the power of reflecting a particular sort of light which excited particular nerves in the eye; sugar possessed not sweetness, but molecules that excited particular taste receptors on the tongue. Such qualities as these, which had previously been a part of external reality, now became illusions constructed by a mechanical body. While the status of reality – mainly resting with an immortal soul rather than physical matter – was still maintained by Descartes, his mechanical vision of the human being as knower was destined to change radically the philosophy of knowing and hence the philosophy of reality.

For the next 250 years, the study of human physiology corrected, verified and refined Descartes' proposal, and at the same time progressively transferred mental functions such as language and decision making from Descartes' 'soul' to the physical brain. The soul withered away and became superfluous for mainstream science, while external reality lost more and more of its seductive qualities and became an arid realm of mechanical operations. Ironically, science in this way removed the one certain reality supposed by Descartes, namely the human soul, the 'I', thus cutting the foundations from the Descartes' whole structure. This would result in scientific materialism, according to which all religious beliefs were illusory.

Immanuel Kant

While science was to move steadily towards a purely mechanical picture, with no place for the reality of the spiritual, in philosophy an entirely new approach entered in 1781 with the publication by Kant of the *Critique of Pure Reason* (Kant, 2003; Savile, 2005). His proposal involved not tinkering with Descartes' approach, but starting again from scratch. Eschewing false modesty, he compared his idea with the revolution wrought by Copernicus in placing the Sun, rather than the Earth, at the centre of the planetary system: both Kant's system and that of Copernicus involved looking at a problem from a completely different point of view.

There were two essential planks to his argument. The first was critical and seemingly negative. The doubts of Descartes and his successors such as Locke, Berkeley and Hume had to be faced with no evasion. Everything we think we know about the world comes through our senses, either by direct perception or by indirect perception using instruments or by reasoning based on these. Religious faith apart, we have no 'hot line' to reality and so we can know nothing of the absolute reality lying behind our senses. This does not mean that we are making it all up: Kant's point is rather that our knowledge is always knowledge of *the world as it appears to us* and not the world as it is 'in itself' (as Kant puts it). Indeed, the world could seem fundamentally different to beings different to ourselves.

Compared with Descartes' positive findings, this seems seriously bad news. But the second plank to Kant's argument turns this conclusion on its head and produces a core of certainty; a foundation on which, Kant claims, we can build science and ethics. For, if the only world we have is the world as it appears to us, this world must necessarily conform to any basic principles that govern the way we experience things.

So a basis for the world as it appears can be found by analysing the bounds and the structure of our own thoughts and experiencing. This is the change of 'centre' that Kant likens to the Copernican revolution. Instead of focussing on the *content* of our experience, we must focus first on the *structure* of our knowing. Here, Kant claims, we can find essential regularities that must necessarily underlie any world that appears to us. Importantly, the aspect of the world that we find by this procedure is not an illusion. It is a genuine aspect of the real world that we can fully grasp by using our understanding to the full. The qualification is that it is necessarily the world's aspect as it reveals itself to us, rather than its aspect as it is for itself.

Kant's picture of how we know the world has several stages. First, our senses give us the raw data of a manifold of constantly shifting forms, which he calls the 'manifold of intuition'. This is so far back in our consciousness that we cannot be said even to be aware of it. Conscious perception then comes from a process of 'synthesising' this manifold to produce things with definite properties. But there is more than this. Our perception is not just a collection of bald images, but it is a coherent picture of a state of affairs, involving objects that endure in time and change in time and are related to each other meaningfully in space. Analysing this situation, Kant identifies two distinct sorts of processing going on, both necessarily to our full grasp of the world. First, the manifold of intuition is ordered by means of the concepts of *time* and *space* which we supply prior to actually having a sensation. The concepts of time and space provide the form for our sensation, irrespective of its content. Second, we bring to this sensation an understanding as to a state of affairs: we exercise *judgement* to form concepts that unite and relate the elements of our sensations. Just as time and space give form to our raw sense data, so there are, he claims, basic types of judgement that give rational, propositional form to a meaningful world.

When it comes to the specification of these types of judgement, Kant reaches for Aristotle's logic and in the spirit of Aristotle lists four basic components that a judgement must have (quantity, quality, relation and modality), each of which can take one of three possible values. Here, his account starts to feel arbitrary and unconvincing from our modern perspective. Kant's enduring legacy is not the details of his logic. Rather, it is the principle that we do not passively image a given world, but we bring to the world a very specific repertoire of processes which involves a whole panoply of concepts and structures, some so basic as to be 'hard wired', and others formed progressively through the application of these basic elements.

The most important of these structures is the unity of our perceptions, which is linked to the concept of a *self*. There is an 'abiding and unchanging 'I' which 'forms the correlate of all our representations in so far as it is to be at all possible that we should become conscious of them' (Kant, 2003, p. A123). This binding together of our objects of perception in a unity, which we can subsequently call a 'self' in the sense of the subject of all experience, is called by Kant 'the first pure knowledge of understanding' (Kant, 2003, p. B137). We see here how far Kant has progressed beyond Descartes. The latter's 'I think therefore I am' seems from the perspective of Kant to be based on little other than the fact that in the French of the first published version of Descartes' work this statement happens to contain the pronoun 'je'.

Reality, Kant claimed, was now on a firm foundation, but it was the foundation of the nature of the human knower.

Philosophy and Science

Kant was a great admirer of Newton, and he believed that his own philosophical derivation of space and time (ingredients that Newton sets out in basic axioms at the start of his main work) would be the prototype of a recasting of science on the basis of his own philosophy. One reason why this failed to happen was that science (or 'natural philosophy' as it was then called) has a life of its own as an activity of a community that has always paid at best only a passing reference to other branches of philosophy. As science and mathematics developed they were to demonstrate that the details of Kant's arguments were simply wrong. Kant, for instance, had argued that space must necessarily conform to the axioms of Euclidean geometry, because these were implicit in the very idea of space. Today 'non-Euclidean geometry' is the basic conceptual structure of Einstein's theory of relativity. Having spent much of my own life working on this, I can testify to the fact that there is nothing *a priori* unthinkable about alternative geometries, Kant notwithstanding. In a great many such details of his system, Kant's assertions that anything other than X is unthinkable can be refuted by thinking Y. \o\

More generally, the development of mathematics and its subsequent applications in science have undermined both Plato's realm of absolute reality and Kant's system of *a priori* human concepts. Alternative logics have been developed distinct from the logic of Aristotle that Kant embodied in his principles of understanding. The most relevant new logics to the theme here are topos logic (Isham and Butterfield, 1998) and bi-logic (Matte Blanco, 1998), the first of which has been found valuable in making sense of quantum mechanics and the second in analytic psychology.

As science has repeatedly *disproved* claims from philosophy either for absolute reality or, as with Kant, for a foundation to the world with an equal status to absolute reality, so the idea has grown that science itself can provide either an absolute reality (the idea of scientific materialism) or at least an increasing 'verisimilitude' to absolute reality (Popper, 1963).

This claim, however, now needs careful examination in view of the direction that science has in fact taken. As Descartes' programme has been pursued, so more and more of the properties of the world that we like to think of as real have been stripped away. First were the senses (colour, smell and so on) which were relegated to 'secondary qualities' of an illusory kind. In the same way, our passions and desires, our hopes and our memories were replaced by impulses in our nerves. Then quantum theory appeared and the idea of solid objects was replaced by a swirling cloud of minute particles in a space that was otherwise almost entirely empty, and finally space and time themselves were replaced by abstract structures of strings or membranes; for a survey, see Kumar (2008). The 'reality' to which science was supposed to be attaining a steadily greater verisimilitude has become a picture that bears no relation whatever either to what we see externally around us or what we feel within us. Science has taken us full circle and, just like Plato, has removed reality entirely from our ordinary experience. Have we learnt anything from this 2500-year trek?

Competing Stories of Reality

I suggest that we have in fact learnt much, but it needs putting together in a new way. And the key to this is Kant's fundamental realisation that 'the world' is in fact 'our world' – the world as it is manifested to the human knower. In analysing what human knowing consisted of, Kant had little to go on beyond introspection and the traditions of his predecessors. We have the advantage of half a century of neuro-psychology and cognitive psychology, much of which has been devoted to just this problem. From this, it has become clear that there are many different systems concerned with making sense of the world. Some, such as those involved in the initial processing of input from the senses, geometrical awareness and some aspects of language processing, are distinguished by being localised in different areas of the brain. Others, such as the interacting cognitive subsystems, are concerned with processing at higher levels. They seem to involve many areas of the brain and are distinguished by the psychological structures of the processes, discussed by Isabel Clarke in her chapter (9) here.

Whereas Kant looked for a single coherent rational system of human knowing, I would advocate now a 'post-Kantian' view in which we apply Kant's thinking to this multi-system conception of our knowing. Kant talked about 'synthesising the manifold of intuition'; that is, processing low-level sense data to produce higher level schemata. Kant assures us that this *is* the reality of the world as it appears for us humans, and ICS reminds us that it consists of both propositional and implicational forms (including, respectively, linguistic and spiritual components). We can then expect that human knowing will be a tapestry woven from the many strands of our cognitive subsystems, and hence the same will be true of 'our world'. I will call these different constructions of our experience 'stories', even though they may not be at all articulated into words. We have different stories corresponding to different ways of knowing, arising from different mental systems. So I am suggesting that we carry around in our mind many different stories, in this sense (including, for me, the scientific story), which will affect where we direct our attention in using our senses, and how we classify and describe the things we see, hear and taste. Some of the resulting thoughts and images will be strong, vibrant and arresting, others will be indistinct and peripheral; but none will have a flag stuck to it saying 'here is unique reality'.

In addition to the particular philosophical trends that I have briefly sketched, there are many others which offer alternative understandings of how we know, and hence alternative understandings of reality. Some of these support the post-Kantian view of reality that I have just outlined. The view has, for example, many elements in common with the philosophers, such as Merleau-Ponty (Langer, 1989), of the school of *phenomenology*, following on from Kant, which moved from the purely logical criteria of Kant to include the sensory component and the place of the body. The ecologically focused philosopher David Abram (1997) has forcefully argued that Merleau-Ponty's approach opens up a much needed way of knowing hitherto 'subjugated' by the dominant way of knowing in our society (see June Boyce-Tillman's chapter in Clarke, 2005).

Other strands originating further back in history rethink the separation between a subjective knower and an objective known that is assumed in most of the approaches described so far. For example: phenomenology often sees the very concept of 'phenomena' as abolishing this distinction (Langer, 1989); Leibniz (1991) saw the universe as made up of worlds that are themselves self-contained subjects; and Spinoza (1989) started from a conception of the world as a single holistically integrated 'substance' – an approach that has influenced the neuropsychologist Damasio (2004). All these approaches offer a way of understanding in which one experiences oneself as united with what is known, with no separation, a way that is sometimes called 'knowing by being' (Clarke, 2005, p. 1), characteristic of spiritual experience. Spinoza's approach, in particular, is relevant to the 'dissolution of boundaries' described by Isabel Clarke in this book (p. 105)

Although I contend that it is no longer possible to stake out a single absolute reality, I would equally strongly oppose the idea that 'anything goes'. Although there may not be degrees of reality, there are degrees of being public, and these matter. In particular, the story embodied by science has been afforded high status in our society because it is based on a discipline that tries to ensure the maximum degree of agreement and internal logical coherence, independently of particular human cultures.

Spiritual stories, by contrast, tend to be mediated by the implicational subsystem. Because of the fluid nature of this subsystem, they are hard to convey to other people, or they get garbled in transmission. They will therefore have a low degree of public acceptance, unless they are linked with public religious narratives that stabilise the fickle implicational system into faith traditions. Because the implicational subsystem is closely coupled with the emotions, spiritual stories will tend to carry a high emotional charge, be it positive or negative. Where the charge is predominantly positive, a spiritual story can be a valuable way of making sense of the world, even though it may be hard to share with others. This scientific/spiritual polarity is another aspect of the dominant/subjugated polarity in ways of knowing referred to above.

I suggest that the post-Kantian approach to reality that I have described at the start of this section could provide a good framework for understanding the range of ways in which people relate to the world, including ways that we label as spiritual or psychotic. The examples of Klotz and Lancaster here suggest, in addition, that as we recover older, richer uses of language we can be 'post' Kant in recognising that the bounds of our knowing are not fixed.

Section 5

Research

When the first edition was compiled, the two chapters by Jackson and Peters represented the sum of mainstream research into the spirituality/psychosis overlap. Since then there has been an explosion of research interest in the area, and what follows is a selection. Peters and Jackson have both inspired and supervised student researchers who have opened the topic up further. Caroline Brett's work is among the most outstanding of these. Her study, based on the familiar comparison between a diagnosed and undiagnosed group of transliminal experiencers, brings into sharp relief the crucial role of social and cultural context in the way people make sense of their experience, and hence of themselves as social beings, with far-reaching consequences for mental well being.

Taking subjective experience seriously is at the heart of this issue, hence the importance of qualitative as well as quantitative study. Warwick and Waldram provide contrasting examples of this, expanding, field of research.

11

Are Delusions on a Continuum? The Case of Religious and Delusional Beliefs

Emmanuelle Peters

"You're trying to climb rain, Peter, or sweep sun off the pavement."

(Retort from a psychotic man in conversation with Peter Chadwick, discussing his endeavours to investigate delusional thinking. Reported in Chadwick, 1992; p. xiv)

The Concept of Schizotypy

The view that there may be a thread of continuity between normality and psychosis is by no means a recent one, and the use of the concept of 'schizoid personality' was reported by Bleuler as early as 1911. Rado (1953) was the first to coin the term 'schizotypal', which he defined as <u>the psychodynamic expression of the schizophrenic genotype</u>. The concept of schizotypy was later elaborated by Meehl (1962) to denote the genetically determined disposition to schizophrenia. This led to the recognition of a spectrum of abnormal perceptions and experience, and the acknowledgement that conventional diagnostic categories do not accurately reflect the variety of malfunction.

The continuity, or dimensionality, of psychotic characteristics is now firmly established amongst psychologists (Claridge, 1997), and, increasingly, amongst psychiatrists (van Os *et al.*, 1999). Thus, <u>psychotic symptoms are recognised as the severe expression of traits that are present in the general population</u>, and which manifest themselves as psychological variations observable among individuals that range from the perfectly well-adjusted to those who, while showing signs of psychopathology, would not be considered clinically psychotic. Thus, <u>the distinction between signs of mental illness (i.e. *symptoms*) and the expression of human individuality (i.e. *traits*)</u> becomes blurred. One major hurdle to the acceptance of

I feel like the distinction is irrelevant. Trait or not, if it's causing suffering then maybe a change in relationship to it would be helpful.

Psychosis and Spirituality: Consolidating the New Paradigm Second Edition   Edited by Isabel Clarke
© 2010 John Wiley & Sons, Ltd.

[handwritten marginal note: Why not correct function to measure in response society's presering?]

dimensional models had been the apparent incompatibility between accepting the view of schizophrenia as a *disease* and regarding psychosis as continuous with psychological health. Indeed, psychotic symptoms represent, for the most part, such extraordinary disturbances of the mind that they may only be readily understood as serious malfunctioning of the brain. However, Claridge (1972; later revised in 1987), proposed a model of schizophrenia/schizotypy that incorporates both the view of schizophrenia as illness and as a psychological dimension (see Chapter 6, this volume).

The notion of continuity in mental illness has since been interpreted in differing ways. Claridge (1994) labels the two viewpoints as 'quasi' and 'fully' dimensional. The former takes the abnormal state as its reference point, and construes the continuity as varying degrees of expression of the clinical signs and symptoms. In contrast, the latter view emphasises dimensionality at the dispositional level, conceptualising schizotypy as a personality trait – albeit deviant – analogous to other individual differences, such as the extroversion–introversion dimension (Eysenck, 1992). A crucial difference is the notion that 'deviant' traits are seen in the fully dimensional model as being represented in personality as healthy diversity, whereas the quasi-dimensional viewpoint conceptualises schizotypy as attenuated psychotic symptoms.

The presence of schizotypal traits in the normal population can now be measured psychometrically from both the 'fully' (Claridge and Broks, 1984; Raine, 1991), and 'quasi' (Chapman *et al.*, 1978; Peters, Joseph and Garety, 1999) dimensional viewpoints. Individuals scoring highly on such indices have been shown to resemble schizophrenics on a number of experimental correlates (Peters *et al.*, 1994; Linney *et al.*, 1998), which provides some evidence for the validity of the concept. In addition, the structure of schizotypy has been found to parallel the multidimensionality of schizophrenia, with three schizotypal dimensions being identified which are comparable to Liddle (1987) three-factor model of schizophrenia: a positive, a negative, and a disorganisation factor (Bentall *et al.*, 1989; Claridge *et al.*, 1996).

Positive Symptoms in the General Population

Much of the work on schizotypy has been concerned with positive symptomatology. For instance, it has been found that certain identifiable groups of people have elevated scores on positive symptom measures, such as those who believe in the paranormal (Thalbourne, 1994); those who have out-of-body experiences (McCreery and Claridge, 1995); members of certain 'cults'[1] or New Religious Movements

---

[1] The word 'cult', as it is used by the media and in popular parlance, tends to be a pejorative term for religious (or 'pseudo-religious') groups (Richardson, 1993a). The term commonly used by sociologists of religions is 'new religious movement' (or NRM; Barker, 1996), and will therefore be the term used in this chapter.

(NRMs) (Day and Peters, 1999); and those who have profound religious experiences (Jackson, 1997). Others have taken actual positive symptoms as their starting point, and investigated their incidence in non-psychiatric or "normal" populations. Romme and Escher (1989), in their influential book 'Accepting Voices', were some of the first authors to point out that many individuals have auditory hallucinations outside the context of a psychiatric illness, which can be construed as beneficial life experiences, rather than as symptoms of an illness.

More recent, large-scale population surveys have confirmed the high incidence of seemingly benign positive symptoms in the general population. At least two studies have found that 10–15% of the normal population has had some kind of halluci-natory experience in their lives (Tien, 1991; Poulton *et al.*, 2000), whereas approx-imately 20% report delusions (Poulton *et al.*, 2000). In all, approximately one in four of the Dunedin Study cohort (approximately 1000 people) reported having had at least one delusional or hallucinatory experience that was unrelated to drug use or physical illness (Poulton *et al.*, 2000). Similarly, van Os *et al.* (2000) found that 17.5% of the Netherlands Mental Health Survey and Incidence Study (NEMESIS) sample (over 7000 people) were rated on at least one symptom of psychosis using the Composite International Diagnostic Interview (CIDI; World Health Organisation, 1990), whereas only 0.4% qualified for a formal diagnosis of psychosis. This suggests that psychotic-like phenomenology is 50 times more prevalent than the narrower, medical concept of schizophrenia. In addition, strong associations existed between all types of symptom ratings on the CIDI and all types of lifetime diagnoses, further suggesting that the boundaries of the 'psychosis phenotype' do not concur with traditional diagnostic labels.

Psychiatric Definitions of Delusions

Jaspers (1913) originally ascribed three defining characteristics to delusions: themes still reflected in modern psychiatric definitions of delusions, such as in the Diag-nostic and Statistical Manual of Mental Disorders-IV (DSM-IV, 1994):

A false belief based on incorrect inference about external reality (*falsity*) that is firmly sustained (*certainty*) despite what almost everyone else believes and despite what constitutes incontrovertible proof or evidence to the contrary (*incorrigibility*). The belief is not one ordinarily accepted by other members of the person's culture or subculture (*my additions in italics*).

This definition poses several problems, ranging from plainly false assumptions to points of vagueness and ambiguity, as well as unjustified theoretical conjectures. First, many delusions do not show absolute conviction, and often conviction in the same belief will wax and wane over time (Brett-Jones *et al.*, 1987; Sharp *et al.*, 1996). Second, it has been demonstrated that delusions are not necessarily impervious to experience, and deluded individuals vary on how much they accom-modate new evidence into their existing delusions (Brett-Jones *et al.*, 1987). There is also now ample evidence that delusions are open to modification through cognitive-behavioural techniques (Chadwick and Lowe, 1994; Drury *et al.*, 1996; Kuipers *et al.*, 1997; Sensky *et al.*, 2000; see also Kingdon, Chapter 19).

Both Brockington (1991) and Bentall *et al.* (1994) have made the important point that delusions need to be understood against a background of thorough knowledge of the psychology of 'beliefs'. There is in fact a large body of work demonstrating the irrationality of so-called normal individuals (Sutherland, 1992). Holding a delusion with absolute conviction is not pathological in itself, because all beliefs which are personally significant or which support self-esteem tend to be held with absolute conviction, such as religious or scientific beliefs (Maher, 1988). Models of normal belief formation and maintenance (Alloy and Tabachnick, 1984) suggest that strong beliefs are typically maintained with little evidential support, and that our existing beliefs influence the process by which we seek out, store, and interpret relevant information. This well known 'confirmation bias' allows us to be impervious to contradictory evidence, and only notice information which confirms our pre-existing beliefs (and of course science is notoriously guilty of this bias!). Therefore, the certainty and incorrigibility traditionally ascribed to delusional beliefs are in fact the normal characteristics of any challenged belief that supports self-esteem.

Perhaps the most problematic statement in the DSM-IV definition is that delusions are 'false beliefs'. First, in some cases the claims of the deluded patient cannot actually be proved as false. The best examples are the paranoid delusions, where individuals report being followed or spied on by such organisations as the CIA or the IRA. The literature contains counter examples (Mayerhoff *et al.*, 1991; Fulford, 1991 for the so-called 'Othello syndrome') and acknowledged uncertainty (van Os *et al.*, 2000).

Second, in many cases the criteria of truth and falsity is just not applicable. Spitzer (1990) argues that one cannot attribute the notion of falsity to statements describing the contents of one's own mental state or mentality (i.e. 'my mind from my own point of view'), because there is no evidence stronger than the evidence of experiencing a thought or sensation. The inherent 'truthfulness' of one's own mental activity, however, distorted from reality, is demonstrated by scanning studies. For instance, Spence *et al.* (1997) showed that passivity experiences (the belief that one's thoughts or actions are those of external or alien entities) are accompanied by hyperactivation of areas of the brain subserving attention to internal and external bodily space, whereas Woodruff *et al.* (1997) found that hallucinations are accompanied by activation of the brain areas which normally process external speech. These studies confirm that the experiences themselves are not false, because they are actually identifiable at a brain level. Rather, it is the unjustified claim that these experiences have some sort of intersubjective validity, and are not recognised as only lying within the scope of one's mentality, which makes a belief delusional. Fulford (1991) also comments that in many cases it is the evaluative rather than the factual component of delusional thinking which is pathological.

Third, even if one could demonstrate that some beliefs were 'false' or irrational, holding false beliefs is still a common occurrence. In fact, delusional themes commonly reflect beliefs held in the normal population and are not culturally atypical. They tend to keep pace with advancing technology and discoveries in the natural sciences, and tend to vary with social background, confirming that they are derived from acquired knowledge (Roberts, 1992). In addition, Bentall *et al.* (1994) point out that many common delusional beliefs, such as paranoid and grandiose delusions, reflect the person's position in the social universe, after all a common pre-occupation. Delusions of reference can stem from a sense of relationship between individuals and the media, which is actively encouraged by many TV and radio shows.

A frequently quoted American poll (Gallup and Newport, 1991) identified that one-fourth of the surveyed sample believed in ghosts; one-fourth believed they had had a telepathic experience; one-sixth believed they had been in touch with someone who had died; one-tenth had seen or been in presence of a ghost; over 50% believed in the devil; one-tenth had talked to the devil; and one-seventh had seen a flying saucer. Western culture is fascinated with 'unexplained' phenomena such as UFOs, the paranormal and conspiracy theories. Many delusions reflect a religious or spiritual theme. The psychiatric profession and its diagnostic tools have been attacked by some authors as medicalising and pathologising participation in certain types of religious groups and experiences (Richardson, 1993b). How does one distinguish between a belief in an 'accepted' God (by the main cultural standard of a particular society), an 'unusual' God (as adhered to by subcultures within a particular society), and an 'idiosyncratic' God (a delusion with a religious content)? Furthermore, how is the mental health professional qualified to make such a distinction?

Psychological Conceptualisations of Delusions

The discussion above illustrates the difficulties inherent in defining delusions, however, readily identifiable clinically. Newer psychological definitions have tended to concentrate on more descriptive, operational criteria (e.g. Kendler *et al.*, 1983; Oltmanns, 1988). Garety and Hemsley (1994), in an influential book, describe delusions as: (i) continuous rather than dichotomous; (ii) multi-dimensional rather than unidimensional; (iii) potentially responsive rather than fixed; (iv) psychologically understandable; and (v) involving rational processes. Perhaps the most important recognition in these psychological definitions is the emphasis on delusions being neither dichotomous nor unidimensional. While the dichotomous view of delusions had been challenged by Strauss as early as 1969, and by Chapman and Chapman in the early 80s (1980), the lack of working definitions had hampered scientific research in this area. However, there is now a growing body of studies that support these claims empirically.

For instance, surveys investigating delusional ideation in the general population. Verdoux *et al.* (1998) found that the range of individual item endorsement on the Peters *et al.* (1996) Delusions Inventory (PDI), in individuals with no psychiatric history, varied between 5 and 70%, whereas Peters, Joseph and Garety (1999) found that 10% of their normal sample had scores on the PDI which exceeded the mean of a psychotic, in-patient group. The percentage of people reporting psychotic symp-tomatology is even higher in psychiatric, but non-psychotic populations (Altman *et al.*, 1997) Many authors have also commented on the similarities between over-valued ideas, obsessions and delusions (Kozac and Foa, 1994).

These findings demonstrate fairly conclusively that there are no clear-cut divisions between normality and delusional thinking, and between delusions and other types of pathological thinking. There is also persuasive evidence for the multidimension-ality of delusions (Harrow *et al.*, 1988; Kendler *et al.*, 1983; Garety and Hemsley, 1987). Throughout these studies, the recurrent dimensions that emerge concern levels of conviction, pre-occupation, and distress. Their importance were confirmed by Peters *et al.* (1999) who found that their normal and deluded samples were differentiated by their scores on the dimensions of conviction, pre-occupation and distress, despite an overlap in the range of scores between the two groups in the endorsement of delusional items.

Empirical Studies Comparing Religious and Delusional Beliefs

The themes of continuity and multidimensionality are of fundamental importance in the literature comparing intense spiritual and religious beliefs with delusions with a religious content. Jackson (1997) attempted to distinguish between psychotic and spiritual phenomena by comparing two groups of individuals reporting such experiences on a variety of psychometric tools. He concluded that there was no clear borderline between the two, with a common, schizotypal personality trait underlying both forms on the spiritual-psychotic continuum. Jones and Watson (1997), on the other hand, found that schizophrenic delusions could be differen-tiated from religious beliefs held by 'normals' on a number of significant variables, such as pre-occupation, speed of formation, perceptual evidence and use of imagination. Such apparent inconsistencies are mostly owing to the types of people under study: whilst Jackson's respondents consisted of individuals who reported unusual spiritual experiences, Jones and Watson's sample deliberately excluded members of religious minority groups. Nevertheless, it should be noted that fewer differences were found between religious and delusional beliefs, than between delusional and control beliefs in the same individuals. Notably, religious and psychotic beliefs were not rated differently in terms of 'truthfulness' or conviction.

Another interesting group to investigate are members of NRMs (see Richardson, 1995, for a review). The groups which have been most studied include the Jesus Movement Group (now disbanded), the Rajneeshees, and Hare Krishna devotees. Extensive data on their personal background and attitudes have been collected (Latkin *et al.*, 1987; Richardson *et al.*, 1979), as well as comprehensive batteries of personality assessments such as the Myers-Briggs Inventory and the Minnesota Multiphasic Personality Inventory (Poling and Kenny, 1986; Ross, 1983). Various measures of subjective well-being such as perceived stress, social support and self-esteem have been reported (Latkin *et al.*, 1987), as well as several aspects of mental health such as depression, anxiety, loss of behavioural/emotional control and life satisfaction (Weiss, 1987; Weiss and Comprey, 1987). The overwhelming conclusions from this extensive body of work are that, on the whole, members of NRMs display group scores indistinguishable from those of normative samples, and are not, as a group, psychopathological, despite their idiosyncratic choice of deity and lifestyle (Richardson, 1995).

Day and Peters (1999) looked specifically at the schizotypal personality traits of individuals belonging to two NRMs, namely Druids[2] and Hare Krishna[3] devotees. They found that the NRMs scored higher than both Christian and non-religious control groups on questionnaires measuring positive, but not other types of symptomatology, and her colleagues (Peters *et al.*, 1999) went on to investigate the level of delusional ideation in the same samples, also comparing them with a psychiatric in-patient, deluded group. The multidimensionality of delusions was also investigated by measuring levels of conviction, pre-occupation and distress associated with such beliefs.

As predicted, it was found that the NRMs group endorsed significantly more items than the two control groups on both questionnaires used [Peters *et al.*, 1996; Delusions Symptom-State Inventory (DSSI); Foulds and Bedford, 1975), and scored higher on levels of conviction. No differences were found between the NRMs and the control groups on levels of distress, supporting previous findings that individuals in NRMs are no more distressed psychologically than normative samples (Richardson, 1995). No differences were found between the Christians and the non-religious on any of the delusions measures, suggesting that being religious *per se* does not account for the NRMs members' scores.

Interestingly, the NRMs group could not be differentiated from the deluded group on their total scores on the PDI. Furthermore, they showed identical levels of conviction about the items they endorsed, indicating that they were as persuaded of the veracity of their experiences as the deluded in-patients. However, individuals from the NRMs were significantly less distressed and pre-occupied by these experiences than their deluded counterparts. This is consistent with Jones and Watson (1997), who found that one of the distinguishing factors between religious

---

[2] Druidry is one of the major Pagan orders, whose ideas are inspired from Celtic traditions of a spirituality rooted in a love of nature. Druids have meetings, called Groves, usually fortnightly. Their beliefs explore sacred mythology, divination and other esoteric teachings. The Druids design and perform magical and religious ceremonies to change themselves and the world. This includes worshipping Old Gods and Goddesses, rites of passage (hand-fasting, child blessings, etc.), and observing eight seasonal festivals during the year (the solstices, equinoxes and the four fire festivals).

[3] The Hare Krishna members studied live communally in a temple, and are free to worship at any time during the day. Although Krishna devotees trace their origins back through the sixteenth-century monk, Chaitanya Mahaprabhu, ISKCON (the International Society for Krishna Consciousness) was not founded until 1965 when His Divine Grace A. C. Bhaktivedanta Swami Prabhupada went to the United States. The movement's philosophy promotes human well-being and the consciousness of God, based on the ancient Vedic texts of India. Its members wear saffron robes, and chant the Maha Mantra around town centres. The Krishnas are vegetarian, do not use intoxicants, do not gamble, and are celibate apart from procreation within marriage.

and delusional beliefs was pre-occupation, but not conviction or 'truthfulness'. The NRMs members also scored significantly lower on the DSSI, which contains items of a considerably more florid nature than the PDI, confirming that they are not floridly psychotic. They also obtained significantly lower scores on Social Desirability, establishing that any differences between the two groups could not be explained by the NRMs members under-reporting their experiences to appear more socially desirable.

Such results support the notion that there is a continuity of function between normality and psychosis, with 'normal' individuals (both non-religious and religious) being at one end of the continuum, the deluded individuals at the other extreme, and members of NRMs at the intersection. Overall, these findings suggest that form may be more important diagnostically than content: it is not *what* you believe, it is *how* you believe it.

What Differentiates Religious and Delusional Experiences?

Empirical studies comparing religious and deluded individuals call into question our existing diagnostic criteria for delusions, which emphasise unduly the content or 'bizarreness' of beliefs to classify them as pathological. Anthropological writings have long recognised that similar mental and behavioural states may be classified as psychiatric disorders in some cultural settings, and religious experiences in others (Bhugra, 1996). Some typical examples include glossolalia (speaking in tongues), common in Pentecostal (or "charismatic") Christianity (Grady and Loewenthal, 1997), or possession phenomena such as the belief in possession by Zar spirits common in Africa (Grisaru *et al.*, 1997; also see Tobert's, Chapter 3, this volume). Indeed, some 'psychotic' experiences (by Western standards) are actually highly revered in other cultures, such as shamanism (Prince, 1992).

Altered states of consciousness, some of which bear close similarity to florid psychotic experiences, have actually been sought after by most societies since time immemorial. Some religious practices and rituals can provide a controlled environment within which individuals can attain such altered states. Some in fact involve the use of hallucinogenics or other potent drugs to enable individuals to reach an alteration of consciousness, required to achieve closeness with their deity, such as the Yanomani tribe in the Venezuelan rainforests. Interestingly, the marginalisation of such experiences in contemporary Western Christianity has been paralleled by a proliferation of alternative subcultures, some spiritual, such as NRMs, and some secular, such as the widespread drug culture. The existence of such sub-cultures, and their pursuit of altered reality experiences, would suggest that we have an almost evolutionary need to 'get out of our minds', be that to fulfil a spiritual or purely hedonistic function.

Several authors have attempted to account for both the resemblance and differences between culturally idiosyncratic psychotic states, culturally validated mystical states, and drug-induced states (Saver and Rabin, 1997; Greenberg *et al.*, 1992;

Jackson and Fulford, 1997). These authors suggest that the characteristics of the two types of phenomena bear many similarities, such as apparent delusions or radical change of belief, hallucinations (voices and visions), strange behaviour and social withdrawal. However, although the content or type of phenomena may not differ, as mentioned in other chapters in this volume, 'abnormal' experiences tend to be sought after in spiritually and drug-induced states, and there is a relatively smooth and controlled entry in and out of those states. In contrast, they tend to be unwanted in psychotic states, and to be out of the person's control.

The above authors further point out that the major differences seem to lie, firstly, in the interpretation and meaning given to the experiences, and, secondly, in the emotional and behavioural consequences of such experiences. Usually spiritual experiences have adaptive and life-enhancing consequences, whereas in psychosis similar phenomena often lead to social and behavioural impoverishment (Fulford, 1989). Lenz (1983) has also suggested that the only difference between a religious belief and delusion is the course of development that the belief takes them. Hope, faith and freedom are found in mystical experiences, while this is not the case in deluded individuals: 'the mystic swims, the psychotic drowns' (Chadwick, 1992; p. 93).

Interestingly, this is not a fool-proof distinction, as indicated by a study by Roberts (1991): he found that a group of chronically deluded individuals had comparable scores to a sample of Anglican Ordinands on 'meaning' and 'purpose of life' questionnaires, coupled with low levels of depression and suicidal inclination, suggesting that objective judgments of functioning may not correspond to the subjective fulfilment experienced by individuals. Similarly, some psychotic patients regard their voices as benevolent (Chadwick and Birchwood, 1994), enjoy their company, and may even actively invoke them (Romme and Escher, A., 1989). Other patients will deliberately stop taking neuroleptic medication, or ingest cannabis or other drugs to induce a delusional atmosphere or restore their psychotic state, presumably because they feel it is preferable to their non-psychotic reality. In contrast, some of the intense spiritual experiences described by Jackson and Fulford (1997) sample were neither solicited nor controllable, and were initially very frightening for the experiences.

I have argued elsewhere (Peters, Joseph and Garety, 1999; Peters *et al.*, 1999) that whether or not one becomes overtly deluded is determined not just by the content of mental events, but also by the extent to which it is believed, how much it interferes with one's life, and its emotional impact. Some religious delusions may not necessarily be 'deviant' in content (e.g. they may adhere to mainstream Christian doctrine, and be based on the Bible), but rather it is the fact that the individual is entirely immersed in his/her religious pre-occupation (e.g. reading the Bible all day), and the potential emotional and behavioural consequences of the beliefs (e.g. extreme distress if the closeness to God temporarily wanes, or self-neglect or complete passivity in the face of God's omnipotence), which make the belief pathological. Indeed, psychological interventions for delusional beliefs usually involve dissociating percepts from beliefs and emotional reactions, as well as exploring alternative coping or behavioural strategies, rather than directly challenging the content of delusions.

Which Factors are Responsible for the Pathognomonic Features of Idiosyncratic Beliefs?

The empirical studies reported in the previous section reflect both the relatedness and distinctiveness of psychotic and religious experiences. On the one hand, they must share some common psychological mechanism, which leads both groups to hold idiosyncratic ideas about the world and be subjected to unusual experiences. One possible candidate is the sharing of a schizotypal central nervous system or personality, as would be suggested by Jackson (1997), and Day and Peters (1999) results. Other possibilities may include cognitive style, such as difficulties in probability judgments and hypothesis-testing, which has been demonstrated in deluded subjects (Garety and Freeman, 1999), people who believe in the paranormal (Blackmore and Troscianko, 1985; Williams and Irwin, 1991), and people who score highly on the PDI (Linney *et al.*, 1998). Of course, these hypotheses are not mutually exclusive, and may in fact be causally related.

On the other hand, there must be some differences that account for the divergence in the emotional and behavioural consequences of the two groups' beliefs and experiences. It is unclear at this stage whether those differences are biological, psychological, or socio-cultural, or indeed a combination of the three. Jackson (Chapter 12) proposes a 'problem-solving' model which can work in a negative or positive direction, so accounting for the psychosis, spiritual experience differential. Gumley *et al.* (1999) suggest that after one episode of psychosis, fear of relapse can produce increased arousal, anxiety, sleeplessness and potentially withdrawal, in itself increasing the risk of relapse, thereby creating a similar feedback loop to that described by Jackson.

Whether a positive or negative feedback loop is triggered could again be determined by a variety of factors. First, it could be that the content of the experiences is more inherently frightening in psychosis: Jackson and Fulford (1997) note that although the spiritual experiences of their small sample could mostly all be classified as psychotic, nevertheless there was a conspicuous absence of common psychotic beliefs such as delusions of persecution. Interestingly, in a study charting the course and outcome of a group of 88 delusional patients, Jorgensen (1994) reported that patients with main delusions of persecution or influence had the most pessimistic outcome. It is possible that some types of delusions, such as persecutory beliefs, are more likely to engender a cyclical process whereby individuals provoke actual rejection and control by others by virtue of their behaviour, thereby providing confirmation of their beliefs and increased social isolation (Roberts, 1992).

Accompanying symptoms such as thought disorder and third person hallucinations were also absent in Jackson and Fulford's spiritual sample, while they are common in psychosis. While this is likely to be due to biological factors, the psychological effect would be to reduce the coping resources of the individual, thus leaving him or her more vulnerable to a positive feedback system. In the study mentioned above, Jorgensen and Jensen (1994) do indeed find that subjective thought disorder is predictive of the persistence of delusional beliefs.

The cognitive resources of the individual may play a part in determining whether s/he is able to make sense of the experiences. Indeed, there are numerous reports of the impoverishment of cognitive functioning in individuals with a diagnosis of schizophrenia (Russell *et al.*, 1997). Interestingly, deficits are particularly marked in tasks requiring cognitive flexibility (Pantelis and Nelson, 1994), a cognitive process that has been identified as a predictor of good response to CBT for delusions (Garety *et al.*, 1997). In other words, it may be that it is a lack of cognitive flexibility that prevents individuals from reframing their beliefs and experiences both at the initial stage and in response to therapeutic dialogue.

Lastly, support and validation within the socio-cultural context of the individual may help to alleviate stress. Again this is supported by Jorgensen and Jensen (1994), where the persistence of delusional beliefs was predicted by living alone and the experience of psychosocial stressors. One pertinent consideration is the potential buffering role of religious affiliations (such as membership of NRMs). Muffler *et al.* (1997), for instance, report that in the experimental *zeitgeist* of the 1960s and 1970s, religious communal organisations assisted large number of young people who were, temporarily at least, 'shaken loose' from their usual social locations.

In addition to offering a protective role in terms of social and emotional support, NRMs may also help with the validation and normalisation of their beliefs and experiences. Thus, a religious interpretation of unusual experiences may help individuals achieve meaning, self-esteem and a sense of control which then increases coping behaviour (Crossley, 1995; Jackson and Fulford, 1997). Indeed, recent approaches to psychosis have been influenced by the Beckian model (Kovacs and Beck, 1978), which postulates that it is the way in which experiences are evaluated, rather than the fact that they occur, which determines their affective and behavioural sequelae (e.g. Chadwick and Lowe, 1994; Garety and Hemsley, 1994). Therefore, the additional role of religious affiliations would be to replace a catastrophic interpretation of the experiences themselves with a more benign evaluation; i.e. as an authentic sign from God rather than as potential symptoms of mental illness. Indeed, Chadwick (this volume) notes how self-doubt was undoubtedly influential in mediating his switch from the mystical to the psychotic, and he has previously reported of his own psychotic experiences: 'I had neither the intelligence nor the conceptual apparatus *nor the spiritual development* to handle the experience that was now going out of control' (Chadwick, 1992; p. 37; my italics). Prince (1992) also points out that cultures which invest meaning into, and provide institutional support for 'unusual states', can channel at least some of the experiences into socially valuable roles. This would suggest that NRMs are in fact beneficial to one's mental health, in contrast to some of the psychiatric writings which have pathologised non-conformity in the religious sphere (see Post, 1992;

Neeleman and Persaud, 1995; Crossley, 1995, for an analysis of the role of religious experience in psychiatry).

Conclusion

Research into schizotypy has shown that certain groups of people have similar experiences to the positive symptoms of schizophrenia while remaining functioning members of society. The specific case of delusions was in this chapter. A number of empirical studies that have endeavoured to distinguish between delusional and religious beliefs were examined. The overall findings from this body of empirical work provide support, firstly, for the notion of a continuum between normality and psychosis, and, secondly, for the necessity to consider the multidimensionality of delusional beliefs. It is argued that what makes people cross the psychotic 'threshold' is not necessarily the content but the consequences of their beliefs: It is not *what* you believe, it is *how* you believe it.

12

The Paradigm-Shifting Hypothesis: A Common Process in Benign Psychosis and Psychotic Disorder

Mike Jackson

This chapter begins with a summary of my original contribution to this collection, which described a qualitative study of the relationship between benign spiritual experience and psychotic disorder. Three emerging themes are developed in terms of more recent research evidence and theory.

1. The phenomenological continuity between benign and pathological forms of psychosis.
2. The psychosocial determinants of benign or pathological outcomes in psychosis, including both the role of developmental factors, and the social context of adult psychotic experiences.
3. The development of an explanatory model for benign psychotic experience as a paradigm shifting process.

Summary of 'Spiritual and Psychotic Experience: A Case Study Comparison'

'Religious mysticism is only one-half of mysticism. The other half has no accumulated traditions except which the text-books on insanity supply. Open any one of these, and you will find abundant cases in which "mystical ideas" are cited as characteristic symptoms of enfeebled or deluded states of mind. In delusional insanity, paranoia as they sometimes call it, we may have a kind of diabolical mysticism, a sort of religious mysticism turned upside down. The same sense of ineffable importance in the smallest events, the same texts and words coming with

Psychosis and Spirituality: Consolidating the New Paradigm Second Edition   Edited by Isabel Clarke
© 2010 John Wiley & Sons, Ltd.

new meanings, the same voices and visions and leadings and missions, the same controlling by extraneous powers; only this time the emotion is pessimistic: instead of consolations, we have desolations; the meanings are dreadful; and the powers are enemies to life ... It is evident that from the point of view of their psychological mechanism, the classic mysticism and these lower mysticisms spring from the same mental level ... That region contains every kind of matter: "seraph and snake" abide there side by side' (James, 1902, p. 426).

James's view that spiritual and psychotic experience are broadly distinguishable, but involve important areas of correspondence, is shared by many subsequent commentators (Arieti, 1976; Boisen, 1952; Buckley, 1981; Campbell, 1972; Jung, 1960; Laing, 1967; Lenz, 1983; Prince, 1979; Underhill, 1930; Wapnick, 1969; Watson, 1982; Wootton and Allen, 1983). This formulation presents us with what might be termed 'the *spiritual-psychotic paradox*': how can two categories of experience, which are defined partly in terms of their opposite pragmatic effects, be so closely related as to suggest the presence of a common underlying process? What determines whether a particular individual's experience falls one side of the line or the other – whether he or she finds 'seraphs' or 'snakes'? How are the apparent benefits in 'benign psychosis' explained in terms of an understanding of psychosis as a form of radical dysfunction?

The original study aimed to evaluate this relationship by comparing two strategically selected groups from the grey area between psychotic and spiritual experience. The first group had never had psychiatric treatment or diagnosis, but were selected on the basis of their relatively 'florid' spiritual experiences. The second group had diagnosed and treated psychotic disorder, but had made substantial recovery by the time of the study, and held a spiritual or paranormal interpretation of key anomalous experiences. Cases were selected from the archives of the Religious Experience Research Centre (now based at Lampeter University), which contained over 5000 first-hand written accounts of contemporary spiritual experience, elicited in national and international surveys. Some additional cases were obtained through a questionnaire survey of spiritual experience in a self-help group for people with psychotic disorders.

A series of eight case studies (four in each group) were presented and a qualitative comparison of the experiences they described in semi-structured interviews was conducted. These will not be reported in depth here, but to give a flavour of the study, two are briefly described.

Penny (62 years) was a widow whose parents were missionaries. She had three manic episodes between the ages of 35 and 45 years, following the sudden death of her husband and the birth of their fourth child. During these episodes, she experienced a strong synchronicity in events and believed that she had a divine identity. She was 'sectioned', treated with mood stabilisers and anti-psychotics, and she made a good recovery between episodes. Since the last one she had worked as a medical social worker, a TM teacher, and an art teacher, and she was active in Green politics and the ecumenical movement. At interview, she had been stable for almost 20 years without medication, and she had recently retired. She was a committed Bahai.

Sean (53 years) was a married insurance salesman, from a working class, atheist family. At 48 years, after suffering a financial and personal crisis, he started to hear voices he described as 'the cosmic CIA', instructing him in a new philosophy of life. These experiences occurred daily for around 12 months, and were largely restricted to a specific locality. He felt that they enabled him to both accept and cope with his adversities. At the time of the interview, these experiences had faded, and Sean was well adjusted, successful and happy. He had never discussed his experiences with anyone before.

Detailed comparison of the experiences described in these two groups found that while most of the distinctions cited in the literature had some value as generalisations, none were watertight in the sense of clearly separating the groups. Phenomenological distinctions concerning the form and content of experiences fared worst, and the benign group met diagnostic criteria for a wide range of delusions and hallucinations (using the Present State Examination: Wing, Cooper and Sartorius, 1974). Neither group felt able to control their experiences, but the benign group were less worried by this. There was a tendency for benign experiences to be more often framed within an accepted sub-cultural context, relatively transitory, and to involve more emotionally positive content. The diagnosed group described experiences which were more idiosyncratic, more prolonged and involved more distress. Crucially, however, for each distinction there were also plenty of exceptions in both directions. Most of those in the benign group could describe times when they had found their anomalous experiences disturbing, and times when they were prolonged over periods of days. Most of the diagnosed group described moments of benign spiritual feelings and anomalous experiences they found helpful.

Although it strongly supported James' view of the closeness of relationship between spiritual and psychotic experiences, the study was limited in a number of ways. The sample was small and highly selected, and as such, of little value for generalising to the wider population. The benign group was relatively extreme in the degree of psychotic content of their spiritual experience and not representative of most people reporting occasional spiritual experiences. In the following, some more recent studies which clarify the phenomenological comparison are discussed.

The original study informally explored the role of childhood experience and attachment in relation to psychotic experience in adulthood. All of those whose adult psychotic experiences involved persistently distressing elements described major trauma in childhood, and in general, this was more severe in those who later developed psychotic disorders. Those who described happy and stable childhoods also described largely positive adult experiences. The apparent neatness of this correspondence was perhaps spurious in part; it could be explained, for example, by systematic biases in either memory or narrative style. However, the degree of correspondence between the two extremes of childhood and adult experience suggested that development experiences should be considered as potential determinants of outcome in adult psychotic disorder. This has been extensively confirmed in more recent research, which is briefly summarised below.

The strength of the qualitative method is that it allows the narrative meaning of the experiences described to emerge. When considered in the context of the person's life and circumstances, many of the significant benign psychotic experiences described contributed to the resolution of underlying problems which they were struggling with at the time. Thus, Sean's voices, for example, helped him come to terms with his problems, and to cope with them in a constructive way: 'it turned me upside down in many ways. It altered my views completely . . . [I] live life now as far as I can by what I'm learning . . . I think I have support and guidance, so nothing in this world can worry me'. Drawing on the wider literature on spiritual experience (Batson and Ventis, 1982; Boisen, 1952; Campbell, 1972; Hay, 1987; Prince, 1979; Underhill, 1930; Valla and Prince, 1989) inspirational creativity (Hadamard, 1945; Harding, 1942; Storr, 1996; Wallas, 1926) the psychodynamic concept of regression in the service of the ego (Freud, 1911; Kris, 1952) and Jaynes' (1976) evolutionary theory of hallucinations, a *paradigm shifting process model* of benign psychosis was proposed. The essential features of this 'PSP model' are that:

1. Benign psychotic experiences are triggered in a normal, adaptive psychological process which serves the function of paradigm shifting – enabling the individual to adjust firmly held values, beliefs and assumptions to resolve a conflict.
2. The process is driven by states of conflict or 'impasse' which create psychological stress.
3. When anomalous experiences are triggered, their emotional intensity is sometimes sufficient to over-rule or reset values, beliefs and assumptions which have been previously firmly held.
4. The content of anomalous experiences can contain insights which are useful and effective in addressing the conflict which drives them. These insights are a form of creativity which reflects unconscious processing of the problem.
5. This allows resolution of the underlying conflict and maintenance of emotional homeostasis, effectively functioning as a *negative feedback loop*.

     Considering pathological psychotic disorder in terms of this model, two ways in which the adaptive PSP process can go wrong were suggested.
6. If the paradigm shift leads to increased conflict with social reality or other firmly held beliefs or values, the process can *increase* psychological stress, and effectively operate as a *positive feedback loop*. This would involve an accelerating cycle of increasingly unhelpful anomalous experiences and stress – a state of florid psychotic disorder.
7. Alternatively, relative stability can be achieved by withdrawing from sources of conflict – most importantly social interaction. This describes the situation of many people living with a psychotic disorder, which is hidden in that they either avoid others entirely, or they avoid disclosure of their beliefs and experiences to others. This could be thought of more as a state of stability with residual symptoms.

This descriptive model of benign psychosis describes a process which has been discussed by many commentators on spiritual experience and inspirational creativity, and has been explicitly related to psychosis by some (Boisen, 1952; Lukoff, 2007a; Grof and Grof, 1986; Wapnick, 1969). In the following discussion, I attempt to articulate this process in more contemporary psychological terms, drawing from recent biopsychosocial models of psychotic disorder. These provide a rich basis of psychological theory, which can be applied to benign psychosis by a straightforward, but critical paradigm shift. Where the psychopathologists' models are constructed to explain a dysfunctional system, in which something has gone wrong, we will consider them as ways of understanding a normal, adaptive psychological function, which is doing what it is supposed to do. Instead of considering the essential features of the processes described in terms of *deficits* in function then, we can consider them as *differences* in function. First, I briefly review some more recent developments in research concerning the psychosis continuum and psychosocial determinants of disorder.

The Psychosis Continuum

Since the original study was conducted, there have been substantial developments in research into the psychosis continuum, and the relationship between clinical psychotic disorder and non-clinical psychosis (for a systematic review, see van Os *et al.*, 2008). This has effectively established the existence of a continuum and the considerably higher prevalence of non-clinical than clinical psychotic experiences in the normal population.

The Dutch NEMESIS study (van Os *et al.*, 2001) involved conducting clinical interviews (CIDI) with a large epidemiological sample ($N = 7076$), checking those which appeared to report psychotic experiences, and repeating the assessments over two subsequent studies. In the baseline assessments, around 17% of the sample reported psychotic experiences which met the criteria for delusions or hallucinations, although most of these were 'not-clinically relevant' (not distressing or problematic). The authors estimate that 'the psychosis phenotype is up to 50 times more common than clinical disorder'.

In their review of the psychosis continuum literature, van Os *et al.* (2008) discuss a series of comparison between 'non-clinical psychosis' and psychotic disorder, each of which provides evidence for continuity. A meta-analysis of all studies of psychotic symptoms in the normal population found a median prevalence of 5.3% across studies, with considerable variation depending on the methodology used to sample experiences. The same demographic characteristics were associated with psychotic disorder and non-clinical psychotic experiences – the prevalence of both being higher in males, migrants, ethnic minorities, unemployed, unmarried and less educated people. Some of the same risk factors were associated both with psychotic disorder and non-clinical psychosis, including exposure to cannabis, traumatic experiences and urbanicity (time spent living in an urban environment during development). Most compellingly, the predictive validity of the continuum concept is confirmed by the finding in the NEMESIS study that when followed-up 2 years later, report of non-clinical psychotic experience at baseline was a robust predictor of subsequent psychotic disorder. Although most of those who had an initial psychotic experience had no further problems, 8% still had 'subclinical symptoms' 2 years later, and a further 8% had developed psychotic disorders. This amounts to a 60-fold increase in risk of developing a psychotic disorder amongst those who reported a psychotic experience at baseline. Similarly, Poulton *et al.* (2000) found that children who reported psychotic experiences at age 11 had a 16-fold increase in risk of psychotic disorder over the next 16 years.

van Os *et al.* argue that these findings support a 'proneness–persistence impairment model' of psychosis, in which 'psychotic disorder may be conceptualised as the rare poor outcome of a common developmental phenotype characterised by persistence of psychometrically detectable sub-clinically psychotic experience'. They suggest that environmental risk factors, such as exposure to cannabis and social adversities, may account for the persistence of psychosis in some individuals.

These are radical conclusions, which represent a massive step forward from a traditional medical model view of psychotic disorders. They establish the existence of a psychosis continuum and the far greater prevalence of 'normal' self-resolving psychosis compared with psychotic disorder. However, the exclusively quantitative method and clinical focus reveal little about the personal meaning of the 'non-clinical' psychotic experiences in question, whether they relate to the concept of spiritual experience, and whether it is more accurate to regard them as 'sub-clinical' (i.e. mildly problematic) or 'benign psychosis' (positively constructive).

Alongside this, a smaller body of literature has developed which more specifically replicates and refines the comparisons made in my original study. Brett *et al.* (2009) has conducted a larger scale and more rigorous replication which is described elsewhere in this volume. While she found a similar picture of strong phenomenological comparisons and psychotic content in the experiences of her 'no need for care' group, she focused specifically on the associated appraisal and metacognitive processes implicated by Garety et al.'s (2007) model of psychotic disorder, discussed below. Andrew, Gray and Snowden (2008), and more recently Thornton (2009), describe more in-depth comparisons of clinical and non-clinical voice hearers. In both studies, the non-clinical groups experienced voices which were not associated with distress or psychopathology. Andrew drew on the spiritualist community for a sample of non-clinical voice hearers, and found that for most of this group, their voices were experienced as helpful and constructive in their lives, and provided them with a valued social role as a medium. Thornton elicited a broader sample of non-clinical voice hearers, including participants with diverse perspectives on their voices. She demonstrated that the non-clinical group had no significant symptoms of mental illness apart from their hallucinations. This group generally found their voices to be constructive, offering advice or reassurance, or at worst, trivial comments. One participant, for example, described how this voice reassured her when she had difficulties with other people, 'One message that comes over and over again is "They do not mean you any harm, it is just their way of doing things"'. By contrast, the patients' voices were generally more distressing, making negative comments about them, e.g. 'You don't belong here, you belong to us. You're useless, you fail everything' and 'You're scum, you should be dead'.

These studies support the interpretation of at least some non-clinical psychosis as 'benign', in that the non-clinical participants were generally comfortable with their voices and valued the experience of hearing them. Given that the individuals in question were not in any meaningful sense 'ill', it is a question of values rather than science as to whether we consider their experiences to be good or bad – but we need to acknowledge that many of them view their voices as benign.

Developmental Determinants of Outcome in Psychosis

There is now a substantial body of research evidence which demonstrates that psychotic disorder is associated with adverse developmental psychosocial factors such as childhood sexual abuse, bullying, neglect and alienation (reviewed in Read *et al.*, 2005). Bebbington *et al.* (2004), for example, in the second British National Morbidity Survey, found that childhood sexual abuse was associated with a 15-fold increase in risk of psychotic disorder.

Consistently with these broader findings, Andrew found that anxiety and depression in her sample of voice hearers was predicted by trauma history. Thornton found that voice related distress was specifically predicted by a history of childhood sexual abuse and disturbed attachment. Interestingly, the most significant parental attachment in her study was *paternal* care – participants who were distressed by their voices had more damaged relationships with their fathers (this echoes a similar finding from Read *et al.*, and challenges the convention of the schizophrenogenic mother).

Non-clinical voice hearers then, had lower levels of physical and sexual trauma, and more secure attachment histories than those who had received diagnoses. Nevertheless, there were indications that they had higher levels of non-sexual trauma than the normal population. Interestingly, in Thornton's qualitative study, some of the non-clinical voice hearers discussed the phenomenon, apparently well recognised amongst mediums, of beginning to hear voices as a consequence of a traumatic event:

> The reason what was happening to me is, apparently, it's quite common, I didn't know but a lot of mediums start working out of trauma. They say to you 'Are you a trauma medium?' And I go 'What does that mean?' and they say 'Did it come on because of trauma?' Now, the doctor said I was stressed when my Mum had the heart attack.

Both of these studies suggest that people who hear voices – benign or pathological – may have higher rates of trauma than normal, but that pathological voices are specifically associated with interpersonal and sexual trauma, which is unresolved. Patients in both studies reported active PTSD symptoms, which were not present in the non-patient voice hearers.

In the context of these specific comparisons and the broader literature establishing the relationship between trauma, attachment disturbance and psychosis, it is reasonable to propose that the tone and outcome of adult psychotic experiences is in part determined by developmental experience. This is developed further in the following section.

A Cognitive Model of Psychotic Disorder

The influential cognitive model of psychotic disorder proposed by Garety *et al.* (2001, 2007) synthesises a large body of research and theory, and provides several hypotheses of the relationship between trauma and psychotic disorder. On this model, vulnerability to psychosis is determined both by biological factors (genetic pre-disposition, early developmental insults) and adverse psychosocial developmental factors such as abuse, trauma and alienation. Vulnerability to psychosis leads to a set of possible 'cognitive dysfunctions', which generate anomalous experiences when the individual is under stress. Negative schematic models about the self or the world (themselves resulting from adverse developmental experiences), underlie psychotic appraisals of these experiences, for example in terms of malevolent external forces. Various related interpretative biases, such as a tendency to jump to conclusions, increase the likelihood of psychotic appraisals. Psychotic symptoms are maintained by adverse social factors such as a high expressed emotion environment or isolation, and by counterproductive coping strategies, including metacognitive strategies such as hypervigilance or rumination, and behaviours such as substance abuse and social avoidance (Figure 12.1).

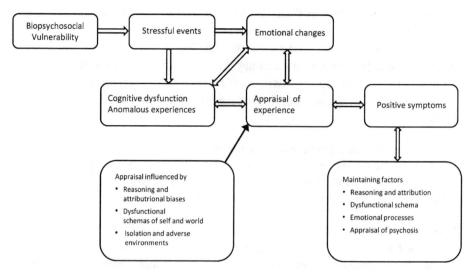

Figure 12.1   A cognitive model of the positive symptoms of psychosis (from Garety et al. 2001, 2007)

A fundamental concept in the cognitive approach to clinical phenomena is that distress does not necessarily follow from an event or an experience directly, but depends on how the individual makes sense of their experience – their appraisals. Furthermore, these appraisals themselves follow from underlying 'schemas' – sets of assumptions and ways of thinking about the self or the world, which have their roots in formative developmental experiences. In Garety's model, the role of negative schematic models of the self or the world in driving appraisal processes is seen as critical: 'earlier social adversity, such as social marginalisation, childhood loss or severe childhood trauma, may create an enduring cognitive vulnerability, characterised by negative schematic models of the self and the world that facilitate appraisal biases and low self-esteem'.

The validity of this model is well supported. Fowler *et al.* (2006), for example, provide direct evidence that, in both clinical and non-clinical populations, paranoia is associated with extreme negative schema, of 'self' as weak, vulnerable or inadequate, and of 'other' as devious, threatening or bad. Freeman *et al.* (2005) found that in virtual reality simulations in which participants encountered 'neutral' avatars, emotional disturbance and a negative view of self predicted paranoid responses. This paradigm controls the contents of the participant's virtual social experiences experimentally, explicating the specific effects of individual differences in appraisal.

In clinical practice, however, and in some of the studies reviewed earlier, it is clear that for many people with psychotic disorders, the contents of their psychotic experiences are unambiguously negative and distressing – voices are often self-attacking, undermining and shaming, for example. These experiences are probably made worse by appraisals, for example, of the voice's power and authority, but the distressing nature of the experience derives at least in part directly from these negative contents.

Within the cognitive model, the contents of psychotic experiences could be viewed either as the sequelae of earlier trauma, or as being driven by underlying schema. Morrison, Frame and Larkin (2003) suggest that in psychosis, 'flashback' memories of traumatic experiences are not recognised as post-traumatic phenomena, but instead are misattributed, for example to supernatural influences. On this view, unresolved traumatic memories generate flashback images and thoughts, which become the immediate content of psychotic experiences. Thus, voices may directly echo what a bully or an abuser used to say to the person, or 'made feelings' may echo actual bodily sensations in previous experiences.

Alternatively, the contents of psychotic experience could be understood as the output of active negative schematic models of the self or the world. These generate a stream of intrusive thoughts, which, especially if experienced with unusual salience and force, may become contents of anomalous experiences such as voices or paranoid delusions. Both possible mechanisms were investigated by Hardy *et al.* (2005), who found that in a sample of 75 people with psychotic disorders who heard voices, a direct association could be made between traumatic events and the contents of their voices for around 12% of the sample; while schematic links could be indentified in around 40%. These preliminary findings provide support for both hypothesised connections between trauma and psychotic disorder, and suggest that the indirect schema route is more common. Within a cognitive model of psychotic disorder then, distress can be viewed as following both from the negative contents of anomalous experiences, and from the ways in which the experiences are appraised. Underlying both kinds of process are traumatic memories, disturbed attachment processes and negative schemas.

By contrast, benign psychotic experiences involve anomalous experiences with more constructive and affirming content. By extension, we can suggest that they are appraised in more benign ways, and that both the contents and the appraisals originate in more adaptive schema, and probably in the absence of severe unresolved trauma. Common features of spiritual experience include a sense of being loved, watched over, protected, or guided; of a nurturing companionship, and a sense that 'all will be well'. Leaving aside more spiritual interpretations, these features strongly suggest the activation of schema related to secure attachments within loving relationships. This would be consistent with Thornton's findings of relatively low levels of trauma and secure attachments in her non-clinical voice hearers.

Interestingly, Brett *et al.* (2009), Andrew *et al.* (2008) and Thornton (2009) all failed to find differences in externalising appraisals between their clinical and non-clinical groups – most participants in each study believed that their voices were external and 'real'. These findings suggest that, against the predictions of the cognitive model, externalising *per se* is not a relevant factor in determining whether a psychotic experience is benign or distressing. Most psychotic experiences, benign or otherwise, involve an externalising appraisal – a sense that this is 'not me' and this in itself is probably not a significant factor in causing distress.

Salience Dysregulation Theory

One of the definitive features of psychosis is a sense of increased significance, meaning or 'salience' in experience; what James called the 'noetic quality' of mystical experience, and what is referred to by psychopathologists as 'delusional mood'. Current theoretical developments in biological psychiatry focus on this feature of 'salience dysregulation' (Kapur, 2003) as a core process in psychosis. The brain system implicated in this is the mesolimbic dopamine system, which becomes dysregulated at high levels of arousal or emotional disturbance such that – 'it fires and releases dopamine independent of cue and context, creating experiences of aberrant novelty and salience'. Dopamine dysregulation – 'the wind of the psychotic fire' – thus leads the individual to interpret their ongoing experiences as being deeply significant, which can lead to delusional explanations.

Salience is understood as signalling prediction error in the broader context of a more general control systems theory recently (and elegantly) explicated by Fletcher and Frith (2009). Based on acquired knowledge about the world, and analysis of incoming perceptual information, the brain generates detailed models of reality, part of which constitute ongoing conscious experience. These models are continually revised and updated in a hierarchy of perceptual and cognitive control systems. Lower level systems, for example, are concerned with details such as spatial positioning and fine motor activity, whereas higher levels systems are more concerned with beliefs, goals, values, self-perception, etc. On this view, lower level perceptual information is used to constantly test and update the internal model of reality being generated, and anything unexpected – an error in the prediction system (our knowledge of reality) – attracts attention, and is coded as 'salient' or significant. This leads to adjustment at some level of the hierarchy, for example to a perception, so that it fits our current model; or to a belief which forms part of the 'model', so that it fits new information. This process thus adjusts and maintains the goodness of fit of our internal models to reality. The more the internal model is challenged, the stronger the prediction error and the resulting salience signal, and the higher up the control system hierarchy the adjustment is required.

Under normal circumstances, our internal models fit the world well, as they have been developed through a lifetime's exposure to it, and consequently only require small lower level adjustments, or what we might consider normal learning, in an essentially 'self correcting' process. Fletcher and Frith suggest that 'In terms of this framework, the problem that leads to the positive symptoms of schizophrenia starts with false prediction errors being propagated upwards through the hierarchy. These errors require higher levels of the hierarchy to adjust their models of the world. However, as the errors are false, these adjustments can never fully resolve the problem. As a result, prediction errors will be propagated even further up the system to ever-higher levels of abstraction'.

On this model, false prediction errors arise because the system which signals error or 'salience' is dysregulated (because of deficits in the prefrontal cortical systems which regulate the system). If we are prepared to take the small step into considering benign psychosis as an adaptive rather than a 'sub-clinical' phenomena, we could suggest that salience dysregulation might at times be strategic and useful. The PSP model proposes that the emotional significance of benign psychosis is necessary for the process to successfully alter firmly held beliefs and values in a 'paradigm shift', and that this is a form of creativity. This clearly fits well with the idea that salience signals lead to cognitive re-organisation, and that this process is triggered by emotional disturbance, and is homeostatic and self-correcting. It differs from the salience dysregulation model, in that the PSP process is conceptualised as happening in a intelligent, selective way – key features of the anomalous experience are felt to be deeply meaningful, rather than a general sense of any random experiences being unusually salient. This might be better described as functionally altered salience – rather than anarchic dysregulation.

Salience dysregulation theory offers an explanation of why anomalous experiences occur in response to stress, why they feel significant and how this leads to belief change. What does it tell us about whether the process is self-limiting or self-perpetuating?

Self-Perpetuating or Self-Limiting Psychosis?

All of these models of psychosis include the concept that stress drives the process which leads to the production of anomalous experiences. From simple control system theory (Mansell, 2005), it is clear that for the process to be self-limiting, the triggering stress has to be reduced to below threshold by the process. The PSP model proposes that this is what happens in 'normal' benign psychotic experiences. These are rare events in most people's lives, occurring at unusual times such as life transitions, particularly adolescence, bereavement, etc. At such times, we are faced with higher order and potentially disabling emotional conflict, and our PSP system resolves this by generating a high salience 'psychotic experience' which allows us to see things differently and to move on. It is proposed that this process underlies Van Os' observation that: 'Subclinical psychotic experiences are prevalent, but mostly self-limiting and of good outcome'.

As we progress along the psychosis continuum, into the grey area between normal benign psychosis and psychotic disorder, we encounter the more extreme, but still benign experiences described in my earlier study, and by Brett, Andrews and Thornton. Many of these describe sequences of experience which occur frequently, and which can be relatively sustained, yet are not overwhelming. For these people, it seems, the process is not self-limiting in the way that normal spiritual experience is. Instead, it seems that their threshold for generating such experience is relatively low, and they are able to have relatively low intensity experiences. Mediums and spiritualists talk about developing 'sensitivity' which allows them to tune into their 'spirits'. This sensitisation is also seen in acute psychotic disorder, to the point that any stimulus can apparently trigger further psychotic experiences. In these situations, clinical experience suggests the need for a very peaceful, calm, unstimulating environment – a haven or asylum. Unfortunately, the NHS is not always able to provide such a context! Fletcher and Frith (2009) suggest that:

> a very small alteration in this mechanism, an alteration that we believe to be fundamental to schizophrenia, can push someone over the edge from a state in which perception/belief formation is altered but still self-correcting to a state in which even increasingly flexible and imaginative inferences no longer accommodate persistent, unreliable prediction error.

The Garety model suggests that, in addition to maladaptive coping strategies, emotional aspects of the social environment, such as critical and intrusive relationships, may help to maintain disorder through continuing stress and physiological arousal. Garety *et al.* (2007) observe that by contrast, supportive relationships should help to reduce anxiety and depression, and this may account for some of the widely observed non-specific benefits of therapies in psychosis.

Of course, for many spiritualists and mediums, there is a social context for their experiences in which they make sense and indeed are valued. This may be crucial in allowing them to contain and manage the experiences. One of Thornton's participants, for example, was an 'animal communicator' – she heard animals' thoughts as a voice in her head. She describes how 'I was really pleased that, when I actually discovered that, a few years ago, that "animal communication" was something. I didn't even know what the name meant "animal communication", I hadn't come across it [...] and came across it purely by chance. People actually want you to do this'. Non-clinical voice hearers in her sample who had disclosed to others about their experiences, all had social contexts where their voices were accepted and where other people had similar experiences. By comparison, the patients who heard voices had not discussed them with others, and did not know others who had similar experiences. Interestingly, within this group there was a more pathologising view of other people who heard voices: 'Yeah, I think it's a mental health problem, yeah, I think they're nuts [...] They're definitely mental in the head [...] I don't class myself as, I class myself as normal, me'.

In the domain of acute and florid psychotic disorder then, there is often no context which allows the acceptance and integration of experience. Instead, psychosis is socially punished through diagnosis and the intrusive apparatus of the mental health system (hospitalisation, compulsory medication, community treatment orders). In terms of the PSP model, this level of invalidation would be expected to lead to repeated cycles of the process, by keeping emotional arousal high.

A second route to stability suggested by the PSP model is avoidance of disconfirmation, either by avoidance of social situations or avoidance of self disclosure. This is self-evident in many cases of clinical disorder, and may be described in terms of 'negative symptoms'. It has also been reported by some of the benign psychosis cases in these studies, who are careful to keep their experiences to themselves, to avoid being pathologised.

A General Model of Psychosis

Most of the explanatory features of models of psychotic disorder seem to have strong application in making sense of benign psychosis, if the pathologising assumptions underlying the models are dropped. Figure 12.2 below sketches out a general model for benign and pathological psychosis, based on the original Garety *et al.* (2001) model.

Depending on the underlying 'unconscious contents', psychotic experiences triggered by emotional arousal can be either constructive and self-resolving, or destructive and self-perpetuating. These cycles will be influenced by the individual's appraisals (in turn following from underlying schema), their behavioural responses and the social responses from others if they disclose their experiences.

Summary

Clinically oriented biopsychosocial theories of psychotic disorder have made substantial progress since the original edition of this book in 2001. The principle

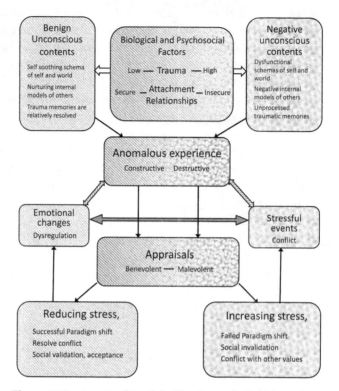

Figure 12.2 A general model of benign and clinical psychosis

that psychotic disorder is on a continuum with 'sub-clinical' psychotic phenotypes is effectively established by large scale, high quality, longitudinal, epidemiological research. The importance of developmental factors such as trauma and alienation in contributing to the development of later psychotic disorder is increasingly well established. The role of ongoing appraisals, interpretative biases, reasoning biases, metacognitions and other cognitive factors in contributing to distress is also widely accepted. These factors are now being linked with dopamine theory through the salience dysregulation hypothesis. These theories of psychotic disorder offer considerable insight into the understanding of benign psychosis, if we utilise the conceptual insights they provide, but instead of thinking about them as explaining a dysfunctional system which is broken, we think of them as describing a psychologically valuable function of the normal system.

Claridge and Beech (1994) discuss this distinction in terms of a debate between quasi-dimensional and fully dimensional models of the psychosis continuum (see Claridge, Chapter 5.). To some extent, this debate reflects a difference in underlying orientation and values as much as in interpretation of scientific findings (Jackson and Fulford, 1997, 2002). If we are concerned purely with the risk of a psychotic disorder developing, non-clinical psychotic experiences are bad news, and perhaps suggestive of a need for intervention. From a more spiritual perspective, they are associated with other valued characteristics such as being relatively intuitive, creative, sensitive and having a deep-seated faith, which may be seen as more important than whether the person is at increased risk of psychotic disorder.

This difference in orientation is also expressed (and perhaps in part derives from) a difference in preferred level of explanation and methodological approach. The 'benign psychosis' view arises from in-depth narrative/qualitative studies which focus on the personal meaning of the experiences for the individuals concerned. The sub-clinical perspective is drawn from rigorous quantitative research exploring statistical associations between cognitive, biological and social variables associated with psychopathology. Each approach is powerful in a different way and each is relatively blind to the findings of the other.

The clinical implications of the extended model suggested in Figure 12.2 particularly concern the role of social feedback (including the process of diagnosis and therapy) in the individual's trajectory through the problem solving process. To slow down or reverse the positive feedback cycle of failed paradigm shifting in psychosis, other than through biochemical means, the model suggests that the individual needs to find a sense of resolution which effectively reduces their level of stress. This indicates the potential for clinical interventions which increase stress, either through invalidating the individual's experience, or through sometimes unavoidable measures such as compulsory hospitalisation, to be iatrogenic. At the same time, it suggests the potential value of cognitive-behavioural therapy for psychosis and similar approaches, in which anomalous experiences are normalised where possible, and an attempt is made to understand the way that they are embedded in the individual's values, goals and needs. Lukoff (2007a) provides a useful review of spiritually based interventions in this area, which aim to reduce stress using alternatives to medication.

For floridly psychotic patients, experiencing an overwhelming and sometimes terrifying sense of the spiritual, there is a need for sensitive therapeutic interventions which involve respect for the personal significance of such experiences. For those of us fortunate enough not to suffer from psychotic disorders, reflection on the intimacy of the relationship between madness and inspiration may help us to approach the unusual experiences of others with the sensitivity and respect they require.

13

Transformative Crises

Caroline Brett

Introduction

The view that psychosis can be understood as a transformative crisis has been put forward by theorists including Jung (1983), Laing (1967), Perry (1989, 1999), and Grof and Grof (1989, 1991), to name only the most prominent. Their work shares a common theme of seeing the experiences of psychosis as contributing to a process with, at least potentially, a positive direction. In this sense, psychosis is seen not just as meaningful and psychologically understandable, as in most contemporary psychological formulations, but also as purposeful. The main differences between these views relate to whether they apply to all or only some kinds of psychosis: whether they involve a distinction being made between psychotic breakdown and transformative crisis.

Because of limited empirical work in this area, many questions still remain about the kinds of presentations which are indicative of a transformative crisis, and how more chronic forms of psychosis differ in their aetiology or process. A principle question to be explored concerns the relative usefulness of aiming to distinguish psychotic experiences from spiritual or transformative crisis, compared with the usefulness of learning about transformative aspects of experiences, however they may be described. One perspective is that it is important to differentiate particular forms of spiritual crisis from psychosis as a mental disorder, on the basis that the current views of and treatment approaches to psychosis are inappropriate and damaging to people undergoing a spiritual crisis. Other perspectives include a wider range of processes within the terminology of transformative crisis, or suggest that there is no difference *in kind* between 'psychotic' and transformative crisis.

Perhaps it is helpful to keep in mind the social construction of labels such as 'spiritual crisis' and 'psychosis', which reflect the context and the outcomes of experiences as much as anything inherently different about the processes involved. Clarke and Jackson in the current volume both emphasise a common process which may result in varying outcomes depending on many factors. The research described

Psychosis and Spirituality: Consolidating the New Paradigm Second Edition   Edited by Isabel Clarke
© 2010 John Wiley & Sons, Ltd.

in the current chapter aimed to examine how those people with a benign outcome of psychotic-like experiences (PLEs) differed from those who were distressed by and showed functional incapacity as a result of their experiences, as well as clarifying the ways in which they did not differ. The ways in which the core experiences contributed to a transformative process are explored with reference to the existing literature. The aforementioned social construction of the term 'psychotic' will be taken as read and henceforth the inverted commas denoting this will be omitted.

Aims of the Research and other Considerations

The concept of transformative crisis is necessarily subjective and value-laden: there can or perhaps should be no objective criteria by which an individual may be judged to have undergone a significant transformation. People are changing all the time, and perhaps no single event or process can be established as a causative factor. Some events or processes involve or may precipitate more change than others, and yet over what period of a person's life should we look for the transformative impact or integration of a set of experiences? As such, the current research was not designed to compare those having negotiated a transformative crisis with those who have suffered a psychotic breakdown, and participants were not selected on the basis of having undergone a transformative crisis. All the participants were selected on the basis of having anomalous experiences usually associated with psychosis (PLEs). An examination of their reports of their experiences led to the identification of transformative elements within their experiences, by their own accounts. The extent to which experiences cut across the divisions between those in need of care and those without, as well as the factors associated with benign outcome, will be reported.

The research elicited both quantitative and qualitative data to develop a close-grained investigation of the intimate phenomenology associated with psychosis and transformative crisis. It is worth noting that, because the data elicited pertained to anomalous experiences, and appraisals and responses to them, the qualitative analysis emphasises forms of psychosis characterised by more unusual experiences rather than non-bizarre paranoid delusions (e.g. involving persecution by acquaintances). People with these beliefs were interviewed, but often reported few unusual experiences and therefore generated less data. For this reason, the report may appear to omit a large proportion of the kinds of psychotic narrative commonly seen within mental health services. It is beyond the scope of the current chapter to explore much of the relationships and distinctions between mundane paranoia and the more florid altered states discussed below; nevertheless it seems important to acknowledge the differences.

Samples and Recruitment

The research is based on two samples: one group who had received a diagnosis of a psychotic disorder, who were recruited through mental health services; and another group who reported PLEs but who had never received treatment for or diagnosis of a psychotic disorder. The differentiation on the basis of diagnostic status was used as an imperfect proxy for distress and functional impairment versus benign outcome, in the context of PLEs. Some of those in the undiagnosed group may have had periods of distress or difficulty functioning, but for none of them had this become so severe that they had required mental health service input. The association between 'need for care' and diagnostic status is imperfect because there are many reasons that impact on a person's receipt of diagnosis, including their social circumstances, responsibilities, and resources, attitudes towards mental health care, and the accessibility of other forms of support and care during difficult times.

The diagnosed (D) group ($n = 35$) was recruited through an inpatient unit for young people in their first or second episode of psychosis, and an outpatient psychology service for people with 'treatment-resistant psychotic symptoms'. The undiagnosed (UD) group ($n = 36$) was recruited through various online, written and personally presented advertisements and word of mouth, focussing on particular interest groups such as new religious movements, and new age community groups. Participants were required to have experienced PLEs for a minimum of 5 years, to lessen the chance that they might require mental health input in the future. They all lived independently and showed good social adaptation. The qualitative analysis also includes data from 20 further participants who were using a mental health service for young people considered to be at risk of psychosis (AR; $n = 20$).

All the participants reported having at least one of the following kinds of experiences: thought transmission/telepathy (self to others, or others to self); thought withdrawal; experiences of being controlled by someone or something external; other passivity experiences of loss of control over movements; ideas of reference of various kinds (e.g. receiving messages in things you hear or see written down; 'synchronicities' where internal and external events appear uncannily connected; feeling that things people say and other events are directed at you); experiences of controlling others with thoughts or causing things to happen with the mind; hearing one's own thoughts out loud in the head; hearing voices, music or other sounds that others cannot hear. For all the participants, it was necessary that they had had these experiences either intermittently but often, or for an extended period of time, and that they were not the result of drug-intoxication.

This was a relatively small self-selected sample recruited from the south of England and may be unrepresentative of the wider pool of 'undiagnosed' individuals with PLEs. Nevertheless, by dint of the shared phenomenology with those considered to have a psychotic disorder, the sample provided salient information for the understanding of this area of human experience.

Data Collection and Analysis

Participants took part in an in-depth interview about their experiences. A semi-structured format was used to elicit data that could be compared quantitatively across participants, as well as including open-ended questions that generated responses for qualitative analysis (see Brett *et al.*, 2007 for a description of the development of the AANEX interview schedule and more information about the scoring methods).

The initial section of the AANEX comprises an inventory of 40 anomalous experiences, for which participants were rated on the basis of frequency/duration of each experience across the lifetime, and for presence at each of several time-points: e.g. the first onset and the time of the interview. The second section of the AANEX elicits how the person made sense of their experiences, the context of their life at the time, their emotional, cognitive and behavioural responses, and what they perceived as the acceptability of their experiences to others in their social group. Further questions ask about the salience of experiences for the person's view of themselves and the world.

The quantitative analysis involved multiple logistic regression analyses to identify odds ratios and significance levels as a way of expressing the relationship between different variables. The qualitative analysis utilised interpretative phenomenological analysis to process taped and transcribed interviews.

Results

Phenomenological Analysis: Different Types of Experiences

The AANEX inventory provided the basis for two principal components analyses which identified clusters of co-occurring experiences: one examined the co-occurrence of experiences within individuals across their lifetime (the 'trait' analysis) and one examined the co-occurrence of experiences at any particular time (the 'state' analysis). The process and details of these analyses are reported in full elsewhere (Brett, Peters and McGuire, unpublished data). This statistical approach is best viewed as exploratory, because it involves judgements regarding the 'best' available statistical solution: expectations were therefore brought to bear on the data based upon existing literature and the qualitative analysis of the dataset.

The best solution for the 'trait' analysis identified five factors of experiences, whereas the 'state' analysis was summarised in four factors. The two sets of factors coming from the trait and state analyses were partially overlapping, suggesting that the traits could be understood as a tendency to experience particular states, although there was some variation. The schematic lists below summarise the anomalous experiences loading onto the TRAIT and *State* factors.

Noetic largely overlapping with MEANING/REFERENCE:

- Spontaneously receiving some knowledge as a revelation or insight
- Spontaneous sense of a mission or task that must be performed
- 'Peak experience' of peace, energy or lightness profoundly different from normal range of emotions

- 'Reference' experiences: words seen or heard or other things perceived in world reflect in an uncanny or striking way the thoughts or concerns of the individual, sometimes in a symbolic or oblique way
- Altered state in which perceptions lack a sense of boundary marked by the physical body
- Unusually speeded thought processes
- Loss or changes in sense of time

Mental Boundary largely overlapping with FIRST RANK SYMPTOMS
Reduced boundary between mental events of person and those of other people:

- Receiving others thoughts
- One's own thoughts received by others
- One's own thoughts stopped, blocked or taken away by something/someone
- 'Reference' experiences (see above)
- Hearing voices
- Sense of being monitored or watched by invisible agency

DISSOCIATIVE/PERCEPTUAL partly overlapping with *Daze* and *Anomalous Perception* (see below):

- Loss of emotions (numbness)
- Depersonalisation
- Oversensitivity
- Changes in hearing so that noises seem louder, more intrusive or distorted
- Feeling cut-off from other people and things around
- Out of Body experiences
- Being emotionally hypersensitive and hyper-reactive

Anomalous Perception partly overlapping with PARANORMAL/HALLUCI-NATORY:

- Altered perception: things not ordinarily felt or seen are experienced visually or physically, including energetic and paranormal phenomena
- 'Derealisation': world seems unreal or profoundly different in some way
- Involuntary/spontaneous physical movements

Additional experiences in TRAIT cluster PARANORMAL/HALLUCINATORY:

- Precognitive experiences (premonitions)
- Causing things to happen or controlling others through the mind
- Being controlled by something or someone external

Daze partly overlapping with COGNITIVE/ATTENTION

Altered state characterised by sense of incapacity and unreality:

- Derealisation
- Depersonalisation
- Oversensitivity to external stimuli
- Difficulty processing information and organising behaviour
- Thought pressure and distractability contribute to decreased ability to control flow and direction of thoughts

TRAIT cluster 'COGNITIVE/ATTENTION':

- Difficulty understanding spoken language
- Taking turns of phrase literally
- Disorientation
- Heightened distractability
- Disturbance of the train of thought by irrelevant or intrusive thoughts
- Frequent loss of train of thought
- 'lost automatic skills' where things that normally could be done without much attention now require all the person's attention and have to be taken one step at a time
- Inability to do two things at once
- Attention getting captivated by irrelevant details of the environment
- Mixed-up emotions that cannot be identified
- A sense of impending doom or disturbing heaviness and lack of energy

What Kinds of Experiences or Contextual Factors are Associated With a Benign Outcome?

Phenomenological Comparisons. Participants from both groups reported experiences of all types, and there were no differences between the groups in terms of the lifetime number of experiences contributing to the MEANING/REFERENCE, FIRST RANK SYMPTOMS or DISSOCIATIVE/PERCEPTUAL clusters. However, the UD group on average reported fewer COGNITIVE/ATTENTION experiences, and more experiences contributing to the PARANORMAL/HALLUCINATORY factor across the lifetime, compared with the D group.

Existing evidence suggests that PLEs occur on a continuum of severity across the population (van Os *et al.*, 2000). Another analysis was conducted to look at differences in the severity or frequency of particular kinds of experiences between the groups, to see whether the D group, for example, had more intense or persistent episodes of the same types of experiences. It was found that the D group reported having MEANING/REFERENCE and FIRST RANK SYMPTOMS experiences with significantly greater frequency and/or duration than the UD group, on average. There were no differences in the intensity of DISSOCIATIVE/PERCEPTUAL or

PARANORMAL/HALLUCINATORY experiences between the groups. This suggests that the experiences or processes contributing to the MEANING/REFERENCE and FIRST RANK SYMPTOMS trait clusters may be more difficult to manage when they happen more often or for longer periods of time.

These analyses took the average frequency ratings for each group; however, it was also found that 45% of the UD group reported MEANING/REFERENCE experiences with equivalent or greater intensity compared with the average of the D group. A smaller subset of 16% had FIRST RANK SYMPTOMS with equivalent or greater intensity than the average of the D group. This suggests that prolonged episodes of extreme psychotic-like phenomena are not always indicative of a need for care, but that it may be more common to end up in mental health care when experiencing persistent loss of mental boundaries or hearing voices and feeling monitored by external entities.

The analysis above aimed, as far as possible, to separate out the structure of experiences from the person's appraisal of them and their responses to them. The next section summarises some of the contextual factors that distinguished the UD and D groups. Scores were calculated for the different *state* factors, that the analyses could control for the different types of experience that the individual was reporting at any particular timepoint in the interview.

Comparison of Contextual Factors and Personal Responses. Individuals from both groups reported having experiences starting around times of significant change, isolation, crisis or impasse and drug use. This corroborates the contexts suggested by Grof and Grof (1991, e.g.) to be common triggers for the onset of PLEs in transformative crises, as well as those situations viewed as stressors which commonly trigger psychotic illness (Corcoran *et al.*, 2003).

It was also found that the kinds of experiences summarised by the *Noetic* and *Anomalous Perception* categories were more likely to occur after periods of focus on spiritual practices (such as chanting or meditations of various kinds), or after the person had come into contact with a social group within which anomalous experiences were discussed, accepted or even encouraged. *Noetic* experiences were also associated with drug use. The UD group was relatively more likely to have started having experiences in the context of spiritual practices or congruent social contexts, but this was explained statistically by the preponderance of *Noetic* and *Anomalous Perception* experiences at the time-points being discussed. This might suggest that the experiences in these clusters may be associated with a particular process or aetiology, relatively distinct from that underlying the *Mental Boundary* or *Daze* anomalies. However, the UD group was also more likely to have had their experiences from childhood, independently of the type of experience.

Another significant difference between those people who ended up with a diagnosis and those who did not was that the former group were more likely to conclude that some other agency was causing the experiences they were having. In particular, appraising experiences as being caused by other people predicted D group membership. People in the UD group did make supernatural and personalising appraisals; nevertheless, making a more 'personalising' appraisal was predictive of greater distress about the experience(s), across the groups.

Space does not permit a full report of the factors found to predict distress about an experience[1]; however, in an analysis which entered all the independently predictive variables into a model to determine which accounted best for the level of anomaly related distress, it was found that appraising anomalies within a 'spiritual' framework (i.e. to do with meaning in life, or some higher order or power) independently predicted lower levels of distress, regardless of the nature of the anomalies (and across the groups). The other protective factors were a higher level of perceived social support and/or understanding regarding the anomalies, and having a higher level of perceived control over their occurrence. However, although the UD group reported higher perceived control than the D group, the average rating for perceived control was 'minimal' (2 on a scale of 1–5). The score for perceived social support rated the extent to which the person felt that other people they knew would understand what they were experiencing (or might have experienced something similar themselves), compared with feeling that they would be better off keeping quiet about them.

Looking at the person's style of response to their experiences, it was found that higher attempted control was predictive of greater distress. The UD group were less likely to try to control or suppress thoughts or experiences, to try to distract themselves or to act on the basis of their experiences; conversely, they were more likely to respond in a neutral way (i.e. trying to neither prevent nor pursue the experiences).

Noetic experiences were associated with an increased odds of making a 'spiritual' appraisal. In other words, participants were likely to interpret experiences of reduced self-world boundaries, ideas of reference and spontaneous 'insights' as reflecting processes involving some higher order or force, or to do with a search for meaning in life, irrespective of diagnostic status. Higher *Noetic* scores were also predictive of a lower likelihood of giving a psychological appraisal, which contributes to the picture of these experiences as inherently pointing to something beyond themselves, rather than being easily amenable to psychological reduction. People with *Noetic* experiences were less likely to report avoidant responses and more likely to act on the basis of their experiences.

How are PLEs Implicated in Transformative Crisis?

While the analyses reported above suggest that certain appraisal and response styles differentiated the two groups, the following analysis looks in more detail at the transformative aspects of the phenomena being discussed.

---

[1] A more comprehensive report of the quantitative analyses can be found in Brett *et al.*, 2007.

Changes in Sense of Self and World: Associations With Particular Experiences

Questions at the end of the AANEX interview enquired about whether the experiences discussed had altered the way the participant understood themselves and the world.

Changes in Sense of Self. Only five of the 91 participants reported that their experiences had had no impact on their understanding of their life or their view of themselves. A perception that the experiences were implicated in a growth process of learning or evolution was present in the accounts of some participants in all groups, including the AR group who were voluntarily seeking help regarding their experiences and had started having PLEs in the last year. For those individuals that held this view, it was something which helped them to tolerate and cope with sometimes intense and disturbing experiences, because there was a sense that it was in the service of some purpose.

> I still feel I've learned a lot....these things, they did all come together into a process of something which did change me fundamentally, and I did learn how to pray like a Muslim ... and how to remember the one thing that is really important, which is to have faith in something that is unbelievable ... I hope that what I've learned from them will continue. I've got to cling to the view that it's a positive experience, when I'm being told everyday by doctors and nurses that I should feel sorry for myself. (18 years, D).

Two frequently expressed and inter-related themes consisted of a shift in the concept of the self: one comprised a shift from a self-image as a physical or psychological being, towards one as a spiritual being. Participants described being in touch with an aspect of self that is infinite and sometimes a concomitant detachment from identification with particular thoughts, feelings or concerns. Experiences like this were therefore 'decentering' in that they loosened fixed ideas about identity and limitations and opened up the possibility of a new sense of self.

Noetic phenomena were often reported as bringing inherent wisdom, or an experience of transcendent aspects of the self, which had a quality of being irreducibly convincing. The non-dual view was sometimes part of this, as were 'insights' into the importance of looking after oneself and others, and the Earth. For some people, this was associated with identifying themselves with various archetypal figures such as Mary, Eve or Christ, which usually brought confusion and distress in the longer term. Some felt that the information had come from other sources:

> Well one time I was meditating and it was off weed as well. It was a release ... and suddenly I felt a burst of power into my room, it wasn't strong, it was releasing, in the sense that it stopped my thoughts; and it did speak but that could have been my mind playing tricks on me, so I won't give you that as evidence ... it felt like aliens had come and done something to me, but really and truly my subconscious had opened up to bare knowledge that's just been stuck in there forever (19 years, D).

The affective component of the *Noetic* state, the experience of 'spiritual elation' was often described in terms of love, unity and beauty. These feelings were universal to all three groups, often alongside other more disturbing experiences, and were described as bringing an expanded sense of self and universe, and of hope and meaning in life. A proportion of the UD group described a process through which they moved on from feelings of low self-esteem, isolation or insignificance after making positive appraisals of their experiences, which introduced an expanded self-concept and sense of increased potential. Another theme among those who reported *Noetic* experiences was a sense of atonement or purification.

The second related theme involved a newly developed appreciation of the essential connectedness of the self with other people, and the rest of existence. Anomalous experiences (particularly reference phenomena and experiences of altered boundaries and causation such as telepathic, receptivity, activity and passivity experiences) were taken as incontrovertible evidence of an inherent connectedness between oneself and other people, and between one's thoughts and feelings and events in the 'external' world. Closely related was a non-dual view of the self, in which distinctions between self and world are seen as relative and illusionary.

The implications of non-dual worldviews seem to be important to the impact of and the sense made out of psychotic experiences. For example, an individual's experience of 'ideas of reference' can be vastly different depending on the worldview that provides the frame of reference. As Peter Chadwick has described in his chapter in the first edition of this volume, it is a short but significant step from '. . .thinking that these coincidences were magically, paranormally or cosmically engineered, a somewhat mystical view. . .' to, '[inferring] that they (surely) must be engineered by people – a psychotic view'. (Clarke, 2001: p. 82).

The contrast between these ways of experiencing *Noetic* or *Mental Boundary* states was demonstrated clearly in the data set. Many of the participants in the UD group described either arriving at or bringing to their experiences, a view of reality in which the erosion of boundaries between and evidence of intimate connectedness between 'inner' and 'outer' was normal. This also links with Clarke's emphasis on the 'both/and' logic of transliminal states: that an individual can understand the experience of seeing personally relevant messages in advertising billboards with exquisitely synchronous timing as *both* the magic of cosmic guidance, *and* a reflection of their own subconscious on their perception of ambiguous information in the world. The condition of being comfortable with this paradox seemed to enable a less emotionally aroused and more adaptive response to the experience of anomalies.

The erosion of a sense of separation was often described as something emotionally positive and valued by the person.

> . . .we're just isolated, skin-encapsulated egos, in a scientific world view and that is terrible for the individual and the culture. And it's such a vast sense of relief for me to find that intelligence in some way extended outside my own ego. Always a vast sense of relief, even if it's scary. (51 years, UD).

People experiencing *Mental Boundary* phenomena sometimes reported feeling positive about their increased perceptiveness, or else they valued the sense of connection and oneness with others. However, this was not universal, and some people made statements suggesting that the experience of reduced separation between self and others can feel like an erosion of personal integrity.

> but picking up from all these people that don't understand and don't have this feeling means that I get out of touch with what was essentially myself. So I lose the capacity sometimes to understand ... that is dreadful, you know (62 years, D).

It was notable that in the accounts of those participants who had received a diagnosis of psychosis, there were more common reports that the experiences had changed the sense of self negatively, in terms of loss of previous self-concepts, feelings of being abnormal, confusion or helplessness in the face of ongoing experiences or the kind of isolation from others that the process had brought. Others talked about the need for time for recovery, and the difficulties of managing the impact of the experiences on the self:

> Basically, I've just been nursing myself over the last 9 years, I've been withdrawn and just trying to recover because it's like a huge ... changeover ... and I'm really only starting to get it together now – going in a new direction (52 years, D).
>
> I think they were like, hitting rock bottom and I had to get myself back up, so it was useful that I decided to do that ... after the relapse was when I was trying to put the pieces back together, that was still difficult. It's much better now (18 years, D).

The 'connecting' experiences of reduced boundaries and increased meaningfulness were also often linked in a positive sense with the sense that events were occurring in a purposeful way, as if according to some intelligence.

> ... well, I started taking risks more, because I felt that, because there was this knowledge of this interconnectedness, well, I felt that strong sense of faith that despite whatever odds we were up against, circumstances would unfold the way we wanted them to. And that did prove to be the case, we were in the Sahara and came up against tremendous difficulties, and we remarkably got through them (32 years, UD).

Of course, it is easy to see the connections between this 'pronoia' and its flip-side, paranoia, which may lead people into a state of intense fear and disability. Perhaps it is relevant that paranoia, which often reflects areas of shame or guilt, does not seem to involve the same shift in self-concept associated with pronoia. Sometimes, however, both sorts of interpretations were seen in the same person.

Participants also described an emerging sense of purpose in life, or awareness that the individual has something to contribute to the world, even if this is not yet clear:

> They've made me think, there is something within me that needs to be unleashed; something that needs to have its place in the world ... I have something to offer that no others can offer (19 years, AR).

Changes in World-View.   Only seven participants reported that their experiences had had no impact on their view of the world; notably none came from the UD group. Many participants in both the clinical and non-clinical groups said that their anomalous experiences had caused them to move away from believing in a purely material world. This is a clear example of the development of new metaphysical beliefs in response to anomalies incongruent with a previous world view.

> Now I look upon those experiences as an illness [voices etc], but I'm reluctant to write off my experience of God as an illness. The existence of a spiritual side to the universe; the existence of God, and the potential of going towards God inside of people. Physical laws are not the whole story (28 years, D).

One major theme was of the perception of unity within things, which reflected the sense of the connectedness of the self with the rest of existence described above, and was related to the same sorts of anomalies that reflect alterations in sense of boundary, agency and also meaning.

Several of the D participants, and two UD participants described experiences of passivity, including a sense of an external presence, and feeling an external influence on their thoughts or behaviour, which was interpreted as experiencing 'God'. Passivity experiences seemed to affect people by changing their conception of the control they have over their lives, and suggesting the existence of intelligent external agencies, which ranged from God to demons, aliens, angels or other immaterial beings.

Other changes to world-view included the existence of life after death, revealed by *Anomalous Perception* experiences such as voices, visual experiences of seeing ghosts, out of body experiences and a variety of energetic experiences. Many participants spoke of perceiving reality in terms of energy as a more basic reality that lay behind what is normally perceived. All of these themes cut across the clinical–non-clinical spectrum, corroborating that externalising appraisals do not define psychotic disorder. For example, two D and one UD participant described experiencing powerful winds, a feeling of burning and/or a voice speaking to them, which they interpreted within a Christian framework as evidence of God or the Holy Spirit.

Conversion-Type Processes.   The transformative process described by many can be associated with the phenomena of religious conversion, as suggested by Jackson in this volume (p. 140). A related theme which arose in the analysis involved a process of searching that the individual was involved in: a sense that there was more to life than the life they were living.

> . . . at the time I was flitting between, my god, what is the point? Why do people carry on? I was doing a job I hate, I'm not doing the things I'm meant to be doing, I don't see why I'm struggling on. I think perhaps it was something I needed to use and believe in cos I was searching desperately for a purpose, for a reason behind it all (24 years, AR).

Religious/spiritual conversion-type phenomena were described by 48% of the current sample: 21 UD participants, 17 D participants, and six AR participants (when cognitive and emotional shifts, involving reorientation to some divine or transcendent reality, are taken as the criteria).

When the time-scale of the conversions was examined, it was found that the clinical and non-clinical groups clearly diverged on this dimension. Sudden conversion phenomena (i.e. experiences of sudden cognitive shifts characterised by periods of extreme anomalies) were described by four UD participants, 13 D participants and three AR participants. In contrast, 17 UD participants described some kind of lifelong or gradual change of beliefs and experiences, compared with only four of the D group, and three of the AR group. In these accounts, the experiences represented either intermittent episodes characterised by cognitive shifts, but building upon a previous orientation towards the 'spiritual'; or the experiences developed gradually to a level of intensity that engendered a significant cognitive or emotional shift, but one which fell short of sudden conversion from complete atheism or agnosticism to full belief.

It was artificial to divide the accounts in this way, because they are better viewed as falling on a continuum. However, it was noticeable that the gradual shifts preponderated in the UD group, and sudden shifts were more common in the D group. This suggested that variation in pre-morbid world-view and the speed and magnitude of the process may contribute to the variation in coping and integration of the experiences by the different participants. For example, those participants who already had access to non-dual or other metaphysical world-views that could encompass PLEs had less difficulty coping with intensification of their experiences when they occurred.

Difficulties Associated with Transformative Aspects. Several aspects of appraisal and response seemed to be associated with difficulties and negative repercussions in the context of the experiences described above. One factor involved an interpretation of PLEs as evidence of special powers particular to the individual, rather than universal dimensions of experience potentially available to anyone. Another factor involved an attachment to pleasant experiences such as the anomalous affective states, or other experiences that were evaluated positively such as insights, or reference experiences. When these states ended, the person became distressed or confused, feeling that something had gone wrong or been lost. In general, a period of doubt and depression often seemed to follow very 'expansive' states, both in the clinical and non-clinical groups, and differences in life circumstances and social support may have played an important role at these times in determining how well the individual was able to cope with them.

Another factor stemmed from conflicts arising in the social environment, because of the individual feeling compelled to 'preach' to other people or behaving in other disinhibited ways.

I tried to be extra nice to people. But I had rows with people, I tried to tell her about God. I just feel it that she don't have peace inside of her, I could feel it when they not honest, they don't have peace, you know. When they honest, then they are relaxed . . . I did need to tell people to sort their lives out, to read the bible and find out what's good for them. Now I am absolutely depressed cos I've got no job, I'm in this hospital for weeks, and I don't know why these things happen to me (32 years, D).

Others became very intolerant of negative thoughts in themselves, or negative actions by other people. This was linked to attempts to control their own thoughts and experiences, or other people, and an associated sense of failure, frustration and distress.

Helpful Factors

The data suggest that more intermittent experiences increase the likelihood of functional adaptation to PLEs; however, within the UD group there was also a subset of individuals who had experienced prolonged and intense episodes of psychotic-like altered states. Some phenomenological differences have also been identified in terms of more benign types of PLE; however, counterexamples within the UD group indicate that distinctions cannot be made on phenomenological grounds alone.

Participants were asked about things that had helped them cope with experiences. Some involved reducing general emotional distress and maintaining a good level of self-care. Other factors provided a helpful frame of reference within which to interpret the experiences, or supported self-esteem and social inclusion through normalisation.

Social Support.   Social support was a predominant theme. People talked about the value of trusted friends who could just be with them and do normal things. Of particular importance were like-minded others who could relate to the experiences the person was having. These were a specific source of help through the normalising effect, which protects self-esteem and may maintain social integration. The opportunity to talk about things with others may be containing and enhance the acceptance of experiences by the person.

It's crucial to actually talk. That alone, to talk to someone who isn't going to be heavy . . . judgemental stuff. It's so difficult to walk around with this stuff in your head. When I was so confused, and lost my perception of who I was, it really relieved me to have that girl talk to me and confirm that I was on a spiritual trip (45 years, UD).

At points of intense altered states, some participants reported being aware that others around them were not in the same state, which got in the way of taking on board others' input. However, very often 'others' input' consists of concern about the individual and their behaviour, which, though well-intentioned, may not help a person who is not in control of the experiences they are having. Those people in the UD group who had been through extended episodes of intense crisis had all been in circumstances where other people looked after their basic needs for sometimes months at a time, or where they had been able to live alone in nature with the means to manage their basic needs. For example, one person had lived in Wales in a tipi, whereas another had lived in a caravan in a field for several months. Another participant had been looked after in a shared house, whereas another was looked after for three months by his parents. In time, these individuals had felt able to begin to either start to take over their own cooking and cleaning, or to start to integrate with others again.

Some individuals, only in the UD group, described finding help from people able to offer specific informed guidance: including teachers or gurus, elders who had had their own experiences of a similar nature, spiritual healers, and anthroposophical doctors. One participant talked about finding a healer with particular experience of altered states:

> I went to see this spiritual healer, and he confirmed that I had opened my third eye, and I was perceiving lots of different energies. I asked him about the darker energies and what to do about them. He took me through something to help close down the third eye to a manageable level – he did something as well, and showed me how to visualise the third eye closing down, and told me that when I feel the dark energy there, to send loads of love to it, to whatever was in and around my being. So I started working with these techniques and it did help, the telepathic experiences were less disorientating and after about 3 months I was back to normal (21 years, UD).

Another talked about the support he found within his own family:

> So the fact that I had that family and that cultural support whereby there were other people in my life, of the older generation, or the generation above that, who I came across, who told me, 'Yes, this is normal, this is normal human evolution; great thinkers go through this. They will be told they're crazy and lots of people won't understand you, and don't worry about it.' So that's helped a lot (27 years, UD).

Integration of Experiences into a Changed Framework of Understanding. Participants talked about how frameworks to understand their experiences, which sometimes developed years after the initial onset of the experiences, helped to contain the experiences, and allowed an integration with 'everyday' life. Some found these through social networks, others through more formal involvement in schools of yoga, xi gong or other energy systems, Wicca, Tarot, Reiki, religious groups, etc. The medical model offered by psychiatric services was reported to be helpful by a proportion of the D group: this framework offers a way of explaining experiences that does not entail any shift in the person's perspective on the world. However, it may entail a shift in perspective towards the self (e.g. as being vulnerable or abnormal), perhaps despite an emphasis on the role of stress in causing experiences, coupled with a strong normalising approach.

I think, knowing that, anybody could get sick, that I am not the only one that this has happened to, has helped me a little bit, in forgetting this issue (24 years, D).

Personal Insight.   Some participants spoke about the way that they had found their own meaning in experiences, often facilitated by diary-keeping, reading around the area or just an ongoing personal process of reflection. This appears to reflect the irreducible aspect of such experiences in terms of their integration with one's emotional life and sense of self. Coming to an understanding or towards resolution of emotional, psychological or practical issues alters the experience of anomalies, as part of the whole life experience. At the same time, the experience of anomalies can be a crucial prompt towards doing this work.

[talking about previously hidden drug addiction] Telling my family, freeing myself from it, telling loads of people; instead of having this mask; lift this mask and show people who I was, and who I'm going to be. It was churning inside me, if that man hadn't said something [referring to voice experience], I would have continued in the same way (35 years, D).

This process often reflected a broader attitude of *learning from experience*. Seeing events, including traumatic ones and anomalous experiences, as learning experiences seemed to be helpful. Taking the perspective that the process could increase self-knowledge created a sense of meaningfulness and hope in the face of challenging experiences, and could also foster an approach of acceptance of new or unusual experiences.

The dimension of *acceptance* was explicitly cited as a helpful factor by several participants, who described a belief that their own openness to their experiences facilitated a good outcome. Potentially, it can also be understood to underlie the value of other factors such as normalisation through social support, and clarity through the development of an explanatory framework or narrative: these factors support the acceptance of the experiences, in contrast to a response of resistance, denial, or ruminative over-involvement. The concept of 'faith' also emerged, which is interpreted as a form of generalised trust that facilitates openness to experiences.

Whatever you do, don't try to stop it, the more you resist the worse it gets . . . I guess I'm talking about the heavy crisis type thing (45 years, UD).
    Well, I think just, having an open mind, you know . . . as opposed to having a resistance or indoctrination that has caused guilt or difficulty towards the experiences, it's been more embracing (32 years, UD).
    Also taking things as they come, that has also helped me (24 years, D).

Self-Care.   People talked about activities and attitudes that were nurturing: including abstinence from drugs, resting, creative activities and having an attitude of gentleness towards oneself. As mentioned above, where the person was not in a state to manage self-care (e.g. not being motivated to cook or rest, or being too disorientated to manage), it was helpful to have this care-taking structure provided by others. Some people talked about the value of structure and simple routines for providing containment and grounding.

> I set myself the task of cooking one good meal a day, and doing the washing up, whatever else happened. Sometimes I did loads of washing up, because I'd do it for everyone else as well. After about another month, I started working, cleaning windows. The structure was really helpful (25 years, UD).

Making a Contribution.   Other people talked about the nurturing effects of making a contribution to the welfare of others, where possible. In the longer term, several talked about working in the area of mental health: this seems to relate to several factors including developing a framework to understand experiences through exploration of literature and contact with others, normalisation and integration of experiences into the life path.

Summary.   The participants' own accounts of what they found to be helpful showed that beneficial approaches address the whole person, rather than just the anomalies they experience. One of the principal themes expressed across the groups was that of coming to a *personal* understanding of the anomalous experiences within the context of one's psychological life and narrative. Those individuals who had developed a way of understanding their experiences that could be *shared* with others, appeared to be protected from some of the distress otherwise experienced. The potential to develop such a shared framework of understanding seemed to be facilitated through extrapersonal factors such as social context, and availability of some form of information about the experiences. Practical support and acceptance were also key for those fortunate enough to receive it.

Discussion and Clinical Implications

The data presented above largely corroborate the findings of Jackson regarding the shared aspects between benign and problematic processes of change involving PLEs, because there were clear overlaps between the phenomenology and transformative impact of the experiences in the two groups. Moreover, only people in the D group said that their experiences had had no impact on the way they understood the world, supporting Jackson's proposal that significant transformations or restructuring actually facilitate a benign outcome of PLEs. More specifically, this study suggests that metaphysical shifts in self- and world-concepts are potentially benign, especially the emergence of non-dual views in the current sample.

The findings also corroborate many aspects of the models of transformative crisis presented by Perry (1999) and the Grofs (1991). Perry's concept of *the renewal process* fits several of the participants in both the UD and D groups who experienced prolonged periods of intense altered states. The self-reported outcomes of a greater sense of authenticity and connection to life purpose fit with Perry's views of the fruits of the renewal process, as well as the subjective sense that the unfolding of the crisis follows its own innate order and intelligence. At the same time, the continuum of frequency and intensity of similar experiences apparent in the sample supports Grof's concept of *spiritual emergence* and *spiritual emergency*, whereby the more rapid the process of change and opening, the more difficult the process can be to negotiate successfully.

The types of triggers for spiritual emergency were corroborated by the contexts of the onset of experiences in the current sample, across the groups. The exclusion from the concept of spiritual emergency of states characterised by marked changes in cognition and attention fits with the finding of significantly fewer of these experiences in those with a benign outcome. Grof also excludes 'delusions of persecution, acoustic hallucinations of enemies with a very unpleasant content' from the domain of spiritual emergency (Grof, 1991: p. 255). These appraisals and experiences also distinguished the clinical and non-clinical groups in the present sample.

However, Grof also excludes those whose experiences are associated with drug intoxication: in the current sample *Noetic* experiences were associated with periods when a person had been using drugs, even though the inclusion criteria for the relevance of experiences stipulated that the experiences must not occur as a direct result of intoxication. Grof also stipulates that the person in a 'genuine' spiritual emergency will have an awareness that their experiences are caused by their own inner processes, rather than being caused by events in the outside world. However, the data presented here suggest that this may be an oversimplification. The current analysis suggests that many of those with a benign outcome and fitting other aspects of Grof's model also attribute some aspects of their experiences to powers or entities outside of themselves, and indeed that the whole concept of inner versus outer may be transcended during the process.

The data suggest that the *Noetic* and *Anomalous Perception* experiences were most frequently implicated in transformative processes involving broadly spiritual themes. Interestingly, the *Noetic* phenomena were found to be more intense on average in the D group. It may be relevant that these experiences were also seen to commence as a result of spiritual practices, especially in the UD group: this context may be associated with the increased likelihood of normalisation of such experiences, helpful frameworks of reference, the availability of social support and specialist guidance. Certainly, the findings suggest that the social and cultural context may be a powerful factor influencing both the outcome of experiences, as well as possibly the form in which they are experienced (e.g. pro- versus paranoia), although this hypothesis cannot be confirmed by the data.

This raises the issue of whether therapeutic interventions should incorporate aspects of such schools of thought to provide the same kind of validation of PLEs that these contexts seem to offer. Miller's *Personal Consciousness Integration* (2000) is one such model of clinical intervention that explicitly provides frameworks of reference drawn from world wisdom traditions, as a means to facilitate normalisation of altered states and non-idiosyncratic interpretations of PLEs. Unfortunately, while containing for some people, illness models of PLE's often tend to entail a sense of entrapment and humiliation for the individual, and a negative transformation of their self-concept to one of vulnerability to breakdown (see Gumley and Schwannauer, 2006). They can also strip entire processes of validity, rather than allowing for certain aspects of episodes to be valued. Greater use of 'experts by experience' who have been through processes of transformation in association with PLEs could be another way to maximise normalisation and provide hope to struggling experiencers.

It feels important to comment on the ways in which the attitude of *learning from experience* cut across the different types of experience, such that individuals who had distressing or incapacitating experiences still spoke of the ways in which they had learned about themselves and, in some cases, changed their attitude to life. In this sense of course, any process may be transformative, and it seems relevant to acknowledge that mainstream psychological approaches which attempt to formulate the beliefs and pre-occupations of the individual in a meaningful way that is connected with their wider life story can be seen as contributing to this transformative potential. In the best case scenario, those who become paranoid rather than mystical when faced with ideas of reference, for example, have the opportunity to recognise and move on from modes of interacting with the self and others that have outlived their usefulness, and this may be facilitated by opportunities to reflect on experience as 'purposeful' in the broadest sense. Recognising this undermines the utility of distinguishing transformative crisis from other forms of psychotic experience, despite the differences that can be observed in terms of elements associated with more or less benign outcomes.

There is a great and understandable desire to be able to comprehend the factors that make an experience 'pathological'. However, in the process of interviewing the participants, I was struck by how in many ways it is not possible to deconstruct a person's experience into constituent parts and say, 'this is why s/he got distressed'. What can really *explain* why one person simply allowed their experiences to unfold without becoming paranoid, and why another person becomes excited by their insights and behaves in such a way that they come into conflict with others; or paranoid about the seeming self-reference of events? While many factors may contribute to these diverging paths, of which several have been suggested in this chapter, ultimately every person has a distinct personal (and possibly, transpersonal) history in terms of their social experience of exclusion, victimisation, empowerment, etc., which will be implicated in the unfolding of their experiences. It feels important to keep sight of the wholeness of an individual's personal experience, and the intimacy of their experience to who they are and their life journey. The most important things to learn, I would suggest, are how to support people to navigate these journeys. There is therefore a clear indication of the need for more research to examine the utility of therapeutic approaches which apply the perspectives contributed by transformative models of psychosis. At present, the agenda of reducing distress and incapacity that understandably dictates mental health care expresses itself in efforts to stop PLEs as soon as possible, where possible. Perhaps evidence gained from people whose experiences have run a natural course can encourage us to explore other models for those who would choose them.

14

Exploring the Transliminal: Qualitative Studies

Sharon Warwick and Roger Waldram

This chapter presents two recent qualitative research projects spanning the areas of transpersonal psychology and integrative psychotherapy. Each paper involved participants whose experiences may be termed paranormal, transpersonal, mystical or anomalous, some of whom became involved in mental health services as a result. Warwick presents a grounded theory of the dynamics between the active seeking of experience and spiritual emergence/emergency, introducing the terms 'psychic surge' and 'tool users' for central aspects of her findings. Waldram's bricolage concerns the potential confusion in the process of anomalous experience, and the implications for humanistic psychotherapy and perhaps psychiatric practice. The authors will explore and discuss the findings and implications of their research.

Sharon Warwick

An area of study and research that overlaps with the psychosis and spirituality debate is that of Spiritual Emergence/Emergency (Grof and Grof, 1987). Here I share some of the key findings from one such study which was undertaken in the context of an MSc in Transpersonal Psychology and Consciousness. A full description of the study and results can be found in Warwick (2007).

I have never had a spiritual emergency (Grof and Grof, 1987) and continue to be surprised when that assumption is made. My decision to study Transpersonal Psychology was based on two things. First, it has a place for anomalous experiences within its frameworks and models. Secondly, my focus was upon exploring the impact of anomalous experience on individuals. This study adds to the theme of the book by illustrating how a number of participants managed themselves through

Psychosis and Spirituality: Consolidating the New Paradigm Second Edition   Edited by Isabel Clarke
© 2010 John Wiley & Sons, Ltd.

significant anomalous experiences, sought and unsought, without the involvement of mental health services. Following this study I trained as an integrative psycho-therapist and counsellor to undertake further research on the subject from a therapeutic perspective.

Context

Public interest in psychic openings, sought and unsought, is evidenced by the proliferation of television programmes, books, websites and workshops offering positive interpretations on 'psychic development'. Little mainstream attention is given to the difficulties associated with psychic opening. The focus of this study was upon exploring the relationship between seeking, psychic opening (Grof and Grof, 1987, 1991; Lukoff, Lu and Turner 1996, 1998) and spiritual emergence(y) (Grof and Grof, 1987). Seeking is a term used across many traditions. The focus of this study was upon intentional seeking by an individual as defined by that individual. Specific attention was initially given to psychic and mediumistic training. However, other activities that the participants defined as part of their seeking were also included.

The 'crisis of psychic opening' is outlined by Stanislav and Christina Grof as one of 10 forms of spiritual emergency involving 'non-ordinary states of consciousness' (Grof and Grof, 1987). Whilst 'psychic or paranormal phenomena' are recognised within a range of spiritual emergencies, the experiences are considered indicative of crisis of psychic opening when, as Grof and Grof (1987) express:

> the influx of information from non-ordinary sources, such as pre-cognition, telepathy or clairvoyance, becomes so overwhelming and confusing that it dominates the picture and constitutes a major problem.

Spiritual emergency is presented by Grof and Grof (1987, 1990) in relation to the concept of spiritual emergence. The relationship between these two concepts is presented as a continuum in which an emergence can become an emergency in the presence of 'rapid and dramatic' development (Grof and Grof, 1987, 1990).

The work of David Lukoff is of great theoretical and practical significance to this area; the introduction of the DSM-IV category 'religious and spiritual problem' being of particular note (Lukoff, Lu and Turner, 1998). Lukoff, in a similar fashion to Grof and Grof, outlines the need for psychic experiences to be considered as a category of problem in their own right in certain circumstances. He explains that whilst occurring in other emergencies 'in the psychic experience type of spiritual problem, psychic events are the central feature of the person's experience' (Lukoff, 2007b). For the purpose of the study all types of experiences mentioned by Grof and Grof (1987), Lukoff (2007b) or Bragdon (1990, 1998), as occurring in crisis of psychic opening, were defined as relevant to the exploration. These included clairvoyance, telepathy, pre-cognition, mediumistic experiences, out of body experiences and synchronistic events. The term psychic and/or mediumistic experience is used here to summarise the above categories.

The research base on spiritual emergency currently tends to focus broadly across all 10 categories rather than on the individual categories. Advice to individuals undergoing emergence(y) mirrors this and is quite broad sweeping, for example suggesting the cessation of spiritual practise and eating grounding foods (Bragdon 1998, Grof and Grof 1990). Beyond that, very little focussed observations or advice are offered on what an individual can do when facing the specific crisis of psychic opening. Literature that does deal with practical issues focuses on what could or should be done 'for' or 'to' an individual to either 'treat' them or allow their process to emerge. Anne Armstrong's (1987) account of her own emergency of psychic opening serves as an interesting case study but its nature precludes the offering of practical advice. In his work 'The spectrum of therapies' (1993, pp.156–159) Wilber comments that the options available for those undergoing 'unsought awakening of spiritual–psychic energies or insights' are that they 'ride it out' with conventional care, risking interpretation as a psychotic break, or that they 'consciously engage this process by taking up a contemplative discipline'. No way of the individual coping with the opening in the absence of a spiritual discipline is offered. The results of this study illustrate such an option being created by individuals.

Approach

Having worked with many research approaches over the years, I consider myself neutral in any qualitative 'versus' quantitative debate. I selected grounded theory methodology and method (Strauss and Corbin, 1998; Glaser and Strauss, 1999) because of its high level of rigour (Braud and Anderson, 1998) and its use and acceptance in related fields. The participants were sourced from two separate sites. Before sampling saturation (Strauss and Corbin, 1998) was reached, eight participants were interviewed using a semi structured interview guide. The interviews were transcribed and the method followed through its many stages. Six of the eight participants had experienced 'crisis of psychic opening' as outlined by Grof and Grof (1987). Five participants had undertaken psychic and/or mediumistic training at some point. The grounded theory analysis process led to the emergence of five themes and a grounded theory.

Central Findings

Here, I will outline the dynamics of seeking and not seeking anomalous experience and introduce the concepts of the 'psychic surge' and 'tool users'. Both these terms were coined as part of the study (Warwick, 2007). By also providing the grounded theory itself, presented as a short narrative, I hope that the reader may get a flavour of the richness of the remaining themes and areas available in the full results. All participant names have been changed.

The Psychic Surge

Several variables of the relationship of psychic opening to spiritual emergence(y) emerged. Only one participant experienced initial psychic opening and initial crisis simultaneously. For Holly, this was an intense extended experience in adulthood:

> [Holly] I had big impacts, I, I mean all sorts was happening then, precognition, seeing auras, feeling people's emotions, . . . I had a real, like psychic . . . I was swamped. . .

However, for the majority of remaining participants, the first psychic opening was not experienced as a spiritual emergency. The experiences started in childhood and were not reported as problematic:

> [Anna] Well, I think I've always had . . . psychic experiences, so as a child and . . . I think I've always assumed that, I think they are quite normal, I think that people sometimes discount them, in a way, which I find quite odd, . . . so I think I just grew up thinking that that's quite normal really.
> [Kelly] but I've had those experiences throughout my life at different times, so . . . when I was seven it was perfectly normal and natural . . .

However, it is crucial to note that early life psychic opening and childhood normalisation of the experiences do not appear to prevent later *crisis* of psychic opening (Grof and Grof, 1987) in an individual. The presence of later crisis appears to be associated with the intensity, rather than the nature of the experience as they are familiar with their general nature. The term 'psychic surge' (Warwick, 2007) was coined to refer to a powerful psychic opening undergone by someone who has previously had similar experiences without crisis. This surge can then affect the person's ongoing relationship to the experiences as they now are associated with new feelings such as terror. Nevertheless participants also go on to have subsequent openings without crisis where intensity is not present.

This supports Grof and Grof's (1987, 1990) concept that emergency occurs in the presence of intense periods of 'development'. The findings stimulate reflection upon what should be considered and defined as a 'psychic opening'. It is unclear whether the term 'opening' (Grof and Grof, 1987), suggests that it is the first occurrence of the experiences and whether once it has occurred someone is then considered 'open'. Participants commented upon experiencing differing types of opening, for example seeing some as being more 'healthy' than others (Sam). This would suggest a sequence of opening and re-opening.

This matter is of significance in terms of potential ways to assist the individual undergoing psychic opening and recovery. One of Lukoff's 'prognostic signs for a good outcome' is 'acute onset of symptoms during a period of three months or less' (Lukoff, Lu and Turner, 1996: pp. 231–249). This has implications for the majority of participants, as they report experiences going back to childhood. The term 'psychic surge' is therefore seen to be of use in identifying individuals who may have 'opened' a long time ago but are currently experiencing an increased intensity of activity that is challenging their usual coping mechanisms. It is suggested that acute onset of the *surge* of experiences, rather than of experiences in general, may be a useful differential. Taking a non-pathologising view of those with long-term psychic and/or mediumistic experiences may open the possibility of individuals sharing their previously effective coping mechanisms, learning and development that may be useful in contributing to their own recovery from the surge. In this way, a more equal relationship with the practitioner focuses on reducing the troublesome surge rather than stigmatising all experiences.

Seeking

The dynamic of seeking or not seeking experience was expressed as a quest rather than a journey; the difference being that in a quest there is no known destination (Keyston, n.d). The context is that the individual does not follow a particular path or tradition that advises them what to do when having experiences, there is an absence of a 'spiritual map' (Lancaster, 2000, 2007). Therefore, in the absence of a such a map, or indeed a non-spiritual map, the individual makes their way through unfamiliar territory through the use of 'tools' (see 'tool users' below).

Rather than meriting the category of seeker or non-seeker, all participants move frequently, between seeking and not seeking, at different points, throughout their quest, which I have named interplay. Turning points for this interplay include the occurrence of particularly challenging experiences or the onset of spiritual emergency. Further factors include: following personal questions, responses to alternating levels of fear and gaining control of experiences through learned techniques. There is a dynamic of 'thirst and unfoldment': thirst relating to times when experiences are pursued and developed, unfoldment describing the periods when experiences and development opportunities are allowed to unfold. This is not a random process; different phases of seeking have different aims. These include seeking to start healing, to explain experiences, to mix experiential with other knowledge, to find ways to embrace energy, seeking home and seeking transformation.

It is worthy of note that these seeking dynamics and motivations do not appear to resonate with the often raised concern of ego-based seeking and ego inflation. Grof and Grof (1990) warn of the problem of once 'familiar and comfortable' with psychic experiences, an individual may 'interpret their occurrence as an indication of one's own superiority and special calling'. There were no indications of this nature within this particular sample group. Ferrer (2002) addresses the issue of the ego and the spiritual path in the concept of spiritual narcissism, which he summarises as 'the misuse of spiritual practises, energies or experiences to bolster self-centred ways of being'. These perspectives however, do not seem to apply to people, such as the participants, who are not pursuing a spiritual path, merely attempting to privately understand, control or transform their natural way of being.

Tool Users

As stated above in the absence of a map, the individuals seek out tools and become 'tool users' (Warwick, 2007). The 'tool user' utilises a variety of activities to heal and recover from the effects of psychic opening and continue with their personal path of emergence. The term tool came from description of development activities by several of the participants. For example, it first appeared in the pilot interview with Sam commenting upon her membership of a group: 'It is a tool, a tool, certainly not the only tool that I use'. Natalie and Anna also contribute to the code:

> [Natalie] You have to learn the tools, somehow, so that again gave me an understanding that you have to learn the laws of the tools and how things work
> [Anna] ... picking different pieces from different things and ... that being a way of putting together a picture of the world really

A tool could be summarised as an activity undertaken to assist the individual with the need for personal 'repair and maintenance' created by psychic opening. Tools used include but are not limited to psychic and mediumistic development training, books and the academic study of a wide range of areas. The selection of tools appears to be based on self-knowledge. This is knowledge of both the openings and the participant's personal biography. Different tools are picked up and put down according to the participant's aims for that particular phase of their quest. Tools are also used in conjunction with each other and sometimes alongside personal therapy (also a tool) to promote an understanding of the experiences in the context of their overall personal history. It appears that the tool user creates and controls an effective personalised programme of self-care and healing.

Prior to sharing the grounded theory, I will share one or two key points from the remaining two major themes. These were entitled 'the role of biography and the everyday world' and 'the role of others'. Given issues around seeking and ego, it was significant that there was complete rejection of the personal label of being a psychic or medium:

[Holly] I was a bit wary about some of this experience, you know and I I . . . didn't want to be a clairvoyant or a medium. . .

[Kelly] . . . and was a bit of a relief that, you know, you didn't have to. . .look at becoming a medium, you didn't have to do that, because it didn't, it didn't sit right for me . . .

The experiences were not utilised to build their own or others sense of their own importance. The process that participants were engaged in was very private. This privacy even continued in groups where others were viewed as having their own paths. There were a few enduring groups but most were fleeting. There was not a sense of joint seeking. This may be related to the finding that the seeking process often included having to work through private personal history, including traumatic events, alongside the other chosen forms of development. These events in some cases were the openings themselves with content such as accurate negative pre-cognitions. It is also of note that changes and challenges in participants' personal life could also act as a trigger for experience and/or crisis. There were some significant others identified such as teachers and therapists but these came and went with the particular phases of seeking and tool use to which they related. Finally, it is of note that personal learning achieved is fed back into the daily life of the individual in a desire to help or serve others.

Theory Building and the Role of the Self

The role of the Self (Jung, 1978) surfaced as a thread throughout all themes as the grounded theory emerged. Processes similar to that discovered concerning the Self are Wilber's "navigator" (2000), Jung's 'unifying function' (Stein, 1998) and Rogers' 're-organisation of the self' (1951). At this stage, the theory is viewed as being 'local' (Strauss and Corbin, 1998) to the participants in the study. The theory was reviewed and supported by the participants and also triangulated well with a variety of professional peers. In subsequent presentations of results to academic, professional and service user audiences, the theory has been recognised by many as representing their path. The theory is the 'Seeker as the healing Self using Tools' and is best expressed in the form of a short narrative. It outlines a personal path of growth, healing and recovery charted by individuals for themselves rather than suggested by a spiritual path or prescribed by any form of practitioner.

Seeker as the healing Self using Tools (Warwick, 2007)

At the centre of all the themes appears to be the Self, Self as Tool and Self as 'Tool user.' This is a Self that knows the individual's biography and secret biography in some cases. The term Self is used instead of ego as there is a rejection of labels such as psychic or medium, a wish for 'abilities' not to be recognised and a concern with a deep level of healing. In the cases explored, this is a Self of an individual without a 'spiritual map'. At certain points in the individual's life psychic opening in the form of psychic and or mediumistic experiences presents challenges or spiritual emergency that trigger the need for healing, answers or understanding. This challenge or spiritual emergency may be stimulated through intensity of experience or through the importance of the experience as gauged by its related outcome. In these circumstances, the Self embarks on a quest that involves taking action whilst remaining open to spontaneous unfoldment. It employs 'Tools' to answer questions and challenges that emerge or that it generates for itself. It goes through a process of healing, gaining understanding and integrating experiential and biographical material.

There is not a sense of the ego selecting at random from the 'spiritual supermarket' here. There is interplay of periods of unfoldment and periods of using seeking in the form of development activities to attend to matters that are known to the self-concerning personal history and psychic and/or mediumistic experiences that they would rather not discuss.

Although the individual attends groups they pick these up and put them down, seeing others in the group as having their own seeking to attend to. Although there may be a common thread of worldview there is not a sense of 'group seeking'.

The individual's quest settles with a sense of a new meaning; of a stronger connection to the daily with a concern to remain grounded. However, there is openness to continued unfoldment and exploration balanced against remaining 'grounded' and 'connected.' (Warwick, 2007)

Roger Waldram

Introduction

From the beginning of recorded time, man and womankind have struggled to understand anomalous experience i.e. 'an uncommon experience or one that . . . is believed to deviate from ordinary experience or from the usually accepted explanations of reality' (Cardeña, Lynn and Krippner (eds), 2000: p. 4). There is a creative tension or potentially destructive polarities among the perspectives of biology, psychology and spirituality. The 'gold' standard is quantitative research often using random control trials in the process of establishing objective 'truth' much beloved by the medical profession, drug companies and the government in what may be seen as a triangle of power. Quantitative research is useful to obtain the 'hard' data of the physical sciences and medicine. However, there is a continuing debate concerning how experience may be understood using quantitative methods perhaps in mimicry of the physical sciences. As a humanistic integrative psychotherapist, I chose qualitative research for my doctoral thesis.

The seed for the research was sown in my psychotherapy training when I attended a psychopathology workshop 'Mental Illness: Mystery or Mis-Story?' (Fantini, 1998). Differences in the treatment of unusual experiences in various cultures were considered. In Western society, mental illness may be diagnosed and this is more likely with black ethnic minorities, elderly women and others who have less power (Newnes, Holmes and Dunn, 1999) whereas in some cultures, having strange experiences, could herald acceptance as a shaman-healer, like the archetypal Wounded Healer of legend. This rang bells and raised a 'What if. . .' question for me. At the age of 20 years, I was unhappy, frustrated, had lost any sense of purpose and began having terrifying experiences that neither others nor I could understand. I could not sleep, was highly sensitive, saw significance and meaning in everything from television programmes to the sound of bubbles bursting on my coffee and felt overwhelmed. I denied *that* reality by stopping my insulin injections (for *diabetes mellitus*), and beginning a journey to reach the sanctuary of a friend's family. My quest ended in diabetic coma, near-death experience, eventual admission to a psychiatric hospital and treatment with Largactil and Electro Convulsive Therapy (ECT) that I hated. My story or the reasons underlying my almost fatal choices seemed only to have been of interest to one nurse. From him, I learnt how to be a 'good' compliant patient within my 'escape plan' and so get discharged. I thought my diagnosis was 'manic depression', although I since caught sight of the words 'acute schizophrenia' in my medical notes. I hated my treatment and thought there must be a better way. There are perhaps signposts to this way in this research.

The Enquiry

I chose to work with those who are now mental health professionals in a form of co-operative enquiry because I was interested in their perspectives on what had happened. The participants included a psychiatric nurse, a psychiatrist, a clinical psychologist, a doctor of psychology, two psychology students, a psychiatric social worker and myself. All work within the UK and American Health Services or support those with mental health problems in a voluntary or paid capacity. Heron and Reason (2001, p. 182), in their discussion of co-operative enquiry, write 'We have not yet heard of any full counterpartal role enquiries', i.e. doctor/patient, or perhaps psychotherapist, psychologist, psychiatrist/client. The research involved a kind of counterpartal role inquiry because it involved participants who know the experience, and are now mental health professionals.

As research preparation, I read widely, including the first edition of this book, and attended a number of workshops including one by Stanley Krippner (2003). The word 'anomalous' to describe experience that is *other than* 'homolous', encompassing both psychosis and spirituality, is my preferred term because it serves to normalise rather than pathologise experience for clients who do not find diagnosis helpful. At the beginning of my research quest, I was astonished by Bentall's (2003) comments about the lack of validity and efficacy of diagnosis and intrigued by the idea of a transliminal domain of experience (Clarke, 2001, 2005). How then to research this domain sometimes said to be beyond words and 'know' others' experience? Reason and Bradbury (2001) mention four forms of knowledge: *propositional* knowing about something as statements and theories, *practical* knowing how to do something, *experiential* knowing through our own experience and that of others and finally *presentational* knowledge through images, symbolically expressed through poetry, dance, drama, and presentations. The design and method included these ways of knowing.

Research Methodology

I wanted to research *with* and not *on* participants and honour them and their experience. 'Honouring' may *not* happen in research. Michelle Fine (1998, p. 130), writes about the process of 'Othering' where qualitative researchers write about 'Others', their research subject, and make the voice of the 'Other' their own, thus denying the 'Other' voice. I wanted to ensure the Others' voice was heard throughout their narrative. The *bricoleur* approach involves using the tools and materials available to extend research and produce a creative *bricolage* (Kincheloe and Berry, 2004). This is perhaps subversive because it challenges existing methods and reductionist approaches. Denzin and Lincoln (1998. p. 425) suggest we may discover in our *bricolage* that there is not one voice or one story, 'but many tales, dramas, pieces of fiction, fables, memories, histories, autobiographies, poems and other texts to inform our sense of lifeways, to extend our understandings of the Other...'

This *bricolage* was carefully chosen to provide the necessary research data. I decided on phenomenological enquiry where every aspect of experience is treated as phenomena for research (Magee, 1998). Phenomenological philosophy represents a return to the traditional task of philosophy as a search for wisdom and a refusal of the subject-objective dichotomy of scientism so that reality is seen within the subjective meaning of an individual (Creswell, 1998). This is the existential phenomenology that Laing (1960) said would provide useful understanding of the symbolic meaning inherent in the subjective experience of 'madness'. Phenomenological enquiry into the participants' anomalous experience held the potential to include the personal truth of the inter-subjective and transpersonal aspects of our field.

A form of co-operative enquiry known as *appreciative* enquiry uses the 'power of the unconditional positive question' to facilitate positive and enthusiastic answers, usually in organisations (Ludema, Cooperrida and Barret, 2001, pp. 189, 191). Appreciative enquiry is 'an intentional posture of continuous discovery, search and enquiry into conceptions of life, joy, beauty excellence, innovation and freedom'. This reminded the cynic in me of an organisational mission statement, and I wanted the whole phenomenology including negative aspects.

Peter Reason (2000, p. 15) links participative, cooperative enquiry to the four paths described by Matthew Fox (1983); *Via Positiva* (appreciative enquiry); *Via Negativa* (a willingness to engage with shadow – ours and others); *Via Creativa* (perhaps to creatively re-vision our shared world), and finally the *Via Transformitiva* ('the concept of "action" includes the development of theory which may illuminate our action, guide it and provide it with meaning'). These ideas structured the interview questions. I used semi-structured open interview questions (McLeod, 1994) to contain and boundary the enquiry process. To avoid this constricting the research, each participant had the opportunity to add their own questions, add to what they said at the time and, after reflection, through my later enquiries.

Just as a shaman has a *native way of knowing* (Krippner, 2003), so my research participants and I have our own knowing from experience, which Moustakas says is an important factor in the heuristic research process (Krippner, 2003). In humanistic and holistic research Barber (2006, p. 23) suggests *'From this perspective, you, your person-hood and humanity are most important tools of enquiry and relationships are the prime medium through which you create research'*. I used myself as research instrument during the interviews and in the subsequent data analysis using reflective listening both for the enquiry and to integrate the phenomenology of the experience.

For the data analysis, I used thematic analysis, retaining participants' terminology. I immersed myself in the data, 'knowing through becoming' by intuitively moving from objective to subjective awareness (Braud and Anderson, 1998, p. 51). I thought it important not to skew participant experience through this later intuitive knowing and used aspects of interpretive phenomenological analysis where themes are grounded in the data of what the participant said, and listed my intuitive responses separately. I sent the thematic analysis back to participants to enquire whether the essence of their experience had been captured, and later offered my intuitive 'knowing' for feedback.

In conclusion, I conducted a heuristic, transpersonal, phenomenological enquiry using semi-structured interview questions, including the iterative process of validating the data with participants. In this way, the similarities and differences in the phenomenology of participants' stories of psychosis and spirituality (or anomalous experience), and the implications for therapeutic practice were explored.

The 'Mis-Stories'

There was some evidence of participants' stories being missed to return to Fantini's (1988) workshop title. It will be interesting to see what those stories were before returning to the question of what qualitative research can tell us. I used the timescale in the following Map of Themes to provide structure for the themes containing the individual stories.

MAP OF THEMES
(Key to type-styles: **Danger/Negative** — Mixed: Caution —*Positive Experience: Choice*)

CHILDHOOD
Loss Abuse — *Creative Adaptation* — **Fear-full Childhood** — *Art of Deceit Escape*

PRE-ANOMALOUS EXPERIENCE
Loss and Stress — **Betrayal** — **Rows** — **Aura of Criticism** — **Not Being Heard**

ANOMALOUS EXPERIENCE
Hyperactivity — **Insomnia** — **Isolation** — Different State/Reality — **Out of Control** — **Hopeless** — Dissociation — Anger — Fear — **Fragmentation** — Belonging — *An Opening* — *Mystical/Spiritual Experience* — *Escape* — *NDE* — *Contact/Connection* — *Sensitivity* — Messages — **Spirit Disappeared** — *Reborn* — *Mission* — Hallucinations/Visions — Synchronicities — *Psychosis* — *Integrated with Mysticism* — **Psychic Pain** — *Night-Blooming Flower* — *Symbolic Meaning* — *Archetypal Journeys* — *Revelations*

PSYCHIATRY
Managing Psychiatry — **Lack of Understanding, Contact, Support** — *Anger Rights* — **Hallucinations/Delusions** — *Exercise* — *Support* — **Indoctrination** — *Rebellion* — *Sanctuary* — *Containment* — *Compliance/Non-Compliance* — *Hope* — *Judgement* — *Symbolic-Benefit* — **Stigma** — **Shame** — **Psychiatric Hell**

RECOVERY
Survival Instinct — *Being in Control* — *Spiritual-Hope* — *Self-Observation* — *Resourceful* — *Psychological Awakening* — *Connection* — *Sanctuary* — *Empowerment* — *Support* — *Meaning & Sense of Purpose* — *Knowing* — *Meeting of Opposites* — *Creative* — *Calling* — *Service* — **Lost Creativity** — **Stigma** — **Shame** — *Continuum of Experience*

TRANSFORMATION
Creative — *Transformation* — *Sceptical*

Childhood

Although the research questions did not focus on childhood most participants began their stories then and spoke of physical or emotional trauma. An inclusive view of trauma is that it can be defined according to subjective experience rather than by the nature of the event or process (see van der Hart, Nijenhuis and Steele, 2006, p. 24).

Pre-Anomalous Experience

Personal crisis, stress or losses were precursors of all participants' anomalous experience. These included adverse relationships, deaths, serious illness, rape, work-related stress, drugs (marijuana, insulin and amphetamine-based slimming tablets), and positive relationships ending. Stress, with its impact on the autonomic nervous system, has been found to play a central role in trauma and breakdown. Bentall (2003, p. 482) comments 'the evidence that trauma can play a causal role in psychosis appears to be surprisingly strong'.

Anomalous Experience

Anomalous experience including hospital admission or involvement with psychiatry for seven of the eight participants was the heart of the research enquiry. All participants retained their thinking although the meaning was often symbolic. As Rob said 'Yeah, that has been my definition of madness. Madness is when other people can't understand you; it doesn't mean you are not understandable'.

Everyone was hyperactive and some spoke of being in a different reality expressed eloquently by Tabitha 'I wasn't real, any more, feeling afraid, numb, dead, lost, not sleeping and having no sense of time'. All six participants who were admitted to psychiatric hospital shared negative experiences of No Understanding, Contact or Support, Indoctrination, and Adverse Judgement. Positive aspects included Support from other patients, a sense of Sanctuary and Hope from an admission psychiatrist who tried to understand, and walking and talking with a male nurse.

Spiritual experiences included a sense of Connection or Oneness perhaps an 'antidote' to the Isolation most shared. After receiving prayer in church, Joy felt lifted as if she were walking 6 feet off the ground, calls bible verses her supportive 'gems' and says 'I can tune into spiritual support'. Joy also made the hope-full statement 'I have been renewed in mind, body and soul over the years because I believe in complete healing, there is a way, and a path and it is the question of finding it. It is an ongoing process and it is still ongoing. Harner's (1990) 'Revelations' in his shamanic journey are reflected in the following themes. Ruth spoke of a Knowing that included 'the cure for schizophrenia lies not in medicine, but in physics'. Nikita's Revelations included 'Science and religion are the same at some point', and 'There is no mental illness, the doctors are wrong and it was just like getting this knowledge from Heaven, and it was just like electricity just flowed, it was just the most wonderful experience'. Her knowing from her experience what hindered her recovery is 'I think the psychiatric system undermines and creates the problem and the system drive you mad'.

Six participants had visions perhaps otherwise called hallucinations that held symbolic meaning. Tabitha saw people trying to shoot her, Gorbachev, Kinnock, bombs and nuclear war that reflected her environment at that time. Ruth heard a voice saying 'Eve, Eve', took a bite from an apple and felt juice running down her chin. Afterward, she said 'Holy Moly where did I go'. She describes this as an Archetypal journey. She understood these experiences were not just for her but to share with others who were afraid and lost. These imaginal dialogues were very useful for all who had them, providing Vocation and Meaning described as Calling, Mission and Service.

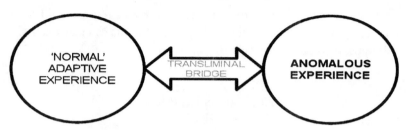

Figure 14.1   The two domains of experience

Recovery

There were a number of important aspects in the recovery phase. Individuals' sense of regaining autonomy was encompassed in the themes of survival instinct, being in control, being a rebel and becoming resourceful. Hope was found through support and encouragement from the *contact* with others human, animal or non-human in the form of Christian god or spiritual other. There was often a practical side to this contact involving housing, working, using bible quotes to challenge negative thought spirals, finding personal sanctuary and finding one's personal story to make sense of the experience. An important aspect of recovery was having someone alongside who could *normalise* what had happened, whether through theory or sharing their personal experience.

Transformation

Transformation was seen in all participants' stories of wound, healing and new knowledge used for the benefit of others. As one example, Ruth said felt changed at a cellular level that layers and layers were peeled away, and her conclusion was that each past deep pain was necessary and purposeful in the process.

What Can Qualitative Research Tell Us About Psychosis and Spirituality or Anomalous Experience?

As a bricoleur researcher who does not like a mono-theoretical research approach or any claim to absolute knowledge I will answer with a number of 'maybes'. I like Clarke's (2001) concept of two domains of experience that is in some ways similar to Huxley's (1994) *Doors of Perception*, written after taking mescaline. As a research map, the diagram below showing two different domains will prove helpful (Waldram, 2007).

'Normal Adaptive Experience' is an individual's state of being as an adult. Some literature and this research points to a perhaps accidentally traumatic childhood

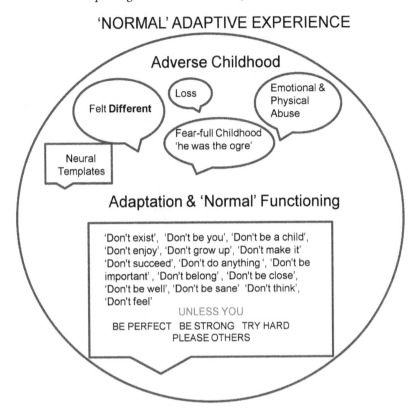

Figure 14.2 The script-beliefs of childhood

laying the foundation for adulthood. Particularly, in USA, genetic and/or biological abnormality is perhaps over-emphasised by drug companies and skews research. 'Normal Adaptive Experience' may not, of course, be a healthy adaptation. The 'Transliminal Bridge' represents ways in which a person may begin to move into anomalous experience. The 'planks' that formed the 'Bridge' for participants included stress-overload from a range of environmental stressors. Other 'planks' included the drugs mentioned earlier. Thus, with too much stress and not enough effective coping, we may lose our ability to think clearly, concentrate or function in our usual way. Perhaps stress overload or stimuli outside *'our window of tolerance'* (Ogden, Minton and Pain, 2006: p. 27) may lead to us being 'rubber-banded back to early childhood scenes' (Stewart and Joines, 1987, p. 111). If we then use the symbolic feeling thinking of childhood for responses in adulthood, there are likely to be problems. Transactional analysis suggests that our adaptation to adulthood may mean living according to the script-beliefs (such as in the figure below) that we previously needed, but may be unhealthy now.

Schore (2003) emphasises the role of early attachment difficulties in impoverishing affect regulation capacity, leading to later psychopathology. Bentall (2003: p. 483) says '... a person who has poor source-monitoring skills will be most vulnerable to hallucinations when experiencing a flood of intrusive thoughts and images. Trauma (we know from the research literature on post-traumatic stress disorder) often has exactly this effect'. If this is so, perhaps stress-management and 'normalisation' may be important interventions.

Anomalous experience may be deemed psychotic or spiritual depending on the context and the perspectives of those involved including, of course, the subjective experience of the individual. For example, Saul's 'road to Damascus' experience meets the criteria for schizophrenia, delusional disorder and somatoform disorder since he had a conversation with God, was struck blind and acted on God's instructions. However, his experience changed his heart, mind and name since as Paul he spread the gospel and laid the foundations of Christianity

The 'planks' providing the bridge to recovery are an important aspect of this research.

Regaining autonomy through the support of others was a common theme. Withdrawal and Isolation were key themes so Re-engagement and Connection fit well with the idea of returning across the Transliminal Bridge into a homolous or shared world. A Halfway House in the community provided Sanctuary, Connection, Hope and Empowerment for Tim. Support, Contact and Encouragement were important themes for everyone. They were provided by other patients, friends, partners, work colleagues, a nurse and animals. Diagnosis enables Sofia to manage her experience and medication. Support, Sanctuary and Accompaniment were important in Harner's (1990) shamanic journey and return after taking *ayahuasca* in South America. Similarly, Tabitha found Sanctuary and Safety when she needed this in psychiatric hospital.

Some literature suggests the importance of relationship for recovery. From his work with attachment theory, Wallin (2007: p. 7) suggests 'As part of what makes the therapeutic relationship a transformative one, the therapist's mindful stance may have a "contagious" quality-kindling the patient's own experience of mindfulness very much as expressions of the therapist's reflective stance help to kindle the patient's ability to mentalize'. In a variety of ways participants found 'good enough' relationships to return to a healthier 'normal' experience.

Jung suggests that our soul daemon may speak to us through our symptoms and voices may indicate a new vocation (Storr, 1998: p. 199). Six of the eight participants decided to undertake training as mental health workers. Lukoff, in his presentation on Recovery (Presentation at Spirituality & Mental Health Conference, Dundee, 2004) said 'Creating a new personal mythology' was the final phase of therapeutic integration and all participants did this.

Ruth did not have hospital admission or contact with psychiatric services. She carefully shared only aspects of her experience with different friends and groups in order not to alarm them. She says there is a tremendous 'energy of calling' and of connection which can be expressed in art with no stigmatisation. When painting or with clay she could express her madness freely and it was appreciated. She attended a conference on mysticism where people speaking of mystical experiences similar to her own served to normalise her experience. Tabitha is Creative through poetry, Tim, Rob and Roger are Creative in written work and Rob also finds dance, drama and campaigning good Creative outlets. Sofia writes what she calls 'nonsense' and sees this as a sign that she requires medication, although this leads to Lost Creativity.

In summary, drawing on participants' wisdom, the 'planks' in the Recovery 'bridge' include regaining autonomy (Control), Support, Good Contact whether human, animal or spiritual, Sanctuary and Safety, using Resource(s), Finding Meaning and Purpose, and finally using Creativity in various ways.

Conclusion

It would perhaps be perverse, on the evidence of this research, to suggest that every psychological crisis, anomalous experience or psychotic episode contains the potential for change and personal growth. Particularly, as my criteria for participation was that participants are now mental health professionals, thus able to work and 'recovered' or 'healed'. However, what made the difference for participants has, in my opinion, potential implications for psychotherapeutic practice with psychosis and spirituality, or anomalous experience.

In conclusion, this suggests a different meta-narrative to that of the body of knowledge; particularly perhaps within the arguably flawed epistemology of the medical model.

A meta-narrative offered by this research is Loss, Stress or Trauma from early development may lead to Anomalous Experience after further Loss, Stress or Trauma at the important later developmental stage of adolescence to 20s. Recovery takes place through Sanctuary, Affect Management (through exercise and mindfulness, e.g. meditation and breathing techniques) and Relationship.

As a post-script, I used participants perhaps quite different to those typically presenting to the Health Service or practitioners like myself. However, perhaps the wisdom from them might usefully be explored through further research.

Acknowledgement

Warwick's research was supervised by Michael Daniels, PhD, School of Natural Sciences & Psychology, Liverpool JMU.

Section 6

Clinical Implications

With three new chapters added to the original two, this section illustrates the blossoming of this perspective within the mainstream (Transpersonal psychotherapists have always been at home with therapy for 'spiritual emergency', while being less welcoming towards 'psychosis'). In particular, the section develops the theme of harnessing the transformational potential of transliminal experiencing through innovative therapeutic approaches. David Lukoff is famous as a pioneer in securing recognition of the transformative potential of 'visionary spiritual experiences' (his phrase) of a sort that invite psychiatric attention. His achievement has been to enshrine this insight within DSMIV. His chapter includes much wise advice on the management of such episodes. Hartley takes the theme further in her workshops which use her own remarkable experience as a starting point to lead other experiencers to reconceptualise their 'breakdowns' as potentially life enhancing, albeit severely challenging, in the pattern of the mythic hero.

Focus on distinguishing spiritual from psychotic experience or treating them as aspects or potential within the same phenomenon divides the contributors to this section. Lukoff with his diagnostic focus, and Kingdon *et al.*, who represent the more mainstream CBT for psychosis approach being the 'categorisers'.

15

'What is Real and What is Not': Towards a Positive Reconceptualisation of Vulnerability to Unusual Experiences

Isabel Clarke

In Chapter 9, a new way of understanding both spiritual experience and psychosis was outlined. Both were identified with the experience of the transliminal, an area that is accessed when the two central meaning making systems of the brain become desynchronised. This chapter outlines how this conceptualization can be applied clinically, in the challenging setting of the acute mental health unit.

Sustained or repeated desynchrony between the two central meaning making systems envisaged by the Interacting Cognitive Subsystem (ICS) model (p.107) is not a situation which makes for good functioning in the ordinary shared world. Such functioning requires the smooth co-operation between implicational and propositional. This smooth co-operation can be resumed without much disruption after a brief period of asynchrony. Such periods of asynchrony bring positives as well as potential dangers. By temporarily stepping out of their experience of a self bounded by individuality, a human being can experience a greatly expanded sense of reality. As well as frequently being an exhilarating experience, this can open the door to personal development, to new insights of wisdom and in some cases, the accessing of psychic powers, as discussed in a number of the preceding chapters. However, such a course is in no way guaranteed. This opening also puts the individual in touch with unresolved issues from their personal past. Where these concern problematic formative relationships and/or trauma this can be highly de-stabilizing. Thus, for many, the journey into the transliminal loses its way; unable to conduct ordinary life with accustomed skill and unable to distinguish between threat and no threat, between danger and safety, the person can flounder around, acting in ways that cause

Psychosis and Spirituality: Consolidating the New Paradigm Second Edition   Edited by Isabel Clarke
© 2010 John Wiley & Sons, Ltd.

concern to themselves or those around them. In our society, this tends to result in the involvement of the mental health system.

The perspective offered above is rather different from the one that will greet someone entering the psychiatric service. Once immediate needs and concerns about safety have been attended to, the first task of the psychiatrist is to give the person a diagnosis. This means questioning them about their experiences, beliefs and behaviour to establish which category of 'mental illness' this qualifies them for, and therefore which medication is predicted to produce the most efficient return to normality. This procedure is reassuring to many, both service users and their carers. It communicates certainty amid confusion and promises 'cure'. However, this comes at a price. A price in terms of self image, and in terms of relinquishing any positives or insights that the journey into the transliminal might have given them, and of labelling their facility to make such journeys as pathological. In terms of social rank and hierarchy, it plunges them instantly into one of the least favoured categories in our society, which is in itself highly destabilising to mental health (Birchwood *et al.*, 2001).

If the perspective offered by this book can contribute anything, it needs to contribute to redressing this balance. While not minimizing suffering and risk, this perspective has the potential to temper the 'illness' message by giving space to the positive potential and association with valued states and faculties such as spirituality, creativity and personal growth. The earlier chapters have laid the theoretical and research context for this re-balancing. This chapter will describe one small programme, delivered in an acute mental health hospital under ordinary conditions (insofar as things are ever 'ordinary' in such settings), that seeks to redress the balance. A small scale evaluation study is submitted for publication at the time of writing, but such is the impact that this programme has already had in the surrounding services, that an extended programme and more ambitious evaluation, in collaboration with service users is already in the planning.

My introduction to the overlap between spiritual and psychotic experience came about through working as a therapist with people who had acquired a diagnosis of chronic schizophrenia, but whose 'illness' had started with mystical experiences as had Peter Chadwick's. It was a small step to start to apply these insights to my practice of cognitive behaviour therapy (CBT) for psychosis, which was in any case very much a developing field at that time (early 1990s). Validating experience and linking it with that of the mystics wherever relevant was an obvious first step. This was coupled with a realistic appraisal of the problems of trying to conduct life from the transliminal (which I often compare with trying to drive a car from the back seat, without proper access to the controls) and encouragement to join the ordinary world along with strategies for managing this.

This more balanced approach encouraged engagement in strategies to gain control over unruly transliminal experiences such as voices and strongly held beliefs not shared by others. While it did not guarantee engagement, as developing a collaborative engagement is a well-recognised challenge in this area, it certainly increased scope for engagement. Once it is possible to negotiate a mutually acceptable language with someone (shared and unshared reality, sensitivity or openness to other ways of experiencing, are phrases I habitually use), it is often easier to persuade them to put in the considerable effort required to maintain contact with shared reality and resist the lure or the bullying of voices and unshared beliefs.

That was 10 years ago and the whole field of therapy for psychosis has moved on. The role of arousal, both high as in stress and low, as in dissociated, hypnagogic states, is recognized. Voices and symptoms (paranoia, unusual beliefs, etc.) groups had become a routine part of psychological therapy programmes, in both in- and out-patient settings. More recently, Chadwick and his collaborators have developed and evaluated mindfulness groups for voice hearers (Chadwick, Newman-Taylor and Abba, 2005; Chadwick *et al.*, 2009). Working in an in-patient setting, it was a small step to develop our psychosis group programme along these lines, but additionally incorporating the normalizing idea of a spectrum of openness to unusual experiences. In this way, the 'What is Real and What is Not' group was born. As length of stay in UK acute mental health units is usually brief and always unpredictable, the programme had to be short. We settled on four sessions, with the option to return to finish the course after discharge. Individual work with people with this type of problem follows the same lines, but allows scope for individual formulation. Ideally, someone both attends the group and has one or more individual session to help them apply the model to their own situation. I will here outline the group programme and its evaluation, followed by the reflections of a participant, some weeks after her discharge from hospital.

Introduction to the Group

The programme is offered to anyone who is prepared to identify themselves as having experiences that others do not share, irrespective of diagnosis. These might be voices or visions (hallucinations, flashbacks), strongly held beliefs (delusions) or fears (paranoia). Group facilitators talk to identified individuals, going through a sheet describing this approach, and inviting them to learn more about it, meet others in the same situation and learn new coping techniques. The fact that someone is in hospital, suggesting others do not share their viewpoint or are concerned about them, can be helpful in persuasion. By these means, it is often possible to engage the interest of people who are otherwise quite alienated by the mental health system, as well as those who are content with it.

Session 1

The approach is characterized by treating participants as the interested and intelligent adults that they are, and so presenting (briefly) the research findings behind the key ideas. Thus, Romme and Escher's (1989) work on recognizing the widespread nature of voice hearing and introducing voice hearers who coped well with their voices to those who did not is presented as the foundation of the programme, with the rider that we extend it to other unusual experiences, unshared beliefs and fears. We then invite participants to give examples of how their experiences might fit into this spectrum, but with no pressure to contribute. Lack of pressure is particularly important, as it is a short group for people at an acute stage of their problems. Attending the groups and not saying a word is perfectly acceptable, but most people feel able to share at least after they have got to know the other participants.

We then introduce the idea of openness to voices and strange experiences – the Schizotypy spectrum (Chapter 7, this volume). The positive and the negative aspects of high schizotypy are discussed, as well as the ways in which even low schizotypes might find themselves plunged into this type of experience (sleep deprivation, hostage experiences, taking street drugs, etc.) The group and facilitators come up with examples of famous high schizotypes; artists such as Van Gogh or celebrities, as Stephen Fry. We then introduce the specific example of a high schizotype who used this to advantage in the singer David Bowie. Bowie surmounted this vulnerability and used his high schizotypy to great effect in his act, adopting varied strange personae, with a theme of being an alien from outer space (Buckley, 2001). This example provides an accessible role model of someone who was able to inhabit both 'realities', shared and unshared; to know which he was in at any one time, and move from one to the other and so operate both creatively in a way that communicated and be effective in the wider world.

The rest of the group programme aims to provide strategies to manage openness to unshared reality and participate in the shared world, without necessarily totally rejecting the transliminal. This contrasts with other mental health programmes which tend to aim at elimination of 'symptoms' (i.e. unshared experiences). For some people, this is what they want. For others, it is not so simple, and much failure to comply with medication, and persistence with drug taking can be explained by this ambivalence.

In this way, the aims of the group are presented as something that will give the participants more control, but without having to reject their unique experiences or to accept a stigmatizing label. Medication can be accepted as one of these possible means of control along with psychological coping strategies. The need to commit to monitoring, to noticing whether they are in shared or unshared reality, is presented as essential to following the programme at this point and monitoring sheets are handed out to be filled in between sessions. Participants are also invited to identify a personal goal for the group. This is rated at the end on a visual analogue line and represents an ideographic evaluation tool (see Durrant *et al.*, 2007: p. 123. for a description of how this is used).

Session 2

This session is organized around the role of state of arousal in increasing or decreasing vulnerability to unshared reality (symptoms), and discussion of ways of managing this. The results of the monitoring (whether actually filled in on the

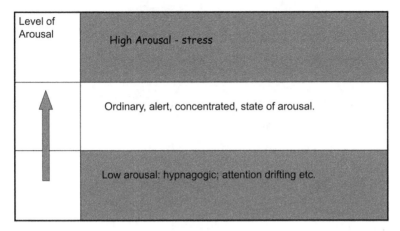

Figure 15.1   The role of Arousal: The shaded area is where anomalous experience/symptoms are more accessible

sheet, or more usually, verbally reported), is used as a basis for this. In a typical group, some participants report having more trouble with voices, etc. at times of stress, but many note that it is when they are trying to get to sleep, or generally in a drifting state of mind that these experiences are most in evidence. This is represented in the form of a diagram (above), which helps to identify the time at which shared reality is most accessible as the alert, concentrated, state in-between the identified states of high and low arousal.

This leads naturally into a discussion of arousal management, whether using breathing control, relaxation, exercise, etc. as means of managing high arousal or engaged activity to avoid low arousal. The latter can present a challenge in hospital!

This simple conceptualization coincides with the conditions leading to asynchrony between the propositional and implicational subsystems in ICS. We do not burden the group with an exposition of ICS, but illustrate the point using an adapted version of Linehan's (1993b. p. 109) 'States of Mind diagram which maps neatly onto these subsystems, with the overlapping 'wise mind' state representing the central engine of cognition when the two central subsystems are working together (Fig 15.2).

The advantage of adapting this diagram is that it is widely employed in the therapeutic programmes run in the hospital, and some at least of the participants in the group will probably be also enrolled in the Dialectical Behaviour Therapy based Emotional Coping Skills group (Rendle and Wilson, 2008).

Session 3

Having introduced ways of avoiding unshared experiences, we now turn to the complementary approach of facing them. In research terms, the elegant study by Haddock *et al.*, (1998) provides a neat introduction. They compared teaching two opposite coping techniques for dealing with voices with the study participants;

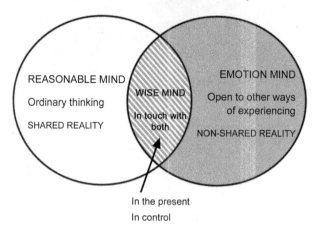

Figure 15.2 Linehan's states of mind applied to psychosis

distraction and focusing. Concentrating on some absorbing task, as recommended in the previous session, would constitute distraction. Focusing means attending to the voices, but in a detached, not an absorbed way. Rather than becoming pre-occupied with what the voice was saying, or the content of thoughts, participants were invited to note the voice, and then turn attention to form and characteristics; loudness, what sort of voice, etc. The group is asked which approach they think was most effective. The answer is a bit of a trick, as both strategies produced a similar decrease in symptoms. However, focusing had beneficial and lasting effects on the self-esteem of the participants.

Since this early research, there has been a blossoming of interest in applying mindfulness to any number of mental health problems (e.g. Kabat-Zinn, 1994; Segal, Williams and Teasdale, 2002), including psychosis (Chadwick, Newman-Taylor and Abba, 2005; Chadwick *et al.*, 2009), and this represents the same principle of detached attention as focusing. This is therefore the point at which we introduce mindfulness as a coping strategy. It is possible that the participants have come across mindfulness before during their stay in the hospital, as it is a basic element of the therapeutic programme.

Before initiating a very brief grounding and mindfulness exercise, we invite a discussion on what might get in the way. Mindfulness in the context of distressing voices or ideas is an exposure technique. The natural reaction is a flinch; avoidance. All the evidence (extensive in the field of anxiety disorders) shows that avoidance responses serve to entrench whatever is avoided. Requiring someone to face the abusive voice, for example, requires courage and we name this and discuss this. Similarly, even where the unshared ideas are not unpleasant, the individual might have identified pre-occupation with them as unhelpful and so be reluctant to engage them. Facing the possibility that a cherished idea is unshared is similarly challenging. Mindfulness requires attention to internal events such as these, along with equal attention to bodily sensation, for instance, breathing, and stimuli from the external world, such as sounds. Starting the exercise with attention to the body and sense stimuli provides a firm grounding that can make the achievement of a different relationship with the unshared experiences more possible to achieve. Once introduced to the exercise, participants are encouraged to practice between groups.

Session 4

This session is an opportunity to review the group, to return to the goals identified in the first session, and to introduce the possibility that openness to these experiences might have a role in the wider context of the individual's life. This aspect is introduced quite lightly in what is a very brief programme. We first initiate discussion into the pros and cons of using coping strategies to manage 'unshared reality', acknowledging that this is a matter of choice and there are arguments on both sides, but that our agenda is to try and coax people to join the shared world. This is made harder where they have been offered a devalued and stigmatized position in this world by virtue of their diagnosis, whereas unshared reality often offers a more exalted position, even if accompanied by frightening experiences.

We then introduce another research based idea: Mike Jackson's problem solving view of psychosis (Chapter 12) and invite discussion around this, suggesting early breakdown experiences as significant. This usually produces a recognition that times of stress, specific trauma or both, preceded the initial breakdown. The more positive perspective introduced in a number of the chapters in this book (e.g. Chapters 12, 13, 14, 16 and 18) that such experiences can be the route to personal growth and an expanded perspective is floated. This resonates with some participants, but not others. We conclude with the participants marking where they have reached on their goal setting visual analogue line and completing questionnaires.

Evaluation

Evaluating any therapeutic activity, whether individual or group, in the inpatient setting is challenging (see Durrant and Tolland, 2008 for more on this subject). A formal evaluation was made possible by the award of a small grant through a stigma reduction programme of the Care Service Improvement Programme (Phillips, Clarke and Wilson, unpublished data). In line with the Recovery idea (Repper and Perkins, 2003) of aiming for adaptation rather than symptom reduction, and being realistic about what can be achieved in a four session programme in an acute unit, we settled for measuring mental health confidence (Carpinello et al., 2000), using the ideographic goal setting measure already referred to and administering a satisfaction questionnaire at the end of the group. Before and after comparison of the Mental Health Confidence and goal setting scales showed significant improvement, and the feedback received from the exit questionnaire (administered by the researcher, not the facilitators) was encouraging. As the sample was small and there was no control group, these results need to be viewed cautiously. To bring the impact of this programme to life for this chapter, I requested an interview with one of the participants, who had followed the group with particular interest and attention; this interview follows now.

Jemma's Account

Jemma is a young woman in her 20s who had a very brief admission to the hospital, with no previous contact with psychiatric services. She was experiencing an acute stress reaction, following a weekend at a festival with friends, which she had found exhilarating and overwhelming, and which had catapulted her into the transliminal in a manner which became stuck and terrifying (no street drugs involved). Psychiatric medication helped to ground her, and she had one session of individual psychology and attended the four session group, returning to complete it after discharge (along with her partner, T, at her request). She was recuperating at her mother's house, with support from the local mental health services, when I interviewed her.

JEMMA: (*describing the onset of the episode*): I felt I got myself into a panic. I couldn't work out what was right, whether I ought to drink or sleep. I got it into my mind that if I went to sleep without drinking enough I would die. I hadn't spoken to my Mum for a while and I had just been to that festival, and it was such an intense experience I didn't want it to end. I didn't want to come back to reality, so I didn't want to go to sleep because I didn't want it to end. That resulted in me not sleeping, and drinking a lot of water, which resulted in me having a lot of experiences that were not real. I don't remember a lot of them, but it was very real to me at the time and it still affects me now.

ISABEL: What was it like coming into hospital?

JEMMA: Awful. I thought I was in hell. I remember looking at the sun and thinking, 'Am I dying? Am I dead?' I remember waking up after an intense dream and nothing familiar around me, and I just freaked out because I didn't know where I was; I didn't know where my Mum was; whether she was dead; whether T was dead, and I was just so scared that I didn't know what to do. Thankfully, the hospital gave me drugs to calm myself down. I am still taking meds. now. Living in reality is kind of . . . it's not great! I am finding it quite difficult to ground myself now. Looking back to going into the hospital feels like a dream now.

ISABEL: What do you remember about the group programme and the individual psychology session?

JEMMA: I felt that I was understood. That is important when you have got family who do not understand what you have been through. To meet someone who does understand, and who understands from an outside perspective was really good.

ISABEL: What gave you the impression that I understood, perhaps differently from the rest of the hospital?

JEMMA: It just made sense, what you said about real and unreal experience/shared and unshared reality, made sense. Because I do take things very seriously, and I sometimes perceive things in a wrong way. The way I perceive things in unshared reality. Since having that, if I take something the wrong way, I say, 'No, wait a minute, that is an unshared reality'. I have a lot of unshared reality moments with people in general.

ISABEL: Recognising that you were sensitive and sometimes picked up more than was actually happening?

JEMMA: Yes, and I have always been like that, so it was a grounding.

ISABEL: Anything else you remember.

JEMMA: The mindfulness. Just coming down and checking where you are. I have been trying to be mindful, but it is quite difficult. Sometimes, I am floating off, and then I will come to sit down, and it is like being a bit drunk and realizing – zoning in.

ISABEL: Because you have that sensitivity it is very easy for you to float off into that unshared reality place.

JEMMA: It is very easy. I am finding it difficult to ground myself, and I have been relying on support from everyone to just come back to reality, because I don't really like reality. It is too easy to just float off.

ISABEL: Is it a bit tempting sometimes?

JEMMA: Oh yes, oh yes, it is very tempting. I am finding the management of it quite difficult. I float off really easily, especially since what happened. I am finding it difficult to slow my mind down and do things.

ISABEL: Do you remember what else was suggested in the group that can help?

JEMMA: The deep breathing. Every time I do it now, T reminds me. It is amazing how much it helps. Taking a step back. I have been doing knitting and sewing.

ISABEL: Doing manageable things in the present.

JEMMA: Yes, and being mindful when you are doing things, like making a cup of tea. I have been trying to be mindful, which makes me go a lot slower.

ISABEL: How do you feel about the illness idea?

JEMMA: That is a difficult one. People said, unlike when you break a leg, no-one knows when you have a mental disorder but you are really unwell. So, take these tablets and you will feel better. I was really grateful for that when things were very bad, because I knew they were helping me. I could see a lot of other patients did not think that they were helping, but I knew their doctors knew how to help them.

ISABEL: Did you see the schizotypy idea as a different way of looking at it?

JEMMA: In a way. It made me feel good, because I thought, I am creative, which means I can do these things, but it also means that I am quite sensitive. Very sensitive, and it has its ups and its downsides. Being creative is exciting, but being sensitive is a weight in a way.

ISABEL: Two different ways of framing the same thing: illness or vulnerability that you have to manage.

JEMMA: The vulnerability idea made me understand it because my Mum was always saying to me, Jen you are too sensitive. I thought, I know I am sensitive, but

I think that is a good thing. In the group, it was nice to meet other people who had been through things and managed to stabilize themselves because I am finding it difficult, and so it was very reassuring. It was interesting learning about the high schizotypy. It was interesting to think about the different types of mind. I have always thought that some people are very creative and some people are very logical. I have always been very creative so it made sense that the high sensitivity went with creativity. I always preferred being around creative people because I can relate to them.

My friend has spoken to me about rational and emotional mind before, so that made sense. Getting to wise mind, getting the balance is quite difficult. Having T in the group with me helped. We can work on getting that balance together. It makes sense

Conclusion

My hope is that Jemma's account has given a better idea of the programme and its potential impact. It has aroused interest locally beyond the hospital service, in particular with the Assertive Outreach Team (AOT), as it has helped to engage previously disaffected service users. As a result, a longer version of the programme has been developed with participation from service user graduates, for AOT and community participants, and the plan is to seek funding to evaluate this properly, in collaboration with service users. In this way, hopefully, some of these ideas can filter through into the literature and evidence base, and start to influence therapeutic practice more widely.

16

Visionary Spiritual Experiences

David Lukoff

The term visionary is used in the anthropological and religious literature to refer to a mental condition that leads an individual to propose changes for an entire culture. However, in most cases, a Visionary Spiritual Experiences (VSE) does not transform the culture, but sometimes adds a new dimension to the individual's spiritual life. This chapter reviews criteria for identifying VSEs and implications for psychotherapy to address the spiritual dimensions of such experiences.

Visionary Spiritual Experiences

Psychotic and spiritual experiences have been associated since the earliest recorded history. The Old Testament uses the same term to refer to madness sent by God as a punishment for the disobedient, and to describe the behaviour of prophets (Rosen, 1968). Socrates declared, 'Our greatest blessings come to us by way of madness, provided the madness is given us by divine gift' (Dodds, 1951). In more recent years, religious institutions and the mental health field – especially in the West – have taken a more dichotomous view of spirituality and psychosis. When spirituality and psychosis overlap, the experience has usually been viewed as pathological. Yet some contemporary clinicians and researchers have also observed that psychotic episodes occasionally result in improvements in an individual's functioning. Karl Menninger, often recognised as a founder of American psychiatry, noted:

> Some patients have a mental illness and then get well and then they get weller! I mean they get better than they ever were . . . This is an extraordinary and little-realised truth (Silverman, 1967).

Boisen (1962), who was hospitalised for a psychotic episode and then became a minister who founded the field of pastoral counselling, maintained:

Psychosis and Spirituality: Consolidating the New Paradigm Second Edition   Edited by Isabel Clarke
© 2010 John Wiley & Sons, Ltd.

Many of the more serious psychoses are essentially problem solving experiences which are closely related to certain types of religious experiences (Bowers, 1979).

But these episodes will resolve spontaneously with appropriate support, and can lead to improvements in well-being, psychological health, and awareness of the spiritual dimension in life. There are scores of self-reports and case studies documenting such outcomes (Chapman and Lukoff, 1996; Dorman, 2004; Lukoff and Everest, 1985). Many view the episode as a spiritual awakening and initiation. Jungian analyst John Perry (1998) noted that after a VSE:

> What remains ... is an ideal model and a sense of direction which one can use to complete the transformation through his own purposeful methods.

Cross-Cultural and Historical Perspectives on VSES

Based on a cross-cultural survey, anthropologist Prince (1992) concluded that:

> Highly similar mental and behavioural states may be designated psychiatric disorders in some cultural settings and religious experiences in others ... Within cultures that invest these unusual states with meaning and provide the individual experiencing them with institutional support, at least a proportion of them may be contained and channelled into socially valuable roles.

For example, anthropological accounts show that babbling confused words, displaying curious eating habits, singing continuously, dancing wildly, and being 'tormented by spirits' are common elements in shamanic initiatory crises. In shamanic cultures, such crises are interpreted as an indication of an individual's destiny to become a shaman, rather than a sign of mental illness (Halifax, 1979).

In Asian cultures, problems associated with spiritual practices are recognised and are distinguished from psychopathology. For example, a well-known pitfall of meditation practice is 'false enlightenment', associated with delightful or terrifying visions, especially of light (Epstein and Topgay, 1982). Beginning in the 1960s, interest in Asian spiritual practices such as meditation, yoga, and tai chi, as well as experimentation with psychedelic drugs, triggered many VSEs, some of which were problematic for their practitioners:

The contemporary spiritual scene is like a candy store where any casual spiritual 'tourist' can sample the 'goodies' that promise a variety of mystical highs. When novices who don't have the proper education or guidance begin to naively and carelessly engage mystical experiences, they are playing with fire (Caplan, 1999: p. 74).

The similarity between psychotic symptoms and mystical experiences has received acknowledgment and discussion in the mental health field (Arieti, 1976; Boisen, 1962; Buckley, 1981; James, 1958). Both involve escaping the limiting boundaries of the self, which leads to an immense elation and freedom as the outlines of the confining selfhood melt down. The need to transcend the limiting boundaries of the self has been postulated to be a basic neurobiological need of all living things (Newberg, D'Aquili and Rause, 2001). However, during psychotic episodes, if 'the sense of embodied self is transcended before it has been firmly established ... disintegration and further fragmentation are the likely results' (Mills, 2001, p. 214).

People who have undergone VSEs have, in ancient western, as well as traditional cultures, been esteemed and enjoyed privileged status as shamans, prophets, or saints. However, in contemporary Western society, experiences such as seeing visions and hearing voices, experiencing oneself communicating with or being a religious figure are viewed as delusions and hallucinations, symptoms of a psychotic disorder. People in the midst of VSEs have difficulty obtaining support from either the healthcare system or religious institutions. 'If a member of a typical congregation were to have a profound religious experience, its minister would very likely send him or her to a psychiatrist for medical treatment' (Grof, 1986). Religion and spirituality have also been suspected of triggering and exacerbating symptoms of a psychotic disorder although comprehensive literature reviews show positive associations between religion and outcomes from psychotic disorders (Koenig, McCullough and Larson, 2001).

Some individuals who have been through it consider religion and spirituality to be integral in the makeup and working through of psychosis (Lukoff and Lu, 2005). Clinicians with this perspective, mainly transpersonal psychologists, have described psychosis as a natural developmental process with both spiritual and psychological components. They have also pointed out and discussed the similarity between psychotic symptoms and spiritual experiences (Arieti, 1976; Buckley, 1981; James, 1958), and have argued that psychotic experiences are better understood as crises related to the person's efforts to break out of the standard ego-bounded identity: 'trials of the soul on its spiritual journey' (House, 2001, pp. 124–125).

Some mainstream researchers and practitioners have also taken a new look at religion and spirituality in persons with psychotic disorders. They have begun to show how religion serves as a resource for individuals coping with psychosis. Mainstream practitioners have recently created therapy programmes for persons with serious mental illness (SMI) that address religious and spiritual issues. These therapists help mental health consumers discover and share their spiritual resources, believing that clients' spirituality can help them grow and cope with their mental difficulties.

If cases of VSE could be differentiated from cases of serious psychotic disorders, the prognosis for such individuals could be improved by providing appropriate treatment consistent with their need to express and integrate the experience in a safe environment. This chapter presents a model delineating the overlap between VSEs and psychotic disorders, and suggests guidelines for making diagnostic and treatment decisions from a psychiatric perspective which recognises this overlap.

Unusual Experiences in VSES

Voices and Visions

Auditory and visual experiences have played an essential role in religion for thousands of years. Accounts range from Biblical prophets and saints to shamans, as well as Socrates's famous Daemon voice that guided him. Later, psychiatrists have retroactively diagnosed all of them to have had mental disorders (Leuder and Thomas, 2000). However, the DSM-IV (American Psychiatric Association, 1994) specifically notes that clinicians assessing for schizophrenia in socioeconomic or cultural situations different from their own must take cultural differences into account: 'In some cultures, visual or auditory hallucinations with a religious content may be a normal part of religious experience (e.g. seeing the Virgin Mary or hearing God's voice' (p. 281). In a study of visions among Hispanic clinic patients, Lata (2005) found that 'psychotic phenomena could occur in connection with spiritual experiences. Visions of loved ones who have died occur constantly, as well as visions of saints, angels, Jesus, and Mary'.

Several survey studies have shown that more than half of the normal population has some experience with voices (Posey and Losch, 1983), and approximately 10% of the general population have the experience of hearing a comforting or advising voice that is not perceived as being one's own thoughts (Barret and Etheridge, 1992). Voices and visions frequently occur in people during bereavement, life-threatening situations, and stressful traumatic situations such as sensory deprivation, sleep deprivation, illness and solitary confinement (Forrer, 1960).

Inner voices have played a significant role in the lives of many noted individuals including Carl Jung, Elisabeth Kubler-Ross, Martin Luther King, Jr., and Winston Churchill. Hearing inner voices is often experienced as helpful by people who are experiencing a spiritual awakening (Heery, 1989).

Unusual Beliefs

The DSM-IV (American Psychiatric Association, 1994) notes that 'Ideas that may appear to be delusional in one culture (e.g. sorcery and witchcraft) may be commonly held in another'. (p. 281). Research has confirmed the overlap between beliefs considered psychotic and spiritual. Peter's chapter (this volume, Chapter 11) reports on studies comparing adherents of New Religious Movements with a diagnosed sample, concluding that those in the NRM group could not be distinguished from the inpatients by their beliefs, but could by their mood and adjustment. Detailed cases show that unusual beliefs can occur in the context of spiritual experiences (Jackson and Fulford, 1997; Lukoff, 1991). Greenberg, Witzum and Buchbinder (1992) described four young men who explored Jewish mysticism and became psychotic. Their voices, grandiose and paranoid beliefs, and social withdrawal were indistinguishable from those of many mystics. Thus empirical studies comparing individuals who are both religious and deluded call into question diagnostic criteria for delusions that emphasise the content (i.e. bizarreness or falsity) of beliefs to classify them as pathological (Brett, 2002).

In addition, holding an unusual belief with absolute conviction is not a sign of pathology in itself because all beliefs that are personally significant tend to be held with absolute conviction (Maher, 1988). A feature of normal cognition is a confirmation bias that allows us to be impervious to contradictory evidence and only notice information that confirms our pre-existing beliefs (Alloy and Tabachnik, 1984)

Differential Diagnosis between Psychotic Disorders and VSEs

Over the past 30 years, there has developed a body of literature on approaches to distinguishing VSEs, particularly mystical experiences and spiritual emergencies, from psychotic disorders. Iatrogenic problems may occur if VSEs are misdiagnosed and mistreated, possibly contributing to poorer outcomes in industrial societies where the rate of full recovery is lower and level of impairment of persons with psychotic disorders is considerably higher than in non-industrial societies. In an interview study, 'the most subjectively frightening aspect of their experience was psychiatric hospitalisation itself' (Jackson, 2001; p. 189). The diagnosis of a mental disorder is still stigmatising in contemporary American culture. The clinician's initial assessment can significantly influence whether the experience is integrated and used as a stimulus for personal growth, or repressed as a sign of mental disorder, thereby intensifying an individual's sense of isolation and blocking his or her efforts to understand and assimilate the experience.

The DSM-IV category Religious or Spiritual Problem (V62.89) is not a mental disorder, but is listed in the section for Other Conditions That May Be the Focus of Clinical Attention. The proposal for this diagnostic category had its roots in concerns about the misdiagnosis and treatment of spiritual emergencies. The inclusion of this new diagnostic category in 1994 marked the acknowledgement that distressing religious and spiritual experiences occur as non-pathological problems:

> Religious or Spiritual Problem (V62.89). This category can be used when the focus of clinical attention is a religious or spiritual problem. Examples include distressing experiences that involve loss or questioning of faith, problems associated with conversion to a new faith, or questioning of other spiritual values which may not necessarily be related to an organised church or religious institution (American Psychiatric Association, 1994, p. 685)

VSEs warrant the DSM-IV diagnosis of Religious or Spiritual Problem even when there may be symptoms present that are usually considered psychotic, including hallucinations and delusions. In this regard, the category Religious or Spiritual Problem is comparable with the V-Code category Bereavement. The DSM-IV notes that even when a person's reaction to a death meets the diagnostic criteria for Major

Depressive Episode, the diagnosis of a mental disorder is not given because the symptoms result from a normal reaction to the death of a loved one. Similarly, in VSEs, transient hallucinations, delusions, bizarre behaviour and interpersonal difficulties occur so frequently that they should be considered normal and expectable features (Lukoff, 1985).

Treatment of VSEs

Interventions range widely: residential treatment, support for a time-limited crisis with involvement of relatives, friends, support groups and healthcare professionals, intensive long-term psychotherapy. Choice of specific interventions depends on the intensity, duration, and type of VSE, and also on the individual and their support network.

Psychotherapy can help people shape their VSE into a coherent narrative, to see the 'message' contained in their experiences, and to create a life-affirming personal belief system that integrates their experience. Depth psychotherapy can help some individuals probe the personal meaning of their symptoms, and also see the universal dimensions of their experiences (Dorman, 2004).

Some residential approaches have also developed. Kingsley Hall, started in England in the late 1960s by R.D. Laing and others who identified themselves as part of an 'anti-psychiatry' movement, was the first attempt to provide alternative non-medical model residential treatment.

Diabysis, a Jungian-based group treatment home people for experiencing a first psychotic episode was started by John Perry and operated in San Francisco during the 1970s. Medications were rarely used. Instead, Perry encouraged clients to express and explore the symbolic aspects of their psychotic experiences. Perry (1992) reported that when clients were treated with this model, most came through their psychotic episodes within 6–10 weeks. Through case studies of approximately 20 psychotic patients, Perry (1974) found themes including the destruction of the world, a cosmic fight between good and evil, the appearance of a messiah that the client identifies him/herself with, and a sense of rebirth of the world into a more loving place. The purpose of these mythic motifs was similar for both the individual and society – a transformation of a way of life (Perry 1974). For these patients who worked through the psychotic experience, a new worldview emerged, one more accepting and kind towards the self and others.

Perry's model is based on the finding that the psychotic phase in some individuals is temporary, a symbolic vision quest that initiates changes that are on the horizon for the person. If the process can be explored instead of squelched with medication and lack of acknowledgment, then a return to higher levels of functioning might be possible. Perry created a group home residence called Diabasis for individuals presenting with recent onset psychosis (Perry, 1974). Only non-mental health professionals were hired to assist the clients, as Perry believed educated clinicians had embedded conceptualisations of schizophrenia that would only interfere with their ability to follow such a novel treatment approach. Perry looked for staff members who were open to diverse life experiences, sociable and good listeners. The staff members' duties included acting as caretakers (helping oversee cooking, cleaning, etc.) as well as functioning as therapists. The residence consisted of a typical living facility (bedrooms, kitchen, living room) with the addition of a 'venting room' that encouraged residents to express their concerns, no matter how intense. Therapy, conducted thrice weekly, consisted of listening to clients and helping them interpret the powerful and spiritual symbols within their hallucinations and delusions.

Diabysis closed down as a result of budget cutbacks in the mental health system. The average length of stay was 48 days. Perry reported that severely psychotic clients became coherent within 2–6 days without medication. The outcomes appeared better for those who had had fewer than three previous psychotic episodes. Unfortunately, other quantitative data were not collected for this sample.

A similar programme, Soteria House, located in San Jose, California, provided more empirical support for this model (Mosher, Hendrix and Fort, 2004). Soteria House ran from 1971 to 1983, roomed six clients, with 3–4 staff on premises at one time. Most staff were non-professionals, chosen because of their lack of exposure to the medical model in mental health treatment (to which Soteria House did not adhere). Other criteria for staff included being 'psychologically tough' (willing to sit with unusual behaviours and beliefs) and good at listening. The staff were trained to recognise that psychotic experiences were a developmental stage that can lead to growth, often containing a spiritual component of mystical experiences and beliefs. Medication was typically not prescribed unless a client showed no improvement after 6 weeks (only 10% of clients used medication at Soteria), because it was believed to stunt the possible growth-enhancing process of the psychotic episode. Limits were set if clients became a danger to themselves or others. A project director and quarter-time psychiatrist were also employed.

Outcomes from Soteria were compared with a 'traditional' programme, a community mental health centre inpatient service consisting of daily pharmaco-therapy, psychotherapy, occupational therapy and group therapy. After a few weeks clients in the traditional programme were referred for outpatient care, including partial hospitalisation or halfway houses. Criteria for admission to either programme required patients to be unmarried, between the ages of 15 and 30, diagnosed with schizophrenia and in need of hospitalisation. Because of practical considerations, random assignment of clients to each treatment programme was not used (at times, there were no beds available in the Soteria programme). However, there were no significant differences across demographic and psychopathological variables at admission between the two groups (Bola and Mosher, 2003). Clients' length of stay was longer at Soteria than in the comparison programme (mean of 166 days versus 28 days). But most of the patients recovered in 6–8 weeks without medication (Mosher, Hendrix and Fort, 2004).

Bola and Mosher's (2003) 2-year follow-up study compared client outcomes across the two programmes. Thirty-three clients from Soteria were compared with 30 clients from a psychiatric hospital. An independent outside evaluation team conducted the assessment, although the authors report it was impossible to make them blind to the treatment. Four major differences were found. First, fewer Soteria subjects were using antipsychotic medication (4%) 2 years after admission than control subjects (43%). Second, Soteria participants were less likely to be using mental health services; this could be interpreted as an indication that clients were not in need of these services. However, an alternative conclusion is that clients were in need of these services but did not utilise these resources. A third divergence between the two groups was that Soteria clients had significantly higher ratings on occupational status at the end of the two-year time period compared with individuals treated in the control programme. The fourth significant distinction was that Soteria clients were more likely to be living on their own or with a peer at 2-year follow-up than were members of the control programme, who were more likely to be living at home with their parents. While both groups had significant declines in symptoms over the 2-year time span, there was not a significant difference on clients' level of pathology. It appears that treatment that allows psychosis to be 'worked through' by treating it as a powerful transformative process can work as well as current mainstream forms of intervention.

A recent meta-analysis of data from two carefully controlled studies of Soteria programmes found better 2-year outcomes for the randomly assigned Soteria patients in the domains of psychopathology, work and social functioning than for similar clients who were treated in a psychiatric hospital (Bola and Mosher, 2003). It does not seem that any residential programmes using this approach exist in the USA, but there are several Soteria homes in Europe (Turner, 2005).

Interventions

The following eight interventions are based on the approaches from Diabysis and Soteria along with case reports of people who have recovered from a VSE (Kornfield, 1993; Lukoff, 1996), personal communications with others who have worked with people in a VSE, consultation with Robert Turner (2005), a psychiatrist and homeopath, on dietary recommendations. However, few systematic studies comparing treatments for VSEs have been conducted.

Normalise

People in the midst of VSEs need a framework of understanding that makes sense to them. The most important task is to give people in crisis a positive context for their experiences and sufficient information about the process that they are going through. It is essential that they move away from the concept of disease and recognise the leading nature of their crisis (Grof and Grof, 1989).

The lack of such understanding, guidance and support can allow such experiences to become more distressful and psychopathological. Brant Cortright (1997), describes the clinical value of educating the client and significant others:

Education about spiritual emergency serves two primary functions. First, it gives the person a cognitive grasp of the situation, a map of the territory he or she is traversing. Having a sense of the terrain and knowing others have travelled these regions provides considerable relief in itself (p. 173).

Create a Therapeutic Container

John Perry (1974) emphasised that when a person's psyche is energised and activated, what he or she needs is contact with a person who empathises, who actively encourages the process, who provides a loving appreciation of the qualities emerging through the process, and who facilities the process rather than attempting to halt or interfere with it. Thus, Perry encouraged expression of the VSE because 'therapy should follow the psyche's own spontaneous movements . . . you work with what the psyche presents'. Depth psychotherapists, particularly those with Jungian and transpersonal training, are uniquely prepared to provide psychotherapy for people in VSEs because of their training in unconscious dynamics.

Help the Person to Reduce Environmental and Interpersonal Stimulation

The person undergoing a VSE needs to be shielded as much as possible from the stimulation of the everyday world, if it is experienced as painful and interfering with the inner process. This may include television, radio and loud music.

Have the Person Temporarily Discontinue Spiritual Practices

Meditation has triggered some reported spiritual emergencies. Meditation teachers who hold intensive retreats are familiar with this type of occurrence, and many such as those at Spirit Rock Meditation Centre have developed strategies for managing such occurrences (Kornfield, 1993). Yoga, Qi gong and other spiritual practices can also be triggers. DSM-IV includes Qi-Gong Psychotic Reaction as a culture-bound syndrome. Usually teachers advise ceasing the practice temporarily. It can be reintroduced as the person becomes more stable.

Suggest that the Person Eat a Diet of 'Heavy' Foods and Avoid Fasting

Grains (especially whole grains), beans, dairy products and meat are considered grounding ('heavy') foods as opposed to fruit and fruit juices, and salads. Sugar and stimulants like caffeine are also not advised.

Encourage the Person to Become Involved in Grounding, Calming Activities

Gardening or any simple tasks, such as knitting, housecleaning, shovelling or sorting can be calming. Encourage the patient to participate in regular exercises. Walks are an excellent way to help a person bring their focus of attention back into their body. Walks in nature have the added benefit of enhancing tranquility and a calm mind. If the patient is a regular participant in other activities such as swimming or biking, they could engage in that. However, competitive sports would be too stimulating.

Encourage the Person to use Expressive Arts Both in the Psychotherapy Sessions and at Home

Drawing, painting, making music, journaling, dancing and other creative arts can help a person express and work through his or her inner experience. The language of symbol and metaphor can help integrate what can never be fully verbalised. A successful case utilising this method was reported by Lindner (1954) who treated a research physicist by encouraging him to fully explore and express his delusional beliefs that he lived on another planet and travelled into other universes. At the end of the therapy, the scientist had achieved a state of objectivity and distance from these experiences which allowed him to return from these adventures.

Evaluate for Medication

Some practitioners, such as John Perry, have argued that medications inhibit a person's ability to concentrate on the inner work and impede the individual's capacity to move the process forward. However, sometimes the process is so intense that the person is overwhelmed and becomes very anxious. That person could benefit from slowing down the process. Bruce Victor, a psychiatrist and psychopharmacologist, recommends using low doses of tranquilising or anti-psychotic medication with some individuals to alleviate some of the most distressing feelings and allow the person to better assimilate the experience.

It becomes a challenge to determine whether the person can actively work with the pain therapeutically toward further psychological growth . . . One important role of pharmacotherapy is to titrate the level of symptoms, whether they be pain, depression, anxiety or psychotic states, so that they can be integrated by the person in the service of growth (Victor, 1995).

Conclusion

Polls conducted over the past 35 years have shown a dramatic increase in the percentages of people who report VSEs such as mystical, near-death, psychic and alien abduction experiences (Gallup, 1987). During the last 25 years, there has also been a significant increase in participation in spiritual practices such as meditation, yoga, qi gong sweat lodges, drumming circles and other practices which can induce intense spiritual experiences. The majority of these experiences are not problematic, do not disrupt psychological/social/occupational functioning and do not necessitate mental health treatment. However, with the increase of such practices, it can be expected that the incidence of VSEs seen in treatment will increase.

James Hillman (1983) pointed out that 'Recovery means recovering the divine from within the disorder, seeing that its contents are authentically religious'. Rarely after a VSE does an individual actually lead a transformative movement for the entire culture. However, through psychotherapy, such individuals may be able to salvage personally valid spiritual dimensions of their experience. By eliciting the client's perspective and offering an individualised, treatment strategy, clinicians are more likely to help people having a VSE control the distressing aspects of the voices and delusions, minimise stigma and discrimination, make meaning of the experience, and achieve a full recovery.

17

Learning to Become Centred and Grounded and Let the Voices Come and Go

Nigel Mills

This chapter will first explore the experience of fragmentation that accompanies, or "is" the psychoses. I will then describe how the use of centring and grounding techniques drawn from the Taoist systems of Qigong and Tai Chi, can serve as a way of anchoring the attention so the person is more able to let psychotic phenomena 'come and go'. The chapter will finally make some links to the Buddhist practice of mindfulness; mindfulness based cognitive therapy and the cultivation of compassion.

Fragmentation

Feeling fragmented or fearing becoming fragmented is a common theme in people with a diagnosis of psychosis. A while ago the National Schizophrenia Fellowship published a collection of first-hand accounts of the experience of schizophrenia. Here are some of the words that came up again and again:

'Disintegrating', 'fragmented', 'out of my body', 'floating', 'all over the place' and for one contributor:

'To be schizophrenic is best summed up in a repeating dream that I have had since childhood. In this dream, I am lying on a beautiful sunlit beach but my body is in pieces. This fact causes me no concern until I realise that the tide is coming in and that I am unable to gather the parts of my dismembered body together to run away. The tide gets closer and just when I am on the point of drowning I wake up screaming in panic. This to me is what schizophrenia feels like; being fragmented in one's personality and constantly being afraid that the tide of illness will completely cover me'.

Psychosis and Spirituality: Consolidating the New Paradigm Second Edition   Edited by Isabel Clarke
© 2010 John Wiley & Sons, Ltd.

In the sections that follow, I will describe how it is possible to encourage a sense of having one's awareness centred and grounded, so as to act as a counterpoint to this fragmentation. If one can learn to anchor one's attention in a more centred way then comes the possibility of feeling safer in ones world and also there is the possibility of noticing things (voices and hallucinations), without being blown away by them. Just as we may watch clouds pass across the sky, so too we can watch the vagaries of our inner world pass too. However, we can only do that if we have our feet planted firmly on the ground, or we will let ourselves think we are floating away on the clouds too!

A Case Example

Robert, in his early 20s, has suffered from 'schizophrenia' for the last 3 years, he is describing a recent situation he found stressful, in which his father was telling him 'how difficult he is'. I ask Robert to re-run the event, slow the process down and to imagine 'if you and your father were engaged in a real physical fight, what would it be like?'

'It feels like he's hitting me over the head with a hammer'.

'And what do you fear is going to happen to you?'

'I'm going to shatter into pieces'.

Robert felt that when his father verbally criticised him, he was in real physical danger, not just of being hit, but of his sense of self, disintegrating somehow. His father never actually had hit him, but the way in which he spoke the words gave Robert that kinaesthetic experience. The perception of 'attack' has previously been identified as an important theme in psychotic episodes. The literature on expressed emotion (Dixon and Lehman, 1995) has described very clearly the role of hostility in family interactions as a precursor of relapse. The E.E. literature is described largely in verbal terms, however, Robert, and almost everyone else I have worked with, readily describe psychological 'attacks' as imagined physical ones. The fact that this is a common experience, not just in psychosis, is suggested by our use of language in such expressions as 'If looks could kill'; 'It feels like a slap in the face'; 'He pulls me down', etc.

Perceived Attack as A Trigger for Disassociation

I would like to suggest there is a difference between the non-psychotic and the psychotic individual in this respect. The non-psychotic person notices the 'attack' element of interaction and whilst feeling uncomfortable with it, they 'know' it is not a physical reality and does not signify real risk to 'self'.

The psychotic person, on the other hand, senses this element of attack and, at some level, makes a judgement that there is real risk to survival of 'self' and so, as has been well documented in abuse survivors (Finkelhor, 1988), they employ the strategy of withdrawing awareness from the current time and place and physical location (of the body). The resulting 'disassociation', may well be related to the development of psychotic symptoms.

How Can Being Centred and Grounded Help?

Many spiritual traditions and paths of personal development talk about the importance of paying attention, in an open way, to our moment to moment experience; becoming aware of emotions, but not being dominated by them; accessing a part of self that is centred, grounded and calm; cultivating the part of ourselves that is beyond the everyday chatter of our minds. There are various routes to this goal. In this chapter, I will focus on the kinaesthetic/sensory route as developed in Tai Chi/Qigong. I first reported qualitative feedback on a group for people with psychosis, employing 'being centred' principles over 12 years ago (Mills and Whiting, 1997). The approach has been refined with over 10 years of practice (Mills, 2007). However, it stays true to the basic principle of helping participants to cultivate a sense of being 'centred and grounded' in order to cope with psychological distress.

Tai Chi/Qigong is an ideal therapeutic approach for people who generally find words difficult and whose experience is often beyond words.

I have now run numerous groups, both in day hospitals and acute admission wards for people with a diagnosis of schizophrenia. The group is usually called 'Tai Chi'. I prefer to avoid the 'Coping with Voices' or 'Relapse Prevention, titles, as I wished to avoid labels that resonate with pathology. Calling the group 'Tai Chi', emphasises that it is about cultivating new patterns, not necessarily trying to get rid of old ones.

As an aside, a disadvantage of calling the group 'Tai Chi' is that is not taken so seriously by other NHS personnel. It seems our mental health culture only values interventions that refer to mental illness.

Grounding

Exercise.   Imagine your awareness searching down, between the rocks, Just as tree roots search for moisture and nutrients so your awareness can search for connection to the earth.

Seek out the grounding influence of the planet beneath your feet.
Sense the molten core at the centre of the earth, let yourself be open to the magnetic pull of the magnetic core.

Imagine yourself to be like a collection of iron filings, allow the magnetic core of the earth to bring all your scattered 'charge' into a more unified pattern.

Feel how you have a tendency to be drawn to the centre of the earth.

This connection with the earth can also be encouraged through activities which remind us of our dependence on the earth like gardening or walking in the countryside.

To cultivate a feeling of safety and shift your nervous system into 'safe mode', it is good to practice this cultivation of connection with the earth on a daily basis, do not leave it until you are feeling anxious. The practice and skill need to be cultivated when you are feeling fairly calm and in a non-threatening environment. When you have developed some skill in increasing your connection with the earth, then it is useful to test it out in an anxiety provoking situation. The task then is to allow the waves of anxiety to travel through the body and to pass into the earth; to allow the earth to soak up the anxiety.

Breathing

If you hold your breath, you would not be able to centre or ground your awareness.

Breathe out! Sigh, yawn, laugh, cry. It is amazing how many people hold on to their breath when they are anxious, or breathe in short sharp breaths. The attention then becomes stuck in the chest, and the ground seems a very long way away.

If a full out-breath has been achieved then the in-breath will follow naturally. This avoids a tendency to suck air in or to pull air in forcibly, which can in itself create a heightened state of tension and anxiety. Allowing a full out-breath, can encourage a general sense of letting go and releasing. There is no need to count breaths or count seconds in and seconds. These forced breathing techniques can set up further anxieties about 'doing it right'.

Let your belly soften, qigong is about allowing things to happen naturally. If you let your belly soften then it will become involved in the process of breathing, expanding on the in-breath and falling back on the out-breath.

In addition to increased oxygenation of the blood and the brain and calming of the autonomic nervous system, this relaxed abdominal breathing also has the effect of anchoring your awareness more fully into the body and away from the 'chatter' of the mind (Frantzis, 1999).

You Have to Come in Before You Can Safely Go Out

For the person vulnerable to psychosis, it is very important that a sense of 'safe self' be established. The psychoses have been described as a process in which the sense of embodied self is transcended before it has been firmly established (Birdfield, 1998). This is in contrast to the transcendence of self ultimately aimed for by a Taoist or Buddhist monk. A Taoist or Buddhist would for many years first practice exercises that gave them a firm sense of being 'in their body' – breathing, grounding and centring exercises, only then would they practise the more advanced skill of 'transcending'. The reader interested in the details of these philosophies is referred to Kabat-Zinn (1994) or Kennedy (1985) for a full discussion. The experience of these traditions is, that if there is not a firm sense of what is being transcended, disintegration and further fragmentation are the likely results. The need is first for a firmer sense of embodiment.

Developing a Sense of Embodiment

At the beginning of the group, we do some simple stretching and loosening up exercises, the external 'form' of these exercises is not so important, it is the way in which they are practised that is important. In our culture, we spend a large amount of time involved in mental activity, – even when we are 'relaxing' we are watching television or scanning the internet – our minds are always busy, and even when we are 'doing' exercises it is often at the 'command' of an active mind.

'I'm going to the gym so that my body will look better and then people might like me. . .'

The body is seldom listened to or enjoyed for its own sake but rather is related to as something which hangs beneath the neck as a functional collection of plumbing and electricity cabling on the inside and a 'shape' to be hated or lusted after on the outside. For a Taoist or Buddhist, this is a tragedy – a tragic loss of the inner life, of the inner sense of 'aliveness' which helps one to feel a resonance with all of nature. So we start the group by trying to re-gain a sense of that embodied 'aliveness' or 'energy'.

An example: Rotating the hands – loosening the wrists. Joint rotation is a movement common to many exercise systems. It is often done with an attitude of 'come on you stupid joint, you're going to loosen up, now' – rather like a sergeant major barking at his new recruits. At the other extreme is the detached, disinterested, limp-wristed attitude of 'I'm only doing this because I'm being told to, I wonder how much longer there is to go?'. Mind chattering away, body doing something – but on a different planet to the mind. In Tai Chi/Qi Gong, – the Taoist exercise system, body and mind are working as one. Mental awareness is concentrated in the body. The attitude is one of 'allowing' the hand to move, and the mind being an acute observer of the inner sensations; of the feel of the muscles, releasing and tightening to enable the movement to occur – of how the blood flow to the fingers is changed with the rotation of the work; of the relationship of breath and movement.

We 'enter' the hands, the shoulders, the hips, the knees, the ankles and the toes, breathing awareness into each part of the body, shifting the balance of 'activity' or 'energy' down from the head and into the body. This in itself is therapeutic – to develop a sense of pure 'aliveness' independent of the 'chattering of the mind' (Mills, 1999).

Moving with Mindfulness: Developing a Sense of Physical Integration

The next step brings these embodied enlivened parts of ourselves together, into movement; to move as a coordinated whole, to develop a sense that the different parts of our body are connected and integral to each other. Why? What is the relevance of that as a 'treatment' programme for schizophrenia? Because the fragmentation I referred to earlier, is not an intellectual idea, it is described by people diagnosed as having schizophrenia as a kinaesthetic reality. Experience of a way of movement which is integrated and has a sense of 'centre' about it can serve as a counter-point to that fragmentation. It is a 'taster' of another way of being in the world; not a new way of being, but there at birth, and for many years afterwards, until for some reason – biological, psychological, social or otherwise the mind decided an alternative strategy was called for – fragmentation. Fragmentation may have been adaptive as a short-term measure, but when installed as a permanent feature it does not seem to have much going for it. So in the group we aim to recreate that choice between staying integrated or fragmenting.

The movements of Tai Chi/Qi Gong are coordinated from a central place – the lower 'dantien' (or sometimes called 'the hara' in the Japanese traditions), approximately one and a half inches below the navel. Taoists place great emphasis on developing an awareness of this location. Placing awareness in the belly means that there is less mental activity – less 'fuel' for the delusions and hallucinations that often accompany psychosis. Here is one way to cultivate awareness of 'centre': through movement:

Session: Movement from a Sense of Centre

Stand with your feet one in front of the other in 'walking stance', begin to shift your weight backwards and forwards but feel that the movement is initiated from your waist, from the 'dantien'. As thoughts come to you let them trickle down from the brain towards your belly. Let the 'dantien' convert these thoughts into the energy of movement. Leaving the mind clear, there is nothing for the head to do except to be taken for a ride on this repetitive movement. The head is passenger, the belly is the driver. Let the arms hang loosely and follow along with the swing. Feel how the whole body is moving 'as one' (Mills and Allen, 2000). One integrated movement led by the 'dantien'. Allow your awareness to inhabit every muscle on the inside and every area of skin on the outside. Feel the movement of the air across your skin. Allow yourself to be present.

Sitting with Awareness at ones Centre

Come to rest, sit, but in such a way that you are supporting your own back. Rest your hands lightly over the lower belly. Give yourself permission to allow a full breath out, as when sighing or yawning. On the next breath-in, allow the breath to go deep into the body. Imagine the breath is passing down through a central channel, right down to the 'dantien' – one and a half inches below the navel. Feel that the breath starts and finishes from the dantien. Notice how the passage of the breath may feel tighter or easier at certain points on its journey down. Give the tight areas some space, cultivate an attitude of 'allowing'. Allowing space to be created, allowing muscles to soften, allowing the breath to deepen.

For a fuller treatment of Taoist breathing, along with CD guides, see Frantzis (1999).

Sensing Your Centre

If you are a sensory or visual person you may prefer to use the following method of centring as a 'way in'. It is important, however, that the connection made with the sense of centre does not remain a merely visual one but 'bridges' into a more kinaesthetic modality, like this:

> Place your finger-tips approximately one and a half inches below the navel, close your eyes, let yourself become aware of the area behind your fingers – inside your body. Imagine this area can act like a receiving reservoir, a reservoir for your energy, a reservoir for your awareness, feel how any excess energy in your body can trickle down like water, and be stored in this place ... Once you have allowed your awareness to gather at this place, feel how you can use this location as a 'base' from which to notice and accept sensations in the rest of the body: Notice them, accept them, let them go, bring your awareness back to centre.

See Frantzis (Frantzis1999, 2006) and Jahnke (2002) for fuller details of the approach sketched here. The important point is that once a sense of centre has been developed, one's awareness has somewhere to rest; a home. If your awareness has no home base then it will be seduced away by the wandering thoughts, voices and images that pass across our minds.

A Link with Cognitive Behaviour Therapy

Of course, it can sometimes feel scary to remain present and centred. When faced with highly charged emotional environments it feels safer to disappear. An unspoken assumption may be something like: 'If I was to stay present in this time and place and keep my awareness in my body then all the emotion flying around will destroy me'. It may feel safer therefore to disassociate, to become uncentred. A pattern becomes established and it is hard to get back to the natural state of being centred and grounded. The intervention, as described in this chapter – of being centred and being present could be seen in cognitive therapy terms, as a behavioural experiment for the client to test out, and disprove, the validity of the above assumption. I have previously (Mills, 2001a) described how body-oriented methods can be incorporated into cognitive therapy and lead to a more multi-modal pathway towards therapeutic change.

How Does This Relate to Mindfulness-Based Cognitive Therapy?

Being mindful entails bringing ones full attention to ones present experience in an accepting, non-judgemental way (Chadwick *et al.*, 2009).

There is now substantial research evidence that 'mindfulness' and related practices are beneficial to mental health. Mindfulness meditation for anxiety disorders has been shown to result in significant improvements which are maintained at three year follow-up (Kabat-Zinn, 1994). Mindfulness has also been researched as a therapeutic approach for chronic depression (Segal, Williams and Teasdale, 2002). Recently, an adaptation of the basic mindfulness programme has been shown to have potential for people with psychosis (Chadwick *et al.*, 2009).

Teasdale, Segal and Williams (1995) provide a theoretical, and cognitive, account of how mindfulness may exert its therapeutic effects. When I wrote the material for a chapter in the first edition of this book (Mills, 2001b) I called the chapter 'The Experience of Fragmentation in Psychosis: Can Mindfulness Help?'. Back in 2001, there had been nothing written about the possible application of mindfulness to psychosis. However, the work of Chadwick and others has recently made some promising beginnings into applying mindfulness-based cognitive therapy (MBCT) to this area. Both MBCT and the approach introduced here are trying to encourage 'an observer' perspective to psychotic phenomena, to help the person watch psychotic phenomena come and go, rather than get too wrapped up in them. The emphasis in this chapter, drawn from the Taoist practice of Tai Chi and Qigong is on developing a body-based sense of grounding and centring; a kinaesthetic route to this awareness. Mindfulness practices go further than qigong in helping the development of compassion (Gilbert, 2006), and I have often found it useful to incorporate compassion based exercises into the 'Being Centred' programme.

Being Centred and the Cultivation of Compassion

Taoism and Buddhism maintain that we all have a natural inclination to be compassionate, it is only our fear or our anger that prevents this quality shining through. Once one has learnt to 'let go' of fear and anger, then compassion emerges as a natural quality.

I have found, again, that the Taoist emphasis on body-based techniques provides an excellent preparation for the more cognitive approach of compassion as facilitated through the practice of mindfulness.

It is hard to allow any compassion to flow through ones being, if one is holding ones musculature very tightly. Compassion requires a softening, requires space for the wave of compassion to flow through. It is only if we can soften that we can receive something nurturing for ourselves. Once the softening has been established then the benefits of spiritual nourishment or personalised imagery for oneself can be received more readily (Mills, 2000a).

Similarly cultivating compassion for others is hard if there is lot of muscular 'holding'.

Let us go back to the example of Robert. In the scenario, I described at the beginning of this chapter, his attention is directed inward – he is focussed on his own fear. After some weeks of practising the above exercises, he reports feeling safer and more centred; more ready to let go and soften. Robert is now ready for the next step, to reach out to his father, to try and understand his father's fears, to develop compassion.

When Robert was asked to describe the situation at home more fully, it became apparent that Robert's father was actually facing pressure from his neighbours who were making complaints about Robert staying up late and having his music on loud. It was a recent complaint that had triggered the hostile interchange between Robert and his father.

In the group (some weeks after he has become used to the 'being centred' practice), I ask Robert to take on his father's role: to stand like his father stands, to describe the clothes his father wears. I address Robert by his father's name and ask him how he feels about his life, his work, his neighbours and his son, Robert. Standard work for gestalt, therapy or certain forms of family therapy (Weiner, 1999).

We de-role and I ask Robert how that felt – Robert looks thoughtful, 'he's got problems, hasn't he?' – Robert, now more firmly rooted in his own centre, can look towards his father, and see not so much an attacking 'ogre' but more: 'man with problems'.

We go back into role, I ask Robert's father (through Robert) 'what do you need right now?'

'I need to know that Robert's going to be OK'.

I ask 'Robert, if you were to create a statue of yourself and your father standing together and you were giving him that reassurance, what would the statue look like?'

'I'd be reaching out to him, hand on his shoulder, rubbing his back, maybe'.

'Let's go back to our original scenario where your father is saying 'how difficult you are', but this time, when you look at him see him as 'man with problems', see that place on his shoulder which needs holding, feel yourself reaching out to rub his back'.

By remaining 'centred' and with his now developed sense of kinaesthetic awareness, Robert is able to imagine himself reaching out with compassion, to his father. Robert reports that this act of extending compassion actually makes him feel braver somehow – his sense of 'energy' is expanding rather than contracting.

Lao Tzu expressed this in 500 BC as follows:

'Being compassionate one can afford to be courageous (Lao Tzu, Lao,1963: p. 129).

For myself role-playing his father, I find it hard to maintain my hostility, something in me softens. As Lao Tzu went on to say:

'Heaven protects with the gift of compassion'.

Over the 9 weeks of the group, we have built up to this point, gradually increasing our sense that it is physically and kinaesthetically safe to remain present and it is safe, even pleasurable, to allow a natural compassion to flow, which in turn increases our sense of positive 'being'.

This same principle, by the way, can be applied to ourselves as therapists (Mills, 2000b).

In Summary: Why is the Practice of 'Being Centred' Useful for Someone Vulnerable to Psychosis?

To summarise, the practice of the exercises relating to 'being centred' have the potential to be helpful for the person vulnerable to psychosis in the following ways:

- Being centred provides a counter-point to the experience of fragmentation;
- Being centred reduces the amount of 'activity' in the brain and therefore gives less 'fuel' for the psychotic phenomenon of delusions and hallucinations;
- Being centred provides a sense of safety, integration and containment;
- Being centred is often accompanied by a 'cognitive shift' to the 'detached observer' position (Kabat-Zinn, 1994). That is, 'my father is angry and is shouting at me and although this feels a little scary I know that I am not at any personal risk'. However, in the approach described in this chapter that 'cognitive shift' is achieved as a by-product of a change in kinaesthetic awareness;
- Being centred is an essential preparation before embarking on more cognitive approaches to the cultivation of compassion.

Acknowledgements

Sincere thanks to the people I have worked with, for 'going with' the process and giving me feedback as to the core issues involved.

Sincere thanks to the teachers of Qigong who have helped me to find my own centre, including Daverick Leggett, Bruce Frantzis and Zhixing Wang.

Sincere thanks to the teachers of psychology who have helped me to describe my experience through words.

18

Mapping Our Madness: The Hero's Journey as A Therapeutic Approach

Janice Hartley

Introduction

This chapter outlines a therapeutic approach I have used in workshops and training sessions at conferences and mental health support groups. It was originally conceived as a therapeutic tool by fellow contributor to this volume David Lukoff (Lukoff and Everest, 1985). Here, Howard Everest, a young man hospitalised with psychosis describes his inner experiences, which Lukoff then interprets in relation to Joseph Campbell's (1993) 'The hero with a thousand faces'. Campbell identifies the Hero's Journey as a consistent theme occurring throughout the myths and legends of the world, suggesting it is a metaphor for a journey into the psyche. Lukoff describes psychosis as an *actual* journey into the psyche and suggests the Hero's Journey idea can help chart the strange experiences of madness in a way that renders them meaningful (Lukoff and Everest, 1985). My own experience of a short psychotic episode also fits this model, and by describing my 'journey' in and out of madness I hope to show how the Hero's Journey can help make sense of psychotic experience and facilitate deeper understanding of mental distress. It is also an excellent concept for anyone wanting to challenge negative conceptualisations of madness, and fight discrimination and stigma in mental health.

The Hero's Journey approach suggests that although someone may be 'out of touch' with consensus reality, they are actually 'in touch' with mythic realms (Lukoff and Everest, 1985). This allows us to accept and learn from psychotic experience, thereby implying a different world view to standard clinical approaches. The Hero's Journey follows a structure, broadly split into three stages: Separation, Initiation and Return. Working with this structure gives people a means to create their own narrative or personal myth, whereby terrifying experiences are rendered less fearful, and eventually come to be valued as achievements or means of inner transformation.

Psychosis and Spirituality: Consolidating the New Paradigm Second Edition   Edited by Isabel Clarke
© 2010 John Wiley & Sons, Ltd.

The connection between insanity and mythology was originally noted by Carl Jung. Jung formulated his concept of the collective unconscious on the basis of similarities between his own inner experiences, those of his psychiatric patients, and his studies in religion, alchemy and world mythology (Jung, 1983). Jung's ideas have unfortunately not influenced modern psychiatry, but the Hero's Journey concept is well known in literature and film. The Arthurian legends, Tolkien's 'Lord of the Rings', and films, 'The Matrix' and 'Pan's Labyrinth' all exemplify the theme. The idea therefore has widespread popular appeal and a whole wealth of relevant resources now exists on the internet.

I will now outline the stages of the Hero's Journey as summarised by Lukoff and Everest (1985), describe and analyse my own 'Journey', and discuss the concept as a therapeutic approach.

The Three Stages of the Hero's Journey

Separation

The hero sets out on a journey leaving the familiar world behind, e.g. Ulysses sets sail from Troy and Buddha leaves the protected environment of his father's palace. This is a time of change, of crossing a threshold, when old and familiar ways become outgrown. There may be a 'calling' or magical encounter. There are parallels with shamanism, in which the role is usually preceded by separation from the everyday world.

Initiation

The hero enters the realm of the supernatural and encounters mythical creatures, gods, demons and magical powers. He or she must complete a series of trials or ordeals and may experience divine protection or assistance. Ulysses battles with Cyclops and other monsters and Buddha battles with Kama-Mara, the god of love and death. There are further parallels with shamanism as the shaman gains new powers to battle with supernatural forces. Lukoff and Everest (1985) identify two key dangers at this stage:

- self-identification with divine or supernatural powers;
- unwillingness to return to the real world.

Return

After completing the trials and ordeals, the hero must return to the ordinary world, relinquish the magical and supernatural, and integrate the experiences into everyday life. Usually, heroes bring back a trophy or something for the benefit of others. Jason brought back the Golden Fleece and Buddha became a healer and teacher. Lukoff states that Return from the psychotic journey is the most important stage, but also the longest and hardest. He stresses that telling the story is vital to complete the process, and integrate it into one's personal narrative. This benefits not only the teller, but anyone who listens, because hearing about another person's mythic journey helps us all to engage with that archaic or mythic part of ourselves. So for modern returning heroes then, their story is the prize which they bring back.

My 'Hero's journey'

Coming out of psychiatric hospital back in 1999, I never expected to be writing about my experience. Madness seemed both shameful and frightening and I was anxious to return to 'normality' as fast as possible. However, although unpleasant, this episode triggered a search for explanation and meaning, and this chapter is the result.

The Beginning. . .

My mother was admitted to psychiatric hospital shortly after my birth, and as I grew up she became 'ill' several times. I never really noticed anything, and it was never discussed, but the stigma affected me badly. I hated my mother being a mental patient and resolved that such an awful thing would never happen to me. And for many years it did not, until. . .

The Separation

It happened completely out of the blue. John and I had been married for 20 years. We had two children, aged 11 and 7 years, and I had a good job in computing. We were happy or at least averagely so. John had had some major health problems, and that had been hard, but now he was in good health at last, and about to start a new job. We were all excited and life was good. But while setting off fireworks one bonfire night, John had a major stroke leaving him paralysed down one side and in a wheelchair. He was 43 years old.

Neither of us could accept what had happened. John was in hospital for 4 months and devastated at losing his mobility. He became increasingly frustrated and depressed while I was exhausted and fearful for the future. I started using self-hypnosis to try to relax and keep going, but inside I just wanted to run away. . .

. . . We had an argument, not over anything in particular, but significant in its emotional intensity, and suddenly, like a coin flipping over, I decided that our 20 years of marriage had been a mistake. While walking along the beach trying to think things through, I found myself running out to an island just off the coast. It felt like running away and the relief was amazing. On the island, I felt I had to get as far away as possible and waded out into the water up to my knees. It was January and freezing cold, but there on what felt like the edge of the world, a flock of sea birds came flying around me, so close I could almost touch their wingtips. I felt completely at one with them and that I knew all their names. The wind eased and shafts of pale sunlight began to filter through. It was mystical and beautiful and I felt somehow new and alive. Searching underneath rocks and boulders at the foot of the cliff I found an oyster shell. It seemed like an important discovery that I had to tell everyone about. Then I met an old man and his dog, and could *feel* the bond of love between them. Everything felt significant and highly charged with meaning.

However, coping with the children was getting difficult, and one morning my 7-year-old refused to get dressed. Something snapped and I screamed at her, striking my fist on the floor. She had never seen me so angry and stood there trembling, a tear rolling down her cheek. Suddenly, it was as if time collapsed and my mother was shouting at me. Who was I now? Who was the scared little girl? Was it my mother, my daughter or me? There seemed to be no boundaries, no 'here', 'now' or 'who'. But I felt the carpet under my fingers and it all came back. Shocked and horrified that I had scared my daughter, I resolved to 'get a grip'. I began taking sleeping pills but they had little effect and I was woken constantly by powerful symbolic dreams. Nevertheless, I had boundless energy and although hardly eating, I felt fine.

The Initiation

One night, I was suddenly struck by some strange and powerful ideas about religion, science and God. It felt as if I had gained access to some strange knowledge and my mind was racing. I realised that the self-hypnosis I had been doing had unleashed something beyond my control and I could not stop it. Seized with panic, I had what I now understand as an out-of-body experience, but back then I did not know this could happen and had no idea what it was. I thought I might be losing my soul and this must be a punishment from God for obtaining some forbidden knowledge, and although not religious I became very afraid. Next morning, I was highly relieved to be back in my body but still afraid it might happen again. This fear persisted and there was no one to ask. Who exactly do you ask about a soul?

I now felt a driving need to visit significant places from my childhood and to find out more about my mother's mental illness (she had died years before), but my father seemed to be evasive and acting oddly. A sense of hidden mystery or plot began to pervade everything. While out with my sister, I felt we were being followed by the police and an innocent dog-walker was an under-cover spy. It seemed that all around me paranormal events were happening, as if I were seeing things in advance. It may have just been déjà vu but it was unsettling and I felt I had lost my orientation in the world. Certainly, my memory was affected and big chunks of time seemed to be missing. Once I found a hot, half drunk mug of coffee which must have been mine, but I had no memory of it at all. It is hard to describe the sense of panic induced by losing one's grip like this. I had always thought of my 'self', as a definite entity or real thing, but now it seemed to be fading away. Fear of losing my soul eventually prevented me sleeping at all and I felt terrible. I spent my last night at home turning on lights, and opening drawers and cupboards to let the light in. When I dialled 999 I was shaking in terror and could barely remember my name. . .

Initially, I was fairly positive about my psychiatric admission. I thought the psychiatrists would be able to stop my mind and body splitting apart, which seemed greatly preferable to losing my soul. They prescribed a drug called Melleril, 'something to help you relax', but the hospital environment reminded me of the film 'One flew over the cuckoo's nest' and I began to feel uneasy. The effects of the medication started rapidly but instead of relaxation, I felt nausea and dizziness. I went to lie down but the window did not shut properly, and a howling gale was blowing in. It was freezing, and the wind lifted the ceiling tiles, which rose and fell with loud bangs. Over the shrieking wind, I heard a child screaming, but the screams were coming from inside my own head. The drug seemed to have made everything much worse. The dizziness and faintness had intensified and it felt like I was breaking up into oblivion. I was also being continually shaken awake, even though nobody was there.

My window looked out onto a ploughed field and in the middle was a solitary tree. Suddenly, I found myself out there underneath it. But the tree was blackened and burnt, and all around was grey and bare. My grandmother was there too, exactly as she was when I sat by her bedside as she lay dying several years before. I had loved my Gran, but here she was an enormous and terrible hag, her dreadful gasps and groans shrieking with the wind. In terror, I felt drawn to her and heard myself promise that she would never die, because this madness which my mother had suffered, and clearly I now suffered too, would pass on through the female line in our family, through me, my daughter and on and on forever. As I spoke those words, I felt for a split second the terror of madness and eternity together. Somehow, I managed to say 'No I won't allow it!' and then found myself back again, on the hospital bed.

Despite this bad experience with the drug, I was lucky to have a good psychiatrist. He explained that my 'out-of-body' experience was actually safe and would not be permanent, thus resolving my fears about losing my soul. I also found a great source of support amongst the other patients, and we all talked openly together, trying to help each other with the various difficulties in our lives.

One man described his admission to hospital. He had become breathless and dizzy while out shopping, and then started shaking and sweating and felt he could not breathe. I recognised the symptoms of panic as similar to what I had experienced, but someone had called an ambulance and here he was several weeks later. All for having a panic attack!

With this realisation, the room suddenly felt too small and I needed to get outside. Out under the stars, I felt an idea come surging like a great burst of electricity. The energy felt amazing, like a great truth blazing out: 'There is no mental illness. The doctors have got it wrong!!' Since then, I have learned that others have expressed the same idea, notably the famous anti-psychiatrist Thomas Szasz, e.g. (1997). But back then the idea seemed so wildly radical, I scarcely dared think it.

Until then, I had felt too afraid to visit my husband, but now, charged with new energy, I went over. It was late and starting to snow but I pushed him in the wheelchair as we went for a walk. I felt I had the whole universe buzzing through my veins and was probably completely crazy. But John did not seem to mind. He was just pleased to see me. We walked under some street lights and they seemed to go off as we passed underneath. It all felt amazing and I just laughed with relief at it all. . .

The Hero's Return

I returned my husband safely to his ward and went back to mine. But something had changed. I had conquered a big fear, and now understood I had to get out of hospital and back to the real world as soon as possible.

I was allowed home after just 1 week and initially it was very hard. I could hardly sleep for constant nightmares, and still experienced hallucinations and panic attacks. However, freed from the terror of losing my soul, I learnt to manage the physical symptoms of anxiety and took steps to re-organise my life. Nevertheless, I was still very shaky and all my senses were in overdrive. I remember driving along and being able to see every blade of grass in the fields alongside. Such hypersensitivity was exhausting and I just wanted it to stop. What exactly were these altered states of consciousness I was experiencing? Had I really experienced paranormal phenomena such as telepathy and pre-cognition? Did the street lights really go out? I needed to know. I was terrified by the hallucinations, by my inability to correctly perceive the world, and I desperately wanted to talk to someone who could explain it all. My husband and I struggled to rebuild our relationship, and although this worked out eventually, it was initially very hard for us both. I felt I needed to get back to work quickly or my job might be at risk, and the sense of shame about having been a mental patient pervaded everything. Every second, I half expected to be carted off back to hospital.

In those early few weeks, I was lucky to have supportive friends and colleagues. But this was a time of critical reappraisal of all my relationships, and although it was hurtful, I had to isolate myself from most of my family. I found that being judged and criticised was something I could not tolerate. Going back to work was very difficult initially, but being back at the job I enjoyed was another huge milestone as I gradually regained my self-respect.

However, in other respects I was deeply unsettled. Traumatised by my experiences in hospital, I felt somehow different, as if I no longer fitted in. It felt like seeing things for the first time, and it was painful, as if a layer of skin had been stripped away. I was granted permission to see my mother's case notes and they made disturbing reading. Between 1958 and 1975, she was treated with heavy duty tranquillisers, ECT, insulin coma 'therapy' and LSD. What terrible treatments and she was never able to tell anyone! I was referred for counselling but there was a long wait, and my need for explanations and answers was almost literally tearing me apart. I got the counselling eventually, and although it was useful, I felt uncomfortable telling the counsellor about my inner experiences.

Very gradually though, I started to make sense of things. Studying parapsychology and transpersonal psychology was enormously helpful, introducing me to new concepts and frames of reference, particularly the ideas of Carl Jung, and this Hero's Journey approach (Lukoff and Everest, 1985). Eventually, I discovered that the revelations and insights I gained through madness, although painful, were actually beneficial, showing me that some of my life strategies were unhelpful, something I do not believe I could have seen any other way. I now feel more 'connected' to the world and to others, and can see that our western view of the 'self' as an isolated rational entity is misleading, with the whole area of selfhood being poorly understood. I no longer fear madness and understand that what happened to my mother was terribly wrong, a wrong which continues to be perpetrated by a misguided and drug-oriented psychiatry. Although I would never have done it by choice, madness has given me a different view of the world, and I value the experience.

Analysis

Lukoff and Everest (1985) demonstrate how psychosis parallels the Hero's Journey by following the three stage structure, and the rich imagery found in myths. I will now analyse my story addressing these points.

Separation

This started with the change in our circumstances caused by John's stroke as I gradually became overwhelmed and isolated. Taking time off work, although necessary, increased this isolation, cutting me off from daily contact with colleagues who were a source of support. However, it was the big row with my husband, and my father's sudden change in behaviour towards me that had the biggest impact, showing that, although we may not realise it, our relationships with significant others are important in keeping us 'anchored' in the everyday world. In retrospect I can now see that the self-hypnosis I was doing contributed to a further disengagement from reality, as I became more connected to my inner experiences (i.e. the powerful and symbolic dreams), and less to the everyday world. The trip to the island was deeply symbolic and meaningful, symbolising a journey or flight, and discovery of something new. After this trip, the sense of 'newness' and 'openness' increased, and I started to feel a strong sense of 'connectedness'. Mostly, this was pleasant, such as feeling the love of the old man for his dog and feeling at one with the seabirds. Lukoff and Everest (1985) describe a predominance of bird imagery in Howard's journey, observing that birds are common figures in the myths of many cultures and in shamanic traditions. Overall, there was a thinning or dissolving of boundaries, not only between myself and others, but also across time, as in the incident with my daughter.

Key elements to this stage were therefore: change in circumstances, disruption to significant relationships, isolation, an 'induction' or mind-altering technique, increased openness and loss of boundaries, mystical experience, sense of significance, and an awareness of newness or change. There was a gradual disengagement from everyday reality, and a merging or blurring of inner and outer experiences as I 'acted out' meaningful inner events.

Initiation

A useful yardstick for this stage is when things begin to get out of control and scary. For me, this started with the out-of-body experience where I became pre-occupied with powerful religious ideas. The loss of personal boundaries intensified and feelings of disintegration became visceral and terrifying. Looking back now the insights about science and religion were indeed significant because I ended up studying these areas in transpersonal psychology! Certainly, a great many *seemingly* paranormal events were happening at this time. In hospital, I received valuable guidance and support from Inspector Morse on television, and useful communications from other patients in what felt like telepathy. I could feel the emotions of other patients and believe they could feel mine. The experience with my dead grandmother under the tree represented a confrontation with evil, and my words 'I won't allow it' were like lifting a curse or breaking a spell. Grof and Grof (1990: p. 119) note the significance of trees in shamanism, where the 'world tree' is an archetypal structure connecting the upper and lower realms. There are also obvious parallels with the biblical tree of knowledge symbolism. On a personal level, this experience portrayed deep-seated unconscious regrets and fears over my grandmother's death and my mother's mental illness. But it also seemed 'collective', as if it was somehow about *everybody's* madness across space and time. It is hard to convey the intensity of that, but I believe it is the loss of boundaries of the psychotic state that allows the personal to be experienced at the collective level. In Jungian psychology, this might be the point where a personal unconscious 'complex' connects with an archetype of the collective unconscious. The revelation about mental illness was of enormous intensity and power. I believe that was also archetypal and the inspiration it gave me has been of demonstrable value. However, I do know I was mistaken a lot of the time and some of my strange ideas, such as being followed by police cars and plain clothes agents were misattributions or delusions.

Key elements of this stage included divine, demonic or magical encounters, battles with good and evil, seemingly paranormal events, revelations, insights and guidance, mystical experience, terror and paranoia, delusions and odd ideas, further loss of boundaries and feelings of disintegration. This was a much further and more turbulent disengagement from reality. The experiences had increased in intensity (both positive and negative) assuming greater significance and power.

Return

Lukoff observes that the lengthy process of the hero's return only *begins* with return to consensus reality because psychotic experiences are fragmentary and disorganised, requiring years of additional work to become properly integrated. Campbell (1993: p. 218) also stresses the difficulties of the return stage both in trying to fit into the normal world again, and in trying to communicate our experiences to others. I can identify with these perspectives in the difficulties I have described. Laing (1967: pp. 23–24) describes normal sanity as a condition of alienation, a product of repression and other destructive actions. This reflects something I felt acutely, but lacked the ability to explain.

The return stage is not about recovery to a previous baseline. The returning hero brings something back to society. This will be different for everyone, but ultimately the hero is transformed, seeing the world differently, which may cause difficulty in readjusting back into pre-existing relationships and roles. The returning hero will also have to fight against all the stigma and prejudice surrounding mental distress. Returning heroes are therefore vulnerable. I thought there would be 'experts' who would be able to explain it all, and it took a long time to realise that while we may obtain valuable help from therapists, psychiatrists, teachers, etc. the real answers are deep within us all along, and we have to discover them for ourselves. A successful hero's return requires finding our own authority and our own personal myth. I have made sense of my own 'journey' in terms of atonement for my mother and all those others who have been damaged by misguided psychiatric treatments and ideas. That is my personal myth and this chapter is the trophy that I bring back.

Key elements of this stage were therefore: Readjusting to the real world, reappraising relationships, accepting, valuing and learning from inner experiences, seeing the world differently, finding one's own authority and personal narrative or myth. This stage is one of struggle and difficulty as prevailing ideas and practices may serve to arrest or frustrate the process.

The Hero's Journey as Therapeutic Approach

The Hero's Journey has two therapeutic aspects:

- reconceptualising inner experience;
- using the three stages as a 'map'.

Reconceptualising Inner Experience

Jung stresses the value of inner experience. In his autobiography, 'Memories, Dreams and Reflections' he writes: 'The years when I was pursuing my inner images were the most important of my life – in them everything essential was decided' (Jung, 1983: p. 225). Jung describes his autobiography as his 'personal myth'. He observes: 'Myth is more individual and expresses life more precisely than does science. Science works with concepts of averages which are far too general to do justice to the subjective variety of an individual life' (Jung, 1983: p. 17).

Familiarity with the Hero's Journey concept enables us to reconceptualise inner experiences using a mythic perspective. This views psychosis, not as 'illness', but as part of the hero's 'Initiation', a legitimate and temporary stage, i.e. the turbulence that is sometimes necessary for personal growth to occur. The returning hero is not simply a recovered psychiatric patient. He or she has experienced the archetypes, the deepest and most powerful structures of the human mind.

Lukoff and Everest (1985) observe that returning heroes need to tell their story to complete the process, but psychiatric patients are usually denied this opportunity. I knew my experiences were deeply meaningful but could not put them into words, partly for fear they would be interpreted as signs of continued 'illness', and partly because I simply lacked the concepts. From the workshops, I have given for service users this seems to be the case for many. Lacking the necessary concepts to explain their inner experiences, and a supportive environment in which to explore them, people can remain trapped and stuck. Thus, there is a real need for new frameworks for understanding, and safe and supportive environments in which to explore psychotic or anomalous experiences.

Reconceptualised in a mythic perspective, more enduring problems can be seen as examples of an incomplete process or unsuccessful Hero's Return. Additional psychotic episodes are therefore not failures, relapses or signs of ongoing pathology, but are simply further ordeals and trials that the hero still needs to face. Instead of reacting with disappointment or further medical interventions, the focus remains on acceptance, exploration and further learning and adjustment. Further 'Initiations' should result in further 'Returns', ultimately resulting in further personal development and growth. The Hero's Journey is ultimately a life-long process, and knowing we are heroes gives us permission to accept our inner trials ordeals and draw on them as sources of courage and inner strength.

The Three Stages as Map

Being lost at the mercy of the powerful forces of the human mind is a terrible experience; but learning that this is a recognised process, which many others have successfully been through, offers reassurance and hope. The three stages offer a broad 'map' similar to stage models of grief, e.g. Bowlby (1980: p. 85), thus the Hero's Journey can be seen as a developmental process with stages that are descriptive and legitimising. The emphasis in the Return stage is on telling our story, and setting it into a personal narrative or myth. Use of the three stage 'map' helps provide structure and reference points, finding where one 'is at' and where one has been. With its broader focus on bringing something back for the benefit of society, the Return stage has a focus beyond the individual, thereby discouraging getting stuck, and facilitating progress and moving on.

With its basis in mythology, the Hero's Journey offers the means to address spiritual experiences in a non-religious way, and wisdom from the various traditions can be valued and explored. For example, Jesus' temptation in the desert can be seen in universal terms as one of the trials of the Initiation stage, rather than an explicitly Christian motif. Various similar examples can be found in Grof's discussion of spiritual emergency (Grof and Grof, 1990). Thus, the Hero's Journey has relevance to people of any spiritual persuasion or none, making it ideally suited to clinical or multicultural settings.

Using the Hero's Journey in Groups

The value of exploring inner experiences in supportive group settings is well established by the mental health support group Hearing Voices Network, and the Hero's Journey provides an ideal framework for a focused group approach. In my workshops, I start by outlining the Hero's journey concept as described earlier. Then I tell my 'story', explaining how it fits into the stages, and we have a discussion where participants consider how to apply their own experiences. In one session, a lady told of how she had felt that Satan was in her bathroom at night, but knowing how ridiculous this sounded she did not dare tell anyone, least of all any mental health professionals. Through learning about the Initiation stage in the Hero's Journey, she could now see this experience differently, as a trial or ordeal she had overcome, and for the first time she was able to talk about it. Sometimes there have been strong emotional reactions, when people see a very different perspective for the first time and realise that they are not alone. There can also be striking similarities, and the fact that these occur I believe demonstrates the validity of Jung's collective unconscious.

I have only ever conducted the Hero's Journey in 'one off' sessions but believe it has enormous potential for continued exploration, i.e. to allow people time to properly digest the ideas and to reframe their experiences. Ongoing discussions could perhaps explore some of the difficulties and pitfalls, such as self-identification with divine powers, i.e. feeling one is Jesus, etc. In the context of the Hero's Journey such experiences are legitimate hazards and pitfalls rather than embarrassing delusions, so people may feel able to discuss them more freely. Further discussions could perhaps focus on failure or unwillingness to return to everyday normality, on why the Hero's Return is so difficult, and what trophies or prizes one can realistically hope to bring back. Participants could consider how to recognise the Separation stage, why it occurs and how to manage it, and how to cope with the turbulence of the Initiation.

The aim of this chapter is for other people to run workshops on similar lines. Facilitators could use their own stories, or this one as an example, but ultimately the aim should be for more people to learn about the hero's Journey concept, and to gain the benefits of telling their stories and formulating their own personal myths.

Using the Hero's journey in Therapy

Psychosis may seem totally alien, impenetrable or even alarming to a therapist. Clients may not feel safe discussing their inner experiences, and therapists may feel uncomfortable hearing them.

Furthermore, standard approaches may perhaps encourage clients to find a meaning purely in terms of their personal biography. However, the ordeals and trials of the hero extend far beyond the individual or personal level. From the archaic or mythic level, they have a *trans*-personal dimension, i.e. across space and time. My experiences seemed to be about much more than just me. I felt they were about reconciliation and atonement for my mother's experiences, and releasing my daughter and future generations from dubious genetic theories of madness. Traditional therapies may not adequately embrace this perspective.

Lukoff suggests that appreciation of the relationship between psychosis and myths may help therapists working with psychotic or post-psychotic individuals. Through the use of case studies such as this one, and Lukoff and Everest (1985), the Hero's Journey offers insight into psychotic experiences and a framework in which to address them.

Conclusion

The Hero's Journey is a developmental approach facilitating recovery, personal growth and transformation. It is also a flexible therapeutic tool, suitable for either individuals or groups. It is easily learnt, with contemporary everyday relevance in literature and film. Crossing the secular – religious divide, it brings Jungian ideas right into the twenty-first century. By reconceptualising psychosis in a positive validating way, we can encourage people to explore and value their inner experiences, and thus create genuine empowerment, and challenge stigma and prejudice.

In highlighting various examples and key aspects of the three stages, I have tried to illustrate the Hero's Journey as a 'map' to help people create their own personal myths, and navigate this difficult territory. Lukoff and Everest (1985) conclude that transformation occurs as a result of contacting that ancient and mythic part of ourselves, and we can all learn from hearing other peoples' stories. The Hero's Journey therefore has benefits for us all.

19

Spirituality, Psychosis and the Development of 'Normalising Rationales'

David Kingdon, Ron Siddle, Farooq Naeem and Shanaya Rathod

Introduction

Spirituality has relevance to psychosis as a component of delusional belief and through the cultural and religious context in which psychotic symptoms arise. Faith organisations and individuals can provide social support and integration although occasionally they can directly or inadvertently contribute to social exclusion. Within the population of Great Britain, it has been reported that up to 73% of the 1983 population said that they believed in God (Webb and Wybrow, 1982) although secularisation and a decrease in this figure may have occurred since that time. Despite this figure, Abrams and colleagues reported that over 70% of the population profess that they seldom or never read the bible and only one of seven report attending church regularly.

Spiritual beliefs can be culturally appropriate or delusional, and differentiation between the two can at times be difficult. Recent research (Siddle, 2000) indicates that if appropriately clear criteria are used then it is possible to reliably distinguish between religious delusions and normal religious beliefs.

Religious Delusions

At their extremes, spiritual and psychotic beliefs are readily seen to be different: the form of the delusion and the belief's content distinguishes them. Spiritual beliefs may be clearly documented and consensus validation within an organisational

Psychosis and Spirituality: Consolidating the New Paradigm Second Edition   Edited by Isabel Clarke
© 2010 John Wiley & Sons, Ltd.

context (e.g. the General Synod or Vatican) provided. Psychotic beliefs may be 'thought disordered' in form: internally inconsistent, idiosyncratic and disordered with expression of new words ('neologisms') or tenuous links ('derailed' or displaying 'knight's move' thinking). They may also be markedly abnormal in content with terms such as God, the Devil or Archangels juxtaposed with aliens, government agencies, etc. The individual may not have ever previously expressed spiritual interest or belief but the origination of their problems, often when under stress, precipitated these beliefs. The beliefs tend not to be recognised by spiritual leaders in their community or elsewhere though the overlap may at times be significant and distinction difficult.

Religious delusions can be defined as strong fixed beliefs causing distress or disability which have a religious content and are not consistent with the beliefs usually associated with that creed. The Present State Examination, a research instrument used to reliably produce psychiatric diagnoses, defines a religious delusion as 'both a religious identification on the part of the subject and an explanation in religious terms, of other abnormal experiences'. This definition implies that there will be essentially two categories of religious delusion; that of delusional misidentification of the individual as a religious figure and religious explanations of other phenomena which may be secondary to other experiences such as hallucinations.

According to Sims (1992), a belief could be characterised as a religious delusion, if it meets the following characteristics:

- Both the observed behaviour and the subjective experience conform with psychiatric symptoms. The patient's self description of the experience is recognisable as having the form of a delusion.
- There are other recognisable symptoms of mental illness in other areas of the individual's life; such as other delusions, hallucinations, mood or thought disorder.
- The lifestyle, behaviour and direction of the personal goals of the individual after the event or after the religious experience are consistent with the natural history of mental disorder rather than with a personally enriching life experience.

Religious delusions can be categorised (Wilson, 1998) as:

- persecutory, often including the devil;
- grandiose, including the messiah complex;
- belittlement, including beliefs that they have committed unpardonable sins.

Figures vary regarding the prevalence of religious delusions in schizophrenia and these appear to depend largely upon the sample studied. Littlewood and Lipsedge (1981) quote figures of up to 45% having religious delusions in a black immigrant sample while they found only 14% of people diagnosed with schizophrenia born in Britain. Tateyama *et al.* (1993) in a study carried out in Japan and Germany found that the incidence of religious delusions in Japanese patients was 7% whereas in the Germany it was 21%. A similar study found higher frequency of religious delusions in Austria, in comparison with their counterparts in Pakistan (Stompe *et al.*, 1999). Other studies have found the prevalence of religious delusions in a sample of Afro-Caribbean patients to be 39% (Gordon, 1965) and 80% (Kiev, 1963). One criticism of these studies is that the researchers used different schemes of categorising religious delusions. Recent research examining religious delusions in a sample of patients admitted to hospital with a diagnosis of schizophrenia (Siddle, 2000) found a prevalence rate of 24% using the criteria identified by Sims.

Impact of Religious Delusions

Although many clinicians will recall instances of patients with religious delusions who for the most part sit and quietly read the Bible, religious delusions can result in risk to the patient and others. Religious delusions have been associated with self-harm (Blackner and Wong, 1963; Field and Waldfogel, 1995; Kushner, 1967; Waugh, 1986; Reeves and Liberto 2006) where individuals have acted on passages from the bible telling them to pluck out offending eyes and limbs. A study of 27 of the most dangerous psychiatric inmates in an American penal institution (Scarnati *et al.*, 1991) showed that over half appeared to have religious delusions. In 12 of these cases, the inmates believed that God or the Devil made them do things, whereas 17 of the inmates (61%) believed that God or spirits communicated directly with them. Folie à deux cases with shared religious delusions may be particularly high risk (Kraya and Patrick, 1997).

Conversely, in some South Asian Muslim cultures, remedies or advice from an elder or Imam is sought as a result of the religious content of delusions. Reciting Qur'an, and wearing armbands, use of charm lockets, talisman, tavees (armlets) to ward of evil spirits with Qur'an verses is used with enormous trust and confidence by South Asian Muslims (Rathod *et al.*, 2009).

Aetiological Considerations

Religious delusions may relate to background influences, e.g. a strong religious background shaping delusion formation, or the circumstances which are currently relevant. Delusional mood may form with religious or other themes. The person is anxious, distressed and often confused with the feeling that something is going on but they know not what. The tension builds to a point where, when a possible explanation emerges, the relief of understanding is profound and reinforces the certainty that the explanation is correct. Someone might be under considerable stress at work and from family. The stress builds but may not be recognised for what it is, and then he 'realises' that this is happening because he is being tested as Christ was tested in the Wilderness, and that he is really chosen by God for a mission which will be revealed to him. Whilst an appreciation of religious themes may be necessary to form the content of the delusions, it may be that idiosyncratic beliefs emerge because of limited knowledge of these religious beliefs.

The experience of hallucinations, visual or auditory or both, can be amongst the most interesting areas where spirituality and psychosis merge. What did Paul see on the road to Damascus? Was that a hallucination, a dream or an illusion, or an angel? He was tired, possibly sleep deprived, maybe food and water deprived – certainly in a high emotional state – and these would all make him suggestible. How much of what is described in spiritual texts is symbolic, misunderstood or misperceived. Does it matter? Why do some people's voices take the form of the devil, god, etc. or their delusions, religious themes? Certainly, this is not always because of their upbringing. Can religious delusions/voices transform to normal religious belief or are they distinct phenomena – i.e. lost when the psychosis remits?

Clinical Aspects

Diagnostic Issues

Assessment of whether someone expressing religious beliefs is psychotically ill therefore depends on:

- Strength: the degree of the person's conviction in the objective reality of the belief.
- Context: how unrelated it appears to be to his situation (the degree of absence of direct cultural or stimulus determination of an experience).
- Pre-occupation: the amount of time spent considering the experience.
- Plausibility: how reasonable.
- Personalisation: believing the experience to be related to the person, themselves.

None of these dimensions alone can determine whether someone is psychotically ill but combining them can allow a judgment to be made. The importance of prior knowledge of the person cannot be over-stressed as psychosis involves a change from previous beliefs and levels of functioning. However, this can be problematic where very gradual change has occurred and beliefs evolved over time. Paradoxically radical change in beliefs, being 'born again', can be a religious experience but can occur with psychotic belief.

Patients present to services because someone has decided that they may be mentally ill. Where this is family and friends, the context and religious background can be determined with reasonable certainty – unless there is conflict between the family and religious organisations with which the person has become involved (Kingdon and Finn, 2006). The relevant religious organisation may be undesirable to the family but belonging to it may be misjudged not psychotic. However, often it is religious leaders or elders who can detect that the beliefs held are beyond their creed and represent a problem. Successful attempts have been made at delivering religiously orientated CBT in anxiety and depression (Propst *et al.*, 1992; Paukert *et al.*, 2009) including the incorporation of mindfulness (Hathaway and Tan, 2009).

Outcome Implications

Religious delusions tend to be held with more certainty than are other types of delusion (Applebaum, Clark Robbins and Roth, 1999). Because of the social acceptability of religious beliefs, individuals with religious delusions or strongly held normal religious beliefs may evaluate their illness differently to those without these symptoms, with consequent effects upon compliance and therefore treatment effectiveness, and the patient's satisfaction with treatment. Lupfer and colleagues (1992) found that moderately religious and non-religious people were more likely to accept a non-religious cause for aspects of their behaviour, whereas highly religious Christians made significantly more attributions of cause, to both God and Satan. Religiously deluded people have been shown to be 2.2 times more likely to have been conventionally religious prior to becoming ill (Siddle, 2000).

It may be difficult to determine exactly when a person started to develop psychotic ideas and it may be that the religiousness which they reported was an attempt to cope with frightening ideas. Many people, including those with psychosis turn to religion or become more religious when they are troubled. If religiously deluded people made their causal attributions to God and Satan, this would have an impact upon their appraisal of their susceptibility to illness. If one attributes the cause of voices to be God, then this appraisal of susceptibility would have an effect upon the individual's perception of the potential benefits and the personal costs of medical treatment and thus adherence to treatment (Wright *et al.*, 2009).

The Religious Beliefs of Mental Health Professionals

The second reason to assume that people with religious delusions would derive less benefit from their treatment than others relates to the nature of the treatment which they receive from the mental health professionals. Religious individuals, although not necessarily religiously deluded individuals, have been shown to be less satisfied with a non-religious clinician than a religious one (Keating and Fretz, 1990). They have specific concerns that their secular clinicians will ignore spiritual concerns, treat religious beliefs as pathological, fail to understand spiritual language and concepts and assume that their patients have shared norms to themselves. Secular clinicians may ask their patients to carry out therapeutic actions which the patient thinks are immoral and they may also make attempts to discredit communications with God (Worthington and Scott, 1983). Psychiatrists have been described as less likely to hold religious belief than the general population (Neelman and King, 1993). However 92% believe in a direct link between religion and mental illness and agreed that psychiatrists should concern themselves with their patient's religious beliefs during assessment and therapy. Other mental health professionals have also been found to be less religiously minded than the population in general (Bergin, 1980), although these differences did not apply to all aspects of religious belief and behaviour (Bergin and Jensen, 1990).

The Effect of Religiosity Upon Therapeutic Relationships

The therapeutic relationship will be affected by strongly held religious beliefs or religious delusions. Counselling clients have been found to be less likely to disclose to therapists who had themselves disclosed their own religious views (Chesner and Baumister, 1985). This may be explained to some extent by the findings that clients are reluctant to disclose to a Christian therapist, because of the rigid moralistic dogma which many associate with institutionalised Christian religion.

Most non-religious counsellors and therapists have been found to be reluctant to challenge even erroneous religious beliefs, and when they do, the most highly religious tend to react negatively (Morrow, Worthington and McCullogh, 1993). As might be expected, most counselling clients preferred counsellors who did not challenge directly their religious beliefs and values.

However, having come to a decision that the beliefs held are not consistent with religious belief but are psychotic, management can be more difficult than with other delusions which are based around situations which are potentially testable, e.g. that the person is being followed, or has a computer chip in his brain. How do you test for the existence of God or the Devil? Where we usually explore with patients the nature of voices: do they sound like someone speaking? Are they clear or mumbled? Can others hear them? If not, why not? Religious voices can be 'plausibly' understood as directed to them alone because that is the nature of the power that God has as demonstrated, e.g. in the Bible. With other sources for voices, explanations of the reason for only the individual hearing voices can be more difficult for the individual to construct and thus some doubt in the external nature of them sewn.

This means that the approach focuses more on the content of the delusional ideas or hallucinations and the mood accompanying them. The statements attributed to God may be derogatory and hostile – exploration of whether one would expect such statements from such a source can be followed through. Derogatory and hostile voices are usually accompanied, as would be expected, by depression. In tracing back their development, they usually seem to commence during depressive episodes, i.e. the depression comes first followed by voices. Taking the person through the course of development can assist in re-labelling the voices as part of their depressive illness rather than as independent external phenomena. The relationship between depression and the voices can often be recognised. Treatment of depression, in itself, using medication may help, but more importantly the development of supportive, consistent, confiding and protective relationships with therapists, general practitioners, friends and mental health staff makes the key difference. At times, the presence of criticism reinforces these beliefs and voices. This may be implicit – from past family relationships – and therefore need exploration and defusing, or explicit and direct work on such 'expressed emotion' may be essential.

Use of 'Normalising'

Applications of cognitive behaviour therapy to psychosis need to consider the factors outlined above as their relationship to management of psychosis is of practical importance. As discussed, differentiation between culturally appropriate and psychotic belief needs to be the first step through a process of assessment using guided discovery. When do you then need to therapeutically intervene? And when can normalising psychotic experiences – for the patient and others – be valuable?

Normalising should not however mean minimising the distressing and disabling conditions that accompany psychosis. The approach used attempts to understand symptoms in terms of commonly accepted, although often, in the strict sense, scientifically invalid, comparisons with widely held beliefs. The similarities with psychotic symptoms of telepathy, speaking in tongues, grandiosity and paranoia are note-worthy. Delusional perception can be clearly related to the concept of spiritual enlightenment. This is a classical symptom of schizophrenia where a consensually validated perception, e.g. seeing a traffic light turn to green, is ascribed personal meaning, e.g. 'therefore I am descended from aliens'. This bears marked similarity to a biblical occurrence, where a bright light shone and Saul knew that he was chosen – the experience of St Paul on the road to Damascus. He was not, of course, diagnosed as having schizophrenia but hailed as a spiritual leader. Thought interference and telepathy can be seen as very similar experiences. Nebuchanezar's vision of seeing writing appearing on the wall is described in much the same way that patients, diagnosed as having psychotic illness, speak.

Religious beliefs are characteristic of mania and cognitive approaches have been developed in this context (Wright *et al.*, 2009). Much of the focus of this work is on relapse prevention but work with the beliefs themselves may be attempted where the episodes are lasting. In all this work, the problem remains of 'What's my territory as a mental health worker, and what not?' with the ethical dilemmas involved in 'thought policing' and infringing religious freedom a constant backdrop.

Managing Psychotic Symptoms

Having made the decision that the beliefs expressed are not culturally consistent, this decision needs to be kept under constant review. However, it is reasonable to explore the nature of the belief – as is described with other delusional beliefs and beliefs about voices (Kingdon and Turkington, 2005). The mechanisms which the patient cites as underlying the phenomena described can be discussed and possible alternatives elicited, or if none can be developed by the person themselves, suggested by the therapist. Normalising information about the incidence of hallucinations, paranoia and delusional belief in stressful circumstances (e.g. deprivation states and after traumatic events) can be described. Appropriate ways of exploring these alternatives may include involvement of the person's spiritual community where they are part of one. Simple 'reality testing' and debate is often ineffective in sowing doubt, but enhances understanding and rapport. At times, it may seem that the therapist is going round in circles or getting deeper and deeper into a quagmire of delusional elaboration. At such times, taking a step back, agreeing to differ but looking for underlying supports to the beliefs – for example, poor self-esteem and lack of confiding relationships, may be productive. It may be necessary to link these to the beliefs, e.g. by inference chaining, i.e. 'if others believed that God spoke to you, why would that be important to you?'. Various answers are possible, but often related to identifiable and persistent life problems, e.g. 'I'd get respect', 'From whom in particular', 'My father'. This issue can then be explored; 'OK, it's difficult for me to do anything about your beliefs about God speaking to you, but maybe we can look at your relationship with your father and see if we can do anything about that'. Typically, this allows a refocusing of the patient onto relevant and sometimes, modifiable issues of profound, and possibly aetiologically significant, issues (see Case).

Conclusions

A continuum exists between psychoticism, normality and spirituality. As mental health professionals are a group less religious than their patients caution is needed in separating normal religious beliefs from religious delusions and trying to work with the religious delusions. In cultures where religious leaders are relied upon, engagement, education and collaboration with spiritual leaders of these communities needs further developing to engage clients from these communities. As yet, there are no clear tested strategies which have been shown to be effective with these delusions, but general CBT approaches have been suggested in this article and have contributed to successful outcomes in studies (e.g. Sensky *et al.*, 2000) in a broader population of patients.

Case Example

MM is a 33-year-old gentleman who had recently started living at the local homeless hostel. He was referred by his general practitioner because of hoarding 'stuff' in his hostel room, including a dead hedgehog and numerous pairs of children's shoes. He had been 'living rough' for a long time prior to this. He stated that his main problem was an inability to sleep caused by society ostracising him for seeing everyone as evil, which he said was what the Bible taught. He went on to say that the true meaning of scriptures enlightened only those who should be enlightened by them, as they were coded. He understood these codes as he was 'the son of God'.

According to him, the rest of the society lived in sin. When asked for a clarification, he stated that, people controlled him through brutality and could also transmit thoughts through the peripherals of his vision and through sound. When asked to elaborate on these, he described seeing two people with wings, at a distance, through his peripheral vision. These were angels in flight, and were big and white. They seemed to be coming towards him and then, would turn into swans.

MM said that the television played games with his psychic self. He had been watching a programme about the Chinese independence day and concluded that the Chinese were going to take over the world.

MM never knew his real father. His mother married a French man when he was 3 years of age. His stepfather was very abusive and used to 'knock him about' a lot. As a child, he felt that everything was wrong and that no one loved him. He was bullied at school as he changed school frequently. His mother was admitted to a psychiatric hospital when he was 10 years, and she never came back, as she had found another partner after discharge. As a result, he started smoking, drinking, stealing and lying. He had also started experimenting with drugs, which he gave up after some years. In his own words, he could not face puberty, experienced self-hatred and remained suicidal. He felt 'God would have loved me but God was not there'. MM married at the age of 20 years for 3 years and he has two children aged 13 and 12 years whom he has not seen for years. He had never worked.

In developing a formulation of his symptoms, pre-disposing factors would include his religious upbringing which may have shaped the religious delusions that he developed. His father and mother's abandonment of him along with his unhappy childhood pre-disposed and may also have contributed over time to precipitating his illness. The lack of meaningful relationships since has perpetuated his symptoms and may be the underlying factor beneath his delusional ideas. It is easy to assume that these beliefs are not related to spiritual belief as opposed to psychotic but this was explored in the context of a Catholic upbringing and understood in managing them. Developing a formulation of his symptoms with him, normalising and exploring the delusions led to engagement with rational exploration and eventually inference chaining to focus on underlying issues directly related to severe childhood adversity. The process successfully engaged him with the service.

20

Endword

Isabel Clarke

My hope is that this volume, in common with the first edition, has served to open up issues and perspectives which will continue to be developed. I will consider two here.

Reconceptualising Psychosis

If psychosis and spirituality are to be reconceptualised as a single, significant, potential of human experiencing, a new understanding of the range of experience labelled as psychosis by the health services is needed to challenge the 'disease model'. This reconceptualisation recognises opening to the transliminal as a part of the journey of life which can be problematic but has great potential. Such openings can compromise normal functioning; they can bring the individual face to face with unresolved issues and be acutely frightening and distressing; however, they can also present the opportunity to break out of a mould that had become constricting and embrace a fuller way of being, through opening the self to the whole.

This conceptualisation is familiar in Grof's terms of 'spritual emergence/ emergency' which is adopted by many of the contributors, but not all. Warwick's research participants and the people who attend the programme in the hospital where I work would find these terms foreign. This volume suggests ways to bring this more hopeful and creative conceptualisation from the margins into the mainstream. Brett's research in particular makes the case that this shift is vital for the effectiveness of the therapy and support offered by the Health Service. This book does not address the immense effort of adaptation that this would pose to our still risk averse and drug-dependent service, although ill effects from standard treatment crop up in the accounts of experience throughout the book. A major contribution of this volume is its justification for a benign and non-pathologising way of conceptualising such experiences. It is not a coincidence that several of the contributors are involved with the early stages of setting up a Spiritual Crisis Network to provide a context for this in the United Kingdom (www.SpiritualCrisisNetwork.org.uk). Where the Recovery movement in the NHS urges service users to take ownership of their own treatment, should we not also be enabling them to take ownership of their own experience and meaning?

The Group and Societal Context

A defining characteristic of transliminal experience is the breaking down of boundaries, including the boundary of the self. Recognising this has far reaching implications. The interface between psychic phenomena and transliminal states is becoming increasingly recognised (Simmonds-Moore, 2009), and is evidenced in Tobert's chapter and by a number of the personal accounts in this book. The discontinuity hypothesis presented in my chapter can be extended to offer a speculative explanation of psychic phenomena via the possibility of interchange of psychic contents when the boundaries between people become weakened in the transliminal state (Clarke, 2009b).

This boundary dissolution has been touched on in a number of chapters (e.g. Tobert and Lancaster) and has far reaching implications (explored more fully in Clarke, 2008). The transliminal mode of experiencing is not a purely intrapsychic phenomenon. Just as moving beyond the constructs implies a dissolution of boundaries within the individual's experience, so it further implies a dissolution of boundaries between minds. The idea of commonality between minds is familiar from Jung's (1956) collective unconscious; from transpersonal theory and Teilhard de Chardin's (1959) no-osphere, to name but three examples. Parapsychological researchers have noted that a meditatative, unfocused state of mind is conducive to connection between minds, as in remote viewing (Rao and Rao, 1982). Group analytic literature takes the concept of a common area of mind operating between and amongst individuals in a group as axiomatic, designated, by Foulkes (1964) as the 'group matrix'.

On a larger scale, people have been noted to respond 'as one' in times of mass political actions, such as revolutions. The utopian phase which often characterises the beginnings of such movements; for instance the French and Russian revolutions, is usually short-lived and tends to be overtaken by bloodbath and tyranny from within, in partial response to attack from outside, but largely generated by a form of internal mass paranoia which can follow hard on the collective experience of liberation. This could parallel the process leading from a euphoric stage in early breakdown to the often terrifying and destructive experiences associated with psychosis, when the boundaries of the individual mind dissolve. Tobert further suggests this extends to boundaries between the living and the dead, the born and the unborn.

There is ambivalence here. Contemplating a time before birth and after death induces feelings of awe and mystery, whereas crowd reactions have traditionally been viewed as regressive [cf. le Bon (1896), as quoted by Freud (1921, pp. 67–144)]. Evolutionarily, our species has probably moved towards finer and finer capacity for discrimination in mental function, but that does not prove that the sort of undifferentiated apprehension, characterised by the transliminal state, is therefore 'inferior'. Such a conclusion falls into the fallacies of assumption-laden language noted earlier. A balancing insight would be to note that as brains specialise in picking up change and movement, they cannot simultaneously take in the whole. From the simple approach, avoidance and habituation responses of the more primitive species, evolutionarily speaking, to the specialisation of cells in our own visual cortex towards registering certain types of edges, the brain has developed as an instrument for making distinctions, and the senses serve this mechanism. The argument of this chapter suggests that as the brain, in its normal mode of operation, thinks by making discriminations, so we only experience the world in terms of discriminations. If we step outside the construed reality, we may well be in a position to apprehend the whole 'as it really is', but are powerless in the face of this reality.

I am suggesting that we need that connectedness with the whole, but not to expect to grasp it with our intellect and our ability to manipulate the environment, as it is literally beyond this grasp. This un-graspability has led to its marginalisation in a technical era. Perhaps we need that connectedness that takes us beyond the individual, towards other humans, other species, and yet wider, within the whole. We need the mystery, the unknowable, to feel at home in the world, with our fellow human and non-human creatures, and with our natural environment; to connect with whatever source of sacredness envelopes all of this. Maybe the technology born of our ferocious power to discriminate and to bend the material world to our will has been able to reach the point where the sustainability of our species is put in question precisely because we have so lost touch with the other half of experience. This potential for transcending our own boundaries can lead to serious reconsideration of the nature of relationship. Perhaps our subjective sense of separateness is more illusory than we would like to think. This idea is pursued in more depth in my book, 'Madness, Mystery and the Survival of God' (Clarke, 2008) and the implications of this viewpoint for the environmental crisis in Clarke (2009a).

The religion and spirituality of our culture have perhaps let us down by concentrating on the fate of the individual soul – whether in the salvation stakes, or in terms of achieving higher states of enlightenment. I am suggesting that the real role for religion and spirituality is to embrace and acknowledge the embededness in the greater whole, and that without in any way failing to recognise the suffering associated with psychosis, we could respect the experience of those suffering in this way for its connection with this sacred state.

References

Abram, D. (1997) *The Spell of the Sensuous: Perception and Language in a More-Than-Human World*, Vintage Books, New York.

Aftanas, L.I. and Golocheikine, S.A. (2005) Impact of regular meditation practice on EEG activity at rest and during evoked negative emotions. *International Journal of Neuroscience*, **115**, 893–909.

Alloy, L.B. and Tabachnik, N. (1984) Assessment of covariation by humans and animals: The joint influence of prior expectations and current situational information. *Psychological Review*, **91**, 112–149.

Altman, H., Collins, M. and Mundy, P. (1997) Subclinical hallucinations and delusions in nonpsychotic adolescents. *Journal of Child Psychology and Psychiatry and Allied Disciplines*, **38**, 413–20.

American Psychiatric Association (1994) *Diagnostic and Statistical Manual*, 4th edn, American Psychiatric Association, Washington, DC.

Andrew, E.M., Gray, N.S. and Snowden, R.J. (2008) The relationship between trauma and beliefs about hearing voices: A study of psychiatric and non-psychiatric voice hearers. *Psychological Medicine*, **38**, 1409–17.

Anthony, E.J. (1987) Children at risk for psychosis growing up successfully, in *The Invulnerable Child* (eds E.J. Anthony and B.J. Cohler), The Guildford Press, New York. pp. 147–84.

Applebaum, P.S., Clark Robbins, P. and Roth, L.H. (1999) Dimensional approach to delusions: Comparison across types and diagnoses. *American Journal of Psychiatry*, **156**, 1938–43.

Arieti, S. (1976) *Creativity: The Magic Synthesis*, Basic Books, New York.

Aristotle (1989) *Prior Analytics*, trans. Robin Smith Hakkett, London.

Armstrong, A. (1987) The challenges of psychic opening: A personal story, in *Spiritual Emergency. When Personal Transformation Becomes a Crisis* (eds Grof, S. and Grof, C.), Jeremy P. Tarcher/Putman, New York, pp. 109–20.

Aung, S.Z., (1910/1972) *Compendium of Philosophy*. Revised and edited by Mrs Rhys Davids. Pali Text Society, London.

Back, K. and Bourque, L.B. (1970) Can feelings be enumerated? *Behavioural Science*, **15**, 487–96.

Bannister, D. (1985) The psychotic disguise, in *Therapists' Dilemmas* (ed. W. Dryden), Harper and Row, London. pp. 167–79.

Bannister, D. and Fransella, F. (1971) *Inquiring Man*, Penguin, Harmondsworth.

Barber, P. (2006) *Practitioner Researcher A Gestalt Approach to Holistic Inquiry*, Middlesex University Press, London, pp. 125–137.

Barker, E. (1996) New religions and mental health, in *Psychiatry and Religion* (ed. D. Bhugra), Routledge, London, pp. 125–37.

Barker, P. and Buchanan-Barker, P. (eds) (2004) *Spirituality and Mental Health: Breakthrough*, John Wiley and Sons, London.

Barnard, P. (2003) Asynchrony, implicational meaning and the experience of self in schizophrenia, in *The Self in Neuroscience and Psychiatry* (eds T. Kircher and A. David), Cambridge University Press, Cambridge, pp. 121–46.

Baron, M. and Gruen, R.S. (1991) Schizophrenia and affective disorder: Are they genetically linked? *British Journal of Psychiatry*, **159**, 267–70.

Barret, T.R. and Etheridge, J.B. (1992) Verbal hallucinations in normals. I: People who hear voices. *Applied Cognitive Psychology*, **6**, 379–87.

Barrett, R.J. (1998) The 'schizophrenic' and the liminal persona in modern society (review essay). *Culture, Medicine and Psychiatry*, **22**(4), 465–94.

Bateson, G. (1991) Ecology of the Mind: The Sacred (lecture delivered at Naropa Institute, Boulder, CO, USA in 1974), in *Sacred Unity: Further steps to an ecology of mind* (ed. R. Donaldson), Harper Collins, New York.

Batson, C.P. and Ventis, L.W. (1982) *The Religious Experience*, Oxford University Press, Oxford.

Battaglia, D. (1990) *On the Bones of the Serpent: Person, Memory and Mortality in Sabarl Island Society*, University of Chicago Press, Chicago.

Beaton, A.A. (1979) Hemispheric emotional asymmetry in a dichotic listening task. *Acta Psychologica*, **43**(2), 103–9.

Beauregard, M. and O'Leary, D. (2007) *The Spiritual Brain: A Neuroscientist's Case for the Existence of the Soul*, HarperCollins, New York.

Beauregard, M. and Paquette, V. (2006) Neural correlates of a mystical experience in Carmelite nuns. *Neuroscience Letters*, **405**, 186–190.

Beauregard, M. and Paquette, V. (2008) EEG activity in Carmelite nuns during a mystical experience. *Neuroscience Letters*, **444**, 1–4.

Bebbington, P.E., Bhugra, D. and Brugha, T. *et al.* (2004) Psychosis, victimisation, and childhood disadvantage: Evidence from the second british national survey of psychiatric morbidity. *British Journal of Psychiatry*, **185**, 220–6.

Benatar, E.L. (2006) Cultural notions of psychopathology: An examination of understandings of spiritual healing and affliction across cultures. *Praxis*, **6**, 58–63.

Bentall, R.P. (2003) *Madness Explained: Psychosis and Human Nature*, Allen Lane The Penguin Press, London.

Bentall, R.P. (2009) *A Straight Talking Introduction to Psychiatric Diagnosis*, PCCS Books, Ross-on-Wye.

Bentall, R.P., Claridge, G.S. and Slade, P.D. (1989) The multidimensional nature of psychotictraits: A factor analytic study with normal subjects. *British Journal of Clinical Psychology*, **28**, 363–75.

Bentall, R.P., Kinderman, P. and Kaney, S. (1994) Self, attributional processes and abnormal beliefs: towards a model of persecutory delusions. *Behavioural Research and Therapy*, **32**, 331–41.

Bergin, A.E. (1980) Psychotherapy and religious values. *Journal of Consulting and Clinical Psychology*, **48**, 95–105.

Bergin, A.E. and Jensen, J.P. (1990) Religiosity of psychotherapists: A national survey. *Psychotherapy*, **27**, (special issue: psychotherapy and religion), 3–27.

Berman, M. (1984) *The Reenchantment of the World*, Cornell University Press, Ithaca, New York.

Berrios, G.E. (1995) Conceptual problems in diagnosing schizophrenic disorders, in *Advances in the Neurobiology of Schizophrenia* (eds J. A. Den Boer, H.G.M. Westenberg and H.M. van Praag), Wiley, Chichester, pp. 7–25.

Bhugra, D. (ed.) (1996) *Psychiatry and Religion*. Routledge, London.

Bhui, K., King, M., Dein, S. and O'Connor, W. (2008) Ethnicity and religious coping with mental distress. *Journal of Mental Health*, **17** (2), 141–51.

Binswanger, L. (1958) The existential analysis school of thought, in *Existence: A New Dimension in Psychiatry* (eds R. May, E. Angel and H.F. Ellenberger), Basic Books, New York, pp. 191–213.

Binswanger, L. (1963) *Being-in-the-World: Selected Papers of Ludwig Binswanger*, Basic Books, New York.

Birchwood, M., Meadan, A., Trower, P. and Gilbert, P. (2001) Shame, humiliation and entrapment in psychosis: A social rank theory approach to cognitive interventions with voices and delusions, in *A Casebook of Cognitive Therapy for Psychosis* (ed. A. Morrison), Psychology Press, London, pp. 108–32.

Birdfield, T. (1998) Symbolisation and integration in schizophrenia. *Dramatherapy*, **20**, 20–23.

Blackmore, S. and Troscianko, T. (1985) Belief in the paranormal: Probability judgements, illusory control, and the "chance baseline shift". *British Journal of Psychology*, **76**, 469–77.

Blackner, K. and Wong, N. (1963) Four cases of autocastration. *Archives of General Psychiatry*, **8**, 169–76.

Bleuler, E. (1911) *Dementia Praecox or the Group of Schizophrenias* (trans. J. Zinkin,1950), International Universities Press, New York.

Boisen, A.T. (1952) Mystical identification in mental disorder. *Psychiatry*, **15**, 287–97.

Boisen, A.T. (1962) *The Exploration of the Inner World*, Harper and Row, New York.

Bola, J.R. and Mosher, L.R. (2003) Treatment of acute psychosis without neuroleptics: Two-year outcomes from the soteria project. *The Journal of Nervous and Mental Disease*, **191**, 219–29.

Bomford, R. (2005) Ignation Matte Blanco and the logic of God, in *Ways of Knowing: Science and Mysticism Today* (ed. C. Clarke), Imprint Academica, Exeter, pp. 129–42.

Boss, M. (1963) *Psychoanalysis and Daseinanalysis*, Basic Books, New York.

Boss, M. (1977) *Existential foundations of medicine and psychology*, Aronson, New York.

Bowers, M. (1979). Psychosis and human growth, in *Exploring Madness* (eds J. Fadiman and D. Kewman), Brooks/Cole, Monterey, CA.

Bowlby, J. (1980) *Attachment and Loss. Vol. 3. Loss: Sadness and Depression*, Hogarth, London.

Boyce-Tillman, J. (2005) Subjugated ways of knowing, in *Ways of Knowing: Science and Mysticism Today* (ed. C. Clarke), Imprint Academica, Exeter, pp. 8–33.

Boyle, M. (1990) *Schizophrenia: A Scientific Delusion?* Routledge, London.

Boyle, M. (1996) Schizophrenia: The fallacy of diagnosis. *Changes*, **14**, 5–13.

Boyle, M. (2007) The problem with diagnosis. *The Psychologist*, **20**, 290–2.

Bracken, P. and Thomas, P. (2005) *Postpsychiatry: Mental Health in a Postmodern World*, Oxford University Press, Oxford.

Bragdon, E. (1990) *The Call Of Spiritual Emergency. From Personal Crisis to Personal Transformation*, Harper and Row, San Francisco.

Bragdon, E. (1998) *A Sourcebook for Helping People in Spiritual Emergency*, Lighting Up Press, California.

Braud, W. and Anderson, R. (1998) *Transpersonal Research Methods for the Social Sciences*, Sage publications, London.

Breggin, P. (1993) *Toxic Psychiatry: Drugs and Electroconvulsive Therapy – The Truth and the Better Alternatives*, HarperCollins, London, (orig. 1991).

Brett, C. (2002) Psychotic and mystical states of being: Connections and distinctions. *Philosophy, Psychiatry and Psychology*, **9**, 321.

Brett, C.M.C., Peters, E.P. and Johns, L.C. *et al.* (2007) Appraisals of Anomalous Experiences Interview (AANEX): A multidimensional measure of psychological responses to anomalies associated with psychosis. *British Journal of Psychiatry*, **191**, 23–30.

Brett, C.M.C., Johns, L., Peters, E. and McGuire, P. (2009) The role of metacognitive beliefs in determining the impact of anomalous experiences: A comparison of help-seeking and non-help-seeking groups of people experiencing psychotic-like anomalies. *Psychological Medicine*, **39**, 939–50.

Brett-Jones, J., Garety, P.A. and Hemsley, D.R. (1987) Measuring delusional experiences: A method and its application. *British Journal of Clinical Psychology*, **26**, 257–65.

Brockington, I. (1991) Factors involved in delusion formation. *British Journal of Psychiatry*, **159** (Suppl 14), 42–5.

Broks, P. (1984) Schizotypy and hemisphere function – II Performance asymmetry on a verbal divided visual field task. *Personality and Individual Differences*, **5**, 649–56.

Buck, L.A. (1992a) The myth of normality: Consequences for the diagnosis of abnormality and health. *Social Behavior and Personality*, **20**, 251–62.

Buck, L.A. (1992b) A proposed category for the DSM: Pervasive labeling disorder. *Journal of Humanistic Psychology*, **32**, 121–5.

Bucke, R. (1961) *Cosmic Consciousness: A Study in the Evolution of the Human Mind*, Concord, MA: Ye Old Depot Press.

Buckley, D. (2001) *Strange Fascination: David Bowie: The Definitive Story*, Virgin Books Ltd, London.

Buckley, P. (1981) Mystical experience and schizophrenia. *Schizophrenia Bulletin*, 7, 516–21.

Bullen, J.G., Hemsley, D.R. and Dixon, N.F. (1987) Inhibition, unusual perceptual experiences and psychoticism. *Personality and Individual Differences*, **8**, 678–91.

Burckhardt, T. (1971) *Alchemy: Science of the Cosmos, Science of the Soul*, Penguin Books, Baltimore, MD.

Burke, T.P. (2004) *The Major Religions*, Blackwell, Oxford.

Burston, D. (2000) *The Crucible of Experience: R.D. Laing and the Crisis of Psychotherapy*, Harvard University Press, Cambridge, MA.

Cahn, R. and Polich, J. (2006) Meditation states and traits: EEG, ERP, and neuroimaging studies. *Psychological Bulletin*, **132**, 180–211.

Campbell, J. (1972) *Myths to Live By*, Viking, New York.

Campbell, J. (1993) *The Hero With a Thousand Faces*, Fontana, London.

Canault, N. (1998) *Comment paye-t-on la faute de nos ancêtres*, Desclée de Brouwer, Paris.

Caplan, M. (1999) *Halfway Up the Mountain: The Error of Premature Claims to Enlightenmen*, Hohm Press, Prescott, AZ.

Caplan, P.J. (1995) *They Say You're Crazy: How the World's Most Powerful Psychiatrists Decide Who's Normal*, Addison-Wesley, Reading, MA.

Cardeña, E., Lynn, S.J. and Krippner, K. (eds) (2000) *Varieties of Anomalous Experience: Examining the Scientific Evidence*, American Psychological Association, Washington.

Carmon, A. and Nachson, I. (1973) Ear asymmetry in perception of emotional non-verbal stimuli. *Acta Psychologica*, **37**, 351–7.

Carpinello, S.E., Knight, E.L., Markowitz, F.E. and Pease, E.A. (2000) The development of the Mental Health Confidence Scale: A measure of self-efficacy in individuals diagnosed with mental disorders. *Psychiatric Rehabilitation Journal*, **23**, 236–43.

Carter, O.L., Presti, D.E. and Callistemon, C. *et al.* (2005) Meditation alters perceptual rivalry in Tibetan Buddhist monks. *Current Biology*, **15**, R412–3.

Chadwick, P.K. (1992) *Borderline: A psychological study of paranoia and delusional thinking*, Routledge, London and New York.

Chadwick, P.D.J. and Birchwood, M. (1994) The omnipotence of voices: A cognitive approach to auditory hallucinations. *British Journal of Psychiatry*, **164**, 190–201.

Chadwick, P.D.J. and Lowe, C.F. (1994) A cognitive approach to measuring and modifying delusions. *Behaviour Research and Therapy*, **32**, 355–67.

Chadwick, P.D.J., Newman-Taylor, K. and Abba, N. (2005) Mindfulness groups for people with distressing psychosis. *Behavioural & Cognitive Psychotherapy*, **33**, 351–60.

Chadwick, P.D.J., Hughes, S. and Russell, D. *et al.* (2009) Mindfulness groups for distressing voices and paranoia: A replication and randomized feasibility trial. *Behavioural and Cognitive Psychotherapy*, **37**, 403–12.

Chadwick, P.K. (1997) *Schizophrenia: The Positive Perspective*, Routledge, London And New York.

Chadwick, P.K. (2001) Sanity to supersanity to insanity: A personal journey, in *Psychosis and Spirituality; Exploring the New Frontier* (ed. I. Clarke), Wiley Inc., Chichester, pp. 75–89.

Chadwick, P.K. (2004) The pen and the spirit: Writing as a therapeutic adventure. *Open Mind*, **129**, 12.

Chadwick, P.K. (2005) Oscar Wilde: The artist as psychologist. *The Wildean*, **27**, 2–11.

Chadwick, P.K. (2006) Oscar Wilde: The playwright as psychologist. *The Wildean*, **28**, 17–23.

Chadwick, P.K. (2007) Freud meets Wilde: A playlet. *The Wildean*, **31**, 2–22.

Chadwick, P.K. (2008) *Schizophrenia: The Positive Perspective*, 2nd edn, Routledge, London and New York.

Chapman, J. and Lukoff, D. (1996) The social safety net in recovery from psychosis: A therapist's story. *Hospital and Community Psychiatry*, **47**, 69–70.

Chapman, J.P., Chapman, L.J. and Kwapil T.R. (1995) Scales for the measurement of schizotypy, in *Schizotypal Personality* (eds. A. Raine, T. Lencz and S.A. Mednick), Cambridge University Press, Cambridge, pp. 79–106.

Chapman, L.J. and Chapman, J.P. (1980) Scales for rating psychotic and psychotic-like experiences as continua. *Schizophrenia Bulletin*, **6**, 476–89.

Chapman, L.J., Chapman, J.P., and Raulin, M.L. (1978) Body-image aberration in schizophrenia. *Journal of Abnormal Psychology*, **87**, 399–407.

Chesner, S.P. and Baumister, R.F. (1985) Effect of therapists' disclosure of religious beliefs on the intimacy of client self disclosure. *Journal of Social and Clinical Psychology*, **3**(1), 97–105.

Cirignotta, F., Todesco, C. and Lugharesi, E. (1980) Temporal lobe epilepsy with ecstatic seizures, so-called Dostoevsky epilepsy. *Epilepsia*, **21**, 705–10.

Claridge, G. (1972) The schizophrenias as nervous types. *British Journal of Psychiatry*, **112**, 1–17.

Claridge, G. (1987) 'The schizophrenias as nervous types' revisited. *British Journal of Psychiatry*, **151**, 735–43.

Claridge, G. (1994) Single indicator of risk for schizophrenia. Probable fact or likely myth? *Schizophrenia Bulletin*, **20**, 151–68.

Claridge, G.A. (1997) *Schizotypy: Implications for Illness and Health*, Oxford University Press, Oxford.

Claridge, G.A. (1998) Creativity and madness, in *Genius and the Mind: Studies of Creativity and Temperament* (ed. A. Steptoe), Oxford University Press, Oxford, pp. 227–50.

Claridge, G. and Beech, A.R. (1994) Fully and quasi-dimensional constructions of schizotypy, in *Schizotypal Personality* (eds A. Raine, T. Lencz and S.A. Mednick), Cambridge University Press, Cambridge.

Claridge, G. and Broks, P. (1984) Schizotypy and hemisphere function. I: Theoretical considerations and the measurement of schizotypy. *Personality and Individual Differences*, **5**, 633–64.

Claridge, G., McCreery, C. and Mason, O. *et al.* (1996) The factor structure of 'schizotypal' traits: A large replication study. *British Journal of Clinical Psychology*, **35**, 103–15.

Claridge, G., Clark, K. and Davis, C. (1997) Nightmares, dreams, and schizotypy. *British Journal of Clinical Psychology*, **36**, 377–86.

Claridge, G.A., Pryor, R. and Watkins, G. (1998) *Sounds from the Bell Jar. Ten Psychotic Authors*, 2nd edn, Malor Books, Cambridge, MA, pp. 227–50.

Clarke, C. (ed.) (2005) *Ways of Knowing: Science and Mysticism Today*, Imprint Academic, Exeter, UK.

Clarke, I. (ed.) (2001) *Psychosis and Spirituality: Exploring the New Frontier*, Wiley, Chichester.

Clarke, I. (ed.) (2002) Taking spirituality seriously. *The Journal of Critical Psychology, Counselling and Psychotherapy*, **2**(special Issue), 201–66.

Clarke I. (2005) There is a Crack in Everything: That's How the Light Gets In, in *Ways of Knowing: Science and Mysticism Today* (ed. C. Clarke), Imprint Academic, Exeter, pp. 90–102.

Clarke, I. (2008) *Madness, Mystery and the Survival of God*, 'O'Books, Winchester.

Clarke, I. (2009a) What we do to the earth we do to ourselves. *Journal of Holistic Healthcare.*, **6**, 19–22.

Clarke, I. (2009b) Transformative and/or destructive: Exceptional experiences from the clinical perspective. Paper presented at: 'First Conference on Health, Mental Health and Exceptional Human Experiences', Liverpool Hope University, September 2009 (to appear in an edited volume, McFarland, Jefferson NC).

Cohen, C.I. and Timimi, S. (eds) (2008) *Liberatory Psychiatry: Philosophy, Politics and Mental. Health*, Cambridge University Press, Cambridge.

Coombs, M. (1996) *Hearing voices: individual psychological factors*, MSc thesis. University of Oxford.

Corbin, H.(1958/1969) *Creative Imagination in the Sufism of Ibn Arabi* (trans. by R. Manheim), Princeton University Press, Princeton, NJ.

Corcoran, C., Walker, E. and Huot, R. *et al.* (2003) The stress cascade and schizophrenia: Aetiology and onset. *Schizophrenia Bulletin*, **29**, 26–92.

Cortright, B. (1997) *Psychotherapy and spirit: Theory and practice in transperonal psychotherapy*, SUNY Press, Albany, NY.

Coyte, M.E., Gilbert, P. and Nicholls, V. (eds.) (2007) *Spirituality, Values and Mental Health; Jewels for the Journey*, Jessica Kingsley, London.

Creswell, J.W. (1998) *Qualitative Enquiry and Research Design*, Sage, London.

Crossley, D. (1995) Religious experience within mental illness. *British Journal of psychiatry*, **166**, 284–6.

Csordas, T.J. (1994) *Embodiment and Experience: The Existential Ground of Culture and Self*, Cambridge University Press, Cambridge.

d'Aquili, E.G. and Newberg, A.B. (1999) *The Mystical Mind: Probing the Biology of Religious Experience*, Fortress Press, Minneapolis.

Dabrowski, K. (1964) *Positive Disintegration*, Little Brown, Boston.

Damasio, A. (2004) *Looking for Spinoza*, Vintage, London.

Davidson, G.M. (1941) A syndrome of time-agnosia. *Journal of Nervous and Mental Disease*, **94**, 336–43.

Day, S. and Peters, E.R. (1999) The incidence of schizotypy in new religious movements. *Personality & Individual Differences*, **27**, 55–67.

Deikman, A.J. (1966a) Deautomatization and the mystic experience. *Psychiatry*, **29**, 324–38.

Deikman, A.J. (1966b) Implications of experimentally induced contemplative meditation. *Journal of Nervous and Mental Disease*, **142**, 101–16.

Deikman, A.J. (1982) *The Observing Self*, Beacon Press, Boston, MA.

Dennett, D.C. (1991) *Consciousness Explained*, Penguin, London.

Denzin, D.K. and Lincoln, Y.S. (1998) *Landscape of Qualitative Research*, Sage, London.

Department of Health (2009a) *Delivering Race Equality in Mental Health Care: A Review* (New Horizons document), product #265605.

Department of Health (2009b) *Religion or Belief: A Practical Guide for the NHS*, product #289752.

Descartes, R. (1968) *Discourse on Method and the Meditations* (trans. F. E. Sutcliffe), Penguin, London.

Descartes, R. (1972) *Treatise of Man*, (trans. Thomas Steele Hall), Harvard University Press, Cambridge, MA.

Dewhurst, K. and Beard, A.W. (1970) Sudden religious conversions in temporal lobe epilepsy. *British Journal of Psychiatry*, **117**, 497–507.

Dixon, L.B. and Lehman, A.F. (1995) Family interventions in schizophrenia. *Schizophrenia Bulletin*, **21**, 631–43.

Dodds, E. (1951) *The Greeks and the Irrational*, Univeristy of California Press, Berkeley.

D'Onofrio, G. (ed.) (2008) *The History of Theology: 2, The Middle Ages* (trans. M. J. O'Connell), Liturgical Press, Collegeville, MN.

Dorman, D. (2004) *Dante's Cure*. Other Press, New York.

Douglas-Klotz, N. (1984) Sufi approaches to transformational movement. *Somatics*, 5(1; Fall–Winter), 44.

Douglas-Klotz, N. (1995) *Desert Wisdom: The Middle Eastern Tradition from the Goddess through the Sufis*, HarperSanFrancisco, San Francisco.

Douglas-Klotz, N. (1999a) *The Hidden Gospel: Decoding the Spirituality of the Aramaic Jesus*, Quest Publications, Wheaton, IL.

Douglas-Klotz, N. (1999b) Midrash and postmodern inquiry: Suggestions toward a hermeneutics of indeterminacy, in *Currents in Research: Biblical Studies* (ed. A.J. Hauser), Vol. 7, Sheffield Academic Press, Sheffield, pp. 181–93.

Drury, V., Birchwood, M., Cochrane, R. and McMillan, F. (1996) Cognitive therapy and recovery from acute psychosis: A controlled trial. I: Impact on psychotic symptoms. *British Journal of Psychiatry*, **169**, 593–601.

American Psychiatric Association (1994) *DSM-IV: Diagnostic and Statistical Manual of Mental Disorders*, American Psychiatric Association, Washington, DC.

Durrant C. and Tolland A. (2008) Evaluating short-term CBT in an acute adult in-patient unit, in *Cognitive Behaviour Therapy for Acute Inpatient Mental Health Units; Working With Clients, Staff and the Milieu* (eds I. Clarke and H. Wilson), Routledge, London, pp. 185–96.

Durrant, C., Clarke, I., Tolland, A. and Wilson, H. (2007) Designing a CBT Service for an acute in-patient setting: A pilot evaluation study. *Clinical Psychology and Psychotherapy*, **14**, 117–25.

Ellenberger, H. (1970) *The Discovery of the Unconscious: The History and Evolution of Dynamic Psychiatry*, Basic Books, NY.

Emmons, R.A. and Crumpler, C.A. (1999) Religion and spirituality? The roles of sanctification and the concept of God. *International Journal for the Psychology of Religion*, **9**, 17–24.

Ensink, B.J. (1992) *Confusing Realities: A Study on Child Sexual Abuse and Psychiatric Symptoms*, VU University Press, Amsterdam.

Epstein, M. and Topgay, S. (1982) Mind and mental disorders in Tibetan medicine. *Revision*, **5**, 67–79.

Evans, J.L. (1997) Semantic activation and preconscious processing in schizophrenia and schizotypy, in *Schizotypy: Implications for Illness and Health* (ed. G. Claridge), Oxford University Press, Oxford, pp. 80–97.

Eysenck, H.J. (1952) Schizothymia–cyclothymia as a dimension of personality. *Experimental Journal of Personality*, **20**, 345–84.

Eysenck, H.J. (1992) The definition and measurement of psychoticism. *Personality and Individual Differences*, **13**, 757–85.

Eysenck, H.J. and Eysenck, S.B.G. (1976) *Psychoticism as a Dimension of Personality*, Hodder and Stoughton, London.

Fantini, P. (1998) *Mental Illness: Mystery or Mis-Story*. Workshop at Sherwood Psychotherapy Training Institute, Nottingham.

Fenwick, P., Galliano, S. and Coate, M.A. *et al.* (1985) Sensitives, 'psychic gifts', psychic sensitivity and brain pathology. *British Journal of Medical PsychOlogy*, **58**, 35–44.

Fernando, S. (1991) *Mental Health, Race and Culture*, Macmillan, Basingstoke.

Ferrer, J.N. (2002) *Revisioning Transpersonal Theory. A Participatory Vision of Human Spirituality*, State University of New York press, New York.

Field, H.L. and Waldfogel, S. (1995) Severe ocular self-injury. *General Hospital Psychiatry*, **17** (3), 224–7.

Fine, M. (1998) Working the hyphens: reinventing self and other in qualitative research, in *Landscape of Qualitative Research* (eds D.K. Denzin and Y.S. Lincoln), Sage, London, pp.130–55.

Finkelhor, D. (1988) The trauma of sexual abuse, in *Lasting Effects of Sexual Abuse* (eds G.E. Wyatt and G.J. Powell), Sage, Newbury Park, CA.

First, M.B., Frances, A. and Pincus, H.A. (2004) *DSM-IV-TR Guidebook*, American psychiatric Press Inc, Washington, DC.

Fletcher, P.C. and Frith, C.D. (2009) Perceiving is believing: A Bayesian approach to explaining the positive symptoms of schizophrenia. *Nature Reviews*, Neuroscience, **10**, 48–58.

Forrer, G.R. (1960) Benign auditory and visual hallucination. *Archives General Psychiatry*, **3**, 119–22.

Foulds, G.A. and Bedford, A. (1975) Hierarchy of classes of personal illness. *Psychological Medicine*, **5**, 181–92.

Foulkes, S.H. (1964) *Therapeutic Group Analysis*, Allen & Unwin, London.

Fowler, D., Freeman, D. and Smith, B. *et al.* (2006) The Brief Core Schema Scales (BCSS) psychometric properties and associations with paranoia and grandiosity in non-clinical and psychosis samples. *Psychological Medicine*, **36**, 749–59.

Fox, M. (1983) *Original Blessing*, Bear & Co., Santa Fe, New Mexico.

Fox, M. (1990) *Prayers of the Cosmos*, HarperSanFrancisco, San Francisco.

Frantzis, B. (1999) *The Great Stillness*, Clarity Press, California.

Frantzis, B. (2006) *Opening the Energy Gates of the Body*, North Atlantic Books, California.

Freeman, D., Garety, P. and Bebbington, P. *et al.* (2005) The psychology of persecutory ideation II: A virtual reality experimental study. *Journal of Nervous and Mental Diseases*, **193**, 309–15.

Freud, S. (1911/1958) Notes on a case of paranoia, in *The Standard Edition of the Complete Psychological Works of Sigmund Freud* (trans. J. Strachey), Vol. **XII**, Hogarth Press, London, pp. 3–84.

Freud, S. (1921) *Group Psychology and the Analysis of the Ego*, Standard Edition XVIII Hogarth Press, London.

Friedlander, S. and Al-Hajj Shaikh Muzafferiddin (1978) *Ninety-Nine Names of Allah: The Beautiful Names*, Harper & Row, New York.

Frith, C. (1995) Functional imaging and cognitive abnormalities. *Lancet*, **346**, 615–20.

Frith, C.D. (1979) Consciousness, information processing and schizophrenia. *British Journal of Psychiatry*, **134**, 225–35.

Fulford, K.W.M. (1989) *Moral Theory and Medical Practice*, Cambridge University Press, Cambridge.

Fulford, K.W.M. (1991) Evaluative delusions: Their significance for philosophy and psychiatry. *British Journal of Psychiatry*, **159** (Suppl 14), 108–12.

Fuller, C.J. (1992) *The Camphor Flame*, Princeton University Press, Oxford.

Gallup, G. (1987) *The Gallup Poll: Public Opinion 1986*, Scholarly Resources, Wilmington, DE.

Gallup, G.H. and Newport, F. (1991) Belief in paranormal phenomena among adult Americans. *Skeptical Inquirer*, **15**, 137–46.

Garety, P.A. and Freeman, D. (1999) Cognitive approaches to delusions: A critical review of theories and evidence. *British Journal of Clinical Psychology*, **38**, 113–55.

Garety, P.A. and Hemsley, D.R. (1987) Characteristics of delusional experience. *European Archives of Psychiatry and Neurological Sciences*, **236**, 294–8.

Garety, P.A. and Hemsley, D.R. (1994) *Delusions: Investigations into the Psychology of Delusional Reasoning*, (Maudsley Monographs 36) Oxford University Press, Oxford.

Garety, P.A., Fowler, D. and Kuipers, E. *et al.* (1997) London-East Anglia randomised controlled trial of cognitive-behavioural therapy for psychosis. II: Predictors of outcome. *British Journal of Psychiatry*, **171**, 420–26.

Garety, P.A., Kuipers, E. and Fowler, D. *et al.* (2001) A cognitive model of the positive symptoms of psychosis. *Psychological Medicine*, **31**, 189–95.

Garety, P.A., Bebbington, P. and Fowler, D. *et al.* (2007) Implications for neurobiological research of cognitive models of psychosis: A theoretical paper. *Psychological Medicine*, **37**, 1377–91.

Geekie, J. and Read J. (2009) *Making Sense of Madness*, Routledge, London.

Geirnaert-Martin, D. (1992) *The Woven Land of Laboya: Socio-Cosmic Ideas and Values in West Sumba, Eastern Indonesia*, Centre of Non-Western Studies, Leiden.

Gilbert, P. (2006) Compassionate mind training for people with high shame and self-criticism: overview and pilot study of a group therapy approach. *Clinical Psychology and Psychotherapy*, **13**, 353–79.

Gilbert, P., Nicholls, V., McCulloch, A. and Sheehan, A. (2003) *Inspiring Hope. Recognizing the Importance of Spirituality in a Whole Person Approach to Mental Health*, NIMHE, London.

Glaser, B.G. and Strauss, A.L. (1999) *The Discovery of Grounded Theory: Strategies for Qualitative Research*, 3rd edn, Aldine de Gruyter, New York.

Glass, J.M. (1993) *Shattered Selves: Multiple Personality in a Postmodern World*, Cornell University Press, Ithaca, New York.

Glock, C.Y. and Stark, R. (1965) *Religion and Society in Tension*, Rand McNally, Chicago.

Good, B. (1994) *Medicine, Rationality and Experience: An Anthropological Perspective*, Cambridge University Press, Cambridge.

Goodwin, F.K. and Jamison, K.R. (1990) *Manic–Depressive Illness*, Oxford, New York.

Gordon, E.B. (1965) Mentally ill West Indian immigrants. *British Journal of Psychiatry*, **111**, 877–87.

Gottesman, I.I. (1991) *Schizophrenia Genesis: The Origins of Madness*, W H Freeman, New York.

Gowers, W.R. (1881) *Epilepsy and Other Chronic Convulsive Diseases*, Churchill, London.

Grady, B. and Loewenthal, K.M. (1997) Features associated with speaking in tongues (glossolalia). *British Journal of Medical Psychology*, **70**, 185–91.

Greenberg, D., Witztum, E. and Buchbinder, J.T. (1992) Mysticism and psychosis: The fate of Ben Zoma. *British Journal of Medical Psychology*, **65**, 223–35.

Grisaru, N., Budowski, D. and Witztum, E. (1997) Possession by the 'Zar' among Ethiopian immigrants to Israel: Psychopathology or culture-bound syndrome? *Psychopathology*, **30**, 223–33.

Grof, C. and Grof, S. (1990–92) *The Stormy Search for the Self: Understanding and Living with Spiritual Emergency*, Jeremy P. Tarcher, Los Angeles.

Grof, S. (1986) *Beyond the Brain: Birth, Death, and Transendence in Psychotherapy*, State University of New York Press, Albany, NY.

Grof, S. (1990) *The Holotropic Mind*, Harper Collins, San Francisco.

Grof, S. and Grof, C. (1986) Spiritual emergency: The understanding and treatment of transpersonal crises. *Re-Vision*, **8**, 7–20.

Grof, S. and Grof, C. (eds) (1987, 89) *Spiritual Emergency: When Personal Transformation Becomes a Crisis*, Jeremy P. Tarcher/Putnam, New York.

Gumley, A. and Schwannauer, M. (2006) *Staying Well After Psychosis. A Cognitive Interpersonal Approach to Recovery and Relapse Prevention*, Wiley, Chichester.

Gumley, A., White, C.A. and Power, K. (1999) An interactive cognitive subsystems model of relapse and the course of psychosis. *Clinical Psychology & Psychotherapy*, **6**, 261–78.

Habid, M. (1986) Visual hypoemotionality and prosopagnosia associated with right temporal lobe isolation. *Neuropsychologia*, **24**, 577–82.

Hadamard, J. (1945) *The Psychology of Invention in the Mathematical Field*, Princeton University Press, New Jersey.

Haddock, G., Slade, P.D. and Bentall, R.P. *et al.* (1998) A comparison of the long-term effectiveness of distraction and focusing in the treatment of auditory hallucinations. *British Journal of Medical Psychology*, **71**, 339–49.

Halifax, J. (1979) *Shamanic Voices*, Dutton, New York.

Halling, S. and Nill, J.D. (1989) Demystifying psychopathology: understanding disturbed persons, in *Existential–Phenomenological Perspectives in Psychology: Exploring the Breadth of Human Experience* (eds R.S. Valle and S. Halling), Plenum, New York, pp. 179–92.

Harding, R.E.M. (1942) *An Anatomy of Inspiration*, W. Heffer and Sons, Cambridge.

Hardy, A., Fowler, D. and Freeman D. *et al.* (2005) Trauma and hallucinatory experience in psychosis. *Journal of Nervous and Mental Disease*, **193**, 501–7.

Hareven, S. (1995) *The Vocabulary of Peace: Life, Culture and Politics in the Middle East*, Mercury House, San Francisco.

Harner, M. (1990) *The Way of the Shaman*, Harper & Row Publishers, New York.

Harrow, M., Rattenbury, F. and Stoll, F. (1988) Schizophrenic delusions: An analysis of their persistence, of related premorbid ideas and three major dimensions, in *Delusional Beliefs* (eds T.F. Oltmanns and B.A. Maher), Wiley, New York.

Hartmann, E. (1991) *Boundaries of the Mind*, Basic Books, New York.

Hathaway, W., and Tan, E. (2009) Religiously oriented mindfulness-based cognitive therapy. *Journal of Clinical Psychology*, **65** (2), 158–71.

Hay, D. (1987) *Exploring Inner Space*, 2nd edn, Penguin, Harmondsworth.

Heery, M. (1989) Inner voice experiences: An exploratory study of thirty cases. *The Journal of Transpersonal Psychology*, **21**, 73–82.

Heidegger, M. (1927/1962) *Being and Time* (trans. J. Macquarrie and E.S. Robinson), Blackwell, Oxford.

Heinze, R-I. (1982) *Tham Khwan: How to Contain the Essence of Life*, Singapore University Press, Singapore.

Heinze, R.I. (1999) Multiplicity in cross-cultural perspective, in *The Plural Self* (eds J. Rowan and M. Cooper), Routledge, London, pp. 151–67.

Helman, C.G. (1985) Psyche, soma and society: The social construction of psychosomatic disorders. *Culture Medicine and Psychiatry*, **9**, 1–26.

Hemsley, D.R. (1993) A Simple (or simplistic?) cognitive model for schizophrenia. *Behaviour Research and Therapy*, **31**, 633–45.

Hemsley, D.R. (1998) The disruption of the 'sense of self' in schizophrenia: Potential links with disturbances of information processing. *British Journal of Medical Psychology*, **71**, 115–24.

Heron, J. and Reason, P. (2001) The practice of co-operative inquiry: Research 'with' rather than 'on' people, in *Handbook of Action Research Participative Enquiry and Practice* (eds P. Reason and H. Bradbury), Sage, London, pp. 179–88.

Hill, P.C., Pargament, K.I. and Wood, R.W. Jr. *et al.* (2000) Conceptualizing religion and spirituality: Points of commonality, points of departure. *Journal of Theory of Social Behavior*, **30**, 51–77.

Hillman, J. (1983) *Healing Fiction.*, Station Hill Press, New York.

House, R. (2001) Psychopathology, psychosis and the Kundalini, in *Psychosis and Spirituality: Exploring the New Frontier* (ed. I. Clarke), Wiley Inc, Chichester, pp. 107–26

House, R. (2002–3) Beyond the medicalisation of "challenging behaviour"; or protecting our children from "Pervasive Labelling Disorder" – Parts I, II and III. *The Mother* 4, 2002, 25–6, 43; **5**, 2003, 44–6, and **6**, 2003, 44–6.

House, R. (2003) *Therapy Beyond Modernity: Deconstructing and Transcending Profession-Centred Therapy*, Karnac Books, London.

House, R. (2009) Diagnosing so-called "ADHD" as a cultural affliction of Late Modernity – Review article. *Ipnosis*, **36**, 22–6, http://www.mentalhealth.freeuk.com/TimimiADHDreview. htm (accessed January 2010).

Hoy, D. (1978) *The Critical Circle: Literature, History and Philosophical Hermeneutics*, University of California Press, Berkeley.

Hudleston, R. (ed.), (1952) *Revelations of Divine Love, Shewed to a Devout Ankress by Name Julian of Norwich*, 2nd edn, Burns Oates, London.

Humphrey, C. (1996) *Shamans and Elders*, Clarendon Press, Oxford.

Hurwitz, T.A., Wada, J.A., Kosaka, B.D. and Strauss, E.H. (1985) Cerebral organization of affect suggested by temporal lobe seizures. *Neurology*, **35**, 1335–7.

Huxley, A. (1994) *The Doors of Perception*, Vintage, London.

Idel, M. (2005) *Kabbalah and Eros*, Yale University Press, New Haven.

Isham, C.J. and Butterfield, J. (1998) Topos perspective on the Kochen-Specker theorem: I. Quantum states as generalized valuations. *International Journal of Theoretical Physics*, **37**, 2669–733.

Jackson, M.C. (1997) Benign schizotypy? The case of spiritual experience, in *Schizotypy. Relations to Illness and Health* (ed. G.S. Claridge), Oxford University Press, Oxford, pp. 227–250.

Jackson, M.C. (2001) Psychotic and spiritual experience: A case study comparison, in *Psychosis and Spirituality, Exploring the New Frontier* (ed. I. Clarke), Wiley, Chichester.

Jackson, M.C. and Fulford, K.W.M. (1997) Spiritual experience and psychopathology. *Philosophy, Psychiatry and Psychology*, **1**, 41–65.

Jackson, M.C. and Fulford, K.W.M. (2002) Psychosis good and bad: Values-based practice and the distinction between pathological and non-pathological forms of psychotic experience (a response to Marzanski and Bratton and to Brett). *Philosophy, Psychiatry, and Psychology*. **4**, 387–94.

Jahnke, R. (2002) *The Healing Promise of Qi. Creating Extraordinary Wellness Through Qigong and Tai Chi*, Contemporary Books, New York.

James, W. (1902) *The Varieties of Religious Experience*, Longmans, New York.

James, W. (1958) *The Varieties of Religious Experience*, New American Library of World Literature, New York.

Jamison, K. (1993) *Touched with Fire. Manic–Depressive Illness and the Artistic Temperament*, The Free Press, New York.

Jaspers, K.(1959 [1913]) *General Psychopathology* (trans. J. Hoenig & M.W. Hamilton), Manchester University Press, Manchester.

Jaynes, J. (1976) *The Origin of Consciousness in the Breakdown of the Bicameral Mind*, Mariner Books, New York.

Jones, E. and Watson, J.P. (1997) Delusion, the over-valued idea and religious beliefs: A comparative analysis of their characteristics. *British Journal of Psychiatry*, **170**, 381–6.

Jorgensen, P. (1994) Course and outcome in delusional beliefs. *Psychopathology*, **27**, 89–99.

Jorgensen, P. and Jensen, J. (1994) What predicts the persistence of delusional beliefs? *Psychopathology*, **27**, 73–8.

Jung, C.G. (1933) *Modern Man in Search of a Soul*, Kegan Paul, London.

Jung, C.G. (1956) *Symbols of Transformation*, Routledge & Kegan Paul, London.

Jung, C.G. (1960) On the psychogenesis of schizophrenia, in *The Collected Works of C.G. Jung*, Vol. **3** (trans. R.F.C. Hull, eds H. Read, M. Fordham and G. Adler), Routledge and Kegan Paul, London.

Jung, C.G. (1961) *Memories, Dreams, Reflections* ed. Aniela Jaffe, Vintage Books. Appendix p. 378.

Jung, C.G. (1978) *Man and His Symbols*, Picador, London.

Jung, C.G. (1983) *Memories, Dreams, Reflections*, Flamingo, London.

Kabat-Zinn, J. (1994) *Wherever You Go, There You Are: Mindfulness Meditation for Everyday Life*, Hyperion, New York.

Kant, Immanuel (2003) *Critique of Pure Reason* (trans. Norman Kemp Smith), Palgrave-Macmillan, New York.

Kaplan, S. (2009) Grasping at ontological straws: Overcoming reductionism in the Advaita Vedanta-neuroscience dialogue. *Journal of the American Academy of Religion*, **77**, 238–74.

Kapur, S. (2003) Psychosis as a state of aberrant salience: a framework linking biology, phenomenology and pharmacology in schizophrenia. *American Journal of Psychiatry*, **160**, 13–23.

Keating, A.M. and Fretz, B.R. (1990) Christians' anticipations about counsellors in response to counsellors' descriptions. *Journal of Counselling Psychology*, **37** (3), 293–6.

Keighley, T. (1999) Woman of Mystery, *Nursing Standard*, **12**, no. 34.

Kendell, R.E. (1991) The major functional psychoses: Are they independent entities or part of a continuum? Philosophical and conceptual issues underlying the debate, in *Concepts of Mental Disorder. A Continuing Debate* (eds A. Kerr and H. McClelland), Gaskell, London, pp. 1–16.

Kendler, K.S., Glazer, W.M. and Morgensetern, H. (1983) Dimensions of delusional experience. *American Journal of Psychiatry*, **140**, 466–9.

Kennedy, A. (1985) *The Buddhist Vision*, Hutchinson, London.

Keyston, J. (ed.) (n.d) *Dialogue with Wolfgang Gigerich*, http://www.guildofpastoralpsychology.org.uk/page9.html (accessed 11 April 2007).

Kiev, A. (1963) Beliefs and delusions of West Indian immigrants to London. *British Journal of Psychiatry*, **109**, 356–63.

Kincheloe, J.L. and Berry, K.S. (2004) *Rigour and Complexity in Educational Research Conceptualising the Bricolage*, Open University Press, Maidenhead.

Kingdon, D.G. and Finn, A.M. (2006) *Tackling Mental Health Crises*, Brunner-Routledge, Philadelphia.

Kingdon, D.G. and Turkington, D. (2005) *Cognitive Therapy of Schizophrenia* (*Guides to evidence-based practice*, Series Editor: J. Persons), Guilford, New York.

Kirkness, B. (ed.) (1997) *Target Schizophrenia*, National Schizophrenia Fellowship, London.

Koenig, H.G. (2007) *Spirituality in Patient Care*, Templeton Foundation Press, Philadelphia.

Koenig, H.G., McCullough, M. and Larson, D. (eds) (2001) *Handbook of Religion and Health*, Oxford University Press, New York.

Kornfield, J. (1993) *A Path With Heart: A Guide Through the Perils and Promises of Spiritual Life*, Bantam Books, New York.

Kovacs, M. and Beck, A.T. (1978) Maladaptive cognitive structures in depression. *American Journal of Psychiatry*, **135**, 525–33.

Kozac, M.J. and Foa, E.B. (1994) Obsessions, overvalued ideas, and delusions in obsessive–compulsive disorder. *Behaviour Research and Therapy*, **32**, No. 3, 343–53.

References

Kraya, N.A. and Patrick, C. (1997) Folie à deux in forensic setting. *The Australian and New Zealand Journal of psychiatry*, **31** (6), 883–8.

Kretschmer, E. (1925) *Physique and Character*, (trans. W.H.J. Sprott), Kegan, Trench, and Trubner, London.

Krippner, S. (2003) *The Epistemology and Technology of Shamanic States*. Presentation at Sci.-Med Network Conference London.

Kris, E. (1952) *Psychoanalytic Explorations in Art*, International Universities Press, New York.

Krishna, G. (1971) *Kundalini: The Evolutionary Energy in Man*, Shambhala, Berkeley.

Krishna, G. (1974) *Higher Consciousness: The Evolutionary Thrust of Kundalini*, Julian, New York.

Kuipers, E., Garety, P.A. and Fowler, D. *et al.* (1997) London-East Anglia randomised controlled trial of cognitive–behavioural therapy for psychosis. I: Effects of treatment phase. *British Journal of Psychiatry*, **171**, 319–27.

Kumar, M. (2008) *Quantum: Einstein, Bohr and the Great Debate About the Nature of Reality*, Faber and Faber, London.

Kushner, A.W. (1967) Two cases of autocastration due to religious delusions. *British Journal of Medical Psychology*, **40**, 293–8.

Laderman, C. (1983) *Wives and Midwives*, University of California Press, Berkeley.

Laing, R.D. (1960) *The Divided Self: An Existential Study in Sanity and Madness*, Penguin, Harmondsworth.

Laing, R.D. (1967) *The Politics of Experience*, Penguin, Harmondsworth.

Laing, R.D. (1970) *Knots*, Pantheon Books, New York.

Laing. R.D. (1972) Metanoia: Some experiences at Kingsley Hall, in *Going Crazy* (ed. H.M. Ruitenbeck), Bantam, New York.

Lamme, V.A.F. (2006) Towards a true neural stance on consciousness. *Trends in Cognitive Sciences*, **10**, 494–501.

Lamsa, G.M. (1947/1976) *New Testament Origin*, Aramaic Bible Center, San Antonio, TX.

Lancaster, B.L. (1997a) On the stages of perception: Towards a synthesis of cognitive neuroscience and the Buddhist *Abhidhamma* tradition. *Journal of Consciousness Studies*, **4**, 122–42.

Lancaster, B.L. (1997b) The mytholoy of *anatta*: Bridging the East-West divide, In *The Authority of Experience: Readings on Buddhism and Psychology* (ed. J. Pickering), Curzon Press, Richmond, Surrey, pp. 170–202.

Lancaster, B.L. (2000) On the relationship between cognitive models and spiritual maps. Evidence from Hebrew Language Mysticism. *Journal of Consciousness Studies*, **7**, 231–50.

Lancaster, B.L. (2004) *Approaches to Consciousness: The Marriage of Science and Mysticism*, Palgrave Macmillan, Basingstoke, UK.

Lancaster, B. L. (2007) *How can spiritual maps guide us through a crisis of meaning?* Workshop Presented at Spiritual Narratives in Psychological Therapies Conference, Cambridge, April 2007.

Lancaster, B.L. (2009) The cognitive neuroscience of consciousness, mysticism and psi, in *Mysterious Minds: The Neurobiology of Psychics, Mediums and Other Extraordinary People* (eds H. Friedman and S. Krippner), Praeger, Santa Barbara, CA.

Lancaster, B.L. (in press) The hard problem revisited: From cognitive neuroscience to Kabbalah and back again, in *Neuroscience, Consciousness, and Spirituality* (eds H. Walach and S. Schmidt), Springer, New York.

Langer, M. (1989) *Merleau-Ponty's Phenomenology of Perception: A Guide and Commentary*, Macmillan, Basingstoke.

Lao, T. (1963) *Tao Te Ching*, Penguin, Harmondsworth.

Laszlo, E. (2009) *The Akashic Experience, Science and the Cosmic Memory Field*, Inner Traditions, Vermont, USA.

Lata, J. (2005) *Visual Hallucinations in Hispanic Clinic Patients: A Need to Assess for Cultural Beliefs*, Carlos Albizu University, Miami.

Latkin, C., Hagan, R., Littman, R. and Sundberg, N. (1987) Who lives in Utopia? A brief report on Rajneeshpuram research project. *Sociological Analysis*, **48**, 73–81.

Lawrence, T., Edwards, C., Barraclough, N., Church, S. and Hetherington, F. (1995) Modelling childhood causes of paranormal belief and experience: Childhood trauma and childhood fantasy. *Personality and Individual Differences*, **19**, 209–15.

Le Bon, G. (1896) *The Crowd*, Unwin, London.

Leibniz, G. (1991) *G.W. Leibniz's Monadology: An Edition for Students*, ed. Nicholas Rescher, Routledge, London.

Lennox, W. (1960) *Epilepsy and Related Disorders* Vol., **I** Churchill, London.

Lenz, H. (1983) Belief and delusion: Their common origin but different course of development. *Zygon*, **18** (2 June), 117–37.

Leuder, I. and Thomas, P. (2000) *Voices of Reason, Voices of Insanity*, Routledge, Philadelphia.

Levin, D.M. (1987a) Psychopathology in the epoch of nihilism, in *Pathologies of the Modern Self*, (ed. D.M. Levin), New York University Press, New York, pp. 21–83.

Levin, D.M. (1987b) Introduction, in *Pathologies of the Modern Self*, (ed. D.M. Levin), New York University Press, New York, pp. 1–17.

Levin, R. and Raulin, M.L. (1991) Preliminary evidence for the proposed relationship between frequent nightmares and schizotypal symptomatology. *Journal of Personality Disorders*, **5**, 8–14.

Lewis, I.M. (1991) *Ecstatic Religion*, Routledge, London.

Liddle, P.F. (1987) The symptoms of chronic schizophrenia: A re-examination of the positive–negative dichotomy. *British Journal of Psychiatry*, **151**, 145–51.

Lienhardt, G. (1990) *Divinity and Experience: The Religion of the Dinka*, Clarendon Press, Oxford.

Lindner, R. (1954) The jet-propelled couch, in *The Fifty Minute-Hour* (ed. R. Lindner), Holt, Rinehart and Winston, New York.

Linehan, M. (1993b) *Skills Training Manual for Treating Borderline Personality Disorder*, The Guildford Press, New York.

Linn, E.L. (1977) Verbal auditory hallucinations: Mind, self, and society. *Journal of Nervous and Mental Disease*, **164**, 8–17.

Linney, Y., Peters, E.R. and Ayton, P. (1998) Reasoning biases in delusion-prone individuals. *British Journal of Clinical Psychology*, **37**, 285–303.

Littlewood, R. and Lipsedge, M. (1981) Some social and phenomenological characteristics of psychotic immigrants. *Psychological Medicine*, **11**, 289–302.

Lowson, D. (1994) Understanding professional thought disorder: A guide for service users and a challenge to professionals. *Asylum*, **8**, 29–30.

Ludema, J.D., Cooperrider, D.L. and Barrett, F. J. (2001) Appreciative inquiry: The power of the unconditional positive question in *Handbook of Action Research: Participative Inquiry and Practice* (eds. P. Reason and H. Bradbury), Sage, London, pp. 189–199.

Lukoff, D. (1985) The diagnosis of mystical experiences with psychotic features. *Journal of Transpersonal Psychology*, **17**, 155–81.

Lukoff, D. (1991) Divine madness: Shamanistic initiatory crisis and psychosis. *Shaman's Drum*, **22**, 24–9.

Lukoff, D. (1996) Transpersonal psychotherapy with psychotic disorders and spiritual emergencies with psychotic features, in *Textbook of Transpersonal Psychiatry and Psychology* (eds B. Scotton, A. Chinen and J. Battista), BasicBooks, New York.

Lukoff, D. (2007a) Visionary spiritual experiences. *Southern Medical Journal*, **100**, 635–41.

Lukoff, D. (2007b) http://www.spiritualcompetency.com/dsm4/lesson3_6.asp.

Lukoff, D. and Everest, H. (1985). The myths in mental illness. *The Journal of Transpersonal Psychology* **17** (2), 123–53, http://www.spiritualcompetency.com/articles.asp.

Lukoff, D. and Lu, F. (2005) A transpersonal integrative approach to spiritually oriented psychotherapy, in *Spiritually Oriented Psychotherapy* (eds L. Sperry and E. Shafranske), American Psychological Association Press, Washington, DC, pp. 177–205.

Lukoff, D., Lu, F. and Turner, R. (1996) Diagnosis; A transpersonal clinical approach to religious and spiritual problems, in *Textbook of Transpersonal Psychiatry and Psychology* (eds Scotten, B., Chinen, A.B. and Battista, J.R.), Basic books, New York, pp. 231–49.

Lukoff, D., Lu, F. and Turner, R. (1998) From spiritual emergency to spiritual problem: The transpersonal roots of the new DSM-IV category. *Journal of Humanistic Psychology*, **38**, 21–50.

Lupfer, M.B., Brock, K.F. and DePaola, S.J. (1992) The use of secular and religious attributions to explain everyday behaviour. *Journal for the Scientific Study of Religion*, **31** (4), 486–503.

Lutz, A., Greischar, L.L. and Rawlings, N.B. *et al.* (2004) Long-term meditators self-induce high-amplitude gamma synchrony during mental practice. *Proceedings of the National Academy of Sciences of the United States of America*, **101**, 16369–73.

Lutz, A., Dunne, J.D. and Davidson, R.J. (2007) Meditation and the neuroscience of consciousness: An introduction, in *The Cambridge Handbook of Consciousness* (eds P. D. Zelazo, M. Moscovitch and E. Thompson), Cambridge University Press, Cambridge, pp. 499–551.

Lutz, A., Brefczynski-Lewis, J., Johnstone, T. and Davidson, R.J. (2008a) Regulation of the neural circuitry of emotion by compassion meditation: effects of meditative expertise. *PLoS ONE*, **3**, e1897.

Lutz, A., Slagter, H.A., Dunne, J.D. and Davidson, R.J. (2008b) Attention regulation and monitoring in meditation. *Trends in Cognitive Sciences*, **12**, 163–9.

Lutz, A., Greischar, L.L., Perlman, D.M. and Davidson, R.J. (2009) BOLD signal in insula is differentially related to cardiac function during compassion meditation in experts vs. novices. *NeuroImage*, **47**, 1038–46.

MacIver, J. (1983) *The Glimpse*, Libra Publishers, Roslyn Heights, NJ.

MacWilliams, S.A. (1983) *Construing and Nirvana*. Paper Presented to The Fifth Congress on Personal Construct Psychology, Pine Manor College, Chestnut Hill, MA.

Magee, B. (1998) *The Story of Philosophy*, Dorling Kindersley Ltd, London.

Maher, B.A. (1988) Delusions as the product of normal cognitions, in *Delusional Beliefs* (eds T.F. Oltmanns and B.A. Maher), John Wiley and Sons, London.

Malinowski, B. (1929) *The Sexual Life of Savages in North-West Melanesia*, Routledge and Kegan Paul, London (1968 reprint).

Mansell, W. (2005) Control theory and psychopathology: An integrative approach. *Psychology and Psychotherapy: Theory, Research and Practice*, **78**, 141–78.

Mason, O. and Claridge, G. (1999) Individual differences in schizotypy and reduced asymmetry using the chimeric faces task. *Cognitive Neuropsychology*, **4**, 289–301.

Mason, A., Claridge, G. and Williams, L. (1997) Questionnaire measurement, in *Schizotypy: Implications for Illness and Health* (ed. G. Claridge), Oxford University Press, Oxford, pp. 19–37.

Matte Blanco, I. (1998) *The Unconscious as Infinite Sets*, Karnac, London.

Mayerhoff, D., Pelta, E., Valentino, C. and Chakos, M. (1991) Real-life basis for a patient's paranoia. *American Journal of Psychiatry*, **148**, 682–3.

McCreery, C.A.S. and Claridge, G.A. (1995) Out-of-body experiences and personality. *Journal of the Society for Psychical Research*, **60**, 129–48.

McCreery, C. & Claridge, G. (1996) A study of hallucination in normal subjects-II. Electrophysiological data. Personality and Individual Differences, **21** (5), 749–58.

McLeod, J. (1994) *Doing Counselling Research*, Sage, London.

McSherry, W. (2006) *Making Sense of Spirituality in Nursing and Health Care Practice*, Jessica Kingsley Publishers, London.

Meehl, P.E. (1962) Schizotaxia, schizotypy, and schizophrenia. *American Psychologist*, **17**, 827–838.

Miller, J.S. (2000) Personal consciousness integration: The next phase of recovery. *Psychiatric Rehabilitation Journal*, **23**, 342–52.

Mills, N. (1999) Encouraging body and mind to work together. *International Journal of Alternative and Complementary Medicine*, **17** (9), 27–28.

Mills, N. (2000a) Working with the clients sense of spiritual nourishment. *Transpersonal Psychology Review*, **4**, 23–5.

Mills, N. (2000b) Therapist burn-out or therapist glow? Some light from the East. *Clinical Psychology Forum*, **146**, 30–33.

Mills, N. (2001). The experience of fragmentation in psychosis: Can mindfulness help? in *Psychosis and Spirituality, Exploring the New Frontier* (ed. I. Clarke), Wiley, Chichester.

Mills, N. (2001a) Working with the body in cognitive therapy. *Clinical Psychology*, **4**, 25–8.

Mills, N (2007) Working with Qi (chi) to help with mental health problems, in *Spirituality, Values and Mental Health* (eds M.E. Coyte, P. Gilbert and V. Nicholls, Jessica Kingsley, London.

Mills, N. and Allen, J. (2000) Mindfulness of movement as a coping strategy in Multiple Sclerosis. *A pilot study. General Hospital Psychiatry*, **22**, 425–31.

Mills, N. and Whiting, S. (1997) Being centred and being scattered: A kinaesthetic strategy for people who experience psychotic symptoms. *Clinical Psychology Forum*, **103**, 27–31.

Moncrief, J. (2009) *The Myth of the Chemical Cure*, revised edn. Palgrave Macmillan, Basingstoke.

Moore, A. and Malinowski, P. (2009) Meditation, mindfulness and cognitive flexibility. *Consciousness and Cognition*, **18**, 176–86.

Morrison, A.P., Frame, L. and Larkin, W. (2003) Relationships between trauma and psychosis: A review and integration. *British Journal of Clinical Psychology*, **42**, 331–53.

Morrow, D., Worthington, E.L. and McCullogh, M.E. (1993) Observers' perceptions of a counsellor's treatment of a religious issue. *Journal of Counselling and Development*, **71**, 452–6.

Mosher, L., Hendrix, V. and Fort, D. (2004) *Soteria: Through Madness To Deliverance*, Xlibris Corporation, Philadelphia.

Muffler, J., Langrod, J.G., Richardson, J.T. and Ruiz, P. (1997) Religion, in *Substance Abuse: A Comprehensive Textbook* (eds J.H. Lowinson, P. Ruiz, R.B. Millman and J.G. Langrod), 3rd edn, Williams & Wilkins, Baltimore.

Mullan, S. and Penfield, W. (1959) Illusions of comparative interpretation and emotion. *Archives of Neurology and Psych.*, **81**, 269–85.

Mullen, P.E., Romans-Clarkson, S.E., Walton, V.A. and Herbison, G.P. (1988) Impact of sexual and physical abuse on women's mental health. *Lancet*, **1** (8590), 841–5.

Nagel, T. (1974) What is it like to be a bat? *Philosophical Review*, **83**, 435–50.

Nancy, J. (1989) Sharing voices, in *Transforming the Hermeneutic Context: From Nietzsche to Nancy* (eds Ormiston, G.L. and Schrift, A.D.), State University of New York Press, Albany, NY, pp. 211–59.

Nasr, S.H. (1968) *Man and Nature: The Spiritual Crisis in Modern Man*, Unwin, London.

Neelman, J. and King, M.B. (1993) Psychiatrists' religious attitudes in relation to their clinical practice: A survey of 231 psychiatrists. *Acta Psychiatrica Scandinavica*, **88**, 420–4.

Neeleman, J. and Persaud, R. (1995) Why do psychiatrists neglect religion? *British Journal of Medical Psychology*, **68**, 169–78.

Newberg, A., D'Aquili, E. and Rause, R. (2001) *Why God Won't Go Away: Brain Science and the Biology of Belief*, Ballantine Books, New York.

Newnes, C., Holmes, G. and Dunn, C. (eds) (1999) *This Is Madness: A Critical Look at Psychiatry and the Future of Mental Health Services*, PCCS Books, Llangarron.

Obeyesekere, G. (1981) *Medusa's Hair: An Essay of Personal Symbols and Religious Experience*, University of Chicago Press, Chicago.

O'Callaghan, M. (1996) The far side of madness: Visionary process and psychosis. An interview with John Perry. *IASP Journal*, **4**.

Ogden, P., Minton, K. and Pain, C. (2006). *Trauma and the Body: A Sensorimotor Approach to Psychotherapy*, Norton & Co., New York.

Oltmanns, T.F. (1988) Approaches to the definition and study of delusions, in *Delusional Beliefs* (eds T.F. Oltmanns and B. Maher), Wiley, New York, pp. 3–11.

Otto, R. (1917/1958) *The Idea of the Holy: An Inquiry into the Non-Rational Factor in the Idea of the Divine and its Relation to the Rational* (trans. J.W. Harvey), Oxford University Press, London.

Pagels, E. (1979) *The Gnostic Gospels*, Random House, New York.

Pantelis, C. and Nelson, H.E. (1994) Cognitive functioning and symptomatology in schizophrenia: The role of fronto-subcortical systems, in *The Neuropsychology of Schizophrenia* (eds A.S. David and J.C. Cutting), LEA, Hove, pp. 215–30.

Pappas, J. and Friedman, H. (2007) Toward a conceptual clarification of the terms "religious," "spiritual," and "transpersonal" as psychological constructs, in *Cultural Healing and Belief Systems* (eds J. Pappas, W. Smythe and A. Baydala), Temeron Books, Alberta, pp. 22–54.

Paris, J., Zweig-Frank, H. and Guzder, J. (1994) Psychological risk factors for borderline personality disorder in female patients. *Comprehensive Psychiatry*, **35**, 301–5.

Parker, I., Georgaca, E., Harper, D., McLaughlin, T. and Stowell-Smith, M. (1995) *Deconstructing Psychopathology*, Sage, London.

Parmenides (1986) *The Fragments of Parmenides: A Critical Text With Introduction, Translation, The Ancient Testimonia and A Commentary* (trans. A.H. Coxon), Van Gorcum, Assen, Netherlands.

Parry, J. (1994) *Death in Banaras*, Cambridge University Press, Cambridge.

Paukert, A.L., Phillips, L. and Cully, J.A. *et al.* (2009) Integration of religion into cognitive–behavioral therapy for geriatric anxiety and depression. *Journal of Psychiatric Practice*, **15** (2), 103–12.

Penfield, W. and Kristiansen, K. (1951) *Epileptic Seizure Patterns*, Charles C. Thomas, Springfield Ill.

Penfield, W. and Perot, P. (1963) The brain's record of auditory and visual experience. *Brain*, **86**, 595–96.

Perry, J.W. (1974) *The Far Side of Madness.*, Prentice Hall, Englewood Cliffs, NJ.

Perry, J.W. (1977–78) Psychosis and the visionary mind. *Journal of Altered States of Consciousness*, **3**, 5–13.

Perry, J.W. (1989) Spiritual emergence and renewal, in *Spiritual Emergency: When Personal Transformation Becomes a Crisis* (eds C. Grof and S. Grof), Tarcher, Los Angeles, pp. 63–75.

Perry, J.W. (1992) Mental breakdown as a healing process, http://www.global-vision.org/interview/perry.html (retrieved 24 April 2003).

Perry, J.W. (1998/9) *Trials of the Visionary Mind: Spiritual Emergency and the Renewal Process.* State University of New York Press, Albany, NY.

Peters, E.R., Pickering, A.D. and Hemsley, D.R. (1994) 'Cognitive inhibition' and positive symptomatology in schizotypy. *British Journal of Clinical Psychology*, **33**, 33–48.

Peters, E.R., Day, S. and Garety, P.A. (1996) The Peters et al. Delusions Inventory (PDI): New norms for the 21-item version. *Schizophrenia Research*, **18**, 118.

Peters, E.R., Joseph, S. and Garety, P.A. (1999) The assessment of delusions in normal and psychotic populations: Introducing the PDI (Peters et al. Delusions Inventory). *Schizophrenia Bulletin*, **25**, 553–76.

Peters, E.R., Day, S., McKenna, J. and Orbach, G. (1999) The incidence of delusional ideation in religious and psychotic populations. *British Journal of Clinical Psychology*, **38**, 83–96.

Pichler, E. (1943) Über Störungen des Raum- und Zeiterlebens bei Verletzungen des Hinterhauptlappens. *Zeitschrift für die gesamte Neurologie und Psychiatrie*, **176**, 434–64.

Plato (1924) *Plato with an English Translation*, Vol **4**, (trans. W.R.M. Lamb) (Loeb Classical Library), Heinemann, London.

Plato (1955) *The Republic*, (trans. H.D.P Lee), Penguin Books, London.

Poling, T. and Kenny, J. (1986) *The Hare Krishna Character Type: A Study in Sensate Personality*, Edwin Mellen, Lewinston, NY.

Popper, K. (1963) *Conjectures and Refutations: The Growth of Scientific Knowledge*, Routledge, London.

Posey, T.B. and Losch, M.E. (1983) Auditory hallucinations of hearing voices in 375 normal subjects. *Imagination, Cognition, and Personality*, **3**, 99–113.

Post, S.G. (1992) DSM-III-R and religion. *Social Science and Medicine*, **35**, 81–90.

Poulton, R., Caspi, A. and Moffitt, T.E. *et al.* (2000) Children's self-reported psychotic symptoms and adult schizophreniform disorder: A 15-year longitudinal study. *Archives of General Psychiatry*, **57**, 1053–8.

Prince, R. (1979) Religious experience and psychosis. *Journal of Altered States of Consciousness*, **5**, 167–81.

Prince, R.H. (1992) Religious experience and psychopathology: Cross-cultural perspectives, in *Religion and mental health* (ed. J.F. Schumacher), Oxford University Press, New York, pp. 281–90.

Propst, L.R., Ostrom, R. and Watkins, P. *et al.* (1992) Comparative efficacy of religious and nonreligious cognitive-behavioral therapy for the treatment of clinical depression in religious individuals. *Journal of Consulting and Clinical Psychology*, **60**(1), 94–103.

Pryor, R. (1998) Mediaeval madness (case description of Margery Kempe), in *Sounds from the Bell Jar. Ten Psychotic Authors* (ed. G. Claridge), 2nd edn, Malor Books, Cambridge, MA, pp. 67–70.

Rado, S. (1953) Dynamics and classification of disordered behaviour. *American Journal of Psychiatry*, **110**, 406–16.

Raine, A. (1991) The Schizotypal Personality Questionnaire (SPQ): A scale for the assessment of schizotypal personality based on DSM-III-R criteria. *Schizophrenia Bulletin*, **17**, 555–65.

Raine, A., Lencz, T. and Mednick, S.A. (eds) (1995) *Schizotypal Personality*, Cambridge University Press, Cambridge.

Ralph, R.O., Lambric, T.M. and Steele, R.B. (1996). Recovery Issues in a Consumer Developed Evaluation of the Mental Health System. Paper presented at the *6th Annual Mental Health Services Research and Evaluation Conference*, Arlington, VA.

Rao, P.K. and Rao, K.R. (1982) Two studies of ESP and subliminal perception. *Journal of Parapsychology*, **46**, 185–207.

Rathod, S., Kingdon, D., Phiri, P. and Gobbi, M. (2009) Developing Culturally Sensitive Cognitive Behaviour Therapy for Psychosis for Ethnic Minority Patients. *Report to Department of Health*.

Read, J., van Os, J., Morrison, A. and Ross, C.A. (2005) Childhood trauma, psychosis and schizophrenia: A literature review with theoretical and clinical implications. *Acta Psychiatrica Scandinavica*, **112**, 330–50.

Reason, P. (2000) Action Research as Spiritual Practice. Prepared for the University of Surrey Learning Community Conference May 4/5 2000. http://www.scimednet.org/Private/privlib/PR1100actionresearch_Reason.htm (accessed 14 March 2009).

Reason, P. and Bradbury, H. (2001) *Handbook of Action Research Participative Enquiry and Practice*, Sage, London.

Reeves, R.R. and Liberto, V. (2006) Suicide associated with the Antichrist delusion. *Journal of Forensic Science*, **51**(2), 411–2.

Reich, W. (1949) *Character Analysis*, Farrar, Straus and Giroux, New York.

Reichel-Dolmatoff, G. (1997) *Rainforest Shamans*, Themis Books, Totnes.

Rendle, A. and Wilson, H. (2008) Running an emotional coping skills group based on dialectical behavior therapy, in *Cognitive Behaviour Therapy for Acute Inpatient Mental Health Units; Working With Clients, Staff And The Milieu* (eds I. Clarke and H. Wilson), Routledge, London, pp. 173–81.

Repper, J. and Perkins, R. (2003) *Social Inclusion and Recovery; A Model for Mental Health Practice*, Bailliere Tindall, London.

Richardson, J.T. (1993a) Cult definitions: From sociological-technical to popular-negative. *Review of Religious Research*, **34**, 348–56.

Richardson, J.T. (1993b) Religiosity as deviance: Negative religious bias in and misuse of the DSM-III. *Deviant Behavior: An Interdisciplinary Journal*, **14**, 1–21.

Richardson, J.T. (1995) Clinical and personality assessment of participants in New Religions. *International Journal for the Psychology of Religion*, **5**, 145–70.

Richardson, J.T., Stewart, M. and Simmonds, R. (1979) *Organized Miracles*. Transaction Books, New Brunswick, NJ.

Roberts, G. (1991) Delusional belief systems and meaning in life: A preferred reality? *British Journal of Psychiatry*, **159** (Suppl. 14), 19–28.

Roberts, G. (1992) The origins of delusions. *British Journal of Psychiatry*, **161**, 298–308.

Rodis-Lewis, G. (1998) *Descartes, His Life and Thought,* (trans. Jane Marie Todd), Cornell University Press, Ithaca.

Rogers, C.R. (1951) *Client Centred Therapy*, 2nd edn, Constable, London.

Romme, M.A.J. and Escher, A. (1989) Hearing voices. *Schizophrenia Bulletin*, **15**, 209–16.

Romme, M.A.J. and Escher, S. (1989) *Accepting Voices*, Mind Publications, London.

Rosen, G. (1968) *Madness in Society*, Harper & Row, New York.

Ross, M. (1983) Clinical profiles of Hare Krishna devotees. *American Journal of Psychiatry*, **140**, 416–20.

Rubia, K. (2009) The neurobiology of meditation and its clinical effectiveness in psychiatric disorders. *Biological Psychology*, **82**, 1–11.

Russell, A., Munto, J.C. and Jones, P.B. *et al.* (1997) Schizophrenia and the myth of intellectual decline. *American Journal of Psychiatry*, **154**, 635–9.

Sabo, A.N. (1997) Etiological significance of associations between childhood trauma and borderline personality disorder: Conceptual and clinical implications. *Journal of Personality Disorders*, **11**, 5–70.

Sannella, L. (1992) *The Kundalini Experience: Psychosis or Transcendence?* Integral Publishing, Lower Lake, CA.

Saver, J.L. and Rabin, J. (1997) The neural substrates of religious experience. *Journal of Neuropsychiatry and Clinical Neurosciences*, **9**, 498–510.

Savile, A. (2005) *Kant's Critique of Pure Reason: An Orientation to the Central Theme*, Blackwell, Malden, MA.

Scarnati, R., Madry, M. and Wise, A. *et al.* (1991) Religious beliefs and practices among the most-dangerous psychiatric inmates. *Forensic Reports*, **4**, 1–16.

Schore, A.N. (2003) *Affect Dysregulation and Disorders of the Self*, W. W. Norton & Co. Inc, New York.

Schrödinger, E. (1967) *What is Life and Mind and Matter?* Cambridge University Press, Cambridge.

Searle, J. (1992) The problem of consciousness, in *CIBA Foundation Symposium no 174, Experimental and Theoretical Studies of Consciousness* (ed. P. Nagel), John Wiley, Chichester, pp. 61–80.

Segal, Z.V., Williams, J.M.G. and Teasdale, J.D. (2002) *Mindfulness-based cognitive therapy for depression: A new approach to preventing relapse*, Guilford Press, New York.

Sensky, T. and Fenwick, P. (1982) Religiosity, mystical experience and epilepsy, in *Progress in Epilepsy* (ed. F. Clifford Rose), Pitman, London.

Sensky, T., Turkington, D. and Kingdon, D.J. *et al.* (2000) A randomised controlled trial of cognitive–behavioural therapy for persistent symptoms in schizophrenia resistant to medication. *Archives of General Psychiatry*, **57**, 165–172.

Sharp, H.M., Fear, C.F. Williams, J.M. *et al.* (1996) Delusional phenomenology – dimensions of change. *Behaviour Research & Therapy*, **34**, 123–42.

Shokek, S. (2001) *Kabbalah and the Art of Being*, Routledge, London.

Siddle, R. (2000) *Religious delusions and religious beliefs in schizophrenia.*, PhD thesis. University of Manchester.

Silverman, J. (1967) Shamans and acute schizophrenia. *American Anthropologist*, **69**, 21–31.

Simmonds-Moore, C. (2009) Exploring ways of manipulating/controlling pathological/ healthy anomalous experiences. Paper Presented at: 'First Conference On Health, Mental Health And Exceptional Human Experiences', Liverpool Hope University. (to appear in an edited volume, McFarland, Jefferson NC).

Sims, A. (1992) *Symptoms in the Mind: An Introduction to Descriptive Psychopathology*, 3rd edn, WB Saunders, London.

Slagter, H.A., Lutz, A. and Greischar, L.L. *et al.* (2007) Mental training affects distribution of limited brain resources. *PLoS Biology*, **5**, e138.

Somerset Spirituality Project Group (2002) It would have been good to talk. *Mental Health Today*, **21**, 18–20.

Spence, S.A., Brooks, D.J., Hirsch, S.R., Liddle, P.F., Meehan, J. and Grasby, P.M. (1997) A PET study of voluntary movement in schizophrenic patients experiencing passivity phenomena (delusions of alien control). *Brain*, **120**, 1997–2011.

Spinoza, B. (1989) *Ethics* (trans. Andrew Boyle), Dent, London.

Spitzer, M. (1990) On defining delusions. *Comprehensive Psychiatry*, **31**, 377–97.

Stein, M. (1998) Jung's Map of the Soul. *An Introduction*. Open Court, Illinois.

Stevenson, I. (1997) *Reincarnation and Biology*, Praeger, Westport, Conn.

Stewart, I. and Joines, V. (1987) *TA Today A New Introduction to Transactional Analysis*, Lifespace Publishing, Nottingham.

Stompe, T., Friedman, A. and Ortwein, G. *et al.* (1999) Comparison of delusions among schizophrenics in Austria and in Pakistan. *Psychopathology*, **32**(5), 225–34.

Storr, A. (1996) *Feet of Clay. A Study of Gurus*, Harper Collins, London.

Storr, A. (1998) *The Essential Jung*, Fontana Press, London.

Strauss, A. and Corbin, J. (1998) *Basics of Qualitative Research. Techniques and Procedures for Developing Grounded Theory*, 2nd edn, Sage publications, California.

Stroop, J.R. (1935) Studies of interference in serial verbal reactions. *Journal of Experimental Psychology*, **18**, 643–61.

Sutherland, S. (1992) *Irrationality*, Constable, London.

Swimme, B. *and Berry T.*, (1992) *The Universe Story*, HarperSanFrancisco, San Francisco.

Swinton, J. (2001a) *A Space to Listen: Meeting the Spiritual Needs of People with Learning Disabilities*, Mental Health Foundation London.

Swinton, J. (2001b) *Spirituality in Mental Health Care: Rediscovering a Forgotten Dimension*, Jessica Kingsley Publishers, London.

Swinton, J. and Pattison, S. (2001) 'Come All Ye Faithful', *Health Service Journal*, 20 December, pp. 24–5.

Swinton, J., Gilbert, P., Coyte, M.E. and Nicholls, V. (2007) *Spirituality, Values and Mental Health: Jewels for the Journey*, Jessica Kingsley Publ, London.

Szasz, T.S. (1974) *The Myth of Mental Illness*, Harper and Row, New York.

Szasz, T.S. (1997) *Insanity: The Idea and Its Consequences*, Syracuse University Press, New York.

Tart, C. (1997) *Body, Mind, Spirit*, Hampton Roads Publishing, Charlottesville.

Tart, C. (2009) *The End of Materialism, How Evidence of the Paranormal is Bringing Science and Spirit Together*, Noetic Books/New Harbinger, Oakland Ca.

Tateyama, J., Asai, M. and Kamisada, M. *et al.* (1993) Comparison of schizophrenic delusions between Japan and Germany. *Psychopathology*, **26**, 151–8.

Taylor, M.A. (1992) Are schizophrenia and affective disorder related? A selective literature review. *American Journal of Psychiatry*, **149**, 22–32.

Teasdale, J.D. and Barnard, P.J. (1993) *Affect, Cognition and Change: Remodelling Depressive Thought*, Lawrence Erlbaum Associates, Hove.

Teasdale, J.D., Segal, Z. and Williams, J. (1995) How does cognitive therapy prevent depressive relapse and why should attentional control (mindfulness) help? *Behaviour Research and Therapy*, **33**, 25–39.

Teilhard de Chardin, P. (1959) *The Phenomenon of Man*, Collins, London.

Terzian, H. (1964) Behavioural and EEG effects of intracarotid sodium amytal injection. *Acta Neurochirurgica*, **12**, 230–9.

Thalbourne, M.A. (1991) The psychology of mystical experience. *Exceptional Human Experience*, **9**, 168–86.

Thalbourne, M.A. (1994) Belief in the paranormal and its relationship to schizophrenia-relevant measures: A confirmatory study. *British Journal of Clinical Psychology*, **33**, 78–80.

Thalbourne, M.A. and Delin, P.S. (1994) A common thread underlying belief in the paranormal, creative personality, mystical experience, and psychopathology. *Journal of Parapsychology*, **58**, 3–38.

Thalbourne, M.A., Bartemucci, L. and Delin, P.S. *et al.* (1997) Transliminality: Its nature and correlates. *The Journal of the American Society for Psychical Research*, **91**, 305–31.

Thomas, P. (1997) *The Dialectics of Schizophrenia*, Free Association Books, London.

Thornton, K. (2009) *Clinical and Non-Clinical Auditory Verbal Hallucinations: A Psychological and Functional Imaging Study of the Psychosis Continuum*. PhD thesis. Bangor University.

Tien, A.Y. (1991) Distributions of hallucinations in the population. *Social Psychiatry and Psychiatric Epidemiology*, **26**, 287–92.

Tobert, N. (2005) Shamanism and consciousness: A review of four books. *Network: Scientific and Medical Network Review*, no. 87.

Tobert, N. (2007a) *In-Sanity: Explanatory Models for Religious Experience*, Occasional Paper no.3, Series 3, Religious Experience Research Centre, University of Wales, Lampeter.

Tobert, N. (2007b) *Interview with Robert Ginsberg*, http://www.robertginsburg.com/InterviewTobert.pdf.

Torrey, E.F., Bowler, A.E., Taylor, E.H. and Gottesman, I. I. (1994) *Schizophrenia and Manic–Depressive Disorder. The Biological Roots of Mental Illness*, Basic Books, New York.

Turner, E. (1992) *Experiencing Ritual*, University of Pennsylvania, USA.

Turner, V. (1968) *The Drums of Affliction, A Study of Religious Processes Among the Ndembu of Zambia*, Clarendon Press, Oxford.

Underhill, E. (1930) *Mysticism. A Study in the Nature and Development of Man's Spriritual Consciousness*, (12th, revised edition) Methuen, London.

Valla, J.-P. and Prince, R. (1989) Religious experiences as self-healing mechanisms, in *Altered States of Consciousness and Mental Health* (ed. C.A. Ward), Sage, London, pp. 149–166.

van der Hart, O., Nijenhuis, E.R.S. and Steele, K. (2006) *The Haunted Self: Structural Dissociation and the Treatment of Chronic Traumatization*, W. W. Norton, New York.

van Gennep, A.(1960/1908) *The Rites of Passage*, Routledge and Kegan Paul, London.

van Os, (2009) A salience dysregulation syndrome, *British Journal of Psychiatry*, **194**, 101–03.

van Os, J., Gilvarry, C. Bale, R. *et al.* (1999) A comparison of the utility of dimensional and categorical representations of psychosis. *Psychological Medicine*, **29**, 595–606.

van Os, J., Hansen, M., Bijl, R.V. and Ravelli, A. (2000). Strauss (1969) revisited: a psychosis continuum in the general population? *Schizophrenia Research*, **45**(1–2), 11–20.

van Os, J., Hanssen, M., Bijl, R.V. and Vollebergh, W. (2001) Prevalence of psychotic disorder and community level of psychotic symptoms: An urban–rural comparison, *Archives of General Psychiatry*, **58**, 663–8.

van Os, J., Linscott, R.J. Myin-Germeys, I. *et al.* (2008) A systematic review and meta-analysis of the psychosis continuum: Evidence for a psychosis proneness–persistence–impairment model of psychotic disorder, *Psychological Medicine*, **8**, 1–17.

Verdoux, H., Maurice-Tison, B. Gay, B. *et al.* (1998) A survey of delusional ideation in primary-care patients. *Psychological Medicine*, **28**, 127–34.

Victor, B. (1995) Psychopharmacology and transpersonal psychology, in *Textbook of Transpersonal Psychiatry and Psychology* (eds B. Scotton, A. Chinen and J. Battista), BasicBooks, New York.

von der Malsburg, C. (1997) The coherence definition of consciousness, in *Cognition, Computation, and Consciousness* (eds M. Ito, Y. Miyashita and E.T. Rolls), Oxford University Press. Oxford, pp. 193–204.

Wagner, W. (1943) Anisognosie [sic; sc.Anosognosie], Zeitrafferphanomen und Uhrzeitg-nosie als Symptome der Storungen im rechten Parieto-Occipitallappen. *Nervenarzt*, **16**, 49–57.

Waldram, R. (2007) *Spirituality and Madness*. Unpublished ISPUK Conference Presentation.

Wallace, A. (1956) Stress and rapid personality changes. *International Record of Medicine*, **169**, 761–74.

Wallas, G. (1926) *The Art of Thought*, Harcourt, New York.

Wallin, D.J. (2007) *Attachment in Psychotherapy.*, The Guilford Press, New York.

Walsh, R. and Vaughan, F. (1993) The art of transcendence: An introduction to common elements of transpersonal practices. *Journal of Transpersonal Psychology*, **25**, 1–9.

Wapnick, K. (1969) Mysticism and schizophrenia, *Journal of Transpersonal Psychology*, **1**, 49–68.

Wapnick, K. (1981) Mysticism and Schizophrenia, in *Understanding Mysticism* (ed. R. Woods), Athlone Press, London.

Warner, R. (1994) *Recovery from Schizophrenia: Psychiatry and Political Economy*, 2nd edn, Routledge, London.

Warwick, S.L. (2007) *Psychic opening as spiritual emergence(y) and its relation to self-defined seeking*. Unpublished Master's thesis. Liverpool John Moores University.

Wason, P.C. (1960) On the failure to eliminate hypotheses in a conceptual task, *Quarterly Journal of Experimental Psychology*, **12**, 129–40.

Waterfield, R. (2000) *The First Philosophers: The PreSocratics and the Sophists*, Oxford University Press, Oxford.

Watson, J.P. (1982) Aspects of personal meaning in schizophrenia, in *Personal Meanings* (eds. E. Sheperd and J.P. Watson), John Wiley, Chichester.

Waugh, A.C. (1986) Autocastration and biblical delusions in schizophrenia. *British Journal of Psychiatry*, **149**, 656–9.

Webb, N. and Wybrow, R. (1982) *The Gallup Report*, Sphere Books, London.

Weill, S. (1952) *Gravity and Grace*, Routledge, London.

Weiner, D. (1999) *Beyond Talk Therapy: Using Movement and Expressive Techniques in Clinical Practice*, American Psychological Association, Washington.

Weiss, A. (1987) Psychological distress and well-being in Hare Krishna. *Psychological Reports*, **61**, 23–35.

Weiss, A. and Comprey, A. (1987) Personality and mental health of Hare Krishna compared with psychiatric outpatients and "normals". *Personality and Individual Differences*, **8**, 721–30.

Wenk-Sormaz, H. (2005) Meditation can reduce habitual responding. *Alternative Therapies in Health and Medicine*, **11**, 42–58.

Wexler, B.E., Lyons, L., Lyons, H. and Mazure, C.M. (1997) Physical and sexual abuse during childhood and development of psychiatric illnesses during adulthood. *Journal of Nervous and Mental Disease*, **185**, 522–4.

Wieser, H.G. and Mazzola, G. (1986) Musical consonances and dissonances: are they distinguished independently by the right and left hippocampi? *Neuropsychologia*, **24**, 805–12.

Wilber, K. (1993) The spectrum of therapies, in *Paths Beyond Ego. The Transpersonal Vision*, (eds R. Walsh and V. Vaughn), Penguin Putman, New York, pp. 156–9.

Wilber, K. (1996) *Up From Eden: A Transpersonal View of Human Evolution*, 2nd edn, Quest, Wheaton, IL.

Wilber, K. (1997) *The Eye of the Spirit: An Integral Vision for a World Gone Slightly Mad*, Shambala, Berkeley, CA.

Wilber, K. (2000) *Integral Psychology. Consciousness, Spirit, Psychology, Therapy*, Shambala, Boston & London.

Williams, L. and Beech, A. (1997) Investigations of cognitive inhibitory processes in schizotypy and schizophrenia, in *Schizotypy: Implications for Illness and Health* (ed. G. Claridge), Oxford University Press, Oxford, pp. 63–79.

Williams, L.M. and Irwin, H.J. (1991) A study of paranormal belief, magical ideation as an index of schizotypy and cognitive style. *Personality & Individual Differences*, **12**, 1339–48.

Wilson, J.S. and Costanzo, P.R. (1996) A preliminary study of attachment, attention, and schizotypy in early adulthood. *Journal of Social and Clinical Psychology*, **15**, 231–60.

Wilson, W.P. (1998). Religion and psychoses, in *Handbook of Religion and Mental Health* (ed. H.G. Koenig), 1st edn, Academic Press, San Diego, pp. 161–73.

Windeatt, B.A. (trans.) (1985) *The Book of Margery Kempe*, Harmondsworth: Penguin.

Wing, J.K., Cooper, J.E., and Sartorius, N. (1974) *The Measurement and Classification of Psychiatric Symptoms*, Cambridge University Press, Cambridge.

Wittgenstein, L. (1967) *Zettel* (trans. G.E.M. Anscombe), University of California Press, Berkeley.

Wolfson, E. (2005) *Language, Eros, Being: Kabbalistic Hermeneutics and Poetic Imagination*, Fordham University Press, New York.

Woodruff, P.W.R., Wright, I.C. Bullmore, E.T. *et al.* (1997) Auditory hallucinations and the temporal cortical response to speech in schizophrenia: A functional magnetic resonance imaging study. *American Journal of Psychiatry*, **154**, 1676–82.

Wootton, R.J. and Allen, D.F. (1983) Dramatic religious conversion and schizophrenic decompensation. *Journal of Religion and Health*, **22**, 212–320.

World Health Organisation (1990) *Composite International Diagnostic Interview (CIDI) Version 1.0*, World Health Organisation, Geneva.

Worthington, E.L. and Scott, G.G. (1983) Goal selection for counselling with potentially religious clients by professional and student counsellors in explicitly Christian or secular settings. *Journal of Psychology and Theology*, **11**, 318–29.

Wright, J., Turkington, D., Kingdon, D.G. and Basco, M. (2009) *Cognitive Therapy of Severe Mental illness: An Illustrative Guide*, APPI, Washington.

Zeki, S. (2003) The disunity of consciousness. *Trends in Cognitive Sciences*, **7**, 214–8.

Zeki, S. and Bartels, A. (1999) Toward a theory of visual consciousness. *Consciousness and Cognition*, **8**, 225–59.

Zohar (1978) (ed. R. Margoliot), 6th edn, **3** Vol, Mosad ha-Rav Kook, Jerusalem.

Index

Psychosis and Spirituality: Consolidating the New Paradigm Second Edition   Edited by Isabel Clarke
© 2010 John Wiley & Sons, Ltd.

Levin, D.M.   91, 94
Liddle, P.F.   128
limen *see* threshold
liminality   45–6, 103
logic   109–11, 122
Lukoff, David   94, 176, 227

MacWilliams, S.A.   105
madness   76, 205
  see also mental illness
magical ideation   83
Malinowski, Bronislaw   40
mania   82, 245
manic-depressive psychosis   77, 82,
  84–5
  see also bipolar disorder
MBCT *see* mindfulness-based cognitive
  therapy
medication   214
meditation
  and spiritual emergencies   213
  changes in brain activity   24–5
  cognitive effects   23–4
  emotional effects   24–5
  'false enlightenment'   206
  mindfulness   224
  value of   21
  Vipassana practice   23
  see also spiritual practices
mediums   44, 145, 150–1
  see also psychics
Meehl, P.E.   127
Menninger, Karl   205
mental health
  and New Religious Movements   137
  and spirituality   37–8
  conventional treatment   91
mental illness   47, 76–7
  aetiology of   83
  and personality   76
  continuum   127–8
  cultural context   183, 206–8
  see also madness
Merleau-Ponty, Maurice   124
meta-awareness   23
  see also awareness
micro-consciousness   28

Middle East
  languages   52, 54 *see also* Hebrew;
    Semitic languages
  mysticism   49–50, 58–61 *see also*
    Kabbalah; mystical hermeneutics;
    Sufism
  worldview   57, 58
midrash   52–6, 58
mind
  common area of   250
  ecology of   60–1
  instruments for understanding   19
  more-than-normal   20
  states of   199, 200
  wild   60
mind-brain-identity theory   11, 17
mindfulness   200–2, 224, 243
mindfulness-based cognitive therapy
  (MBCT)   224
mood
  control   14
  delusional   148, 241
  elevation of   12
  in psychoticism   82
  positive   13, 24
  swings   78, 96–7
multiple personality disorder   91
mystical experience
  and temporal lobe epilepsy   12,
    14–16
  association with right
    hemisphere   13–14
  brain activity during   17, 25–6
  compared with delusions   134–5
  compared with schizophrenia   85–6
  drug-induced   17, 134–5
  features of   12–13
  ICS model   109
  in general population   12
  noetic quality   148
  relation to psychosis   84–7, 135,
    206–7, 208
  see also religious experience; spiritual
    experience; visionary spiritual
    experiences
mystical hermeneutics   52–4
  see also midrash; ta'wil

CPSIA information can be obtained
at www.ICGtesting.com
Printed in the USA
FSHW021441190821
84180FS